D1498442

SOWING THE WIND

Also available:

A Report from Ralph Nader's
Center for Study of Responsive
Law on Food Safety
and the Chemical Harvest

Sowing the Wind

by Harrison Wellford

Grossman Publishers
New York
1972

All royalties from the sale of this book will be given to The
Center for Study of Responsive Law, the organization established
by Ralph Nader to conduct research into abuses of the public
interest by business and governmental groups. Contributions to
further this work are tax deductible and may be sent to the
Center at P.O. Box 19367, Washington, D.C., 20036.

Acknowledgments

This report was prepared with the research assistance of the following persons:

Deborah Luxenberg, Case Western Reserve University, B.A., research coordinator;

Joe Tom Easley, Texas A&M, B.A., University of Texas Law School, J.D.;

Bernard Nevas, University of Michigan, B.A., Harvard Law School, J.D.;

Polly Roberts, Radcliffe College, B.A., for general editorial and research assistance on pesticide problems;

Robert Vaughn, University of Oklahoma, B.A., J.D., Harvard Law School, LL.M., legal advisor and investigator of meat inspection problems;

Connie Jo Smith, Production Manager.

For assistance on special projects, I wish to acknowledge the following:

James Hanks, Jr., Attorney, for legal advice on freedom of information problems and for service as counsel in *Wellford* v. *Hardin*;

William Dobrovir, Attorney, for service as counsel in the 2,4,5-T case, *Wellford* v. *Ruckelshaus*;

Jerrold Oppenheim, Harvard University, B.A., Boston College, J.D., for research on federal poultry inspection;

Barbara Haroz, Western Maryland College, B.A., Boston University M.ED., for research;

Katherine Montague, for administrative assistance.

The National Wildlife Federation, for assistance in the production of the preliminary draft of this report.

viiiACKNOWLEDGMENTS

Special Advisors:

Samuel Epstein, M.D., Chief, Laboratories of Environ-
    mental Toxicology and Carcinogenesis, Children's
    Cancer Research Foundation, Boston, Massachusetts;
Albert Fritsch, Ph.D. in Organic Chemistry;
Michael Jacobson, Ph.D. in Biochemistry.

This book is dedicated to
Connie Jo Smith, Deborah Luxenberg,
and Sue and Susannah Wellford—
blithe spirits in spite of it all.

Introduction
by Ralph Nader

Ever since foreclosures and migrations afflicted rural families during the depressed thirties, city dwellers have been hearing about the technological convulsions down on the farms. They have, more often than not, failed to relate these changes to the safety, quality, and price of foods they consume. While the growth of mechanized, corporate farms and ranches swallowed up small farmers with drastic social consequences for the nation, a parallel growth of chemical technology occurred with equally unexamined secondary consequences for public health and the environment. Pesticides, fertilizers, antibiotics, hormones, additives, and other applications do more than reduce costs and increase sales. They can injure and they can defraud. When these costs do occur, their victims have found the administrative and legal remedies for holding agribusiness* accountable either weak or nonexistent.

In the summer of 1969, a group of law, science, and undergraduate students, under the direction of Harrison Wellford, began a study of these technologies and the political and economic processes that shaped them. In particular, the study focused on the U.S. Department of Agriculture (USDA)—the major institution invested with the duty of determining responsible uses of chem-

---

* The term "agribusiness" refers to corporate enterprises engaged in the processing, marketing, and occasionally production of farm commodities, and in the supply of services and technology to producers of these commodities. The term includes chemical companies selling pesticides and fertilizer, drug companies selling antibiotics and hormones, meat packers and processors, feed companies, and sellers of farm machinery. It does not include family farms, agricultural production units operated by one or more farm-operator families.

icals through a balancing of the public interest against the interests of those who depend on agriculture and its markets for their wealth or livelihood.

Three areas—pesticides, meat, and poultry inspection—were chosen for investigation. Mr. Wellford and I met with Secretary Hardin and several of his chief associates to discuss the project and the Department's cooperation. Although much had been written about these subjects, it was clear from the guarded response we received at that meeting that USDA officials silently agreed with our belief that only the surface had been touched. This Report finds out much more about how these subjects intersect areas of public concern than has been reported before. It is a second-stage investigative effort, penetrating deeply into the interaction of business and government at federal and state levels and into the intricate techniques developed to deny citizens the right to know and the power to act.

The Report is more than a static description of that which was hitherto publicly unknown, for it conveys a sense of pace to the growth of injustice for the unrepresented and to the heightening of technological risk for the future which result from USDA's uncritical promotion of special interest constituencies, such as the chemical industry. The use of pesticides, for example, has nearly doubled since Rachel Carson finished her manuscript *Silent Spring* more than a decade ago, and immensely more toxic brands and aggressive merchandising are present to victimize the farmer as well as the consumer.

Considerable attention is given to the Department of Agriculture which stands, enmeshed in the agribusiness world, as a mockery of its original inspiration 110 years ago described in Lincoln's founding address as "the people's Department." As befits a bastion of corporate socialism, the USDA has very elaborate screens of secrecy, from the deliberations of its powerful advisory committees to the Office of Inspector General. Beset with conflicting constituencies (farmers, processors, consumers, the rural poor, cooperatives, conglomerates, among others), USDA has traditionally ruled for the powerful and wealthy from which many of its temporary political appointees hail. The producer and processor corporations and their trade organizations have a network of early information, preferential Departmental access, and Congressional alliances which have rendered them almost impregnable to scrutiny, much less to countervailing democratic influence.

The entrenchment is continuing. USDA policies have been anything but alleviative of the rural poor's plight, and by their subsidy policies and other practices have assisted the enormous concentration of land ownership. Yet the Department refuses to disclose pertinent data about land concentration, which in large regions of this country is comparable to some underdeveloped countries about whom USDA's Foreign Agricultural Service has such detailed information available. Vertical integration by food conglomerates, as in the poultry industry, has moved with great speed in the sixties. Yet this incredible "poultry peonage" of the chicken farmer, described so closely in the Report, has spread almost without notice by urban America.

Many points of potential access to the USDA by the citizen or aggrieved consumer or small farmer are blocked—including indirect ones such as Congress (monopolized by House and Senate Agriculture Committees and their respective appropriations subcommittees), state government agencies, or by appeal to the Civil Service Commission for personnel accountability. Going through the regulatory procedures of the Department dealing with pesticides (now transferred to the Environmental Protection Agency) or meat and poultry regulation requires power, presence, purse, and persistence—none of which consumers or other unrepresented citizen constituencies possess.

The impacts on consumers are such that they are exceptionally undramatic, invisible, and unreachable at their sources. How, for example, can the housewife detect and do something about residues of hormones, antibiotics, pesticides, and nitrites in the meat she purchases, or the added water in the chickens, hams, and processed meats, or the microbial contamination of growing concern to the public health officials? How can the citizen or citizen group obtain the facts about the pesticide fraud and propaganda that have duped farmers and legislators alike?

The chemical industry and its pesticide pushers have ensured that USDA go slow on research for alternative and safer methods of insect control or eradication, and ignore notorious overselling and overapplication of pesticides which exploit the farmers' fears.

Yet there are detailed avenues of hope in the Report. To its imaginative credit, the Report describes the process of inquiring into USDA and EPA, the problems encountered, and the solutions developed. In short, it shows how stamina, study, and moral concern can get at the facts and even develop supporters within the Federal bureaucracy who previously were reluctant to take stands or speak out.

The process of democratizing meat and pesticide regulation is also suggested throughout the study: Freedom of Information suits, providing due process and defense for the inspector corps in meat and poultry divisions who want to do the right thing, legal challenges to rule-makings and proposing rule-making, and developing rights and remedies by aggrieved citizens against Department officials who violate their own standards of conduct and oath of office by systematically avoiding enforcing the law or by suppressing information critical to health, safety, and consumer economics.

Increasingly, as more information is available to farmers about deceptive sales practices and of negligently produced pesticides, the courts will witness more product liability litigation against chemical companies and their distributors. New detection instruments, such as sensitive and rapid analysis of residue levels or contamination of meat and poultry, will revolutionize law enforcement against violators. Corporate employees in the sciences will begin to hear more insistently the call of professional conscience and refuse to be so pliant, or have their integrity exploited in the testing of pesicides. And Congress, in its halting but continuing advance toward decentralization of power through procedural reform and new displays of courage by some legislators, will improve that institution's supervision of the agencies despite the intransigence of the jurisdictional committee chairman.

It can be said that the behavior of the USDA (and now EPA, as far as pesticide regulation is concerned) brings together the forces in the consumer, poverty, and environmental movements as no other Department can. This emerging coalition should not neglect, however, the effective allies which can be developed within the Department's ranks (conscientious meat and poultry inspectors) and within the agricultural economy (new and older cooperatives, farmer organizations, and farm groups struggling against monopolistic trends in agribusiness). This Report should help the understanding of those Americans who want to do something progressive about this historic sector of our economy, the impact of which on all citizens has increased even as its activities have become more remote and inexplicable. It is time for a new populism, this time uniting the city and rural America. The spread of agribusiness has in effect provided the bond between these two groups.

Washington, D.C.

Contents

Preface

*The real enemy is not evil but irresponsibility.
Responsibility in America is so diffused that no one
is accountable. At the top, people say they did not
know what was going on. At the bottom, they
say they were just following orders. Everyone has his
own best reasons for not being a man.*
                                        —Gordon Sherman

In June, 1969, Joe Tom Easley, a young law student
from Texas, walked into the office of the director of
the Pesticide Regulation Division in the Department of
Agriculture and asked for an appointment. The secretary smiled, opened an appointment book, and asked:
"Which chemical company are you with?" Two years
later, another visitor to the same office also requested
an appointment. The secretary paused, looked him
over, and asked matter-of-factly: "Which chemical company are you with, or are you with Nader's Raiders?"

In the world of public interest advocacy, this greeting
is the equivalent of knighthood by the Queen. It was
earned by two years of research and advocacy in the
area of federal regulation of agribusiness, particularly
the meat and pesticides industry. This effort was sponsored by the Center for Study of Responsive Law. It
was conducted by an interdisciplinary task force of
young professionals trained predominantly in law and
science. Its members engaged in administrative, legal,
and, upon invitation, Congressional proceedings on a
wide range of issues, from the fat and chemical content
of hotdogs and the gothic politics of fire ant control to
information suppression and the potential birth defect
hazards of pesticides. This report is based, in part, on

the insights gained from this combined strategy of action and research.

Two concerns inspired this study: first, the recognition that the most challenging and risky government decision-making outside of national defense is often found in federal regulation of the technology and corporate practices of food production, particularly the application of chemical technology to food and agriculture; and second, the realization that the objectivity and public-mindedness of federal regulators is often undermined by an advocacy gap in the representations which private and public groups bring to bear on the agencies, a gap perhaps wider in the regulation of the food and chemical industries than anywhere else in government.

Federal officials daily make decisions about pesticides, animal drugs, and food additives with only a vague idea of their consequences for human health. In 1969, the Secretary's Commission on Pesticides and Their Relation to Health marveled at the "absurdity of a situation in which 200 million Americans undergo lifelong exposure to chemical pesticides; yet our knowledge of what is happening to them is at best fragmentary and for the most part indirect and inferential." As the cases of DDT, cyclamates, mercury pollution, and thalidomide show, the introduction of chemical technology without adequate anticipation of its long-term effects is a form of Russian roulette with the environment and human health. Too often by the time the environmental impact is assessed, damage has already occurred and the technology has become allegedly "indispensable" to the industry which uses it.

The position of the federal regulator who must balance the risks and benefits of chemical technology is not to be envied. When he weighs the short-term economic benefits of a pesticide, there is an industry advocate at his side to quantify them to the second decimal point. When he weighs a pesticide's long-term hazards to health, he finds they are often theoretical, potential, and vague, and there is usually no public advocate on the scene to help prepare his case. The citizen is usually content to leave these judgments to the experts. But they are not strictly scientific or technical questions, a point supported in a recent report on environmental carcinogens by an ad hoc committee of the United States Surgeon General:

Society must be willing to accept some finite risk as the price of using any carcinogenic material in whatever quantity. The best that science can do is to estimate the upper probable limit of that risk. . . . While science can provide quantitative information regarding maximum risk levels, the task of ultimately selecting socially acceptable levels of human risk rests with society and its political leaders.[1]

The evaluation of the balance of benefits and risks by the regulatory agencies is not immune from politics, no matter how esoteric and technical it may seem on the surface. The manufacturers of chemical technology know this and maintain a large corps of Washington lobbyists as a result. Their stock in trade is their ability to make it seem that decisions which serve the narrowest corporate self-interest are compelled by technical criteria beyond dispute.

The fact that the chemical industry has sown the wind with the unforeseen consequences of its technology is in part a function of an advocacy gap in the federal regulatory system. This regulatory process is heavily premised on the operation of an effective adversary system of representation and advocacy for just and equitable results. This premise is seriously flawed in practice. There are nearly 8,000 practicing lawyers in Washington, D.C., whose daily absorption is directly or indirectly to obtain what their clients desire from the agencies and their political environments. Yet less than fifty full-time professionals represent the public. In the field of meat and pesticides regulation, the number is less than twelve.

The result is that while the clamor of advocacy before the agencies gives the appearance of pluralism at work, a growing number of unrepresented interests suffer from an advocacy gap. In the sector of agribusiness, these include, among others, the consumer's interest in wholesome meat, the meat inspector's interest in enforcing the meat laws, the public's interest in preventing long-term hazards to human and environmental health from agricultural chemicals, the farmer's and farm workers' interest in safe and ecologically sensitive pesticides, and the chicken contract farmer's interest in escaping the status of corporate peonage. For these groups, the pluralism of pressures in the agencies is evidence, not of countervailing powers at work but of logrolling among the special interests.

In this study, we have tried to convey information about these unrepresented constituencies. We have also tried to free the officials of the erroneous information which convinces them that problems do not exist. Charles Frankel, in his memoir of his service in the State Department, gives a rationale for this effort:

I used to imagine when the government took actions I found inexplicable, that it had information I didn't have. But after I had served in the government for some months, I found that the issue was more complex: often the government does know something that people on the outside don't, but it's something that isn't so . . . After a while I came to suspect that I might not be dealing with hard facts but rather with a world created out of hunch, hope, and collective illusion.

In this study, the concept of public interest is given a procedural, rather than a substantive meaning. The public interest is not an absolute set of values to be dogmatically urged on whoever will listen. It is, instead, what emerges when all legitimate interests have a chance to compete and be heard on a particular issue. Because the forces of advocacy have been so unbalanced, the agencies which regulate meat and pesticides have more often subverted democracy than promoted it. As this report will show, consumer and environmental victories which the public wins with the power of the ballot are often lost when they are interpreted by the regulatory bureaucracy.

A great many people have selflessly contributed time and energy to this report. I want to acknowledge particularly the efforts of Sue Wellford, whose research skills and sound judgment both inspired and disciplined the author. The writing and emphases of this study are, for better or worse, my own.

Note on Sources

Any report which discusses problems of professional ethics and conflicts of interest in government and private industry is based in part on information supplied by persons who must, for the time being at least, remain confidential. Federal meat inspectors, chemists for pesticide companies, and many public servants have supplied information which, if acknowledged, would jeopardize their jobs and in some cases their personal safety. These sources will be identified in later editions of this report if and when their personal situation allows. We have verified these reports by cross-checking with other professionals in the fields concerned.

SOWING THE WIND

I

The Politics of Meat

There is no more visceral consumer issue than contaminated meat. The consumer movement, to a significant degree, was founded and later resurrected on complaints about rotting and diseased meat. Americans are emotional about meat, perhaps because they consume so much of it (nearly 116 pounds of beef and veal and fifty pounds of poultry per capita each year), and because they feel peculiarly defenseless against its adulteration and contamination. At least since the U.S. Army served rotten canned meat to American soldiers during the Spanish-American War, the threat of unwholesome meat, whether real or fancied, has provoked politically potent outpourings of grass-roots protest. In 1970, for example, when word leaked out that the Department of Agriculture might permit the sale of chickens with cancerous tumors,* the President's consumer advisor, Mrs. Virginia Knauer, was deluged with angry letters which, for pure vitriol, surpassed comments received on any other consumer issue. (Messages from the White House to USDA, we are told, were only slightly more polite.) Because of such incidents, the head of federal meat and poultry inspection, the nation's chief guardian of meat purity, sits in one of the hottest and least secure seats in government.

With the exception of federal controls on banks and railroads, meat inspection is the nation's oldest regulatory system. As early as 1865, a federal law was passed prohibiting the importation of diseased cattle and swine. At its best, meat inspection is a classic regulatory

* For a full discussion of the chicken cancer affair, see Chapter 4.

function, protecting the ethical businessmen from being undersold by less scrupulous ones and protecting the citizen where he cannot protect himself.

The ingenuity of food chemistry and processing technology long ago overwhelmed the consumer's natural detection devices—seeing, smelling, tasting—which might have protected him from bad meat. Seasoning agents, preservatives, and coloring agents can now serve effectively as cosmetics to mask the true condition of meat products.[1] The use of cheap fillers and additives such as water, cereal, and fat, unless carefully controlled, gives the consumer less and less protein for his dollar. A case in point is the hotdog, the fat content of which increased from 19 percent to 33 percent between 1937 and 1969.

The total effect of unwholesome meat on human sickness can only be estimated. National health surveys estimate that five to ten million cases of acute intestinal illness, many of them meat related, occur annually in the United States, but most go unreported in official records.[2] Meat animals harbor a number of diseases potentially harmful to man. Trichinosis and hog cholera in pork, brucellosis in beef, and staphylococcus and salmonella bacteria in processed and fresh meats may be directly harmful, while animal cancer—103,000 cattle carcasses were held back by federal inspectors in 1969 for removal of carcinomas and cancer eye—poses potential long-term risks according to some scientists.

Poultry is an even more fertile breeding ground for disease organisms affecting man. Twenty-six diseases are known to occur in both man and fowl—the most serious of which are salmonellosis, psittacosis, and Newcastle Disease.[3] Meat inspection is also necessary to protect the consumer from hidden chemical contaminants such as mercury, PCB (polychlorinated biphenyls), stilbestrol, and other synthetic hormones, antibiotics, and chlorinated hydrocarbons such as dieldrin and DDT. With the widespread and often careless use of these chemicals, it has become increasingly difficult to keep them out of the food supply.

The ease with which meat can become adulterated and contaminated, coupled with the extreme competitive pressures in the industry, makes it a risky candidate for self-regulation. Profits are among the lowest of any major industry.* As a result, the industry tends to be subject to Gresham's law, with bad meat driving the good out of circulation in the marketplace. While the consumer's need for something more than corporate ethics to protect him from unsafe meat now seems obvious, it was not always so. In the nineteenth century, inspection was limited to meat slaughtered for export. The meat packers themselves initiated the legislation to protect the image of American meat in world markets,[4] but they strenuously opposed extending the same protection to the American people. Albert Beveridge, the Republican Senator from Indiana, who was an early consumer champion, gave this reaction to the primitive state of meat inspection at the turn of the century:

I looked at our own meat inspection laws, and was horrified to find that, while our laws demanded careful inspection of meats intended for foreign consumption (simply because other countries would not otherwise take them), there was practically none at all for meat sold our own people.[5]

The first law requiring mandatory inspection of domestic meat came about, as did the Wholesome Meat Act sixty years later, through the efforts of a few crusaders who skillfully converted information to action while capitalizing on a national mood for reform. In 1906, Beveridge became an active supporter of meat reform after reading Upton Sinclair's sensational novel, *The Jungle*. While Sinclair conceived his book as an attack on capitalism per se, its larger message was lost in the public indignation provoked by his lurid description of filthy conditions in the Chicago stockyards:

There would be meat stored in great piles in rooms, and the water from leaky roofs would drip over it, and thousands of rats would race about on it. It was too dark in these storage places to see well, but a man could run his hand over these piles of meat and sweep off handfuls of the dried dung of rats. These rats were nuisances, and the packers would put poisoned bread out for them. They would

* In 1969, the meat packers had a 1 percent return on sales and a 9.6 percent return on net worth. By comparison, the drug industry had a 9.6 percent return on sales and 19.9 percent on net worth.

die, and then rats, bread, and meat would go into the hoppers together. This is no fairy story and no joke. The meat would be shoveled into carts, and the man who did the shoveling would not trouble to lift out a rat even when he saw one. There were things that went into the sausage in comparison with which a poisoned rat was a tidbit.

*   *   *   *

There were open vats near the level of the floor; their peculiar trouble was that they [men] fell into the vats; and when they were fished out, there was never enough of them left to be worth exhibiting; sometimes they would be overlooked for days till all but the bones of them had gone out to the world as . . . "pure leaf lard."

Reading these passages, it comes as no surprise that meat consumption in the United States fell by 25 percent in the year following publication of *The Jungle*.[6]

Public opinion, aroused by Upton Sinclair and other muckraking journalists, overcame the opposition of the House Agriculture Committee, which tried to bottle up the meat reform bill. The crucial factor was the active support of President Teddy Roosevelt who had read Sinclair's book in manuscript and secretly commissioned a study of the Chicago meat packers which confirmed the scenes in *The Jungle*. In June, 1906, Roosevelt signed into law the Meat Inspection Act which, he assured the public, would "insure wholesomeness from the hoof to the can."

The meat act, which remained virtually unchanged for the next sixty years, is regarded by historians as a critical achievement of the reformist spirit, which, leavened with suspicion of big business and hostility to corruption became known as Progressivism. With the Pure Food and Drug Act passed the same year, the meat act was the first consumer protection measure instigated by grass-roots consumer protest. Unfortunately the consumers tended to view the act as a symbol that bad meat was no longer a problem and ceased their vigilance after the act was passed. In the ensuing decade, the public continued to be victimized by rotting, diseased, and contaminated meat.

The failures of the original meat act were due in part to weak enforcement and to inspectors who conspired with large meat packers to evade its standards, but more important, there was a major loophole in the law. The early legislation applied only to meat sold in interstate commerce. Meat packers and processors who sold their meat within the confines of a single state were exempt from federal inspection. As late as 1967, nearly 15 percent of the meat slaughtered in the United States and 25 percent of the processed meat were not inspected according to federal standards. In many cases it was not inspected at all.

The states were loath to assume responsibility for this meat. In 1967, twenty-two states did not require mandatory inspection of livestock before and after slaughter; and eight states had no meat inspection at all.[7] The danger to the consumer was especially great in fourteen states, where nonfederally inspected meat accounted for over 40 percent of all meat slaughtered. A 1963 USDA survey of state plants, kept secret until 1967, revealed deplorable conditions which would have shocked even Upton Sinclair. In Delaware, the survey records:

In addition to the very grave and urgent problem posed by the distribution of food derived from diseased animals, the attached report details extremely bad and revolting dirty food handling methods without any regard for rudimentary sanitation. Rodents and insects, in fact any vermin, had free access to stored meats and meat products ingredients. Hand washing lavatories were absent or inadequate. Dirty meats contaminated by animal hair, the contents of the animal's digestive tract, sawdust, flies, rodents and filthy hands, and the tools and clothing of food handlers were finely ground and mixed with seasonings and preservatives. These mixtures are distributed as ground meat products, frankfurters, sausages and bologna. Due to the comminuting process and seasoning of these products, most of the adulteration could not be detected by the consumer.[8]

A second investigation in 1967 confirmed this abysmal picture. A USDA investigator in Norfolk, Virginia, reported: "I found abscessed beef and livers, abscessed pork liver, parasitic livers mixed with the edible product. The owner was with me at the time. On being questioned on the mixture, he said, "These will be rechecked later.""[9] At a North Carolina state inspected packinghouse, an observer reported instances of "snuff spit on the floor, sausage meat fallen on the same floor which was then picked up and shoved into the stuffer."[10] These conditions, described by veteran USDA inspectors, were repeated with revolting consistency in many of the intrastate plants surveyed by USDA.

The surveys clearly showed that Sinclair's work remained unfinished. In 1967, a tiny coalition of reformers dedicated themselves to cleaning up the state inspected plants. In doing so, they revitalized the consumer movement, and gave it a broader base than ever before.

The pooling of forces by labor, public interest lawyers, consumer oriented Congressmen and journalists, their imaginative use of the media to take the message of reform directly to the people, their readiness to use proper names in describing the abuses of Swift, Armour, and other national companies, became a model for public interest advocacy in the sixties. And yet their success, which expanded the sense of the possible for a new generation of "muckrakers," was far more difficult to preserve than it was to win. The campaign for passage of the Wholesome Meat Act in 1967 and its subsequent fate in the hands of the meat inspection bureaucracy in the Department of Agriculture, give revealing insights into the strengths and weaknesses of the consumer movement.

The First Skirmishes

The USDA state surveys were the catalyst for meat reform in 1967. The meat packers learned that USDA inspectors were reporting filthy and tainted meat from state plants as early as 1963, and they began to prepare their defenses. Their strategy was to disperse the forces of consumer reaction by creating state meat packing associations which would lobby aggressively in state legislatures for state inspection programs and thus escape tougher federal scrutiny. Pressured by the various trade groups of the meat industry and by the State Commissioners of Agriculture, USDA kept its surveys secret for four years.

Whenever questions were raised about the adequacy of inspection in state plants, the trade groups scrupulously avoided any description of actual conditions. But there were occasional glimpses of the public's defenselessness. Aled P. Davies, Vice President of the American Meat Institute and the unofficial leader of the meat lobbyists in Washington, inadvertently dramatized the consumer's plight in a 1967 House committee hearing. Under forceful questioning by Representative Tom Foley (D.-Wash.), he suggested that consumers worried about uninspected meat should carry their hamburger with them on trips across state lines:

FOLEY: "Can you tell me a good way to determine what is interstate and what is intrastate in a hamburger?"

DAVIES: "Ask to see the package from where it came."

FOLEY: "But you are a great deal more skilled in knowing what you are doing than most citizens."

DAVIES: "I can smell."[11]

Mr. Davies in fact was underestimating the skill of his constituents in the meat industry. Intrastate packers using antibiotics, preservatives and seasoning agents, and other additives banned under federal law had more than enough chemical ingenuity to mask the odor of decaying meat.

The execrable conditions in state inspected plants undermined the standards of the entire meat industry. These plants provided an outlet for the sale of what the industry called "4-D meat" (for dead, dying, diseased, and disabled) which could not pass federal inspection. It was not immediately clear why large meat packers opposed upgrading the state plants, for most of their plants were already federally inspected.[12] The answer was relatively simple: the competitive advantage which 4-D meat enjoyed over more wholesome products attracted not only marginal operators, but also some of the largest meat packing firms in the country. The Department of Agriculture surveys included reports on Armour, Swift, and Wilson and Company, which operated nonfederally inspected intrastate processing plants to compete in local markets where, as Senator Mondale reported, "out of reach of the federal government" they could reap profits "by passing off sick meat to consumers and by using additives not permitted under Federal regulations."[13] In their defense, the large packers claimed they were forced into this practice because their federal plants faced serious competition from unregulated establishments. The fact that major packers whose names were household words were implicated in the deliberate sale of unwholesome products undercut the traditional defenses of the meat lobby. These practices could no longer be dismissed as the work of small fly-by-night operators.

The conditions in the state plants were still secret when Congressman Neal Smith (D.-Iowa) first began to call attention to Upton Sinclair's unfinished business in 1960. As a farmer who used to attend cattle sales as a young man, he discovered that the same people always seemed to step forward to buy diseased cattle when they appeared on the block. He investigated and found that they were buyers for packing plants which did not come under the federal meat inspection law. Concerned, he introduced legislation to eliminate these practices in 1960—and reintroduced it each year for seven years afterwards. The House Agriculture Committee just as persistently refused to hold hearings on the bill.

Smith's dedication was shackled by his preference for working with the "system" of the House. As one observer put it:

Neal kept doing favors for the boys in the club [the House Agriculture Committee], and hoped they would give him hearings in return. But they were just stringing him along.[14]

His campaign was stymied until 1967, when Congressman Harold Cooley (D.-N.C.), a rigid foe of consumer legislation, stepped down as chairman of the full committee after losing his seat in the mid-term elections. Robert Poage (D.-Tex.), a slightly more flexible man with some Populist leanings, took Cooley's place, but the key change was in the chairmanship of the Subcommittee on Livestock and Grains, which had jurisdiction over meat inspection. This post went to

Graham Purcell (D.-Tex.), a responsible legislator who had both Poage's and Neal Smith's respect.

Smith now saw his chance to break the logjam on meat reform and he took it. He was ably assisted by Ed Mezvinsky, a young lawyer from Iowa, who joined Smith as his legislative assistant in 1967. Alert and quietly aggressive, Mezvinsky used the information Smith had gathered and went outside the committee system to publicize the need for meat reform. One of the men he informed was his occasional handball partner, Nick Kotz, a reporter for the *Des Moines Register*. Another was Ralph Nader, fresh from his automobile safety campaign, who had been looking into poultry inspection at the time.

On February 16, 1967, President Johnson gave a mild blessing for a meat bill in his consumer message to Congress. Consumer protection was a good consensus issue, and Johnson was looking for new approaches. After a blitz of major social legislation, the Great Society had bogged down. Consumer issues carried the promise of new constituencies. However, according to Joseph Califano, Johnson's top domestic advisor, the White House staff was not really persuaded that the time was right for strong consumer legislation. In fact, meat reform had such low priority in the White House that Secretary of Agriculture Orville Freeman, whose Department drafted the Administration's bill, did not even have to check it out with the White House staff.[15]

The political stakes shifted in the summer of 1967 when Ed Mezvinsky's lobbying began to pay off. At a luncheon on July 16, arranged by Mezvinsky, Nader and Kotz persuaded Representative Thomas Foley (D.-Wash.), a member of the vital House Agriculture Committee, to sponsor Smith's reforms in the committee. Nader and Kotz provided the opening shots for the meat fight with articles in the *New Republic* and the *Des Moines Register* respectively. Checking up on allusions to conditions in state plants which he noticed in speeches by several USDA officials, Nader obtained alarming data on unsanitary practices in state inspected plants, although he had not yet seen the actual reports. His article of July 15 focused attention on the state

surveys and compared them to conditions which had
led to passage of the Meat Inspection Act in 1906:

It would be misleading to compare such intrastate operations
today with those conditions prevailing at the turn of the
century: As far as impact on human health is concerned, the
likelihood is that the current situation is worse. The foul
spectacle of packinghouses in the earlier period has given way
to more tolerable working conditions, but the callous misuse
of new technology and processes has enabled today's meat
handlers to achieve marketing levels beyond the dreams of
their predecessors' avarice. It took some doing to cover up
meat from tubercular cows, lump-jawed steers, and scabby
pigs in the old days. Now the wonders of chemistry and
quick-freezing techniques provide the cosmetics of camou-
flaging the products and deceiving the eyes, nostrils, and
taste buds of the consumer. It takes specialists to detect the
deception. What is more, these chemicals themselves introduce new and complicated hazards unheard of sixty years
ago.

Simultaneously, Nick Kotz, acting on tips from
USDA inspectors, was conducting his own investigation. On July 14, someone in USDA leaked to Kotz the
Department's confidential reports on intrastate plants
in several midwestern states. Kotz and Nader then went
to USDA together to demand release of the rest of the
state surveys. At first, Rodney Leonard, Administrator
of the Consumer and Marketing Service, denied their
existence.* An inquiry by Senator Mondale (D.-Minn.)
got the same reply. Eventually, Kotz and Nader did receive a copy of the state reports from USDA but the
Department still refused to make them public officially.

During this period, a meat reform bill was taking
shape in the House. The parent bill, H.R. 12144,
initially supported by the Administration, was sponsored by Congressman Graham Purcell and drafted
largely by his assistant, John Rainbolt. While an improvement on earlier drafts proposed by USDA, the
Purcell bill still did not require any action from the
states. Instead, it attempted to cajole the states into
reform by promising to pay 50 percent of the costs if

---

* Leonard now acknowledges that political and industry pressures
dulled his sensitivity to consumer problems in 1967. After leaving the
Department, he became a leading consumer advocate on food issues.

they decided to accept federal standards. Consumer and labor groups backed a much stronger bill, H.R. 12145, known as the Smith-Foley Amendment, which promised to make federal inspection mandatory in state plants grossing $250,000 a year.*

Opposition to the bills was led by the three major meat packing associations: NIMPA (National Independent Meat Packers Association), the AMI (American Meat Institute), and the WMPA (Western Meat Packers Association). At the state level, the State Commissioners of Agriculture represented by NASDA (National Association of State Department of Agriculture) opposed the bills on the grounds that the federal government should not interfere in state affairs.

At the federal level, the Department of Agriculture was very ambivalent about its own stake in the struggle. Although USDA had had damning information on the state plants since 1963, it gave only a summary report to the House Appropriations Committee and withheld details about specific conditions in specific plants. In a letter to the House Committee on Agriculture on July 20, 1967, Nader described the costs of this policy of secrecy:

Unfortunately, the Department lost an important opportunity to give momentum to its findings because it did not release the state-by-state backup studies which would have given specific substance to the general conclusion. Numerous, concerned employees of the Meat Inspection Service surveyed the respective states where they were stationed. By and large, these state reports are the product of sensitive, observant public servants who wanted a sickening situation remedied. Their high superiors in Washington, however, placed other considerations above prompt and full disclosure.

USDA's reluctance to release the reports was in part a result of pressure from Jamie Whitten, chairman of the House Appropriations Subcommittee on Agriculture,

---

* Many long strategy sessions by the consumer coalition preceded the introduction of this bill. According to Richard Falknor, an assistant to Congressman Foley and a key figure in these discussions, some suggested that FDA, not USDA, be put in charge of the meat program and that failures in the federal system as well as the states be exposed. Ultimately, the decision was made to keep the strategy simple: emphasize the virtues of federal meat inspection and push it as a model for the states. As it turned out, this simplicity of approach was vital to the success of the media campaign.

and Harold Cooley, when he chaired the House Agriculture Committee. Both were afraid of embarrassing state programs. USDA was also motivated by the conflict of functions which keeps a strong consumer orientation from developing in the Department: it is charged with promoting the *sale* of meat as well as conducting its *inspection*. While in fact strong meat inspection promotes the sale of beef in the long run, most meat packers had a shorter-range view and saw the surveys only as a potentially costly embarrassment. Their view was effective, for in 1967 as today, the meat packers and the cattlemen are much more formidable adversaries for USDA officials than the unorganized consumer.

For the most part, the Department played the classic bureaucratic role of the "man in the middle," reeling from pressure on all sides. From a narrow organizational viewpoint, the federal meat inspectors might have been expected to see the meat bill as an opportunity to do a little empire building. This did not prove to be the case. Jurisdiction over intrastate plants would add to their bureaucratic turf, to be sure, but this consideration was outweighed by others. First, even if the consumer coalition managed to pass a strong bill over the opposition of the farm committees, the purse strings for the new program would be securely held in the committees' unsympathetic hands. The inspectors anticipated a nightmare where vast, new responsibilities over thousands of small plants would be thrust upon them with no guarantee of adequate funds to do the job. And it was the meat bureaucrats, not the consumer champions, who would have to defend the program year after year behind the closed doors on Capitol Hill.

There was also a factor of convenience: meat inspection under the best conditions is a rough and dirty job, with the inspector under constant pressure from the plant managers. Few wanted assignments to the smaller and dirtier state plants, where managers were unaccustomed to the discipline of federal standards and where at least in some states political manipulation was a way of life.

They were uneasy for another reason as well. No

one was more aware than the federal inspectors themselves that filthy, adulterated meat, while more common in state plants, was also present in some federal
establishments. If they assumed responsibility for the
state plants, they could expect that the consumer
investigators would soon begin to look at inadequacies
in the federal plants as well. The inspectors ran the
same risk, however, if the debate on Capitol Hill
was prolonged. Public exposure of conditions in the
state plants therefore made them very nervous. As one
retired Consumer and Marketing Service (C&MS)
official said: "We read Nick's [Kotz's] columns with
a grin and a prayer." In retrospect, Ralph Nader described the attitude of USDA's meat division toward
the Wholesome Meat Act as "a ball of putty pulled
this way and that by each new pressure."

Secretary of Agriculture Orville Freeman was less
ambivalent. In his ceaseless effort to give his department a low profile with vested interests and thereby
spare his President controversy, he was not about to
tackle the whole agribusiness establishment, from the
meat packers through the State Commissioners of
Agriculture to the farm committees, for the sake of a
consumer bill. He actively opposed mandatory meat
inspection, even after the White House was prepared
to yield. Moreover, according to one observer on the
White House staff Freeman—and many of the career
bureaucrats for that matter—felt that Congress was
being steamrollered by the hysteria of a handful of
militants: "Orville just didn't think there was a problem,"* said one former aide.

Freeman's main ally was the National Association of
State Departments of Agriculture. NASDA had strong
organizational and political reasons for opposing mandatory inspection. Aled Davies, of the American Meat
Institute, testified before the House Agricultural Subcommittee on July 17, 1966, that "representatives of
the State Departments of Agriculture are in a better

---

* Freeman played much the same passive role in the hunger controversy one year later. He was incredulous that severe malnutrition
could really exist in the Mississippi Delta, until the hungry poor
camped on the doorstep of his Department during the Poor People's
March in 1968.

position than we to comment on the adequacy of their
meat inspection programs," but that was just the problem. Many State Commissioners of Agriculture ran
their inspection programs like private duchies where
political patronage, not professional qualifications, determined an inspector's chances of advancement.* In
many states, the commissioners are statewide elected
officials supported by an agribusiness constituency
which makes them independent of their governors.
According to Congressman Neal Smith and other
observers, the slaughterers and processors who had a
financial interest in weak meat inspection at the state
level frequently made campaign contributions to the
commissioners in some states. In Georgia, in particular, meat inspection reform became a hostage of local
politics.

One of the most vocal opponents of federal inspection was Phil Campbell, the State Commissioner of
Agriculture for Georgia. (President Nixon later appointed Campbell Under Secretary of Agriculture in
1969 and he is now, according to many observers,
the dominant influence on meat policy in USDA.)
For more than a decade, Campbell had been a powerful force in Georgia politics and was widely regarded
as a future gubernatorial candidate. Campbell objected to federal interference and charged USDA
with failing to help state inspectors improve their own
systems. He vigorously defended his state inspectors
against charges of the USDA state surveys. In 1967,
he charged that USDA had threatened him with
retaliation if he testified in defense of the state inspectors before the Senate Subcommittee holding hearings
on meat. In a telegram to Secretary of Agriculture
Orville Freeman after the hearings, he stated:

Many times prior to my testifying before the Senate Subcommittee, I and many other Commissioners of Agriculture
of the United States received long distance telephone calls
from personnel in USDA threatening us with a smear
campaign and stating that things would get very nasty if we
testified. Within two days after my testimony on November

---

* California, New York, and several other states with strong meat
laws and high professional standards for their inspectors were exceptions which did not fit this picture.

15, Federal personnel of the USDA Meat Inspection Division in Atlanta received orders to find something wrong in nine federally inspected Georgia plants. I presume they are now making an effort to follow these orders. Mr. Secretary, you know me well enough to know that regardless of the consequences, I cannot be blackmailed.

A skillful politician, Campbell knew his opposition to the federal government was good politics in Georgia but his posturing had little effect on the outcome of meat reform in Congress. Privately, Campbell told USDA officials he was not really opposed to the Wholesome Meat Act, but was only trying to "protect my boys."

Campbell's performance illustrates the fact that opposition to mandatory federal inspection of intrastate plants was firmly rooted in local politics throughout the nation. Nearly every district had a small packing-house operating antiquated equipment whose manager felt threatened by federal meat standards. The House of Representatives is notoriously receptive to this kind of pressure, especially on matters falling within the jurisdiction of the agricultural committees. It was business as usual, therefore, when the House passed the weaker Purcell Bill on October 31 with a 403–1 vote, but defeated the Smith-Foley Amendment 140–98. This outcome was heavily influenced on the eve of the vote when the State Commissioners of Agriculture, often with their governors on the line, deluged their Congressional delegations with calls demanding that they vote against the stronger bill.

Nevertheless, in some quarters, the vote was a surprise. While it was predictable that the House Agriculture Committee would strongly oppose mandatory extension of federal inspection, few observers thought that a majority of Congressmen would dare to vote against the consumer on the floor of the House. They were saved embarrassment because the meat bill went before the House on a teller vote—not a roll call.* When tellers are used, House members are counted as they file quickly down the middle aisle. Their names

* The teller vote, one of the many anachronisms in the House rules which shield Congressmen from public accountability, was abolished in the House rules reforms of 1971.

are not recorded and no one except observers on the scene can be sure how they voted. Before the teller vote, meat lobbyists led by Aled Davies and representatives from NASDA buttonholed Congressmen in the corridors and cloakrooms and then watched from the gallery to make sure they voted against mandatory federal inspection. Only 238 of the 435 members of the House voted. After the vote, Neal Smith noted:

Some members told me they wanted to help by at least staying off the House floor on the crucial teller votes. But they said they couldn't because the meat lobbyists were in the House gallery watching them.[16]

The consumer coalition was defeated in the House because they could not counter the local pressure on Congressmen organized by the State Commissioners and the meat lobbies. If they were to resurrect the concept of mandatory inspection in the Senate, they would have to personalize the need for reform at the local level. Here the USDA surveys, which revealed revolting conditions in hundreds of state inspected meat plants around the nation, were the key. By an imaginative use of the media to publicize the surveys, the reformers set out to make the struggle for mandatory federal inspection an intimate local concern. This campaign went into high gear in November after defeat of the Smith-Foley Amendment. It was led by a coalition of journalists, Congressmen, and consumer advocates. In addition to Nick Kotz and Ralph Nader, Arnold Mayer of the Amalgamated Meat Cutters Union, Congressmen Neal Smith and Tom Foley (and their legislative assistants, Ed Mezvinsky and Richard Falknor) and Senator Walter Mondale (D.-Minn.) were key participants.*

Kotz pressed his investigations and alone wrote more than fifty pieces on the subject of meat inspection. More than any other single journalist, he insured passage of the Wholesome Meat Act (he was rewarded with a Pulitzer Prize). Ralph Nader conceived the plan of sending detailed reports on individ-

---

* Senator Joseph Montoya (D.-N. Mex.) was also prominent but considerably less militant than this group. He initially opposed any mandatory federal inspection but later amended his position.

ual plants verified by the USDA surveys directly to their hometown newspapers. Many newspapers picked up the story and began to investigate local plants, generating a whole new wave of exposés.*

Nader and Kotz constantly pressed USDA for more information. In November, 1967, Kotz uncovered USDA lab tests of meat products from intrastate plants collected in nationally known supermarkets. Of 162 samples, 123 had not met federal standards. This injected a new public concern. The housewife could no longer assume she was protected merely by buying from prestige national chains. Bad, nonfederally inspected samples were found at Safeway, A&P, Kroger, and other national stores. By constantly hammering home these reports, they began to build momentum nationwide for new meat legislation. Most significantly, they made meat reform good politics at the county courthouse level.

At first, the national media were slow to pick up the story. The break came on November 12 when Public Broadcasting Laboratory devoted the first of three programs to the need for nationwide meat inspection. Other programs followed on November 17 and 26. It was a graphic series which showed what public television can do when it focuses on a flagrant public abuse. Before these programs, with the exception of Cowles Publications (for which Kotz wrote), the *New Republic*, and *The Nation*, the printed media were largely silent. *Life*, *Look*, and *The Saturday Evening Post*, the big circulation magazines, gave no sign of recognizing that a vital consumer issue was at stake. The women's magazines stayed true to the timorous tradition of avoiding controversy with the food industry and shielded their housewives from the bad news about this basic consumer commodity.** But after the first PBL program, the three major net-

---

* The women's page editor of the *St. Louis Globe-Democrat* received 1,379 letters and 229 telephone calls from anxious housewives who had read an account of conditions in state inspected plants in the St. Louis area. She reported this response to the annual meeting of the American Meat Institute.

** This was not always so. In 1906 when Upton Sinclair was leading the first meat crusade, the *Ladies' Home Journal* and *Collier's* were famous muckraking magazines.

works felt obliged to follow its lead, and prospects for an effective bill steadily improved.

The meat fight reached its climax in November. The consumer coalition's effort in the House, while it failed, at least insured that meat reform would be a major issue in the Senate. The publicity barrage organized by the reformers after the defeat succeeded in arousing public opinion and the meat industry suddenly found itself under attack in many forums. Senate mail was heavy with demands that all meat up to retail level be inspected. But the question still remained: who was to inspect, the states or the federal government?

The bills before the Senate Subcommittee on Agricultural Research and General Legislation reflected the shift in the national mood. In addition to H.R. 12144, the House-passed bill, there were two other bills: S. 2218, known as the Mondale bill, which would have authorized immediate federal inspection of all state plants which did not meet federal standards; and S. 2147, introduced by Senator Montoya, which embodied the House bill, but allowed for federal take-over if the states could not come up with a mandatory system at least equal to federal standards within three years.

Most observers agree that a key figure at this stage was Aled Davies, Washington representative of the American Meat Institute. Davies is one of the most astute lobbyists representing any industry in Washington. Quick to react to the flow of power on any issue, he shifted his position three times during the meat fight. At first, he was opposed to any bill. Then after the first batch of Kotz's stories, he came out in support of the Purcell bill, which would throw a bone to the consumers by giving lip service to state reform but left compliance strictly voluntary. When the bills reached the Senate, he literally sat in Senator Montoya's office and directed the forces against any immediate requirement of mandatory federal inspection of substandard plants.[17] Davies's shifts were given a forceful prod when Kotz got hold of the American Meat Institute's secret membership list and matched it with the USDA surveys of filthy plants.

Fifty of its members, the cream of the industry, saw their corporate names, many of them household words, linked firmly to rotting and diseased meat.

The key arena at this point was in the White House. The Administration was committed to some bill, but how strong a bill no one knew. Davies's views had a powerful sponsor in the person of Mike Manatos, a White House staffer who handled the Senate for Presidents Kennedy and Johnson between 1961 and 1968. When the Purcell bill passed the House, Manatos, at Davies's bidding, tried unsuccessfully to ram it through the Senate by getting a vote on the Senate floor without referral to Committee.

This unusual procedure was stopped by Senator Walter Mondale, who informed the Senate Committee on Agriculture that he would take the Senate floor and filibuster the bill if the Committee went along with Manatos's plan to avoid hearings. In the White House Manatos was opposed by Sherwin Markham and Larry Levinson, two young lawyers on Joseph Califano's staff. They decided early in the game that the White House had nothing to lose and much to gain from a strong consumer bill.

The public response to the meat exposés by Nader and Kotz and especially the fact that activist Senators like Walter Mondale had joined the outcry made meat reform seem far more promising politically in November than it had at the time of the President's consumer message in January. The President needed a new domestic issue, and he needed a Congressional victory. The Great Society's poverty and civil rights programs were now on the rocky road to implementation, but Congress was increasingly reluctant to act on new initiatives from the White House.* And the Vietnam conflict, now a major war, with escalating inflation as well as violence, was rending what remained of Johnson's "consensus." Meat reform had the double advantage of being a new consensus issue (nobody was really for bad meat, at least in public, and public opinion was far more tolerant to-

* According to the *Congressional Quarterly*, the success box score of Presidential legislative initiatives had declined from nearly 70 percent in 1965 to 47 percent in 1967.

ward extensions of federal power in 1967 than it would be two years later) and being relatively cheap, at least compared to the domestic reforms of 1965 and 1966.

These considerations may help explain why Califano, in October and November, became increasingly opposed to USDA's position against mandatory inspection. When Tom Hughes, one of Freeman's aides at USDA, sent a memo to the White House asking for opposition to the Smith-Foley bill, Markham stopped it cold. There was, as one observer noted, "one hell of a fight in the White House."

Betty Furness, the President's consumer advisor, eventually became the public spokesman for the group nicknamed (only half facetiously) by Freeman's assistants as Califano's White House Mafia. When appointed in March, 1967, she seemed a most unlikely candidate for this role. A former television personality, she had replaced the doughty Esther Peterson who, as the first consumer advisor to the White House, had become a sort of consumer's Jeanne d'Arc through her vigorous attacks on corporate fraud and malfeasance. In the political climate of 1966 and early 1967 she came to be regarded as a political liability to the President, particularly after she used her White House forum to support a national boycott of supermarkets. Out of loyalty to Esther Peterson, most consumer activists dismissed Miss Furness as a sham and tended to ignore her.

Ralph Nader, however, saw Furness's tenuous position as an opportunity to put pressure on the White House. The occasion for turning the screw was apparently fortuitous. Shortly before the House vote on the meat reform bills, Arnold Mayer, lobbyist for the Amalgamated Meat Cutters and Butchers Workers, convened a quiet strategy session of labor and women's groups. When the press unexpectedly showed up, Nader seized the occasion to throw down the gauntlet to Miss Furness and demand that she live up to her role as consumer advocate by supporting a strong bill. Whether this sudden splash of limelight influenced her is not known, but in any case on October 30, the day before the House vote, Miss Furness surprised everyone by contradicting the Department of Agriculture and announcing her personal support for mandatory inspection. No one knew, at that time, where the President stood.

When Betty Furness was called to testify before the Senate Agricultural Subcommittee on November 15, the White House was suddenly faced with a deadline for commitment it could not escape. Califano's staff wrote Betty Furness's statement, and she gave the administration's endorsement to S. 2218, which called for immediate federal take-over of all plants operating with inspection below federal standards. Only six days before, Rodney Leonard, presumably speaking for the Administration, had endorsed the weaker S. 2147, the Montoya bill. Queried as to the reason for this sudden shift, Miss Furness won applause and laughter with her reply: "I don't think we should have to be looking askance at our hamburgers and frankfurters for another two years." Nick Kotz later said of Furness's performance: "She really proved herself before that Committee. She was great in the testimony, and handled the questions like a pro." From that point on, the President's Special Assistant for Consumer Affairs was a staunch ally of the consumer coalition and gained stature for herself and her office.

Her statement naturally left Freeman frustrated and angry. Several days before, acting on the assurances of Freeman and Manatos, Senator Montoya had claimed before the same Committee that the White House favored his bill. Moreover, Califano had failed to screen Furness's statement with Freeman in advance. Freeman, with good reason, felt he was being undercut by the White House staff.* Freeman was so angry that he sent a telegram to the heads of the state meat inspection programs reiterating his support of the weaker Montoya bill. Once again, the question became who speaks for the President. According to Califano, he took the issue to President Johnson, who decided to go with

* This was not the first time Freeman felt betrayed by the White House staff. In early 1966, against his better instincts he was ordered by the White House to call a press conference and express his pleasure at a recent decline in food prices. This statement helped the President, but Freeman was harshly attacked by every agriculture interest group in the country, and never really got over it.

the tougher bill, S. 2218. Califano then told reporters
that Betty Furness spoke for the White House.

At this point, the conflict between White House staff
and the Secretary of Agriculture became bitter indeed.
After consultation with Senator Walter Mondale, Califano decided that the Administration should send a
letter to Public Broadcasting Laboratory endorsing the
Mondale bill (S. 2218) on the next program in its series
on meat inspection. He thought the letter would have
greater impact if it came from the Department of
Agriculture. But when Califano asked Rodney Leonard,
the Administrator of the Consumer and Marketing Service, to send the letter, he refused. Freeman, Leonard
warned, was absolutely adamant. Califano then sent a
member of his staff over to USDA to get a sample of
official Departmental stationery. Califano's aides, Markham and Levinson, drafted a letter to PBL, then called
Leonard over to the White House late one evening and
ordered him to sign it. Freeman, by all accounts, was
livid. A few days later at Freeman's instigation, Senator Spessard Holland, a patriarch of the agriculture
establishment in the Senate, personally attacked Califano's staff in the Congressional Record, charging that
a little group of northern liberals in the White House
was leading the Administration astray by pushing for
a strong meat program which they knew nothing about.

These shifts in the White House's position and the
legions of incriminating facts, marshaled against the
meat industry by Nader, Kotz, Public Broadcasting
Laboratory, and finally, the major networks and mass
circulation magazines, broke down the resistance of the
large packers. Consumer confidence in meat was shaken
and the packers began to fear that the continuing struggle on Capitol Hill might affect sales.

One turning point occurred on November 2, when
Kotz revealed a startling blunder by Blaine Liljenquist,
head of the Western States Meat Packers Association.
On the eve of the House vote, Liljenquist solicited meat
packing companies to contribute to a fund for Congressmen who were working "to preserve our free
enterprise system," a code phrase for Congressmen who
opposed mandatory inspection of intrastate plants.
Robert Poage, Chairman of the House Agriculture Com-

mittee, and Aled Davies correctly sensed that Liljen-quist's clumsy act might threaten the integrity of their effort. They first tried to cover up for him, then expressed outrage. Davies repudiated his colleague's letter "as a most unfortunate, ill-timed and utterly stupid activity," and the meat lobby's solid front began to dissolve in internal feuds.

By mid-November, Aled Davies decided to cut his losses. He lectured the other trade associations that if they did not "move forward firmly and honestly, we have only ourselves to blame." He criticized the House bill as containing "lots of carrots but not much stick." When he persuaded Swift and Armour to support a strong bill in the Senate, opposition in the rest of the industry folded.

Here was the inside power of the lobbyists put to work for a public good. Davies personally delivered the key votes in the House and Senate Agriculture Committees. In rapid succession, he persuaded them to be for no bill, then a weak bill, and finally a relatively strong bill as he dealt with changing levels of public concern.

In the end, a compromise was reached.* Mondale's plan for immediate take-over of all intrastate plants which did not have federal standards was scrapped, but the principle of mandatory inspection for all meat was established. The states would be given two years to develop an inspection program at least equal to federal standards. The federal government would pay 50 percent of the costs to do so. If the states were well on the way to developing a meat program on December 15, 1969, they would be given an additional year to comply. If not enough progress had been made, the federal government would take over. The Secretary was empowered to require immediate federal inspection of *any* plant which he found producing meat dangerous to public health. This was a great improvement over the

* During the House-Senate conference on the bill, efforts to weaken it were intense, Mondale and Foley asked Kotz to ask Nader for his advice on the proposed compromises. The message came back: "Do what you think is best." In leaving them on their own, Nader was putting his former allies on notice that, as far as the consumer movement was concerned, there would be no permanent entangling alliances.

House bill which lacked any mandatory provisions for federal take-over of intrastate plants. The compromise bill, however, gave the Secretary of Agriculture great discretion (with its possibilities of delay) in determining how states measured up to federal standards.

On December 15, 1967, President Johnson signed the Wholesome Meat Act into law. Upton Sinclair, in a wheelchair, was at his side. A coalition of consumer and labor groups and crusading journalists had shown that even without initial Administration backing, a major piece of consumer legislation could be pushed to enactment in a six month period, once attention focused on the issue. Most impressive of all, they did it over the opposition of the committees on agriculture in the House and initially the Senate.

This victory, especially the techniques used to win it, became a watershed for public interest advocacy and the consumer movement. The reformers had applied the classic strategy of divide and conquer. They divided the executive branch by using the White House to neutralize the Department of Agriculture; they divided the meat industry and the farm committees into warring camps. Second, they freed food protection of its abstractions and made meat reform good politics at the local level and a brand-name embarrassment at the corporate level. Finally, by holding back some information and pacing their exposés, they kept their momentum up and their opponents off balance. The lesson of the meat fight was that disclosure of facts to the public, especially the technical detail of issues usually reserved for industry and government insiders only, could generate an overwhelming political leverage for reform.

The success of this approach was entirely unexpected in 1967. It is fashionable among political scientists, historians (such as Richard Hofstadter), and many political analysts to stress the irrationality of politics, to downgrade the value of getting facts to the people. They point to many elegantly conceived proposals for reform, from taxes to campaign financing, which bring no response from the public. Real power, they say, resides in the "insiders" world of closed committee sessions, special interest lobbies, and the special relationships between the career bureaucrats and sub-committee chairmen. Focus on this arena naturally breeds a contempt for public opinion. In 1967, this view was the source of the conventional wisdom among Washington political pros which held that consumer protection could never be good politics on Capitol Hill. The meat reformers in 1967 went over the heads of the insiders. They gambled on the ability of the public to respond if the need for reform were personalized at the local level.

The Wholesome Meat Act was a *bona fide* accomplishment for the consumer movement. But in the continuing effort to assure the purity of meat and poultry, the victory was only a skirmish. Reminiscing about the meat fight three years later, Ralph Nader put the struggle for the Wholesome Meat Act in perspective when he said of Aled Davies: "The meat packers never realized how much he saved them. At first we had concentrated on standards of sanitation. The other issues—chemical adulteration of meat, microbiological contamination, misuse of hormones and antibiotics, pesticide residues, ingredient standards—we were just getting into that when the meat lobby decided it was time to put the lid back on the meat industry's Pandora's box. Filth became a shield against even more serious revelations. Congress relieved itself with the Act and forgot about the rest of the mess."[18]

The depressing sequel to any victory like this is that consumer groups do not follow up. The massive publicity which attends one of their successes masks the fact that their advocacy resources are very slim. The constituency which supported the cause of pure meat in 1967 was, as the saying goes, "a mile wide and an inch deep." With a few exceptions, it was (and is) a public *unorganized* constituency whose only form of political power was public opinion. It lacked a Washington association and paid lobbyists to represent its interests in the agencies, to make personal contacts with influential political leaders, or to offer or withhold campaign contributions for Congressmen or Presidents. It lacked newsletters or trade journals to keep its members informed about the fate of its legislation or to mobilize its power when a threat arises.

Thus while public opinion without organization may be effective in achieving passage of a law, it is often futile in influencing the administration of the law after it passed. Consumers lack the manpower to ride shotgun for the Act as it passes through the appropriations committees and the bureaucracies in the following months. On these fronts, there is a perpetual advocacy gap between the representatives of consumer interests and of private industry. As one Civil War buff on the House Agriculture Committee stated (for some reason "off the record"):

You guys are like Lee's Army of Northern Virginia. You can gather your forces and pull off a big one, but on all the other fronts, our boys keep coming on.

As we shall see, the subsequent history of the Wholesome Meat Act gives these words the ring of prophecy.

2

Metamorphosis: From Promise to Enforcement

The Wholesome Meat Act was hailed as a grass-roots consumer victory against formidable Congressional, agricultural, and packing industry opponents, and justifiably so. But consumer victories are never actually won, for they are not self-enforcing. Triumphs like the Wholesome Meat Act are merely events in the continuum of federal interaction with private power. Their impact depends on regulatory institutions whose *modus operandi* is not changed overnight by the passage of law. The promises of the Act would have to be implemented by the federal meat bureaucracy and here the struggle for the Act's integrity would begin anew. While the consumer campfires were still glowing on Capitol Hill, the Act was given over to a suspicious and reluctant meat inspection agency to be defined, interpreted, and enforced.

In the next four years, while the Act inched its way toward implementation, it underwent a gradual but startling metamorphosis. By 1971, there were signs that USDA had shifted the emphasis of the Act from the goal of uniform federal standards and instead was using it as a pretext for decentralizing the federal system and sharing inspection control with the states. To make the change complete, the consumer interests now find themselves allied with their old rivals, the American Meat Institute, in resisting this trend. As we shall see, consumer victories like the Wholesome Meat Act often have a lot in common with old soldiers: they just fade away.

On December 15, 1967, the day the Wholesome Meat Act was passed, the expectation of consumers was high. Two years from that date, 15,000 plants previously selling intrastate meat with weak or no standards would have inspection "at least equal to" federal requirements. Their state inspection systems would be officially "certified" as equivalent to the federal. States which could not meet these standards were to be taken over (or "designated") by the federal government, with one exception: in special cases, if the Secretary of Agriculture had reason to believe that a state was well on its way to meeting federal standards, it could have an extension until December 15, 1970.

During 1969, as the December 15 deadline approached, USDA issued press statements suggesting that most states would be able to meet the deadline. Assistant Secretary of Agriculture Richard Lyng stated: "The states individually and collectively have worked hard and have made encouraging progress toward accomplishing the objective sought by the Act."[1] At the same time, however, a USDA survey of state inspection systems was judging otherwise. It found, as Senator Montoya summarized, that states were acting "as if they had been given a free ride for two years." Early in 1969, Ralph Nader was predicting that no state would be able to meet the original December deadline.

Despite these warnings, the general public was unprepared for the Department's surprise announcement in November, 1969, that only three states could meet federal standards by the deadline: California, Maryland, and Florida. Even the certification of these states as "equal to" federal standards was, as a high official in the Meat Inspection Division said, "a big joke among all C&MS personnel. There are no supporting documents such as sufficient plant reviews to back this up."

Some observers charged that the certification of even these states was governed by Departmental politics rather than merit. California probably deserved it but Maryland and Florida probably did not. Arnold Mayer, the studious legislative representative of the Amalgamated Meat Cutters Union, when he heard of the Maryland decision, asked a USDA official whether "they did it for Agnew." Others suggested that Senator Spessard Holland, Chairman of the Senate Appropriations Sub-committee for Agriculture, won Florida its award. One C&MS official confirmed this skeptical feeling by quoting George Orwell's aphorism that "everyone is created equal but some are more equal than others."

Only one state, North Dakota, had its system taken over by the federal government. On December 15, 1969, the target deadline for compliance with the Wholesome Meat Act—18 of 216 plants surveyed in North Dakota were "found to be operating in such a manner as to endanger public health."[2] For the remaining states, as so often happens in federal enforcement procedures, the exception became the rule. Forty-six states were granted the one year period of grace—a postponement originally designed for extraordinary cases where states were on the brink of compliance and needed only a little more time.

The degree to which USDA bent over backwards to extend the deadline is illustrated in Massachusetts. Here USDA's leniency towards state compliance with the Act, and its willingness to accept any verbal assurances from state officials was indelibly clear. In August, 1969, a USDA official charged with evaluating the Massachusetts system, condemned the "deplorable unsanitary conditions" of its meat processing plants and slaughterhouses, and estimated that unsanitary conditions characterized 30–50 percent of these establishments. George Michael, head of the state meat inspection service, conceded that the "situation in the packing plants of slaughterhouses is . . . a threat to public health."[3] A special inspection by Governor Sargent in October, 1969, found that thirty-one of fifty-seven plants inspected had unsatisfactory conditions.[4] The Governor closed eleven meat plants and demoted Michael, who had not closed a plant in more than a decade.[5] In hearings on October 15, Dr. Polansky, a former federal meat inspector who had also been a state inspector, testified that "state meat inspection as practiced in Massachusetts is of no value at all." He told a special commission investigating meat: "I'd say anything goes in a state plant." He recalled that sick cows and hogs—rejected by him at a federally supervised plant—"will be taken down the road to the state slaughterhouse and get passed by the inspectors at the state plants." He startled the commission by telling of one ingenious state inspected processor who salvaged cancerous tumors cut from diseased cattle and sold them as brains or sweetmeats to Boston supermarkets. "It would make your hair stand on end," he said redundantly.

Why had the state meat inspection system failed? Another Massachusetts state inspector gave this answer: "This is politics. If I condemned an animal, I'd lose my job."[6] Nevertheless, USDA judged the state system as capable of rapid renewal. Less than a month after these revelations, USDA classified the Massachusetts meat inspection system as having made substantial progress toward meeting federal standards and gave it a year's extension. Thirteen months later, USDA had to admit its confidence was misplaced. In January, 1971, its inspectors found the Massachusetts system was still below federal standards. USDA did not panic, however. Its calm was deafening. Rather than take over the state system as the Wholesome Meat Act intended, USDA announced it was still studying the situation. On May 18, 1971, USDA announced it would take over state inspected plants, effective in thirty days. Then on May 28, it revoked this notice and certified the state.

USDA's Jobian patience with noncompliance was not limited to Massachusetts. The final deadline for compliance passed in December, 1970, with two-thirds of the states still in limbo, neither certified nor designated. Secretary of Agriculture Clifford M. Hardin, having waited so long to prod the states to implement the Act, now was faced with a clear-cut legal mandate to declare these states "equal to" or seize them. He delayed again. In February, Hardin announced that he "intended" to take over inspection in fourteen states at some future date but that more surveys were required. The remaining states were certified as "at least equal to."

Requiring the states to have programs "at least equal to" federal standards is not the same as requiring them to be "identical to." The vagueness of the governing phrase allowed USDA much discretion in deciding the fate of individual states. There is much reason to doubt whether meat processed in state plants will in fact be up to federal standards. The doubts are reflected in USDA's still confidential criteria for certification.

Although the Department refuses to release them, instructions for certifying state plants as "equal to" have been in existence since at least 1969. The Task Force obtained a copy of the "Instructions and Procedures for Reviewing and Certifying State Meat and/or Poultry Inspection Programs." The Instructions state that the "equal to" determinations are to be based on:

(1) the adequacy of the state law and regulations in meeting federal standards;
(2) the adequacy of the appropriation and staffing of the state inspection program;
(3) the adequacy of the administration of state programs.

The General Counsel's Office in USDA has made the comparison of state and federal laws and regulations. It sent its findings directly to the Consumer and Marketing Service, and did not publish a report. The adequacy of state administration is based in part on a random sample of state plants, which are rated in several dozen categories. A plant is judged "equal to" if it has a total score of 70 out of a possible 100. All plants in the sample must be judged "equal to" before the state as a whole can be certified. Finally, there are seven basic requirements—e.g., "a potable water supply," "operational sanitation," "control of vermin and insects"—which are a *sine qua non* for certification.

Judgments of "equal to" by these criteria are necessarily highly subjective, especially in the comparison of state and federal laws and regulations and judgment of the adequacy of state administration. It should be noted that not all state plants were surveyed, and that even those plants which were selected in the random sample were given an additional five days to comply if they fail the initial survey (in early drafts of the criteria under which some states were certified, the period of grace was thirty days). Requirements for enforcement remain very vague and states do not have to have a compliance and evaluation project of their own to be judged "equal to."

USDA officials will have to rely on rigorous surveillance of state enforcement to prevent slippage from
the goals of the Wholesome Meat Act after certification.
This raises the question: what sanctions can USDA
bring to bear on certified states which subsequently
fail to measure up to "equal to" standards? Here is the
Achilles' heel of the Wholesome Meat Act. If the state
fails to act against a plant found by federal inspectors
to be below federal standards, the only sanction available to the federal government is to threaten federal
take-over, not of the plant, but of the entire state
system.[7] This puts USDA in the role of the muscle-
bound nuclear giants of the 1950s who tried to discourage guerrilla war by brandishing atom bombs. The
threat is not likely to be believed.

A powerful incentive for USDA to stall take-over of
state plants all along has been budgetary constraint,
particularly in providing an adequate number of inspectors. It has been very difficult for the Department to
find just the twenty-three inspectors for North Dakota
alone. The decision has already been made to take over
poultry inspection in fourteen states in addition to meat
inspection in fourteen additional states. The Office of
Management and Budget, as well as the Agriculture
Appropriations Committees, has worked behind the
scenes to encourage USDA not to take on these additional burdens. These facts lay behind a prediction
made by one division chief in the Consumer and Marketing Service before the December 15, 1970, deadline:
"If the states can show enough appropriations and
enough inspectors, they will be declared O.K." USDA's
incentives to stall were increased because enforcement
of the Wholesome Meat Act was ideologically out of
tune with the Nixon Administration's emphasis on reduced federal intervention in state affairs.

Without a strong push from USDA, the states had
many reasons to drag their feet in raising their inspection standards. In two years, they had to develop programs equal to federal standards which had been
developed over sixty years. They were faced with the
task of inspecting 15,000 small plants, some of which
slaughtered only one animal a day, under a program
that had been primarily designed to regulate large

well equipped interstate operations such as Hormel's, with $695,000,000 in annual sales. Texas provides an interesting example of the challenge of compliance for the states. In 1967, when the meat act was passed, the state had roughly 2,200 plants, only fifty-five of which were being inspected at the time. Inspection was voluntary. By July, 1969, six months before the Act's first deadline, Texas had not passed a state inspection act. The fact that the Texas legislature meets every other year, instead of every year, helps explain the delay. Thus one and a half years after the Act was passed, the Texas Health Department (which regulates meat inspection) lacked funds and the legal framework necessary to begin compliance. Many states faced similar problems.

The states also had an economic incentive for noncompliance. If the states reformed their programs to meet federal standards, the federal government would pay up to 50 percent of the cost of the program. If the state failed to develop a program, the federal government would pay the total cost and take it over.

Under these circumstances, one wonders why any state bothered to comply. Dr. Kenneth McEnroe, the new chief of meat and poultry inspection, attributes the states' aversion to federal take-over to the grassroots fear of federal interference in local affairs. But basically the strong and continuous opposition to federal control of state plants and to the Wholesome Meat Act has political and economic roots. State meat inspection is closely tied to the position of the state commissioners of agriculture which can be a source of extraordinary political power with patronage benefits. Phil Campbell, who was State Commissioner of Agriculture for sixteen years in Georgia, used his position as a stepping stone to becoming Under Secretary of Agriculture. In recent years, the commissioners' power base has dwindled as the farm population declined; but they are fighting a rearguard action to preserve their meat bureaucracy. The commissioner of New Jersey won a major victory last year for those in his state opposed to federal meat inspection. When Governor William Cahill sought to have the federal government take over meat inspection in the state, the commissioner of agriculture, allied with the numerous small intrastate meat packers, successfully thwarted the Governor's efforts. He was aided by USDA Assistant Secretary Richard Lyng who made a special trip to New Jersey to dissuade Cahill from requesting a federal take-over.

The state commissioners of agriculture lobbied hard to prevent passage of the Wholesome Meat Act, and when it was passed the National Association of State Directors of Agriculture (NASDA) opened an office in Washington in January, 1968. Ostensibly NASDA was a lobby for all state issues, but a primary goal of NASDA has been to keep meat inspection under the control of the state commissioners.

NASDA's chief hope is that state plants, which now ship meat only within the state, will be allowed to ship in interstate commerce as soon as their systems are deemed "at least equal to" federal standards. They argue that state plants spending large sums of money to upgrade their program should in fairness benefit from a broadened market. Their position may seem logical on the surface, but it ignores the abuses long associated with the state inspection system. After all, it was the failure of state inspection which prompted passage of the Wholesome Meat Act. In 1967, as we have seen, USDA inspectors surveyed hundreds of state plants and found in virtually every jurisdiction instances of unsanitary meat, unwholesome meat, unsanitary packing conditions, adulteration with water and fillers, and misleading labeling. Moreover, in January, 1968, federal inspectors found that 20 percent of all chicken not federally inspected was unfit to eat by federal standards. They found inspection "errors" such as passing products with gross lesions of disease, failure to remove infectious processes, and contamination of the body with stomach contents and fecal material.

Many states have upgraded their systems since these surveys. But while more inspectors and tougher inspection regulations will help, they will not compensate for the fact that meat inspection by the states becomes part of political systems notoriously reluctant to regulate business aggressively. Certainly times have changed since one could say, as did Judge Gideon Tucker of New York one hundred years ago, that "no man's life, liberty, or property are safe while the legislature is in session," but it is still fair to say that the instinct for larceny is potentially more restrainable at the federal level than in many statehouses.

In terms of effective supervision of meat regulation, most state legislatures cannot compare with the federal government. The Citizens Conference on State Legislatures, after the most comprehensive survey ever made of state lawmaking processes, recently concluded that many legislatures were understaffed, underpaid, inept, and in "disarray." How much supervision of meat inspection can Alabama legislators give when they meet only thirty-six days, divide into fifty-two separate committees, have no permanent offices, and rely on four elderly women for research? The same may be asked of Wyoming where the legislature meets only forty days, employs not a single researcher to help members understand pending legislation, and is forbidden to conduct studies when not in session. The legislators' pay (as low as $100 a year in New Hampshire but as high as $19,000 in California) is usually insufficient to help them avoid undue influence from the meat packers or any other regulated interest. Without staff help, they often rely on lobbyists for fact gathering, bill analysis, and even legislative drafting.

The advantage of state government is supposed to be that it is closer to the people and therefore more responsive than the federal "big brother" hundreds of miles away. In practice, this is often not the case. Many state governments are even more hostile to public inquiry than the federal, in part because they are so unaccustomed to it. Most states lack a "freedom of information" act to give even the semblance of protection for their citizens' right to know about their government.

Enforcement of the federal meat standards by the states, therefore, threatens to be the weakest link in implementation of the Wholesome Meat Act. Any standard is only as good as the men who enforce it and state inspectors have traditionally been more subject to political manipulations and other pressures than the federal corps.

Congressman Neal Smith warns:

As a practical matter, these state programs may not always measure up on all respects to federal standards, and when the state legislature fails to appropriate funds for enough inspectors or inspectors for any reason become less effective, it may take several months to correct the situation. These more politically vulnerable state inspectors also may not condemn labeling or the mixing of large portions of fillers.[8]

This warning was recently echoed by a meat processor in New Haven, Connecticut, reporting on inspection in his recently certified state:

As you know politics plays a big part in the running of the state inspection programs and the word is out that whoever is under state inspection can always reach somebody at the statehouse if and when difficulties are encountered.

Meat inspection in Connecticut in February, 1971, illustrates some of the differences between state and federal systems—which remain three years after passage of the Wholesome Meat Act. Federally inspected plants in Connecticut are inspected continuously. The federal government pays for eight hours of inspection per day; if a plant works another eight hours, the federal inspector works overtime with the plant paying the bill. In a state inspected plant, according to reports from meat processors, the inspector often goes home after seven hours and the plants operate as long as they want without any inspection. Much of the work in these plants is put off until the inspector is gone. According to Connecticut observers, "such items as sausage and ground meat are not mass produced until the inspector goes off duty" so that fat and water in excessive amounts may be added. Now that Connecticut has been certified, these shortcomings of state inspection are supposed to have been eliminated, but only time will tell. The fact that they exist two years after the original deadline for application of the Wholesome Meat Act does not speak well for any rapid change.

USDA appears to have telegraphed its lack of good faith in enforcing the Act in its budget requests. In December, 1969, USDA was faced with the possibility of having to take over inspection in over 12,000 intrastate plants within the next twelve months. There was a strong likelihood of take-over in fifteen to twenty states, given the widespread failures in state inspection reported to Congress by USDA in 1969 and 1970.[9] In its 1971 report, USDA was still publicly acknowledging that it may have to seize inspection in fourteen states. It is strange, therefore, that USDA made little allowance for take-over in its budget requests:

USDA BUDGET REQUESTS FOR MEAT INSPECTION

Program	FY 1971	FY 1972
Federal Program	$68,424,000	$73,434,000*
Money to Designate States	$ 3,416,000	$ 3,416,000

* This $5 million increase appears to be for increased costs of inspection in plants already under federal control.

Three million dollars could pay for take-over in one or two small states at best. The decisions whether to designate or certify a state inspection system were supposed to be based on the merits of its programs, but these figures suggest that USDA had prejudged what its investigators would find.

Given the explicit nature of the Act's language, one can only marvel at USDA's skill in evading its intentions. Section 301(c) states:

If the Secretary has reason to believe, by thirty days prior to the expiration of two years after enactment of the Wholesome Meat Act, that a State has failed to develop or is not enforcing, with respect to all establishments within its jurisdiction. . . , requirements at least equal to those imposed under [the Federal Meat Inspection Act] . . . he shall *promptly* after the expiration of such two-year period designate such State as one in which the provisions . . . of this Act shall apply. . . : Provided, That if the Secretary has reason to believe that the State will activate such requirements within one additional year, he may delay such designation for said period. . . . The Secretary shall publish any such designation in the Federal Register and, upon the expiration of thirty days after such publication, the provisions . . . shall apply. . . . (Emphasis added.)

The intent of the Act is clear. State inspection systems found lacking in December, 1969, were to be promptly taken over by federal inspectors, except in a few extraordinary cases. Not only did USDA violate the intent of Congress in delaying designation for virtually all noncomplying states, but when the final deadline arrived in December, 1970, USDA once again evaded the requirement to designate (with its thirty-day time limit for take-over) by issuing instead notices of "intended" designation which had no deadline but simply launched another series of costly surveys.

The "notice of intention to designate" sent out by USDA as evidence of its good faith in enforcing the Act was another in the long series of stalling tactics employed by the Department after its final deadline had passed. As the Colorado case shows, the notices did not mean that the federal inspectors move in immediately to take over inspection in below-standard states. Notices of designation, as opposed to "intended designation," require take-over to follow within thirty days. In testimony before the House Agriculture Committee on March 24, 1971, Assistant Secretary Lyng revealed that data on the fourteen states found to have inspection below federal standards in January and February, 1971 and, therefore, subject to federal take-over were still being reviewed. Final decisions on take-over would be made "shortly," he said. The Department used "intended designation" the same way it used the one-year extensions in December, 1969—to stall in the hope that noncomplying states would take the minimum steps necessary to allow the Department to describe them as "equal to" with a straight face.* As a result of delays by USDA, nearly 25 percent of the states found to be processing meat under substandard conditions in 1967, confirmed to be doing so in 1969 and officially notified as doing so in February, 1971, were still doing so through March, 1971, nearly three and a half years after the passage of the Wholesome Meat Act. As of May, 1971, notices of designation had gone out to only five states and territories: Minnesota, North Dakota, Montana, Kentucky, and Puerto Rico. Ten other states—Ohio, Indiana, West Virginia, Texas, North Carolina, Hawaii, Louisiana, New Hampshire, Colorado, and Massachusetts—which USDA intended to take over as late as February, 1971, have now been hastily certified.

* The difference is that the extensions were authorized by the Act while the notices of "intended designation" are not.

The state of Colorado perhaps best exemplifies the charade of certification. Up to the December, 1970, deadline, Colorado had made almost no attempt to bring the state inspection up to federal standards. Then upon threat of a federal take-over, a crash program was instituted by the Colorado State Senate. The State hired seven new lay inspectors who were given eight days training in federally inspected plants before being placed alone in isolated plants around the state. (After eight days, as one federal inspector said, "they won't even know how to keep knives sharp!") On January 18, 1971, USDA issued a "notice of intention to designate" and began conducting lengthy surveys to determine how federal take-over should proceed. These studies, which should have been conducted at least twelve months earlier when Colorado missed the first deadline, led to months of further delay. In the meantime inspection in Colorado remained under state control. Three months later, USDA changed its mind and certified state meat inspection in Colorado as up to federal standards after all.

Certification of meat inspection in Louisiana and Texas may also warrant scrutiny. In February, 1971, USDA announced that it intended to designate the inspection systems in these states. Texas at that time had 599 plants, Louisiana 270. These would have been by far the biggest state systems taken over by the federal government. Nevertheless it appeared that USDA had no choice. In its annual report to the House and Senate Committees on Agriculture, which it released during this period, USDA stated that its surveys showed that these states had "critical deficiencies in plant sanitation and inspectional (*sic*) controls over processing operations." Approximately three months later, USDA rescinded its notice of "intent to designate" and certified these states. It is at least questionable whether all of these plants, many of which were structurally defective, could have made the investment necessary to achieve the required standards in the short period between notice of intent to designate and certification, particularly when they had failed to do so for three years.

Nebraska and Missouri provide other examples of on-again off-again certification. USDA certified Nebraska meat inspection as "equal to" despite persistent reports from its own inspectors that the program was not adequately staffed or administered. In the summer of 1971, when USDA was finally forced to take over the system, it had to double the staff Nebraska had deemed adequate. USDA certified Missouri's meat inspection program in September, 1970. Less than a year later, in August, 1971, acting on tips from the field, USDA wrote to the Missouri Department of Agriculture (MDA) requiring that it review operations in all state inspected plants within thirty days or be "designated" for federal take-over. By the time MDA completed the required review, 146 out of 464 intrastate plants in this "equal to" state had been closed down.*

In early October, a Missouri newscaster telephoned USDA in Washington to ask whether or not Missouri would be "designated" for federal take-over or recertified. A secretary told him that Missouri was on a list of states designated for federal take-over. The same day, USDA denied that a decision had been made but confirmed that the information on that list had been correct. The newscaster then spoke to the Commissioner of MDA, who indicated that feverish negotiations concerning the status of the Missouri program were under way between USDA and MDA. Two days later, Missouri was certified as "equal to" federal standards.

The final irony in USDA's implementation of the Wholesome Meat Act is that certification, with all its question marks, is now being touted as justification for allowing state inspected meat to cross state lines and for possible defederalization of the whole meat inspection program. Senator Charles Mathias (R.-Md.) in 1971 tried to clear the way for state meat to cross state lines by successfully amending the agricultural appropriations bill on the floor of the Senate. The amendment was killed in the House-Senate conference committee, but it is by no means dead. In a meeting with USDA officials on January 18, 1971, we were informed that Under Secretary Campbell had sent a letter to the Congressional farm committees saying that USDA would support such an amendment in the future.

* While most of the closings were very brief, fifty-five plants were still shut down almost a month later, and some are still closed.

Assistant Secretary Lyng agreed that the Department had changed its mind about keeping state inspected meat out of interstate commerce. The National Meat and Poultry Inspection Advisory Committee, made up of state inspection officials, recommended to Secretary Hardin on February 18 that meat processed in "equal to" plants be allowed to cross state lines and that federal funding of state inspection be increased to at least 80 percent. These plans have been temporarily derailed on Capitol Hill. The House Agriculture Subcommittee on Livestock and Grains, led by Representative Graham Purcell (D.-Tex.) and Representative Thomas Foley (D.-Wash.), has put the Department on notice that it opposes any such change in the Act until it is absolutely sure that state inspection programs are operating on federal standards.

USDA is not content just to give state inspected meat federal privileges, however. Despite all denials to the contrary, it is proceeding ahead with plans to turn federal meat inspection back to the states. At a meat industry trade meeting in November, 1970, Assistant Secretary Lyng made it clear that decentralization of interstate meat inspection was his personal preference but that it had not yet been approved by the Nixon Administration. Lyng's plans harmonize well with Nixon's New Federalism and its corollary revenue sharing.* A high level USDA task force, chaired by Adrian Gilbert of the Forest Service, has proposed "Project No. 4," a confidential plan to decentralize meat and poultry inspection.[10] As a step toward this goal, it urges the cross-utilization of state inspectors to supervise meat processing in some interstate plants. It also calls for increasing federal funding of state inspection from 50 to 80–100 percent. The Task Force consulted no consumer representatives before making its report.

USDA continues to deny publicly that these plans exist. On December 29, 1970, Dr. Kenneth McEnroe, Deputy Administrator for Meat and Poultry Inspection, disclaimed any intent to dismantle the federal program. His superior, Dr. Clayton Yeutter, however, said just

---

* Federal take-over of state inspection is an embarrassment for President Nixon's New American Revolution. It leads to increased federal control, not less, and takes more money away from the states.

the opposite in a meeting with council presidents of the meat inspection lodges of the American Federation of Government Employees. At a meeting in his office, Yeutter is said to have advised the council presidents that he was under orders from the Administration to move swiftly toward the ultimate goal of turning over the federal program to the states. Carl Barnes, Chief of Personnel for the Department of Agriculture, acknowledged these plans at the meeting on February 8, 1971, and tried to reassure the council presidents by saying that he would do everything possible to arrange for the states to "blanket-in" the federal inspection into the state system with, he hoped, no reduction in grade or salary.

In resisting this trend, the consumer does have two strong and unusual allies. The American Meat Institute, the trade association of national meat packers which opposed the Wholesome Meat Act, is now mobilizing to defend its goals of uniform inspection with federal standards. For the large packers, fifty different state inspection systems would be a nightmare. The lack of uniformity in the enforcement of federal regulations is the packer's chief complaint against federal meat inspectors. If decentralization goes through, the large packers will have to contend with not only the vagaries of individual inspectors interpreting the same handbook of regulations, but with different inspectors interpreting different regulations in fifty different states.

The federal meat inspectors are also disturbed by the prospect of defederalization. The inspector corps takes pride in the sixty-five-year history of federal inspection. Despite their occasional failures, they have attained a professionalism and independence from politics which is not matched in any state inspection system.*

* State inspectors already inspect meat in intrastate plants in several states, under auspices of the Talmadge-Aiken Act. This Act encourages states to cooperate in the inspection or grading of various agricultural commodities. Under the Act, some state inspectors are assigned to federally inspected plants. States are reimbursed on a 50–50 basis. Talmadge-Aiken is, in effect, a loophole, which, if widely used, might allow USDA to defederalize gradually without going back to Congress for new legislation. A Government Accounting Office survey released in June, 1970, found significantly more inspection failures in Talmadge-Aiken plants than in Federal plants.

Despite the delays in enforcement, the Wholesome Meat Act does have some success to its credit. The funds budgeted for state inspection programs have increased markedly, from $12.4 million in fiscal 1968 to $38 million in fiscal 1970. There has also been a 60 percent increase in the number of meat plants inspected by the federal government. Refurbishing of old plants and the building of new plants to federal specifications will ultimately mean a more efficient meat industry with a higher quality product for the consumer. These accomplishments were achieved under the threat of federal take-over. Whether they will be maintained if enforcement of the meat laws is given over to the states remains to be seen.

There are also some sound reasons for preserving state inspection when it does meet federal standards. Not only is it cheaper than federal inspection, it is also potentially more responsive to local problems, particularly those involving small plants where state inspectors have the most experience. In the case of the locker plants and custom slaughterers, which provide valuable services to small towns and rural communities, the states may be better qualified and more flexible in applying federal standards in ways that allow these businesses to survive without subverting the goals of the act. But in trying to preserve the state systems, USDA should not throw out the baby with the bath water. The goal of the Wholesome Meat Act is to insure that all meat consumed in this country has been inspected and processed with uniformly high standards. Turning all meat inspection over to the states or allowing state-inspected meat to cross state lines, which would encourage large packers to go shopping in search of compliant state governments, would threaten this goal.

If the federal inspection system becomes an offering on the altar of the New Federalism, the Wholesome Meat Act would in effect be turned on its head. An act, which originally promised to extend uniform federal standards to the 25 percent of meat not processed under federal control in 1967 may result in all meat being processed in fifty separate state controlled systems. It would be ironic indeed if consumer legislation made necessary by the failures of state government provides a pretext for turning the whole inspection system over to state government.

The alchemy which the Department of Agriculture has performed on the Wholesome Meat Act is not unique. It is a form of bureaucratic lawlessness depressingly familiar to followers of other consumer and safety legislation, particularly pipeline safety and coal mine safety. As one observer has noted, lawlessness in the government occurs when statutes (what Congress says it wants to do) fail to correspond with realities (what the bureaucracy *does not* want to do).[11] The consumer coalition which passed the Wholesome Meat Act was aware that USDA did not fully endorse its goals, but it lacked the resources and persistence to follow it through to enforcement. It would have had a hard time arousing public concern in any case. Emasculation of a consumer law is, unfortunately, a very boring affair. When bureaucrats blink at the law in this matter, their evasions and delays are gradual and technical; they rarely make news.

The need for a permanent corps of public interest advocates to defend the integrity of meat inspection is starkly evident in USDA's evasion of the Wholesome Meat Act. But protecting legislative intent is only one phase of the struggle. Even if all meat plants were uniform in their processing equipment, training of inspectors, and regulations, the effectiveness of the law would still be hostage to the integrity of the individual inspector. While the failures of federal inspection pale in comparison to the real and potential breakdowns in most state inspected plants, the federal failures are still very serious and highlight the need for a stronger *federal* inspection system. The federal inspector, as we shall see, suffers from the same advocacy gap which imperils enforcement of the Wholesome Meat Act.

3

The Forgotten Man:
The Federal Meat
Inspector

I am asking for help in an effort to protect the consumer; and terminate some of this pressure from Industry on USDA personnel. . . . Please hold this letter in confidence, since my job would be at stake. My sincere hope is that you . . . will get the public's opinion and support for better Inspection backing. At the present, the Poultry Industry has pressured and manipulated the personnel until I feel that the Inspection Program has deteriorated substantially in recent months.

This plea, from a federal inspector at a Central Soya chicken plant in a Southern state, highlights a cardinal principle of the regulatory process: consumer laws are only as strong as the men who apply them at the plant level. In the drama of getting food safety bills passed in Congress, the consumer often forgets that the integrity of even the most carefully drafted legislation ultimately rests in the hands of an obscure GS 12 inspector who carries his handbook of regulations into a meat or poultry plant, and makes the hard decisions about contaminants, sanitation standards, and condemnations for cancer and other diseases. The principle holds true for the other regulated areas as well. Wherever there is a regulated industry—from coal mines and nuclear power plants to soup factories and sausage plants, the inspectors are the front line in the citizen's struggle for responsible regulation of private power.

The key men in enforcing meat and poultry regulations in the plants of the meat processors are the
inspectors-in-charge, veterinarians by profession who
supervise inspection activities, and the lay inspectors
on the meat production line who do the dirty work of
carcass examination and handling. In performing this
duty, the inspector exercises formidable discretionary
powers. He must apply dozens of regulations to thousands of carcasses a day. In a poultry plant, for example, the inspector, in less than three seconds per bird,
must use sight, feel, and smell to examine all organs
and tissues of the carcass, including the heart, liver,
spleen, kidneys, lungs, air sacs, and skin.[1] He is
expected to protect the consumer from cancerous
tumors, breast blisters, male sex organs, fecal contamination, feathers, lung tissue, and other unsanitary
or diseased chicken parts. The job requires extraordinary concentration and skill.

For instance, the inspector must condemn all chickens with avian leukosis, or chicken cancer, considered
a possible threat to human health. Avian leukosis is a
systemic disease and may affect virtually any organ
or tissue of the bird. The tumors are often microscopic
and even large ones may be missed by the untrained
eye. Even the most dedicated inspector does not catch
all leukosis-diseased chickens, and lax inspectors let
many slip by. According to a group of inspectors in
North Carolina, it is not uncommon for them to spot
the grayish or yellowish lymphoid masses or tumors of
leukotic chickens in stores and supermarkets in that
state (see Chapter 4 for a fuller discussion of chicken
cancer).

Airsacculitis is another common poultry disease
which challenges the skill of federal inspectors in protecting the consumer. The disease is somewhat like
pneumonia in human beings and causes a bacteria-
laden mucus to collect in the chicken's air sacs. Unlike
chickens with cancer, chickens with airsacculitis may
pass inspection, provided that all diseased tissue and
mucus are completely removed. This is easier said than
done. Attempts to clean out the diseased parts with air
suction guns often break the sacs and spread bacterial
contamination from the mucus throughout the interior

of the chicken. The inspector has little official guidance in deciding whether such contaminated birds should be thrown into the "condemn" barrels or salvaged and sold as cut-up chicken.

With so much discretion and responsibility, inspectors work under intense pressure. Moreover, the job is always noisy (men must shout to be heard a few feet away) and often dangerous (meat processing ranks among the top four industries with the highest accident records). And through it all, the inspector engages in a perpetual jousting with plant officials looking for new ways to enhance their profits.

It is ironic that the inspectors, who are closer to the source of regulatory problems than anyone else, have become the forgotten men of the consumer movement. Unfortunately, consumers still suffer from the Progressive's fallacy that law plus bureaucracy equals change and therefore pay little attention to enforcement. In practice the equation more often reads: law plus bureaucracy plus pressure by the regulated interests equals *status quo*. Knowing this, the meat processors take a great interest in the minutiae of enforcement by inspectors, for their judgments can quicken or slow the pace of profit in a plant. The inspector has the power not only to condemn birds but, in rare cases, to suspend inspection, closing the plant down. After consumer safety legislation becomes the law, the inspectors naturally become prime targets for the same vested interests which unsuccessfully opposed safety legislation when it was proposed on Capitol Hill. But at the inspector's level, the pressure tactics are more direct and crude than the campaign contributions and discreet influence peddling preferred by lobbyists in Congress. To win over inspectors, plant managements have cajoled them with direct bribes such as contributions in kind (all the chicken or steak they can eat) and extra overtime (paid for by the plants), and deferred bribes such as promises of future employment. They have intimidated them with verbal abuse, threats to use influence in Washington to have them transferred, investigations of their personal lives, and threats of violence.

After the editorials have been written, the Pulitzer

Prizes awarded, and the consumer champions departed for new crusades, it is the inspector who takes the heat from the packers. Because of these pressures, the single most corrupting force in federal meat inspection is the failure of the meat bureaucracy in Washington to back its inspectors in disputes with plant management. This failure, when it occurs, is not a private personnel matter between the inspector and his superiors. The consumer's interest is very direct. The quality and safety of the meat which goes to the consumer depend on the inspector's morale:

In the plainest of words . . . things are in a hell of a mess! Morale is worse than under Somers.* Only a GAO investigation will spark any real action. There are those of us that are about to throw in the towel.[2]

I am trying to do a good job, to get the regulations followed. Then I get the word to lighten up. You get the feeling: what the heck! In the last twelve months, we have lost a lot of ground.[3]

The pressure on meat and poultry inspectors intensifies whenever profit margins narrow for the meat processors, as they did in 1970–1971. During this period, many inspectors experienced a crisis of confidence prompted by the fear that their superiors will not support them in any dispute with a plant. Left unchecked by USDA this trend has reduced the quality of meat the consumer buys.

The present morale crisis in the meat inspection service must be understood in the context of a tradition of "past acceptance at all levels within the Consumer and Marketing Service of inadequate performance by plant management," as the General Accounting Office described the atmosphere in C&MS in a 1970 report.[4] Few regulatory agencies in the federal government have been as regularly embarrassed by General Accounting Office and Congressional investigations, and none as apparently incapable of constructive response as C&MS. Even when repeatedly warned by its inspectors in their official reports, it permitted grossly unsani-

* Deputy Administrator for Consumer Protection (meat and poultry inspection), Consumer and Marketing Service, 1965–1969.

tary conditions to exist for years in many meat and poultry plants.

In 1959, the General Accounting Office, which oversees federal regulatory activities for Congress, reported that 120 of 255 meat plants visited by its investigators were operating under unsanitary conditions. In 1965, the Office of the Inspector General, USDA's internal watchdog, found unsanitary conditions in a large number of plants, including inadequate vermin control, filthy saws and meat carts, flaking paint directly over exposed meat, and dragging meat products on the floor.[5] Another report by the Inspector General in 1969 found conditions little improved in red meat plants and also reported widespread failures in the sanitation practices of poultry plants on Maryland's eastern shore. Still another group of investigators, the Washington reviewers of the Consumer and Marketing Service, reported serious sanitation deficiencies in *all* regions of the inspection service in both 1967 and 1969. The cleanliness of carcass coolers—a critical stage in the processing of ready-to-market meat products, one in which harmful bacteria often build up—was found unacceptable in 25 percent of plants surveyed in 1967, 29 percent of the plants surveyed in 1968, and 42 percent of the plants surveyed in 1969.[6]

The General Accounting Office renewed its monitoring of meat inspection in 1969 when it examined forty poultry plants which since 1967 had been identified by USDA as chronic violators of minimum standards. C&MS was aware of the violations, but by March 1, 1969 had terminated inspection at only one of the forty plants; six plants either voluntarily withdrew from inspection or ceased operating; thirty-three of the chronic violators continued to process poultry with no improvement. The GAO concluded that the failure of C&MS to suspend or terminate inspection services at these plants probably exposed the consuming public to poultry unfit for human consumption.[7]

A follow-up inspection by a C&MS review team in 1970 found twenty-eight of the forty plants still operating. Although this was only one year after the GAO report, the team found it necessary to suspend inspection at thirteen of these plants and observed contaminated products at nine of the plants. Finally seventeen of the remaining twenty-eight chronic violators were reinvestigated by the GAO in visits ending in March, 1971. Once again, they had to suspend inspection at thirteen of the seventeen plants. GAO also visited fifty-one additional plants selected at random. Of sixty-eight total plants visited in 1970–1971, GAO observed contaminated products at thirty-five.

The GAO's latest report on red meat plants, released June, 1971, has the same monotonous theme of failure. Of forty plants selected for study because of repeated complaints from inspectors, the GAO found that thirty-six were still sending meat to the consumer under unsanitary conditions. These plants accounted for nearly 8 percent of all cattle and swine slaughtered in the United States. In thirty of the forty plants, the GAO found conditions which permitted meat to be contaminated with such exotic matter as rodent urine, metal shavings from carcass splitting saws, fecal material, hair, rust, condensation, dead flies, and cockroaches. The GAO also criticized the use of dirty equipment and unsanitary carcass coolers in these plants. Although these conditions had existed for up to three years, C&MS had not suspended inspection at any plant up to the time of the report and refused to do so afterwards as well. C&MS's overwhelming reluctance to allow its inspectors to use the suspension power has greatly reduced their leverage in pressing the plant for reforms.[8]

USDA's inaction has one basic cause: the ex parte pressures of the meat processors with their large cadre of Washington representatives and their political influence on agricultural committees in Congress can make life more uncomfortable and insecure for top meat officials than can the complaints of their own inspectors. Although the GAO reports to Congress, the agricultural appropriations subcommittees which oversee meat inspection have shown little interest in following up its findings in their hearings on funding for the inspection program.

It is therefore no great surprise that the inspectors do not always get a fair hearing in Washington when they have disputes with a plant. In 1970, the inspectors' lack of confidence in their superiors had become so pervasive that top USDA officials on several occasions had to take the extraordinary step of reassuring the meat inspection corps that USDA, in fact, does intend to enforce the meat and poultry Acts. Dr. Gilbert Wise, Chief of Inspection Services in June, 1970, informed his personnel:

Some of you have expressed to me directly and others indirectly, concern that should you take positive actions to correct [sanitation] deficiencies, you might not be upheld at higher levels. Let me state as emphatically as I possibly can . . . C&MS and the Department will maintain its policy of requiring continuously adequate sanitation in all federally inspected plants.

On July 16, when L. H. Burkert temporarily took over Wise's job, he found it necessary to inform the inspectors that the policy remained in effect. The following month, Assistant Secretary Richard Lyng, at a meeting with regional directors of the inspection programs, once again told the inspectors that he would back them up in assuring that "only a clean and unadulterated product is produced." The minutes of the meeting touch on the source of the inspectors' grievances:

When reports [from plant management] of some consequence reach Mr. Lyng, he will ask us [the regional directors] to look into the problem. When doing this, neither Mr. Lyng nor the administrator's office is "second guessing" anyone. In 99 out of 100 cases, when inquiries are made, it will probably stop there.

A major reason why the inspectors need so much reassurance is that departmental inquiries into industry complaints against inspectors do not stop where Mr. Lyng thinks. There are of course problem inspectors but too often these complaints are fabricated to muzzle inspectors who are trying conscientiously to enforce standards in problem plants. Unfortunately, C&MS responds far more quickly to the plant's complaints about the inspectors than to the inspectors' complaints about the plant.

When top officials in a federal agency must constantly remind their subordinates that the agency really does intend to enforce the law, morale in that agency must be dangerously low. In fact, in the last five years the morale problem of federal inspectors has been recognized by a succession of investigating groups. In October, 1965, the Office of the Inspector General, USDA, in its report on unsanitary conditions in federal meat plants, concluded that a major cause of these conditions was a passive attitude on the part of meat inspectors conditioned by fear of conflict with plant management. In 1970, the Inspector General and C&MS regional personnel suggested the following reasons for inadequate enforcement of sanitation regulations:

Lack of support from higher levels of management within C&MS when inspectors attempted to require correction of deficiencies.

Inspectors' reluctance to incur the displeasure, irritation, or antagonism of plant management that might result from enforcing the regulations.

Past acceptance at all levels within C&MS of inadequate performance by plant management.

The GAO's report on the red meat inspection in 1970 concluded that the inspectors' uncertainty as to what action to take when they discover sanitation failures was the principal cause of laxity in enforcement.* More recently, the Associated Press conducted interviews with over a dozen poultry inspectors in North Carolina in August, 1971. A principal reason for inspection breakdowns in the state, according to the interviews, is the inspectors' fear of reprisals from superiors in USDA, if they inspect "by the book" and raise complaints from plant management.

In sum, C&MS's massive inertia in using its enforcement powers saps the spirit of the entire inspection system, as this GAO report of a discussion with the inspectors at a large meat plant indicates:

---

* The GAO noted that when inspectors reported unsanitary conditions in a plant, they were not required to indicate what corrective action, if any, had been taken. C&MS management had no way of knowing whether the inspector had succeeded in cleaning up a plant or needed help from Washington. "Action taken" is now an essential part of weekly sanitation reports prepared by inspectors in the plants, but is still not required by Washington and regional personnel.

A meeting was held with the processing inspectors on the night of June 12, 1969. Many of them complained about past lack of support from the Officer in Charge (the traveling official who supervises the inspectors of the several plants which make up a meat inspection circuit), the Regional Office and Washington level. They complained bitterly about previous actions taken by them to correct deficiencies in the plants on this circuit that were not supported by any level of management. . . . Although the inspectors were enthusiastic in attitude toward doing a good job of inspection, they voiced much skepticism concerning [promised] support at a higher level.[9]

In its latest report on poultry inspection released on November 16, 1971, the GAO found that inspectors still were uncertain whether C&MS really wanted strict enforcement of sanitation standards. Merl Mitchell, Chairman of the National Joint Council of Food Inspector Locals, which represents the lay inspectors, was so alarmed by this situation that he held a press conference in September, 1971, to warn that the authority of field inspectors is being undermined by their USDA superiors and that morale is at an all-time low.

Four Case Studies

The inspectors' morale is threatened from two directions: from Washington, when superiors fail to suspend or otherwise discipline plants reported by inspectors to be chronic violators of the meat laws; and from the plant itself, when management, emboldened by C&MS's passivity, harasses, intimidates, or subverts the inspector as he tries to do his job. The second is more insidious for it corrupts the individual as well as the system.

Reports from meat and poultry inspectors reveal numerous instances of verbal and physical assault by plant employees against federal inspectors. In 1967, at a chicken plant in Shelbyville, Tennessee, the manager hired a bouncer who threatened federal personnel and finally beat a line inspector unconscious in a dispute over regulations. In Gainesville, Georgia, the manager of a Pillsbury poultry plant was replaced after one of his employees pushed an inspector into a picker, a rapidly spinning machine with hard rubber "fingers" which flay the feathers from birds. A leading official of a poultry inspectors' union reported that inspectors frequently work in plant environments made deliberately hostile by managers who hope to keep inspectors off balance and wear them down. He had experienced a variety of major and petty harassments, ranging from leaving the plant and finding his automobile tires flattened to actual assault by plant employees wielding knives and steel drums.*

Congress recognized in the passage of the Wholesome Meat Act and the Poultry Inspection Act that those who administered the inspection program would be subject to immense pressure. 21 U.S.C. §662 provides penalties for the offer and acceptance of bribes to influence meat inspection officials. 21 U.S.C. §461(c) makes it a criminal offense for anyone forcibly to assault, resist, oppose, impede, intimidate, or interfere with any inspector in the performance of his duties. The Act provides for a $5000 fine and imprisonment up to three years or both for violators. USDA may also withdraw inspection when intimidation occurs.

This clause was put into the Act in recognition of the fact, as stated by the GAO, that "the effectiveness with which . . . standards are enforced will be dependent on the resolve of Consumer and Marketing Service personnel at each and every level—from the plant inspectors to the Washington officials."[10] Clearly nothing erodes a regulatory agency's resolve more rapidly than intimidation of its inspectors by the interests it regulates.

In practice, the law has failed to protect the inspector, either from a hostile plant management or from dishonest or timid superiors. Only in cases of violent attack is the law really effective, and here the victim may use the legal remedies available to any other citizen. A federal inspector at a North Carolina chicken plant, for example, was threatened when the owner's brother, an eviscerating foreman, became infuriated at the inspector's criticism of his work. The foreman invaded the inspector's trailer home at night, threat-

---

* These reports come from confidential communications from inspectors in the field.

ened the inspector and his wife, and damaged the trailer. USDA failed to act, and the plant did not lose a day's production as a result of the incident. The inspector, however, sued the company and won an out-of-court settlement. In such cases, the inspectors do not need the "intimidation clause" of the federal meat law to protect them.

Instead the clause is needed to protect the inspector against the subtle forms of intimidation and harassment which fall short of physical violence; here it has failed. The only records made public by the Meat and Poultry Inspection Division show that fifteen cases of inspection harassment or intimidation have been reported since November, 1970, and that three of these have been referred to the Department of Justice for prosecution under the Act. In one case involving the Marshall Durbin Company of Jasper, Alabama, the plant manager *twice* threatened the life of the federal inspector. USDA let the company off with a letter of warning. The warning was conveyed by a "Dear Marshall" letter from Dr. McEnroe, USDA's meat inspection chief, to Marshall Durbin, Sr. Durbin is an old acquaintance of McEnroe and is a leading industry spokesman. His son is now Vice-President of the National Broiler Council, the industry trade association. Shortly after the letter of warning to Durbin, the National Broiler Council, in July, 1971, stated that charges of inspector harassment were "ridiculous," "union inspired," and "dated." At that time Durbin's letter of warning was still secret.

Unfortunately, threats to inspectors short of actual violence are also not treated seriously by the federal courts in some cases. In a recent case involving the Carr Packing Company of Albany, New York, the federal district court let the company's president off with a warning on the charge that he had repeatedly harassed federal inspectors, but fined him $200 for unauthorized possession of a federal meat inspection stamp.

It would be inaccurate to suggest that all or most packers are guilty of threatening or illegal conduct toward inspectors. Some plants in fact go far beyond USDA regulations in trying to turn out a wholesome product. For example, the Swift Company turkey plant in Wallace,

North Carolina, has up to six men rechecking the birds for defects *after* they have passed the federal inspectors. In some plants, when conflict does occur, the grievances are not all on the side of the inspector. Some packers are occasionally victimized by the incompetence or personality quirks of inspectors, and by the failure of the Consumer and Marketing Service to develop criteria to give more uniformity to inspection in different plants.

Plant managers are also occasionally justified in criticizing the inspectors' competence. Unfortunately federal veterinarians are not required to meet the same standards as their peers in private practice. In most states, a vet must pass an examination by a board or committee of his peers before he can open his door to the public. But any vet who has his DVM can enter federal service without further screening.

Plant managers frequently complain that inspectors are sent into plants without proper training. In some plants, inspectors are barely able to speak the English language, in others they have been left in charge with only ten to fifteen minutes orientation. It is difficult to expect the packers to cooperate if they are assigned unqualified inspectors. USDA must take steps to see that high standards for vets and lay inspectors are protected by examinations and other methods of review. These certifications of competence will protect the consumer and increase the inspectors' authority in the plants.

Better training is no panacea, however. Often it is the more highly qualified inspector who takes his job seriously who gets into conflict with the companies. Problems usually arise for the following reasons. First, the meat industry is relatively competitive, with large volume and narrow profit margins. The competitive pressure is felt most intensely at the plant manager level. He has strong career incentives to make his unit as profitable as possible. If things are not going well, he may try to make the inspector a scapegoat. Company headquarters, while they may be very protective of their product's image, often do not effectively monitor their plant managers. Second, the temptation for hard-pressed companies to corrupt or intimidate inspectors may be irresistible if they feel USDA will not stand behind the inspectors. Third, when disputes between inspectors and plants develop, there is an advocacy gap between resources available to the plant—with its Washington representatives and trade associations—and those available to the inspector. This gap, because it cripples the inspector's ability to present his case, creates an institutional bias in favor of industry.

The inspector's plight is examined in more detail in the following cases. It should be noted that the problems discussed here are more common in poultry plants than in red meat plants. First, unlike federal meat inspection, which dates back to the period of Teddy Roosevelt, poultry inspection is a relative newcomer to the regulatory scene. Prior to 1958, poultry inspection was voluntary and was sold to the slaughterhouse as a service by USDA. Since a plant could discontinue the service if the inspector became too tough, thereby depriving the inspector of his job, industry pressure on the inspector was extremely effective. Passage of the Poultry Products Inspection Act in 1957 placed interstate plants under mandatory federal inspection, but the tradition of "close relations" between inspector and plant continued. Until 1969, poultry inspection was an independent division within C&MS entirely separate from the red meat program. The poultry industry vigorously opposed the consolidation of meat and poultry inspection in 1969, which placed them under the leadership of officials trained in the red meat inspection traditions. According to many inspectors, some chicken plant managers act as if they were still "ruling the roost." Second, there are fewer diseases to look for in hogs and beef than in chickens and turkeys, and the diseases of the former are easier to identify.

The Case of Inspector A: Transfer[11]

Inspector A was the chief inspector at a Central Soya chicken plant in North Carolina. The plant is large, processing a daily average of 48,000 birds. As inspector-in-charge, he supervised five lay inspectors who checked the birds for disease and contamination as

they moved along the conveyor belt of the production
line at an average speed of 100 birds per minute.

After the birds have been eviscerated, their lungs,
gizzards, and livers removed, and certified free of cancer, excreta, spillage from the intestine, feathers, and
other diseases and contaminants, they are supposed to
be "ready to cook." The next step is for the birds to
go into huge ice-water tubs called chillers and then
to be boxed for shipment to the supermarket.

The chiller may hold 4,800 birds or more at one
time. The birds are shaken in the chiller allowing its
water to penetrate deeply into the tissues of the bird.
One unfit bird coming off the production line may
contaminate hundreds of others as its bacteria dis-
perses in the waters of the tank. After the birds
emerge from the chiller, a few are sampled by the
inspector-in-charge as a final check. In the Central
Soya plant a sample of twenty-five birds is examined
four times a day. The purpose of the sample is to
measure the effectiveness of inspection. If the birds in
the sample are unfit, the sample may be condemned
or sent back for reinspection. If the percentage of
birds showing defects is high, the inspector may require the plant to slow the production line speed to
allow the plant employees to do a more thorough
job.

In September, 1970, Inspector A faced a crisis at
this particular chicken factory. Central Soya installed
a new management at a time when falling poultry
prices were increasing the pressure to expand the output of chickens. The new management was not only
new but as one observer put it, as "green as grass."
Before coming to this plant, the manager had previously dealt only with live poultry, the plant manager
had only maintenance experience, the quality control
foreman had been a field man for the Sunnyside Egg
Company, the picking foreman came directly from a
coffee plant in Louisiana, and the packing foreman
was fresh from East Carolina University with no
poultry experience.

By mid-September Inspector A found so many unfit
chickens coming off the line that he was forced to
reduce the line speed several times a day. A slower

line means less profit and the inspector found himself in an escalating conflict with the new manager who was trying hard to impress his superiors by increasing output. By the end of September, the manager was making frequent complaints to Inspector A's superiors.

On October 7, Inspector A's immediate superior, his subcircuit supervisor, found a solution to the problem. He met with the general manager and agreed that in the future the plant, not the inspector, would control the line speed. In the prosaic world of poultry inspection, this was a subversive act. In one swift stroke Inspector A's supervisor had taken away one effective tool for enforcing quality in the plant. This act directly contravened the Poultry Inspector's Handbook which states:

While it is recognized that there is a physical limitation beyond which adequate inspection is impossible or unlikely, it is deemed impractical to establish a specific maximum rate of production applicable in all official plants and under all conditions. *It is, therefore, necessary that each inspector-in-charge determines the maximum speed at which inspection can be properly performed at his specific plant under the conditions prevailing at any specific time.*[12] (Emphasis added)

The Handbook goes on to state that "the quality of birds and the incidence of disease have a direct influence on attainable line speeds."[13]

During the next month (October 7–November 7) with the plant in control of line speed,* the ready-to-cook percentage of birds sampled by the inspector at the end of processing declined. On an average day, more than a third of the birds had defects, such as excessive feathers and other unsanitary conditions, with dips to less than 50 percent on several days. USDA regulations make no allowance for such a massive percentage of defective chickens:

Therefore it is necessary to use as the standard for operating the lines, the rate at which the end product shows zero

---

* The lay inspectors could still control the line at the point where they examined the birds' organs. The plant controlled the line both before and after this stage, when the feathers, crops, lungs, and hearts are removed.

incidence of error in inspection, and at which the products
are so eviscerated that they meet ready-to-cook requirements.[14]

Dr. Harner, the Mid-Atlantic Regional Director,
agrees that 100 percent error-free birds is the goal
but since this is not attainable, "it's up to a man's
judgment." He indicates that the normal range of
acceptance is 5–25 percent errors.

This situation continued until December 15 when
Inspector A cut it short by taking a personal risk.
On this day, so many birds were coming off the line
with feathers (which are bacteria carriers) and other
defects and carrying their contaminants into the chiller
that he could no longer stand aside. Disobeying the
orders of his supervisor, he ordered the plant to slow
the line speed. When the plant manager refused,
Inspector A legally took his inspectors off the line,
temporarily suspending inspection in the plant. Central Soya's manager, in an act of self-destructive
defiance, then destroyed 13,000 pounds of chicken by
processing them without inspection, after which they
had to be condemned.

In a subsequent hearing, Inspector A's lawyer cited
this action as evidence of the plant's arrogance and
its intention to incite and harass a federal inspector.
Mr. John Tromer, the personnel chief of the Consumer and Marketing Service, brusquely dismissed this
contention. In doing so, he suggested that attempts to
slip uninspected birds past inspectors are routine hap-
penings in federal poultry plants. "It's just a business
decision, a business risk," he said, "but we usually
catch them and condemn the chickens." It is difficult
to see why profit-conscious plants would take such
risks if they are usually caught. The danger is that
when the inspectors' personnel chief describes the
packers' attempt to violate federal law as "just a business decision," this attitude passes on to the inspectors
down the line.

In late December, 1970, the meat inspection division's regional office in Raleigh, North Carolina, reviewed Inspector A's decision to suspend inspection at
the Central Soya plant. The regional director, Dr.

George Harner, agreed that the inspector had acted properly in this case, but then rewarded him with a notice of transfer. In an unusual act, the lay inspectors in the Central Soya plant sent a formal protest to Raleigh, protesting Inspector A's transfer and backing his decisions in the plant. Such loyalty of lay inspectors to a veterinarian superior is extremely rare in the federal inspection service.

Upon learning of the inspector's plight, Robert Vaughn, a young lawyer from Oklahoma working with the Public Interest Research Group in Washington, D.C., agreed to go to North Carolina to represent the inspector. This was the first occasion when a public interest group intervened in the regulatory process in this way. As a result, a rare inside look at how inspectors may be intimidated in pursuit of their duty was obtained. The chief charge against the inspector was that he could not get along with plant management. His transfer, said Dr. Harner, was necessary to restore the mutual harmony between industry and agency which is vital to effective regulation. The meat inspection officials agreed that the plant had tried to bait the inspector and that such harassment may damage the inspection service. But according to the chief USDA investigator in this case, the remedy is not to discipline the plant but to have inspectors who can discipline their temper—so as not to react: "management must consider that these practices exist and where they do it behooves the Inspection Program to staff these establishments with people who can cope with such tactics." The danger is that inspectors who "cope" in this manner do so by easing inspection at management's request.*

In disputes of this kind, the inspector finds himself the victim of a peculiar double standard. Central Soya's manager was inexperienced and uncooperative. According to the inspector, he had boasted of his

---

* One of the incidents cited by Dr. Harner to show Inspector A's inability to cope with pressure occurred in 1969 when the inspector sold a piece of property to a black man. A white woman employed at the plant also wanted the property. When she learned of the sale, she assaulted the inspector with an extraordinary barrage of invective and obscenities. The inspector lost his temper and threatened to retaliate against the plant.

power to have inspectors transferred and had used threatening and abusive language. USDA, however, does not have the authority to order a hostile and vituperative plant manager removed as a condition of providing federal inspection. All it can do is to suspend inspection altogether, a rather drastic step it has been historically reluctant to take. In practice, therefore, the high premium USDA puts on cooperation with industry often means that an inspector will be sacrificed for the sake of harmony if any prolonged dispute with the plant develops.

Vaughn pointed out to USDA that the plant management was green, that nearly 40 percent of the chickens leaving the plant were probably unfit by USDA regulations, and that the inspector had consistently tried to correct these deficiencies in a hostile atmosphere. Nevertheless, the original decision to transfer the inspector was upheld.

Inspector A is a classic example of the responsible whistle-blower, a man who had worked for reform through channels and now, suffering reprisals, needed to go outside for help. In going outside, the inspector was not acting disloyally to his department. Repudiation of myopic or negligent leadership in an organization is not the same as repudiation of the organization.

Vaughn discovered, however, that whistle-blowing in the meat inspection service is a risky and lonely business, with a stacked legal deck. The transfer of an inspector, while it can cause him great hardship and uproot his family, is classed as an administrative decision, wholly within the discretion of the agency. The inspector, therefore, has little due process available to him if he wants to resist. The formal due process of civil service regulations which apply to a dismissal do not operate here. The inspector may file a grievance within USDA, but this act does not stay his transfer. If he wants to appeal his transfer, he must do so after the fact, from his new post.

In the past, the inspector who wanted to fight the system had virtually no one to give him advice and encouragement. The plant manager who feels that an inspector is too rigorous in enforcing the regulations has at his disposal the American Meat Institute, the

Western Meat Packers Association, the National Broiler Council, and other trade associations, as well as the Washington representatives of national companies such as Central Soya, Swift, Hormel, Ralston-Purina, to mention only a few. These groups can and do bring pressure directly to bear on the inspector's superiors in Washington.

The inspector has no outside constituency to speak up for him—not the consumer, certainly. Few if any purchasers of contaminated chicken trace it back to the processing plant or complain to USDA. Complaints, when they arise, are directed at the retail outlet. Ordinarily there is no complaint because the consumer is usually a silent victim, with no way of knowing that his disease or food poisoning may have been caused by hidden contaminants in the chicken or that part of his food dollar went for excess moisture instead of for meat. The National Association of Federal Veterinarians, a professional organization to which most inspectors-in-charge belong, lacks the legal resources to help him. The American Federation of Government Employees has been considerably more active in defending inspectors within USDA, but this group represents only lay inspectors, not inspectors-in-charge such as Inspector A, who is a veterinarian.

While it is probably desirable that inspectors be transferred or rotated from plant to plant, it appears that in Inspector A's case the transfer was a reprisal. Inspector A's transfer was dictated by a meat processor who wanted to escape strict enforcement of the regulations. As a result, the consumer's interest and health may have been jeopardized.*

The Case of Inspector B: Dismissal

The risks which inspectors run when they push for reforms from within are further illustrated by the case of a poultry inspector in Mississippi in the fall of 1970. On January 19, 1970, Inspector B received a USDA career-conditional appointment as a veterinary medical

---

* Conditions at this Central Soya plant have improved since the incident above. USDA has taken a special interest in the plant, and the company has brought in more experienced personnel.

officer, after graduating third in his class at the poultry
training school in Gainesville, Georgia.

His first assignment was as inspector-in-charge at a
poultry plant in Canton, Mississippi. At first, he got on
well at the plant, receiving praise from his superiors
as one of the hardest working inspectors on the circuit.
But after five months, he ran into trouble. In his words,
he decided

to cut the production of this plant by 10 percent in order
that we might turn out a ready-to-cook product as near
perfect as a human can produce. I met with immediate
reprisal from the President of this company in the form of
running in the government office speaking vulgar language
in loud tones.

This occurred on August 6, 1970. Soon afterwards, the
inspector requested transfer to another plant. His new
post was at a poultry plant in Morton, Mississippi. Here
he was an assistant to the inspector-in-charge. Soon
after his arrival, Inspector B noticed several infractions
of regulations and reported them to his superior but
received no response. When the inspector-in-charge
went on vacation to the annual Tennessee Walking
Horse event, he instructed Inspector B to man his chair
but to be alert for the GAO or other federal investigators. "I was informed," the inspector said, "that I
must keep my mouth shut." On September 3, he wrote
a letter to the General Accounting Office which made
the following points about his plant:

(a) ready-to-cook poultry being ice-packed with better than
17 percent moisture retained in the carcass [only 11–12
percent moisture is permitted];
(b) poultry being cut up and being frozen for school lunch
and defense contracts with very excessive amounts of moisture;
(c) carcasses being retained in picking room and rehung
at their convenience;
(d) I have known these carcasses to lay on the floor for
up to two hours without ice or any means of cooling;
(e) flies crawling on cut-up products which are being packed
for consumption. Dirty ice being used to chill and ice pack
products going for human consumption;
(f) excessive line speed causing the birds to be picked, drawn
and presented in such a way as to make it impossible for

USDA inspectors to make proper disposition of diseased and contaminated carcasses. This line's speed also makes it impossible for plant personnel to properly trim undesirable parts from these birds.[15]

He concluded his letter by saying:

My career with the USDA has been jeopardized by my trying to get these conditions cleared up at plant level. There has never been any room in this plant for any inspector who wanted to follow the instructions of the Poultry Products Inspection Act.

On September 11, a letter of dismissal was hand-delivered to Inspector B by a relief veterinarian for his circuit. The letter was dated September 1, two days before the inspector's letter to the GAO, but had *no* postal mark. The messenger had received the call to pick up the dismissal letter from the officer-in-charge of his circuit on September 11,[16] after USDA had had time to learn of the complaint to GAO. The letter alleged certain acts of misconduct which Inspector B committed, not at his present plant, but at the plant of his first assignment.

It charged that the inspector had been observed to have liquor on his breath, and to have granted special favors to plant employees. Because he was on probation as a first-year man, the inspector could appeal the charges against him only on the grounds of racial discrimination or political interference. Otherwise he could not obtain a hearing.

Without a hearing and thorough investigation of the inspector's activity in the two Mississippi plants, it is impossible to know for sure whether the inspector is a victim of industry influence, or of his own personal failures. The timing of the letter is suspicious, however, as is the fact that at no time while he was at the Canton plant was the inspector reprimanded by his superiors for the acts alleged in the letter of dismissal. What is clear is that the lack of due process accorded him invites false charges and makes it dangerous for any inspector to stand up to his superior or plant management during his probationary first year.

The extraordinary defenselessness of an inspector in the first year helps instill a spirit of servility which may shape the values of his subsequent career. In such cases, inspectors are much more likely to make accommodations to industry pressures which are not in the public interest. No one likes to work in a hostile environment, especially when he may be transferred or lose his job as a reward for strict enforcement.

Trim Girls, Overtime, and All the Meat You Can Eat

On October 13, 1970, two federal meat inspectors in Baltimore, Maryland, along with five former officials of one of Maryland's largest packinghouses, were indicted on sixty-seven counts of conspiracy, bribery, and violations of federal meat inspection laws. The Grand Jury indictment alleged that the plant had shipped thousands of pounds of uninspected meat in interstate commerce "fraudulently labeled" as pork meat which was not pork, sold lower grade products as higher grade, and used uninspected meat to fill orders placed by the Defense Department.[17] The two inspectors allegedly received "substantial quantities of meat" for their parts in the conspiracy. In the fall of 1971, forty inspectors, nearly one-half of the federal corps in the area, were indicted in Boston for accepting bribes of money, meat, and liquor from meat processors for periods of up to five years.

A graphic account of bribery is given by an inspector in Wisconsin who reports:

I was in a plant that the officer in charge and his boss from the area office had a recreation cabin and boat together. . . . I knew the DVM (veterinarian) was accepting free chicken. This DVM had to have a purchase order to get it out of the plant. These order blanks were 2½ inches by 4 inches. One day the cleaning lady had a wastebasket in the hall outside the main office. I saw a large amount of order slips with the DVM's name on them. I grabbed a handful; I don't know if I got every one, and put them in my pocket and walked on so I wouldn't look like a fool digging in the wastebasket (the order blanks were changed to [appear] to be for advertising). I took these slips and wrote a one-page letter and sent them to what I thought were the proper people. There were so many 2½ by 4 inch slips, that I had to put extra postage on it. And this is what happened; I was sent on a wild-goose chase hundreds of miles on Labor Day . . . to a plant that really didn't need me, just for harassment. A man came to talk to me there and asked me if I would like to retract this letter. I said "What is there to retract? I think I did right." This man babbled on as to that I shouldn't dig in wastebaskets, etc., etc., and his last words were "I will let you slip by this time, but after this keep your (dirty word) nose clean."[18]

As these cases show, industry pressure, especially when accompanied by low morale, sometimes makes individual inspectors easy marks for plant managers seeking to evade meat and poultry regulations. Few men in any profession have the courage and persistence of Inspector A. Many more succumb to conflicts of interest and the various blandishments which the companies may offer in payment for relaxed inspection. According to reports from inspectors, some poultry inspectors are allowed to raise chickens on their own or on contract to a poultry processor. They are not supposed to sell their chickens to the plant where they work but it is doubtful that this rule is rigidly enforced. They also report that part-time inspectors are allowed to inspect in plants where their wives or other close relatives are working.

The companies' attempts to seduce inspectors sometimes take quite literal forms. One inspector reports:

Poultry inspectors are customarily assigned a "girl" by plant management to trim bruises etc. at the points of inspection. Reportedly these "trim girls" are assigned on a twenty-four hour basis—day and night as the inspector so desires. This reportedly is another reason that poultry inspectors resist rotation—they don't want to leave their "trim girls."[19]

Less exotic and more common bribery is the overtime and free meat which the plants sometimes provide. The costs of inspection during regular working hours are paid by the federal government; when plant production schedules run overtime, the company must pay the inspector time-and-a-half. The meat packers claim that inspectors sometimes cheat and force overtime, but they fear retaliation from the inspectors if they complain. There is an inherent conflict, however, whenever the policed are paying the policeman.[20] The company can win special favors from the inspector by arranging to give him overtime. In some cases, a blue-collar GS 12 refuses promotion to a higher grade because he does not want to give up the opportunity for overtime, which may mean an additional $3–5,000 a year.[21]

The Hormel Case

The low morale of the inspector corps and the lack of leadership in Washington have resulted in serious enforcement failures in meat as well as poultry plants. A most notorious case occurred in 1969, when Ralph Nader charged before a Senate Subcommittee that the George A. Hormel Company plant in La Mirada, California, was taking stale meat returned by retail stores, repackaging it and reselling it to other outlets, without reinspection. The report created a sensation because it implicated one of the nation's leading interstate meat packers, not an intrastate or fly-by-night operation. The La Mirada plant, less than two years old at the time of the hearing, was considered a show place, a plant worthy of guided tours and public inspection.

Meat in the Los Angeles area, where the Hormel plant is located, is sold on a concession basis. If the meat is not sold at the retail level, it can be returned to the plant by the sellers. When the meat is returned, samples from it are subject to reinspection by the USDA officer in charge. If the meat still meets acceptable standards of wholesomeness, it can be resold to a different customer. The process has no definite limits. The meat can continue to recirculate in the marketplace as long as it meets acceptable standards. This returned meat has a trade name which gives some indication of its quality. It is called No. 2 meat. Nader explained the pricing policy of No. 2 meat by quoting from a Hormel salesman who sold a great deal of the meat to San Diego schools. Responding to a memo from his superior complaining that the prices for the No. 2 meat were too low, the salesman replied: "I sell all the junk I can for as much as I can get for it. I can't do more."[22]   When the original customers returned the meat to Hormel, they used the following terms to describe it: "moldy liverloaf, sour party hams, leaking bologna, discolored bacon, off-condition hams, and slick and slimy spareribs." Hormel renewed these products with cosmetic measures (reconditioning, trimming, and washing). Spareribs returned for sliminess, discoloration, and stickiness were rejuvenated through curing and smoking, renamed Windsor Loins, and sold in ghetto stores for more than fresh pork chops.[23]

Hormel's sale of No. 2 meat illustrates the charge of Congressman Tom Foley, one of the most effective consumer watchdogs in Congress, that the poor are the most likely victims of unscrupulous purveyors of substandard meat, because they are the least likely to complain, and are generally the purchasers of the lowest cost products. No. 2 meat was sold to supermarkets and schools in the Watts area of Los Angeles. One supermarket not far away from the Watts riot area bought Hormel's No. 2 meat almost exclusively. No. 2 Kolbase, which it bought from Hormel at $0.30 a pound, was sold to the poor for $0.90 a pound.[24]

USDA's response to the Hormel revelations was one of studied disbelief. The Consumer and Marketing Service seemed less concerned about Hormel's violations than they were about the "impropriety" of the manner in which information about the violations was leaked. Eventually, however, testimony presented at the Ribicoff hearings became too serious to ignore. USDA's Inspector General Nathaniel Kossack conducted a two-month investigation of the Hormel plant, and subsequently turned the case over to the Department of Justice for "consideration of possible court action." The records which showed that Hormel had sold uninspected returned meat to public schools and Vandenberg Air Force Base, acts which would have led to serious criminal charges and a $10,000 fine if proven, were omitted as evidence in the federal prosecution of Hormel because they were supplied by an informer within the Hormel plant. (Other federal agencies, including the FBI, routinely use information obtained by informers in federal prosecutions.)

On May 11, 1970, one year after proceedings were initiated, Hormel pleaded guilty to three misdemeanor counts of violating the Wholesome Meat Act, and was fined $3,000 in an out-of-court settlement. Don Russell, an assistant to the director of C&MS emphasized that $3,000 was a big fine; the usual fine for similar action is $50.[25] USDA did fire the inspector-in-charge of the plant on October 3, 1970. The plant had paid the inspector $6,000 annually in overtime. Hormel fired its plant manager.

The Hormel case was the first public exposure of massive failures in federally inspected plants owned by national companies. The Consumer and Marketing Service tried at first to play down the Hormel case as one incident in one plant caused by the failure of one inspector. The Office of the Inspector General, however, anxious to see if the Hormel case was in fact an isolated incident, initiated a survey of federally inspected plants, primarily in California. The Inspector General found deficiencies in twenty-five of thirty plants surveyed: rough spots on walls and railings, meat cuts rubbing across railings or door jambs, knives sterilized too infrequently, and meat remaining uncovered while being transported within the plant.[26] The Hormel case also triggered a GAO investigation of conditions in federally inspected plants which concluded that the Consumer and Marketing Service was not enforcing meat standards.[27]

The Hormel case was valuable in alerting consumers, Congressional committees, and federal investigators to the fact that conditions in federal plants could be as bad as those in state plants. The financial penalty for Hormel, however, was minimal. This plant, part of a company with $695 million dollars in sales a year, was fined only $3,000 for its violations of the Act. Without public disclosure, federal enforcement alone would offer little deterrent for corporate violators of meat legislation.

Problems with the repackaging of returned meat appear to be perennial in the red meat industry. Inspectors in North Carolina report that companies repackage unsold meat without having it rechecked by the inspector. An Associated Press reporter, visiting three meat packaging plants in August, 1971, saw bacon, hams, wieners, and cold cuts which were rotten a solid green with mildew stacked on return tables. Since federal inspectors only spot check the packaging plants, the meat can be cleaned up and sold as new stock with no one the wiser.

The May-Bernard Report

The Hormel incident, along with the blistering GAO reports on poultry inspection, persuaded C&MS's leadership to resort to the bureaucratic equivalent of the psychiatrist's couch: analysis by handpicked consultants. In April, 1970, the agency hired Dr. Phillip J. May and Dr. Alfred Bernard to conduct a reorganization study of itself. The consultants made several valuable recommendations which C&MS adopted in a major reorganization begun in November, 1970. To put more emphasis on sanitation in the plants, C&MS established a separate division for sanitation and plant facilities in the Field Operations office in Washington and in each regional office. A sanitation specialist is now available in each of these offices to provide continuous attention to sanitation problems.

To give the Administrator of C&MS better intelligence on the inspection programs, all of C&MS Washington inspection and review staffs are combined into a single unit reporting to the Administrator. Similar streamlining of the chain of command was introduced at the regional level. These shifts were designed to eliminate in part the cobwebbed communications from Washington to the regional officers which have contributed greatly to the leadership failures of C&MS. Before the reorganization, a regional supervisor of meat and poultry inspection had to take orders from four different bosses: the Chief of the Slaughter Division, the Chief of the Food Processing Division, the Chief of the Technical Services Division, and the Deputy Administrator for Consumer Protection. The circuit supervisors were so overburdened with reports and special programs from Washington that they lacked time to evaluate inspection programs in the plants. Even in the plants, there was often no centralization of authority and responsibility, with conflicting lines of authority between veterinarians and food inspectors.

The flood of paper from the field failed its mission— to inform Washington about conditions in the plant. Bernard and May made the remarkable discovery that *no one* in the meat and poultry inspection divisions of C&MS was regularly assigned to monitor field inspection reports continually and to see that plant deficiencies were corrected. It is no wonder that the inspectors felt that USDA was slow in responding to their complaints: in some cases, their reports were not read, or if read, in even more cases, they were left suspended in administrative limbo and not followed up.

As a result of the May-Bernard report, C&MS has begun to reform its grossly inadequate supervisory structure. When the reorganization is completed, one man—an "Inspector in Charge"—will be held responsible for inspection in each of the 4,000 federally inspected plants. Circuit supervisors will be relieved of office work to spend full time in the field on plant supervision. The regional offices are being divided into thirty-two area offices to allow for closer supervision of circuit supervisors. At the Washington level, a Field Operations office has been created to centralize all communications between federal headquarters and the field. The area directors now report to one Washington office rather than three or four. Finally C&MS has consolidated all supportive functions in two divisions. The Standards and Services Division prepares proposed regulations, develops food standards, monitors labels, etc. The new Laboratory Division, for the first time, centralizes federal surveillance of chemical residues in meat, a highly important step.

C&MS's Administrator, Clayton Yeutter, deserves praise for this administrative streamlining, but it still misses the core of the problem. Streamlining reports is futile if C&MS fails to act on the information they contain. Here we must look at one of the recommendations by May and Bernard which Yeutter did not adopt.

Conflict of Interest

May and Bernard recognized that there is an inherent administrative conflict between C&MS's marketing and consumer protection activities and recommended that meat and poultry be moved to a separate agency within USDA. It is clear they did not go far enough. Meat inspection should be removed from USDA altogether.

Meat inspection will not have strong leadership as long as this public health service remains a subdivision of the Department for agribusiness. Now that pesticide regulation has been shifted to the Environmental Protection Agency, meat inspection has become the outstanding example of the conflict of interest which develops when the same agency is responsible for promotion and regulation of an industry.

With nearly 10,000 full-time employees, the meat and poultry inspection bureaucracy is larger than the entire Food and Drug Administration, yet it retains a subordinate status as only a subdivision of the Consumer and Marketing Service, which is itself only one of USDA's many agencies. The chief of meat inspection reports to the Administrator of C&MS, whose mandate is riddled with internal contradictions. To serve his most vocal and organized constituency, the chicken and red meat producers and processors, the Administrator directs a variety of marketing activities designed to keep meat prices high. He is expected to give meat a wholesome image. Strict regulation of meat processing and especially vigorous enforcement against violators not only reduces the profits of the first constituency; it also generates unfavorable publicity which the producers fear will undermine consumer confidence in their product.

The close personal connections between the top meat regulators and the meat industry should be noted. Dr. McEnroe, the meat inspection chief, owns a Hereford cattle ranch on the Oklahoma prairie and was formerly a consultant to Peterson Farms, an Arkansas firm with large poultry and cattle interests. His predecessor, Roy Lennartson, left USDA to become the Washington lobbyist for the Western Meat Packers Association. Clifford

Hardin, the former Secretary of Agriculture, left USDA to become vice-president of Ralston-Purina, a major meat processor.*

The Administrator's other constituency, the meat consumer, is much less organized. Because the consumer's interest is not focused into intense rays of pressure on the Administrator, he has positive incentives to keep regulatory action "administratively confidential," to hold back on enforcement, to be in effect "a satisficer" who reacts to inspection problems only when bludgeoned by outside criticism.

This conflict has been recognized by several prominent observers of the regulatory scene. Joseph Califano, testifying against a proposed Department of Consumer Affairs on the grounds that most consumer programs can best be administered by on-going departments, made an exception for the Department of Agriculture:

I recognize that there may be cases where placing a consumer program in an existing agency creates a practical, if not legal, conflict of interest. The most obvious example may be the wholesome meat program in the Department of Agriculture. In such cases those programs can be transferred to another department or regulatory agency. In the case of wholesome meat, the Department of Health, Education, and Welfare seems an ideal candidate.

Califano, who as President Johnson's chief domestic advisor witnessed at first hand the imperial agony of former Secretary of Agriculture Orville Freeman in dealing with his Department's contradictions, believes such a move would be in the best interest of the Secretary:

I use meat as an example. I would not put the Secretary or his staff in what I consider to be essentially a conflict position. . . . I think when the Secretary of Agriculture has to deal with people who are producing meat, who are quite properly under our system trying to maximize their profit

* At a recent poultry industry meeting in Kansas City, Dr. McEnroe was introduced as "one of the best friends feathered folk ever had." Such compliments from the regulated to the regulators are not uncommon. Several federal inspectors in top management jobs have been given "Poultry Man of the Year" awards. These include Dr. Harry Gaskill, Associate Regional Director in San Francisco, and several others of officer-in-charge, Deputy Director, or equivalent status.

on meat production, he has an awfully difficult time administering the Wholesome Meat Law. I wouldn't put him in that position.

Meat inspection officialdom is a very inbred bureaucracy, whose outlook has been molded by years of one-sided advocacy by the meat lobbies and producer-oriented Congressmen. Rodney Leonard, who was humbled by this bureaucracy during his tenure as Administrator of the C&MS, warns that even a consumer champion in the Secretary's office will make little headway with reform:

The bureaucracy develops the regulations, the policy control within an agency—I was the only noncivil servant in the Consumer and Marketing Service. *The entire staff the Secretary of Agriculture has for policy review is less than twenty people.* And that is in an agency that has somewhat close to 100,000 employees. This means that the bureaucracy . . . develops the proposals, bureaucracy holds the hearings, bureaucracy, in effect, does all the work in getting things done. You can review what they do, and you can change some things, but you simply don't have time to do the kind of thorough review they do themselves. They are subject to enormous pressures from the interest groups, from groups that have very great economic interests at stake. It is only right that these groups have access to the regulatory process. *Our problem is that where we provide access to special interest groups, we have to find a different way of encouraging and providing access to consumers who are not well organized.* (Emphasis added)

The presence of meat inspection, a public health function, in the federal department for agribusiness is an anachronism. It should now be removed to a public health agency where the bureaucratic ambience and committee supervision will make the consumer's health the commanding priority.

The Need for Consumer Advocacy

There is a fundamental structural fault in the C&MS which tends to put its leadership at odds with the responsible inspectors and which cannot be resolved by the minor reforms proposed by the May Committee. The plight of the honest inspector is directly related to the absence of consumer advocacy in the Department. The pro-industry pressures bearing down on the meat regulators are so one-sided that they have molded the frame of reference of top administrators to the consumer's detriment.

This set of attitudes is revealed in the shibboleths which frequently appear in conversations with USDA officials: "Well, you have to remember, the inspectors have their hands in the company's pockets"; "effective inspection is dependent on the cooperation of the plant management"; "we have to move the inspectors out of some plants for their own protection—they don't want to work in a hostile environment"; "the inspectors always claim they are being transferred because of pressure in Washington—in fact I estimate of every twenty-five requests for transfer that we get from the processors, we only transfer about one inspector."

When there is no countervailing pressure from consumers, the constant hammering of industry complaints —about the effect of inspection on their profit margins, about the alleged hostility of individual inspectors, about lack of uniformity in inspection, about requests for transfers—becomes a war of attrition on objectivity and public-mindedness of top meat officials. In this context, the regulatory official's claim that he is competent to protect the public interest without help from outsiders is a frail support for the consumer to lean on. Regulatory officials live in a political world. Like the President or any politician, they are constantly looking for clues as to where the consensus lies. Yet unlike the President, their role is largely passive. They respond when an organized interest knocks on their door. Stressing that the absence of consumer advocacy was the greatest single barrier to effective consumer programs while he was Administrator of C&MS, Rodney Leonard has described opinion-making in the meat bureaucracy as follows:

They respond to pressures. They look at the Congress, they look to see how much the Congress appropriates for various programs, because it is a signal to them to indicate what the consensus should be. They look to their Department Secretary to see what he does. They look to the White House to see what pressures they bring; what interests they have. They are constantly bombarded by various interest groups.

For a remedy, he urges to "increase the pressure from the consumer sector":

The Secretary of Agriculture is a Secretary not of farmers but of food, food policy. The problem is, he is not being subjected to the pressures from the whole spectrum.

An independent office of consumer affairs, which would create a corps of advocates to represent the public interest in the agencies, would help remedy this situation. A separate consumer safety agency to have responsibility for all food inspection activities of the federal government is also a necessary step. Neither organization will be a panacea, but they would help bridge part of the advocacy gap in the federal agencies and eliminate some of the more egregious conflicts of interest between food inspection and agribusiness.

A Sanctuary for Whistle-Blowers

The plight of the honest meat inspector in the Department of Agriculture is common to many scientists, engineers, and other professionals concerned about destructive or unethical practices in their organizations. Most professionals have codes of ethics which require them to speak out against unethical practices, but in practice the law provides little protection to the person who blows the whistle on his employer. The meat inspector, for example, is subject to the Code of Ethics for Government Service, which states that "any person in government service should put loyalty to the highest moral principles and to country above loyalty to party or government department." But as Professor Arthur S. Miller of George Washington University Law School pointed out at the Conference on Professional Responsibility in 1970, when the chips are down, "the employee of public government who snitches can expect to be fired, cast into some obscure limbo, or criminally punished. If he is wrapped in the security of Civil Service regulations, he might even have his job abolished." Miller concludes that "a secrecy syndrome affects our public and private bureaucracies, backed up by law."

All regulatory agencies would benefit from an "ethic

of whistle-blowing" where the professional finds his
duty to dissent protected by organization of his peers
(as the American Association of University Professors
protects the academic freedoms of university professors)
and by new laws guaranteeing him due process. The
National Association of Federal Veterinarians might
play this role for federal meat inspectors, although up
to now it has not realized its potential in this area. Senator William Proxmire (D.-Wis.) plans to introduce
legislation aimed at safeguarding the rights of government employees who speak out against waste and corruption. The legislation would allow any federal
employee punished for whistle-blowing to file a civil
damage suit against his immediate superiors and against
his own agency.

4

Little Victories: Consumer Participation in Meat Regulation

The federal officials in USDA, assigned to protect food quality, exercise a startling degree of discretion with an even more startling lack of accountability to either Congress or the public. They determine the amount of water in hams and poultry, the level of fat in hamburger and hotdogs, the criteria for condemning diseased animals, the number of hairs and insect remains allowed in canned meat—decisions important to every consumer —but few people outside government and industry circles know how these decisions are made.

Yet the consumer *is* entitled to know what he is eating, to know how decisions are made which affect the quality of what he eats, and to have his interests represented in these decisions. Important health interests are at stake. Medical research on primates and epidemiological surveys of human populations have revealed a strong association between the level of animal fat in the diet and heart disease. But fat, and other nutritional components like protein and water, are constantly manipulated up and down by the meat industry. Similarly, the definition of "wholesomeness"—e.g., whether cattle with cancer eye or chicken wings with small tumors are deemed fit to eat—is constantly in flux.

When consumer pressure is lacking, USDA tends to adapt new standards proposed by industry or to ratify prevailing manufacturing practices, often without consulting health officials, nutritionists, or consumers. These decisions are highly discretionary, particularly when they can be made without worry about feedback from consumer choices in the market. Few consumers for example can detect the substitution of chicken for beef and fat for protein in the hotdog.

The few opportunities for consumer participation in food decision-making which exist have rarely been tested. The weak advocacy of the consumer interest in the Department results in part from policies of secrecy maintained by the meat bureaucracy. The following cases illustrate some of the ways in which consumer advocates have tried to influence their decisions.

On January 25, 1970, Colonel Sanders's fried chicken empire and the housewives of America were jolted by an AP story headlined "USDA Approves Sale of Chickens with Cancer Virus." On the New York Stock Exchange, Kentucky Fried Chicken dropped nearly 10 percent in a single day. The next morning the poultry industry bounced back with a bold demonstration of the resiliency of the free enterprise system. A full-page ad in the *San Antonio Express* declared:

Handy Andy tells it as it is. Regardless of a future ruling that could change poultry inspection standards to permit the sale of chickens or any poultry with cancer viruses. . . . Handy Andy Pledges: *We will not offer such poultry for sale in our supermarkets!*

The Handy Andy Company, in its rush to get a competitive edge from the cancer scare, made a claim it could not support. Most chickens contain the virus of avian cancer in their blood. Less than 2 percent, however, develop tumors from the viruses. The Department of Agriculture has authority to decide whether birds with these tumors are fit for human consumption.

The chicken cancer issue began six months earlier when an advisory panel of veterinarians and animal disease specialists, many with close ties to the poultry industry, secretly recommended to the Department that condemnation of chickens with cancerous tumors be relaxed. Under the old system, an inspector condemned the whole chicken if he found a tumor on any part of it.

The committee now recommended that if a bird were found to have cancerous tumors on its wing or any other part, neither the part, much less the rest of the chicken, should go to waste; the cancerous part should be cut off and used in such products as hotdogs and the rest of the bird should be sold as cut up chicken.

This issue was important, both for its substance and for what it tells about the procedures used by USDA in making decisions about food quality. The committee of veterinarians based its advice on the assumption that cancer in chickens is not a human health hazard. No one in USDA apparently questioned the competence of animal health specialists to make recommendations about human risks. According to the panel, condemnation was warranted on aesthetic grounds alone; the committee acknowledged that many consumers would find chickens with obvious tumors revolting. Therefore, it recommended that a chicken should be passed for human consumption unless its tumors were so large that a consumer might notice them.

There was nothing unusual in USDA turning to such a committee for advice. The advisory committee is a fixture of virtually all regulatory agencies in Washington. Its function is to give the agency the benefit of outside views on regulatory issues. Often, however, the advisory committees become vehicles of privileged access for vested interests. The Advisory Committee on Criteria for Poultry Inspection was established on April 25, 1963, to advise the Department of Agriculture on criteria for judging the wholesomeness of poultry and poultry products under the poultry inspection program.[1] In creating this panel, USDA was asking for a public health judgment of great economic importance to the poultry industry from a committee made up of veterinarians and consultants to the Southeastern Poultry and Egg Association, Holly Farms Poultry Industries, Inc., Vantress Farms, Inc., and other branches of the industry. Its members may not consciously promote the industry's point of view, but factors of background and professional training make it difficult for them to give the consumer's interest a fair hearing. At the least, they are likely to decide borderline cases in favor of the companies that pay them. Their meetings are held in secret, and no transcripts or minutes are available for outsiders. While their role is theoretically advisory, in practice the committees often make policy. Rejection of a recommendation from an official advisory panel is a rare event in USDA.

Cancer in chickens is, with the exception of over-production and low prices, the greatest problem of the poultry industry. Poultrymen estimate the annual loss from cancerous chickens, which must be destroyed, at $150 million. Thirty-seven million young chickens were condemned in 1969, roughly 1.5 percent of all chickens slaughtered. Avian leukosis, the scientific term for cancer in chicken, refers to a complex of diseases known as lymphoid leukosis and Marek's disease. In the last five years it has become the leading cause for the rejection of chicken by USDA inspectors. It appears to be related to the stress caused by crowding chickens together in small spaces to maximize production.

Because the chicken growers operate on very narrow margins of profit, these losses have become a major anxiety for the industry. For years it has pressured the Administrator of the Consumer and Marketing Service to ease the ban on chickens with cancer. Rodney Leonard, Administrator of the Consumer and Marketing Service when Orville Freeman was Secretary of Agriculture, described these efforts in testimony before the House Government Operations Committee:

The poultry industry brought constant pressure on the office of this administrator, and the poultry inspection staff was constantly defending its inspection criteria and standards from allegations that it caused the industry to lose too many birds. The pressure obviously continued after January because this summer [1969] a new committee of poultry veterinarians was named to review the criteria.[2]

Reflecting on the new committee's recommendation, Leonard concluded:

The industry expects the program to adjust to the economic needs of the industry rather than the health needs of consumers.[3]

The poultry industry's influence on USDA increased under Secretary of Agriculture Hardin. A survey of members of the condemnation criteria committee under

Secretary of Agriculture Orville Freeman and members appointed by Secretary Clifford Hardin revealed that six of the eight members who favored retention of the strict ban on chickens with cancer were dropped from the new committee by Hardin. Three new members were added, all of them favoring relaxation of condemnation standards. The committee changed from 8–4 favoring no changes in condemnation standards to 6–2 favoring relaxation of standards. This large a turnover in committee members is highly unusual. In 1967, for example, eleven of the twelve members were routinely reappointed.

The recommendation to ease the ban on cancerous chickens created a crisis for Richard Lyng, the Assistant Secretary in charge of food protection in USDA. Lyng is an intelligent and acutely political Californian who is probably slated for higher posts in the Department. The continuing failures of meat inspection in his Department had made him sensitive to consumer issues. He immediately saw that acceptance of the panel's recommendation could be political dynamite for the consumer movement. At the same time, Lyng was whipsawed by strong pressure from the Georgia Congressional delegation (more chickens are grown in Georgia than in any other state, and it is powerfully represented on the farm committees of the House and Senate), and from the office of the Under Secretary, Phil Campbell; all wanted to give the poultry farmers a break. To his credit, Lyng was genuinely puzzled about the scientific and health merits of the recommendation.

In the end he was faced with two choices: he could accept the recommendation and try to implement it in secret with no one outside the industry noticing, or he could reject it and pay the political costs of disappointing the poultry interests in the Department and on Capitol Hill. Favoring the first course was the fact that a change in the condemnation standards guiding poultry inspectors could be made without informing the public in the *Federal Register*. The Department has discretion to classify such changes, despite their impact on the consumer, as internal inspection procedures beyond public review. Since few citizens have access to poultry inspection manuals, read the poultry trade journals where such changes might be discussed, or can identify a cancerous lesion when they see it, tumorous chicken could reach the dinner table with no one the wiser.

Against this approach was the fact that the Agribusiness Task Force at the Center for Study of Responsive Law had learned (at the beginning of August, 1969), that the cancer condemnation standards were being reviewed. Investigation revealed many scientists who were alarmed at the prospect of increased human exposure to infected chickens. Characteristic of these views was the opinion of a molecular biologist at Michigan State University:

We have no proof that avian leukosis-type viruses cannot cause cancer in man. Therefore, the spectre of long-term contact with the viruses is not encouraging. My professional opinion is that we have something to worry about.[4]

Dr. Ludwig Gross, who received the United Nations prize for work on cancer virus in animals, wrote:

Under present laboratory conditions, it appears that . . . the chicken leukemia virus is pathogenic only for chickens. We may well learn, however, in future studies, that this is not necessarily true and that under certain conditions the chicken leukemia virus may be able to pass the species barrier. Its possible harmful effect for humans has yet to be determined.

Feeling this issue needed further study which was devoid of any suggestion of a conflict of interest, the Task Force began to interview USDA officials to learn more about the panel's deliberations. By the middle of August, its interest in the panel's recommendations was well known within the Department. The Department was therefore on notice that any attempt to adopt the recommendation in secret would fail.

Ultimately, Lyng made an intelligent political decision. He protected himself and Secretary Hardin by taking the decision out of USDA hands and placing it in the lap of the Surgeon General. In a letter to Dr. Richard Prindle, Acting Surgeon General on August 21, 1969, he requested:

(1) a discussion as to whether or not diseases of the avian leukosis complex should be considered malignant;

(2) a summary of evidence relating to a possible association or lack of association between diseases of the avian leukosis complex and leukemia and/or lymphoma in man;
(3) a summary of the evidence regarding the transmissibility of the avian leukosis complex viruses to man.

Just reading these points makes clear how inappropriate it was for a USDA panel composed of veterinarians to have been the primary consultant on these public health questions. The Surgeon General appointed a committee of leading cancer specialists, virologists, and veterinarians to review the panel's recommendation. Their deliberations lasted nearly five months.

The Agribusiness Task Force was content to wait for the Surgeon General's report and see what response USDA made to it. In the meantime, it continued to survey scientific opinion on the issue. Before the Surgeon General's committee reported, however, details of the USDA panel's recommendation broke in the Associated Press, apparently as a result of a slip by Lyng in an interview. Mistakenly assuming the reporter was already informed on the issue, Lyng acknowledged that the Department was considering the advisory panel's recommendation. The resulting uproar rocked the industry. Not since Herbert Hoover promised a chicken in every pot was poultry such a fashionable topic. An aide to Virginia Knauer, the President's Consumer Advisor, noted:

The letters we have received are the most virulent that have come in on any topic. The housewives are really enraged at the possibility the ban will be relaxed.

The impact on the industry, for all its pain, had a positive side, as indicated in this statement from an industry leader:

For a long time, some of us have had a deep-seated fear that leukosis in poultry might be linked to human health, with or without justification. What is it going to take, in Heaven's name, to get our industry aroused to the point of giving adequate attention and support to this problem?[5]

The controversy cooled on February 3, 1970, when the Surgeon General of the United States recommended to the Secretary of Agriculture that any chicken with

visible evidence of cancer should be regarded as totally
unfit for human consumption. In his statement of reasons, he stressed the lack of conclusive safety data:

We may simply not know enough about the oncogenic
potential and host range of avian viruses; it is certainly possible that new strains of avian tumoviruses, which at the
present time appear not to be oncogenic for man, may arise
which may indeed attain the capacity to induce cancer in
people; throughout the animal kingdom, there is much
precedent wherein viruses predominantly of one animal
species will not only replicate but infuse disease in animals
of other species including man.[6]

In summary, the Surgeon General said that consumption
of infected poultry appears to be safe, given the present
state of knowledge, but that continuing surveillance
and research are necessary to develop conclusive data. In
the meantime, human consumption of cancerous chickens should be kept at a minimum.[7] On February 6, at
Lyng's urging, Secretary Hardin accepted Steinfeld's
recommendation and announced that the Department's
ban on cancerous chicken would remain in force.*

The most remarkable feature of the chicken cancer
case is what it reveals about USDA's internal procedures
for making decisions of vital interest to consumers.
First, the recommendation was made in secret. No minutes or any other records were made available to the
public or outside scientists. Second, the panel which
made this decision affecting the scope of federal regulation of the poultry industry was staffed, in part, by industry consultants. Remarkably, even though the panel
was making a judgment about potential risks to the
consumer's health, no consumer representatives, public
health specialists, or cancer experts were present. If
Secretary Lyng had not submitted a recommendation to
the Surgeon General for review, the panel's decision
would not have been subjected to the rigor of discussion
and debate in the wider scientific community. Third, if

---

* A vaccine for chicken cancer has recently been developed by Dr.
Ben Burmester at the regional poultry research laboratory of the
Agricultural Research Service at East Lansing, Michigan. The vaccine,
which is now available for growers, promises to prevent the cancerous lesions from developing in chickens infected with Marek's
disease.[8]

the decision had been approved, it could have gone into effect secretly without any requirement that the public be informed of the change.

The chicken cancer decision was a consumer victory because inquiries from consumer advocates helped persuade USDA officials to have the advisory panel's recommendation reviewed by public health scientists outside the Department and because disclosure in the press made Hardin's acceptance of the Surgeon General's advice a political necessity. The point of this case is clear: but for the accidents of these outside interventions and the presence of an alert administrator (Richard Lyng), the recommendation to ease the cancer ban might well have been adopted without comment from the public or scientists outside the agribusiness establishment.

The Fatdog

The decision to retain the ban on chickens with cancer took place in the interplay of secret advisory panels, confidential committees of scientists, and quiet lobbying by representatives of the poultry industry. USDA's discretion in this vital rule-making was virtually unlimited. At no point in the procedures was there a formal opportunity for consumer advocates to make their views known.

In most cases, however, the Department of Agriculture maintains at least the façade of consumer participation. The public is notified and invited to comment on most changes in USDA's regulation of the food industry through publication in the *Federal Register*. By the time USDA publishes such a proposal, however, it is very late in the game. A proposal is a distillation of staff memos, letters and visits from industry lobbyists, and reports of advisory committees which take place over months and sometimes years. The public is given only thirty to sixty days to respond. When USDA makes its final decision, after supposedly reviewing the comments, it does not have to issue a statement to show the evidentiary basis of the decision. In many cases, the request for comments from the public is a charade, masking the fact that a decision has already been made.

Ironically, this route of access to USDA is most

heavily used by the interests least in need of it—the trade associations of the meat industry. Consumers rarely read the *Federal Register,* and would have difficulty interpreting its opaque syntax if they did. The *Federal Register* is, in effect, an insider's newsletter.[9]

USDA does have the power to open up its proceedings and broaden consumer participation when it chooses. In June of 1969, USDA took the unusual step of holding a public hearing to receive comments on its proposal that the level of fat in hotdogs be limited to 33 percent. Consumer representatives were invited to testify and allowed to cross-examine industry and USDA witnesses. The result was a highly publicized debate which unveiled a startling picture of how the meat industry had gradually undermined the food value of America's most popular meat product. More significantly, it set a precedent for consumer intervention which, if expanded, could help erect barriers against the erosion of food quality.

USDA's proposal to limit the fat in hotdogs derived from its authority to define and promulgate standards of identity for popular food products, and to assure the integrity of their labels. Standards are established by defining the composition of each meat product for which a specific name has been approved by the Department. In arriving at a standard, USDA is supposed to look not only at practices in the food industry but also read cookbooks and other data to get an idea of how much meat the consumer intuitively expects will be in his canned spaghetti, tamales, or beef stew. There are now hundreds of such standards which determine, for example, that chile con carne must have at least 40 percent meat; that corned beef hash can have no more than 15 percent fat or 72 percent moisture; that hamburger can have no more than 30 percent fat; that chow mein can have no less than 12 percent meat.[10]

USDA publishes proposed standards in the *Federal Register* and requests comments. One might expect that, given the chance to help determine the amount of fat in his hamburger or hotdog, the consumers would deluge USDA with comments. In fact, few even know that USDA has such authority. The preponderance of comments comes from the makers of processed food, who have an interest in reducing meat content; very few come from ordinary consumers.

Official standards of fat, meat, and water levels in processed food are a relatively new feature of USDA's consumer protection program. Until 1970, there were "standards of identity" for only three products—oleomargarine, corned beef hash, and chopped ham. Forty other products, like hamburger, had a published meat requirement or other composition standard. Now, since the regulations of October 3, 1970, have gone into effect, fixed standards protect hundreds of products from adulteration with excessive water or fat. The momentum for setting these new standards was largely generated by the much publicized effort to reform the "fatdog."

The hotdog is the classic case of the gradual double-barreled inflation becoming more and more common in the food industry: as the hotdog's price has risen, its nutritional value has declined. Traditionally, the frankfurter has been the meat industry's catch-all for bits and pieces of meat which it could not use elsewhere. According to the regulations, it is allowed to contain, among other things: meat from hearts, tongues, tripe, lungs, lips, eyes, ears, stomachs, snouts, udders, bladders, and the esophagus.[11] Under present regulations, hotdogs may contain up to 10 percent added water, bringing its total water content to between 55 and 60 percent; 3.5 percent salt, spices, and curing agents; as much as 2 percent corn syrup; and 3.5 percent extenders, such as milk products, cereal, and soy flour.

The meat in the hotdog may be only faintly related to the pork with which it is often identified in the public mind. Goat meat and mutton are permissible ingredients, and the hotdog may be labeled "All Meat" and contain up to 15 percent chicken.[12] Until 1969, however, the fat content of hotdogs was not regulated at all.

The nutritional value of the hotdog has been declining for over 30 years. A comprehensive analysis of trends in the composition of frankfurters was undertaken in 1968 by R. H. Alsmeyer, of the Consumer and Marketing Service's Standards Group. Alsmeyer found that between 1937 and 1967, the protein content of frankfurters had decreased from 19.6 percent to 11.8

percent while the fat content had increased from 18.6 percent to 31.2 percent. In 1950, the frankfurter was 20 percent fat and 14 percent protein, but by 1969, the figures were 33 percent fat and 11 percent protein.[13]

The public health implications of this development are remarkably wide. The hotdog is the favorite lunch of school children for example. According to a USDA survey in 1969, the average school lunch is 40 percent fat. Children typically require at least 75 grams of protein a day, but the fat adulterated hotdog contains only about six grams of protein.[14] It is also a staple of the low income diet—where nutritional deficiency exacts the largest health costs. It is by far the largest selling meat product in the country.

The trend to increased levels of fat was accelerated in the fifties by new processing techniques imported from Germany and the discovery of new fat emulsifiers by Oscar Mayer and Company. These developments made it possible to incorporate vastly increased amounts of fat (some products tested had as much as 51 percent), without disturbing the appearance or taste of the sausage. Because sausage production is a highly competitive industry, sausage makers who cut production costs by increasing the fat and lowering the meat content forced other firms to follow suit.

The consumer is defenseless against this subversion of the hotdog's nutritional value. When he purchases steaks, roasts, chops, and similar cuts, he can control the intake of animal fats by trimming. In meat products prepared from emulsified meat mixtures, such as frankfurters, it is impossible either to estimate the fat level or to separate it. Because the percentage of fat is not listed on labels, consumers are denied the opportunity to accept or reject sausage products from the standpoint of fat content. This situation has been decried by medical experts concerned about the level of fat in the American diet. The American Heart Association and the American Medical Association advise the public to avoid excessive intakes of saturated fats, such as are found in meat products. A 1970 report of the Inter-Society Commission for Heart Disease Resources strongly urged that fat amounts be labeled on meat products. The Commission encourages the manufacture of nutritious products low in saturated fats "because so much evidence already points to the diet's implication in the large number of heart attacks in the U.S."[15]

As early as 1958, some USDA officials recognized the need for consumer protection in this area and urged that the fat content of sausages be limited to 30 percent. This proposal met stiff opposition from the sausage industry, however, and was not made a formal requirement.[16]

In 1968, Rodney Leonard, Administrator of the Consumer and Marketing Service under Orville Freeman, renewed the Department's efforts to set a fat limit on hotdogs at 30 percent. He directed that public hearings be held at four places in the country in early 1969 to listen to consumer and industry comments on this proposed regulation, as well as another proposal that chicken be allowed in hotdogs with an "All Meat" label. Leonard left the Consumer and Marketing Service in early 1969, before the hearings were convened. After complaints from the meat industry, which regarded Leonard's preference for open forums as highly irregular, Roy Lennartson, President Nixon's appointee as Leonard's successor, decided to put off the hearings.

The food industry saw the public hearings as a threat to its influence in the Department. Blaine Liljenquist of the Western Meat Packers Association spoke for many meat processors when he advised the Department that "there was no need for a hearing and no need for the government to get involved in processing formulas that can best be solved through the miracle of free enterprise."[17] The American Farm Bureau agreed, arguing that no one "in agriculture has anything to gain from a public fight over the kind of new materials that may be used in the production of sausages."[18]

Nevertheless, the hearings had been too well publicized to be shelved altogether. The hotdog hearing was rescheduled for June, 1969, but at only one place, Washington, D.C. At the same time, USDA postponed indefinitely the public hearing it had promised on the poultry industry's proposal that chicken meat be included in hotdogs up to a level of 15 percent.

Between December and June, the Nixon Administration made another concession to the meat industry and raised the proposed fat ceiling from 30 to 33 percent. Officially, the Consumer and Marketing Service explained that a 33 percent fat content "represents the maximum fat content that is currently normal to these sausage products,"[19] but a brief prepared by the USDA's Technical Services Division for the outgoing Rodney Leonard on January 6, 1969, showed an industry norm of 30.6 percent fat. Aside from this shift in positions, it is interesting to note the fact that USDA accepted as its standard the industry norm—the level of fat in sausage being currently produced. Industry, nevertheless, held out for 35 percent.

Consumer representatives were shocked at this approach. Edward Berlin, general counsel for the Consumers Federation of America, noted:

We begin with the premise that when the consumer purchases sausage products, she assumes that she is purchasing meat, not fat. Therefore, fat should be a permissible ingredient only to the extent that its presence is established as necessary. This should be the thrust of the Department's investigation, not an inquiry to establish prevailing industry practices and then merely ratify them.[20]

At the June hearing, the Consumers' Federation of America and other consumer groups justified the meat processors' fears of public discussion by urging a 25 percent fat ceiling and percentage labeling of hotdog ingredients. Supporting the 25 percent level was an ad hoc committee of health and nutrition experts appointed by the Secretary of Agriculture to study the nutrition of the school lunch. Support also came from Dr. Jean Mayer, the President's special assistant on nutrition, who spotlighted fat consumption as a primary contributor to increased heart disease among American men.

The value of consumer participation in an adversary setting became evident when the meat lobbies tried to justify a fat ceiling of 35 percent. Under cross-examination, the Western Meat Packers and American Meat Institute conceded that the industry consulted neither nutrition experts nor medical professionals in choosing this level. Instead, the sausage makers rested their case on the alleged sovereignty of consumer taste. The

American Meat Institute commissioned a survey by Peryam and Kroll Research Corporation to find out "what does the consumer really want?" It suggested that the wide range of fat content in hotdogs (from 14 to 51 percent) was dictated as much by subtle differences in consumer tastes as by production economics: "The fat content of a given brand is determined to some extent by economics and production capabilities, but it also may represent the end result of certain theories held by the manufacturer about what his customers want and adjustments made in the attempt to provide satisfaction."[21] The Western Meat Packers also conducted a taste test at the University of California. The frankfurter judged best by a panel of students contained 13.9 percent protein and 26.9 percent fat. The Association then fed the hotdogs to a panel of "experts" (qualifications not defined) who preferred 12 percent protein and 33.6 percent fat.[22] In fact, the reason fat has increased is that fat is cheaper than meat. The consumer cannot tell the difference, so it is good business to fatten the dog.

When food decisions are made through private, off the record negotiations between industry and government, devices like these "taste tests" may be politely accepted, but they could not stand the scrutiny of an adversary proceeding. Dr. Leighty, Chief of USDA's Technical Services Branch, during cross-examination by consumer lawyers, revealed that USDA's own surveys showed that "high levels of fat contribute little to taste value. Other factors such as seasoning appear to be of greater importance."[23] Leighty also revealed other USDA surveys which showed that consumers were willing to pay more for hotdogs with low fat.

Leighty also conceded that the Department had not at any time consulted with health and nutrition experts either inside or outside of the government before making its proposal of a fat ceiling at 33 percent, but was content to consult industry practice alone.

These facts might have remained confidential if USDA officials had not been cross-examined in an open adversary process. A public hearing has many obvious advantages for the consumer: it creates a public record of the considerations behind an agency decision, and

puts individual officials on record. It reduces the ano-
nymity of the decision process. It also educates the individual consumers and the press about important issues
of food quality. The anatomy of the hotdog became a
cause célèbre of the women's pages of newspapers
throughout the country. Most significant, this public
exposure put politicians on the spot. A number of
Congressmen endorsed the low fat hotdog, but the most
dramatic moment in the hearings occurred when
Virginia Knauer, the President's Consumer Advisor,
appeared and supported a 30 percent fat level, over
the vigorous objections of the Consumer and Marketing
Service. For a brief time, there was a family conflict in
the Nixon White House: who spoke for the President,
the Agriculture Department or his Consumer Advisor?
The issue was definitively answered at 6:30 P.M. one
June evening, when the telephone rang in Virginia
Knauer's office. The President was calling. "Virginia,"
he said, "I just wanted you to know I'm with you 100
percent on the hotdog. I'm on a low cholesterol diet
myself."[24]

Once the low fat hotdog had become good politics,
the decision was no longer in doubt. In September,
1969, USDA announced that it would set the limit in
hotdogs at 30 percent. USDA's latest estimates show
that the average fat content of hotdogs has now declined
to 28 percent.

The other issue in dispute, whether the relative per-
centages of the hotdog's ingredients should be labeled,
was ruled out of order by the USDA hearing officer, and
has not been revived.

Even in the absence of a public hearing, consumers
have the right to challenge USDA's food quality decisions in court. Because of the delay and expense
involved, such suits are extremely rare. The only one in
recent years involved a challenge of USDA's use of the
label "All Meat" on hotdogs. For years USDA allowed
"All Meat" to be used when the sausage contained 10
percent added water, two percent corn syrup, or 30
percent fat, but it could not be used if dried milk or
nonfat dry milk is included. The consumer paid a higher
price for the "all meat" hotdogs but their fat content
was higher, usually 2.5 percent higher than for nonfat

dry-milk franks. Thus the consumer was paying more for "All Meat" but receiving more fat and less total protein than when purchasing the less desirably labeled frankfurter. The use of milk products in hotdogs raises their protein level by at least 10 percent. An example of the difference in quality between the more expensive "all meat" hotdogs and those with added milk products can be seen in the table below.

NUTRITIONAL ANALYSIS OF HOTDOGS

	Name	Total Protein	Water Added	Fat
Franks with at least 3.3% nonfat dry milk.	Colonial Extra Milk Frank	13%	6.9%	26.9%
	Fernandez Skinless Franks	13.5%	8.9%	22.3%
"All Meat" Franks	Armour All Meat Hotdogs	10.9%	6%	35.5%
	Grand Union All Meat Franks	11.8%	9.8%	28%
	Swift Premium All Meat	10.5%	7.3%	37.7%

Source: USDA Quarterly Analysis of Hotdogs, 1969 (before 30 percent ceiling went into effect).

These arbitrary labeling distinctions, which reduce the nutrition value of the consumer's dollar, were successfully challenged by the Federation of Homemakers, represented by attorney Ed Berlin. USDA turned down his petition to eliminate the "All Meat" label. Berlin then sued in federal district court and in April, 1971, was awarded the decision.

Few consumer groups have the resources to press an issue for over two years, as this victory required. Unfortunately, the great majority of the Department's name games with meat products go unchallenged by consumers. In 1971, for example, a group of Texas meat packers petitioned USDA to allow goat meat to be labeled "mutton" or "chevon." Why "goat meat" should not be labeled "goat meat" is not immediately clear.

The hotdog, chicken cancer, and labeling decisions were influenced by the research and advocacy of a few small consumer groups with headquarters in Washington. While this kind of intervention, with help from the press, can win occasional victories, it only ripples the surface of the food industry's influence in the Department of Agriculture. A case in point is the fact that the hotdog hearing was the last public hearing held by the Department on a food issue. The proposal to permit 15 percent chicken in the hotdog was adopted without the previously scheduled public hearing taking place. In September, 1971, USDA put more "feathers" in the hotdog by allowing 15 percent *cooked* poultry to be added, the equivalent of 21 percent raw poultry. This bonus to the poultry industry was accomplished quietly by a change in the Manual of Meat Inspection Regulations. No formal proposal appeared in the *Federal Register*. After the embarrassment of the hotdog hearing, USDA has apparently retreated to regulation by stealth.

The meat packers have tried to use their success in weakening federal meat standards to offset stronger regulations in some states. Michigan legislators moved, says one observer, by a combination of nostalgia and patriotism—if the hotdog is subverted is anything sacred? —have passed a law requiring at least 12 percent protein and fresh meat only in hotdogs and sausages. The "federal" hot dog averages only 10.5 percent protein.

The Hormel, Armour, and Wilson meat-packing companies recently went to court to set aside the Michigan standards. They argued that the more lenient federal law had preempted stronger standards by the states. A federal judge held that the meat packers were less concerned with uniformity than with maximizing their profits and upheld the Michigan law.

Remedies

The failure of consumer representatives to develop effectual countervailing power in meat regulation is based in part on a lack of information. The need for an informed consumer presence in the Department of Agriculture has been best described by Rodney Leonard, often a target for consumer wrath when he was Administrator of the Consumer and Marketing Service:

I discovered during my service in the Department of Agriculture that many officials and employees of the Department . . . seek to minimize the information made available to the public in order to shield their decisions and actions from questioning and frequently to cover up mistakes and misjudgments in the administration of public programs. In a very real sense, the Administrator lacks information and analysis . . . which are not clothed in the self-interest of agency bureaucracy.

On December 19, 1961, the Nader Task Force sued under the Freedom of Information Act to force the Consumer and Marketing Service to release data which would inform the public about certain alleged consumer protection programs in USDA. The suit* asked the United States District Court for the District of Maryland to order the Consumer and Marketing Service to release the following data:

(1) the results of USDA analyses of the ingredients of hotdogs and other cooked sausage products by brand name;
(2) the letters of warning sent by the Department to intrastate meat and poultry processors suspected of sending nonfederally inspected meat across state lines;
(3) the name of each meat and/or poultry slaughterer or processor who had had meat detained by C&MS since January 1, 1965, the reason for the detention, and the ultimate disposition of the product.

The purpose of this suit was to put some teeth in the heretofore empty jaws of the Freedom of Information Act.** This information was denied by USDA. The results of government analysis of hotdog ingredients were said to be "trade secrets" which might harm the market position of the sausage companies and the letters of warning and the detention of data were considered to be investigatory files which might jeopardize USDA's prosecution of meat law violators.†

After the suit was filed, USDA conceded the first point and in 1970 made public its quarterly analyses of

* The suit was filed under the Federal Freedom of Information Act by James J. Hanks, Jr., a Baltimore attorney representing the Nader group.
** For a fuller discussion of the Act, see Chapter 12.
† The suit also asked USDA to make public the bi-weekly reports of the Slaughter Inspection Division and the minutes of the National Food Inspection Advisory Committee meetings. The District Court upheld USDA's claim that these were intradepartmental memoranda and therefore exempt under the Act.

brand name sausage products, one of the few times the
federal government has given the consumer access to
data from its testing of consumer products. On June 26,
1970, Judge Northrop of the U.S. District Court in
Baltimore in a surprise decision ordered that the letters
of warning and information on the detention of meat
and poultry products be made available to the Nader
group.

The information on detained meat is the first time
the Department has been forced to reveal the brand
names of various meat and poultry products suspected
of violating federal meat laws. Judge Northrop noted
that the "investigatory file" exemption under the Freedom of Information Act was not intended to exempt all
government information about private enterprise, and
stated that the possible embarrassment of the firms
which had violated meat laws was not a justification
for this exemption.*

The Department of Justice appealed and on May 25,
1971, Judge John D. Butzner of the U.S. Court of
Appeals for the Fourth Circuit affirmed Judge Northrop's decision. Butzner's decision significantly widens
the public's right to information about enforcement of
regulatory laws. He held that the investigatory files
exemption did not apply to letters of warning and
administrative detention information, because the contents of such records are already known by the companies who were warned or whose products were
detained. Publication therefore would not reveal any of
USDA's secret investigative techniques. The Freedom
of Information Act, according to Butzner, was designed
"not to increase administrative efficiency but to guarantee the public's right to know how government is dis-
charging its duty to protect the public interest."

Release of this information has a double benefit.
First, it allows the consumer to evaluate for himself the
services of the Consumer and Marketing Service's consumer protection program. Disclosures of the letters of

* Judge Northrop found that the exemption was intended only to
prevent persons against whom the government was enforcing the law
from obtaining an advance look at the government's case. It did not
apply when firms which were the subject of government action had
already received letters of warning or had their products detained.

warning, for example, put USDA officials on notice that no improper efforts to protect industry would be tolerated. In addition, disclosure encourages obedience to the meat laws. The packers will be much more likely to clean up their own operations if they know their letters of warning are going to be made public. Armed with this information, the consumer can avoid the chronic violators of federal inspection laws and make the marketplace an effective regulator of meat and poultry quality.

USDA had argued that disclosure of this information might make meat and poultry processors less willing to cooperate with federal inspection programs. Rodney Leonard disagrees:

To the best of my knowledge, cooperation by industry is not essential to the proper administration of the inspection programs. The cooperation of the regulated should not be vital to the success of a regulatory program.[25]

As these cases show, responsive government in food protection requires that the conduct of federal officials be continuously scrutinized and challenged by an informed public. An effective consumer voice must await major structural change which will be discussed later in this study. One procedural reform, however, would help greatly to overcome the information gap:

All proposed changes in meat and poultry regulations, standards of identity, or labeling must include a "statement of consumer significance" published in the Federal Register *and by press release.* The National Environmental Policy Act of 1969 requires federal officials who propose a project such as the SST, a new dam, the Cross Florida Barge Canal, the Alaska pipeline—any activity with significant impact on the environment—to prepare a statement describing its potential risks and benefits. The policy should now be applied to food protection decisions in USDA. All proposed changes in food protection procedures should contain a statement on the following points:

(a) *the consumer impact of the proposed action;*

(b) *any adverse public health or economic effects on the consumer which cannot be avoided should the proposal be implemented;*

(c) *alternatives to the proposed action;*

(d) *its contribution to the goal of a more nutritious food supply;*

(e) *any commitment of either government or private resources which will make the proposed action difficult to change if implemented.*

Such a statement, published early in the agency's consideration of a proposed action, would inform the consumer of his stake in food quality decisions. It would promote consumer participation as well as education, and it would institutionalize consideration of the consumer's interest in the agency.

As the cases above illustrate, the dynamic technology of the meat industry can be used to adulterate meat quality as well as enhance it. In the case of the gradual fattening of the hotdog, we saw how the technological reach of the meat industry can exceed the regulatory grasp of USDA when a strong consumer presence is lacking in the agency. Adulterated hotdogs are only one result of the meat industry's excessive influence in USDA. It can also have profound social and economic consequences as well. The rapid changes in the technology of meat processing have been paralleled by a revolution in the corporate structure of meat production. In this development, agribusiness has an interface with farmers at the supply end of the meat chain, rather than consumers at the retail end, and here it benefits from an advocacy gap even wider than with consumers. The following chapter discusses chicken farming in the Deep South. As we shall see, the problems of the poultry grower have a common cause with the problems of consumers, farm workers, and environmentalists when they confront this nation's agricultural establishment: organized bargaining power is heavily weighted on the side of agribusiness.

5

Poultry Peonage

*Us folks in the chicken business are the only
slaves left in this country.*

—*Crawford Smith,
Alabama contract farmer*

The dirt-poor hill country of Northern Alabama was the
scene of bizarre events in the spring of 1970. Its poor
white chicken farmers, rugged individualists to a man,
had organized and were out on strike—the first time
for farmers anywhere in the South. These family farmers with their rough blue overalls and Jeffersonian
agrarian values, walked picket lines before the gates of
Pillsbury, Ralston-Purina, and the other food conglomerates which bought their chickens for processing. Equally
unprecedented was the decision of federal meat inspectors in the chicken plants to honor the pickets and
refuse to enter the plants. Strangest of all, truckloads
of black industrial unionists from Birmingham arrived
at one plant to cheer the farmers on. The locals swore
that the ghosts of Tom Watson and the Populists could
be seen dancing in the shadows, their dream of a
labor-farmer coalition against the trusts come true at
last.

These events were stimulated by profound economic
grievances which foreshadow problems for the consumer as well. A study by USDA economists recently
reported that poultry growers in Northern Alabama
work for an average of *minus* 36 cents an hour.[1] They
survive in the short run by living off the depreciation

on their houses and equipment or by going deeper into debt; in the long run, they sell out to larger growers or go bankrupt. Their economic plight reflects the outcomes of the farmers' encounters with the integrated corporations which buy their chickens.

The concentration of meat production and marketing power in relatively few food conglomerates over the last two decades has not been matched by compensatory restructuring of consumer and farmer power. In dealing with the farmer suppliers at one end and the consumer at the other, Swift, Pillsbury, Ralston-Purina, Central Soya, and the other agribusiness giants still maintain a man-to-man contact with unorganized individuals. The unequal relationship encourages an irresponsible marketing power which permits the corporation to pass the costs of its mistakes and excessive profit margins either forward to the consumer or backward to the supplier. This imbalance assumes classic proportions in the chicken country of the Deep South.

The corporations see nothing improper in their refusal to deal with debt-ridden farmers except as individuals. The Operations Manager of the Pillsbury Company, after refusing to meet with a grower's association, explained:

Our position continues to be that we will gladly meet with any grower *on an individual basis* to discuss problems, complaints, or questions. . . .[2]

A Wisconsin turkey grower describes the farmer's leverage in this situation:

What farmer would want to buck up against a big corporation to fight for his rights, with probably $18 in his checking account, against a staff of twenty-five attorneys, to which money doesn't mean anything. How can a small farmer compete in this situation?[3]

The infiltration of the corporate state into agriculture is having a profound effect on the economic and social relationships of rural America. As large integrated companies move in, they force more and more family farmers to lose their independent status and become, in effect, organization men in overalls. Large corporations have recently moved into cattle ranching, cotton growing, orcharding, and other kinds of farming. Dow Chemical now grows catfish in Texas; Purex is growing vegetables on thousands of acres in the Southwest; American Cyanamid and John Hancock Mutual Life Insurance Company have a joint venture to grow corn, wheat, and soybeans on a 35,000 acre farm in North Carolina. Swift, Tenneco, Textron, Campbell Soups, Ralston-Purina, Pillsbury, and Central Soya dominate the beef and chicken industry. When corporations of this size go into farming, they pull the whole agricultural establishment in their wake. Congressional committees and the federal farm bureaucracy become more attuned to the interests of corporate agribusiness and less sensitive to the needs of small farmers, the rural poor, and the consumer.

The corporatization of agriculture has been more rapid in the chicken industry than anywhere else. The chicken farmers of Mississippi, Georgia, Alabama, and Arkansas provide a melancholy model of what the new industrial state may hold in store for rural people. For readers of Southern fiction, this has a special irony. The chicken farmer, while he often cuts a ludicrous figure, was at least his own man farming his own land. He grew chickens in a back lot, fattened them with diets of home-grown cornmeal and mush and sold them at auction at the county market when he was ready. As late as 1959, nearly 60 percent of all broilers were still grown by independent farmers and then purchased in the open market by large processors for slaughter. By 1970, the situation had drastically changed. Over 98 percent of all chickens are now produced under contract to large integrated corporations.

In contract farming, the corporation contracts for use of the farmer's land and its production resources. The corporation provides inputs such as seeds, feeds, medicines, and chicks or other livestock while the grower supplies the land, labor, and management. In this system, the corporation gains many of the advantages of family farming (primarily cheap labor) without taking from the farmer the costs and risks of capital ownership. The farmer sells the commodities directly to the packer or processor at a fixed price agreed on in advance. The farmer is, in effect, paid as a wage laborer on a piecework basis.

In ten years from 1954 to 1964, the broiler industry went from 3 to 98 percent integrator controlled. Mergers of processing and slaughtering firms increased at a rate of 41 percent during the four years 1960–1964.[4] As a result, the open market, the traditional cushion between the farmer and his corporate buyers, is gone. The chicken farmer is no longer protected by competitive bidding in the marketplace. If a farmer wants to sell chicken, he must sell to a corporation through a contract with a fixed formula price or not at all. There is still an open market for hogs and cattle but it too may succumb to contract agriculture, as Swift and other companies increasingly buy fed cattle directly from the feedlot at a fixed price. The American Agricultural Marketing Association estimates that 50 percent of American food will be produced by farmers under contract to corporations in 1970–1980 and that within fifteen years, 75 percent of agricultural production and marketing will be cornered by contracts.[5]

Until the early fifties, the chicken industry was fragmented with hatcheries, feed companies, growers, and processors all operating more or less separately. Gradually, large companies began to integrate these elements. Feed companies like Ralston-Purina and Pillsbury integrated forward to develop markets for their feeds, while poultry processors integrated backward as a means of controlling costs. Eventually the largest companies absorbed all the stages of chicken production, except the actual raising of the birds. The "integrators" found it more profitable to contract with independent farmers to do that. In broiler integration, therefore, the big companies grow the feed, hatch the chicks, and slaughter and process the mature birds. The farmer furnishes his land, building, equipment, and labor to feed the chickens for eight weeks until they grow to marketable weight of three and a half pounds.

On one level, the integrated chicken industry is the great success story of American agriculture. Before World War II, chicken was still a seasonal dish. Families looked forward to "spring chicken," a by-product

of the spring hatch from farm flocks of layers. As
demand increased, a few producers began raising chickens not as egg producers but as fryers for the market.
Spurred on by World War II, when people turned to
chicken while other meat was scarce, broiler production climbed steeply after the Depression. From 1939 to
1958, poultry sales increased an average of 14 percent
each year.[6] Production reached nearly 3 billion birds
in 1970, up from 310 million in 1947. The American
who ate eighteen pounds of chicken a year in 1940,
consumed thirty-nine pounds a year in 1969. Market
specialists estimate that he will consume forty-five to
fifty pounds by 1980.

As a result of rapid technological development in
genetics, feeds, animal drugs, and economies of scale,
the price of chicken has actually *declined* as consumption has gone up. In 1950, broilers cost the consumer
$0.60 a pound; in 1970 the price was $0.42 a pound.
The price received by the grower has plummeted from
$0.29 to $0.15 a pound in the same period.[7] It is important to note that while retail prices declined 33 percent,
payments to growers declined nearly 50 percent. Retail
prices for beef, by comparison, have increased from
$0.67 a pound in 1955 to nearly $1.00 in 1969.

The farmer has stayed in business by increasing the
efficiency of the process by which chickens convert
feed into meat. No animal surpasses the chicken as a
meat factory. While it takes eight to ten pounds of feed
to produce a pound of beef, it takes only 2.4 pounds*
to produce a pound of chicken, down from four or five
pounds in 1950. The time needed to grow a broiler to
market weight has also declined, from ten to twelve
weeks in 1950 to eight to nine weeks in 1969.[9]

The chickens themselves have become computerized
units in a factory environment. The chicken which
used to run free to scratch and root in the soil until
time for slaughter, now spends its short life in a 12" by
18" cage crowded up against three other birds. His day
may consist of sixteen hours of artificial light in a
totally programmed environment. Crowding favors
disease by creating stress and aiding the buildup of

* The figure is 3.5–4 pounds of feed if the broiler breeder's feed
requirements are included.[8]

harmful bacteria and parasites, such as *coccidia.* The
chicken's feed, therefore, is sprinkled with antibiotic
drugs. Other drugs, including arsenic and antibiotics,
such as nitrofurans, are fed to increase the rate at
which the chicken matures and gains weight. Before
going to market, chickens may also be bathed in tetracyclines (antibiotics) or sorbic acid to extend their
shelf life. In addition, the birds' chemical diet may contain coloring additives to give their flesh a desired
yellowish tint. They are also sprayed regularly with
pesticides. With this medicine chest of ready chemicals,
the poultryman can cheat on sanitation without suffering severe flock losses, but at the risk of chemical contamination of the final product.* Stress also induces
cannibalism. Chickens are, therefore, debeaked to keep
them from destroying their neighbors,[10] and in some
cases given tranquilizers.

One indication of how far the chicken industry has
come from the barnyard is the development of what
must be one of the world's most exotic and highly
specialized professions: chicken sexing. For economic
reasons, chicks must be segregated by sex at birth.
Chicken genitalia being what they are, it is virtually
impossible for the untrained eye to distinguish the sex
of a day-old chick. But in 1925, the Japanese discovered
some telltale sign of sex in the chick's anatomy which
they jealously guarded as a trade secret. As a result,
no modern hatchery is complete without its chicken
sexor imported from Japan. The best can sort 800–1000
baby chicks an hour. The Japanese sexors have recently
founded the American Sexing School in Lansdale,
Pennsylvania, and will let anyone in on their secret for
$1300 and an eighteen-week course. To keep their pro-
fessional standards high, they have, in the best American tradition, formed the American Chicken Sexing
Association.

The technical sophistication of chicken growing,

---

* The growers' extreme economic deprivation caused in part by in-
equitable contracts with the integrators leads some of them to cut
corners with drugs. They can ignore withdrawal periods and recommended dose levels in applying this chemical technology to their flocks,
with little chance of being caught by USDA residue samplers (see
Chapter 6).

especially in disease control, gives an impetus to concentration in the industry. According to Dr. Philip Raup, Professor of Agricultural Economics at the University of Minnesota, one of the determinants of the most effective size of firm in poultry production and beef feeding is a scale of operations large enough to support a resident veterinarian.[11] Without expert advice, the typical farmer cannot develop the skills to use chemical technology effectively. Much of the effort at farmer education in the use of feed additives, farm chemicals, and drugs is conducted by private companies who prefer to concentrate on volume users. Dr. Raup notes that our ability to produce this technology has outrun efforts to distribute it in packages useful for the small farmer. He blames the Federal Extension Service and agricultural experiment stations for the failure to develop an effective extension program in animal health.[12]

The pyramiding of economic power in the chicken industry has created a vicious marketing system which can be turned against the consumer as well as the farmer. Up to now, many of the benefits of cost-reducing technology have been passed on to the consumer. But as concentration increases, this may cease. The history of concentration in other industries—the making of automobiles is a classic example—shows that when a few firms dominate the production field, many of the rewards of technological advance are captured by the firms and not passed on. At the same time, a technological rigor mortis may set in as the firms, freed of competitive pressure in pricing, devote more energy to corporate risk-reduction than to product improvement.

In the chicken business, Pillsbury, Swift, and Holly Farms may soon compete in the manner of the soap, detergent, and breakfast food makers—by using advertising to create the illusion of differentiation in essentially similar products. The advertising costs to create the image of "brand name" poultry will be passed on to the consumer.[13] The Pillsbury chicken may soon rival the NBC peacock as the nation's most ubiquitous TV fowl.

Thus far, however, the full weight of the food conglomerates' market power has been turned toward the supplier, not the consumer.

An Honest Day's Pay

Despite the broiler industry's modernization and growth, the growers have not shared in its prosperity. Of all the links in the chain of chicken production, the actual growing of chickens has the lowest profit margins. As one observer noted: "If the growing of chicks were profitable, it would have been integrated long ago."

This situation exists because the relationship between the farmer and the companies is so extremely one-sided. Even though the farmer has invested nearly 50 percent of his industry's capital, he is hardly an equal partner. The growers have little bargaining power in setting the contract price. Companies deny that they stake out exclusive claims for specific territories, but the fact is that with the exception of Gainesville, Georgia, and a few other areas, many growers face local monopoly situations where there is only one company to deal with.[14] The contract price from company to company varies very little. Usually the contract is drafted by the company and presented to the grower on a take it or leave it basis. One California grower, in a letter to Congressman B. F. Sisk (D.-Cal.) in October, 1971, described contract bargaining:

. . . in today's market, the grower dare not bargain for decent pay lest he be cut off [by the integrator]; his mortgage, land, home, and everything are threatened if he so much as asks for a better deal than these phony contracts which are not contracts at all but merely unilateral work rules imposed from on high.

In 1969–1970, the grower received between one and three-fourth cents and two cents per pound for birds he raised. The American Farm Bureau estimates that the *break even* point for the average grower is $0.0229 per pound. Robert Troy, a skilled observer of the Southern poultry scene, gave this description of the economic plight of one Alabama grower, a Mr. Thurmond Banks, who grows chickens for Spring Valley Farms in Empire, Alabama:

For eighty-four days Mr. Banks and his family fed, watered, housed, and looked after 22,500 chickens. Mr. Banks estimated his total labor at a minimum of 588 hours. His gross receipts minus direct cost yielded him a net of $317.67, which works out to be $0.25 an hour for his investment of labor and capital. But depreciation and tax costs, which the grower rarely takes into account, would come to about $370.00 on his equipment. Thus Mr. Banks and his family were actually making about minus $0.08 an hour, which would be a windfall if the negative income tax were enacted.[15]

Many growers are not sophisticated enough in budgeting to realize that a year's net cash flow, without deductions for fixed costs such as depreciation on his buildings and equipment, is a poor measure of income. There is a story about a lady chicken grower who was asked by a labor organizer how she was doing with her chickens. "Great," she said. The surprised organizer then asked if she had figured out her direct and indirect expenses. "Lord no," she answered. "I wouldn't have nothing then."[16]

The fact is that most growers have been working for almost nothing.[17] The Economic Research Service of USDA has estimated that poultry farmers in Georgia earned only $0.53 an hour for their labor in 1952, and that income then *declined* in the next decade to reach a low of $0.01 per hour in 1964. They rebounded to $0.54 an hour in 1965.[18] Testimony in Senate hearings on the Agricultural Fair Practices Act of 1967 showed that many growers were forced to live off their depreciation. Conditions have not improved much since. These dismal figures are not confined to the South. Congressman Sisk of California recently estimated that California growers receive an average of $0.30 an hour. As these figures indicate, a major advantage of contract farming to the integrator is that it allows them, in effect, to hire workers while legally evading the minimum wage laws.

1969 was a record year and yet the net return to the average farmer was approximately $2,000 per year, a three-fold improvement since 1960–64, but an income which still puts him well below the poverty line.[19] (These figures do not include depreciation and interest payments. They were figured on the very unlikely assumption that the farmers were debt free.) This represented total farm income for broiler growers and was calculated at $0.021 per pound of broilers sold.

An Alabama study of cash flow budgets for broiler growers found that a farmer with a 20,000 bird capacity who produced three batches of broilers in 1969, ended up $628 *in the red*, after payments on housing and equipment loans, depreciation, and other fixed costs were taken into account. If production was expanded to four and a half batches a year, the farmer came out ahead but just barely. His net return to labor and management was $890. The return on the chickens themselves was only $90; he earned the other $800 by selling the chicken's manure.[20]

If the farm unit had a 45,000 bird capacity with four and a half batches a year, the total return was $2,000 per farm in spendable and nonspendable income, a modest return to say the least for a businessman with a $40,000 investment in housing and equipment alone. If manure sales and increases in net worth—the nonspendable income—are not included, the farm was over $4,700 in the red.

When this example was cited before the Senate Agriculture Committee in 1969, spokesmen for the integrators said it was unrealistic because it depreciated chicken houses over five years rather than ten.[21] It is true that the growers' profits improve with ten year depreciation. His average spendable income is now a "realistic" $374.62 for the year or $31 a month. He has additional nonspendable income of $1,800 from 360 tons of manure.[22] Whether the depreciation is figured at five or ten years, the result is the same: the growers' profits are *literally* chicken shit.*

The integrators fare differently, to say the least. James Finlayson, a leading poultry consultant for Pillsbury, estimates that on a five year average, pub-

---

* Some growers have suffered because chicken manure is not always readily convertible into cash, but help is on the way. The FDA is considering a proposal to use the manure as *feed* for chickens, cattle, and hogs. The manure must be pasteurized to eliminate bacteria and chemical residues must be removed, but these problems are manageable. "This is the recycled generation," says Joe Claybaugh, a poultry consultant for DeKalb Ag-Research, Inc. "Can you envision a 750 steer lot tied to a 100,000 layer operation?" This recycled manure would reduce feed costs 60 percent or more.

licly held companies essentially in the broiler business, can average 23–24 percent return on invested capital before taxes each year.[23]

The chicken farmer is convinced that his small profits are caused as much by the way they are calculated by the integrator as by market conditions. Here the grower has been totally at the mercy of the integrator. The National Broiler Council, the major association of integrators, publishes a code of ethics which states that its members should give the grower a written contract with full documents on his flock, showing the amount of feed used, the condemnation rate, the weight and number of birds slaughtered, and a settlement sheet giving the calculations used in reaching payment. The only problem with the Code of Ethics is that few integrators have observed it.[24] From the beginning of his association with the integrator, the grower is kept in a state of ignorance. According to J. B. Noblin, President of Scott County Farm Bureau in Forest, Mississippi:

There are no broiler contracts in this area. Integrators simply give the producer a sheet showing what would be paid per pound, based on the feed conversion. The terms of the so-called contracts are not discussed with the producer, nor is it signed by the integrator or producer.[25]

The Packers and Stockyards Administration of USDA reported in 1967 that the grower frequently did not know how many chickens the integrator brought to him, nor how many were eventually taken away, nor how much they weighed. Chickens are neither counted nor weighed at the farm. He has had to take the word of the company on all of these matters. The grower is not permitted to inspect the scales of the integrator. Frequently, he has been forbidden to see the USDA condemnation and grading certificates on the chickens he markets even though all condemned birds are charged to the grower.[26]

Growers are forced further into debt by the company's requirement that they install expensive equipment such as automatic feeders and elaborate insulation, as condition for receiving the chicks. Ralston-Purina in the mid-sixties would only contract with growers who agreed to a tie-in purchase of company equipment.

During the National Food Marketing hearings in 1966, a grower in East Texas testified that "Purina" made him buy a fan worth $19 at any 5&10¢ store for $50. The National Farmers Organization charges that the companies deliberately increase the growers' indebtedness with these measures so they will be forced to take chickens at any price. The companies claim that their only interest is to improve the quality of the chicken houses and cut their losses.

In many cases, the grower's contract is so unequal that he has been compared to the sharecropper in both his status and his poverty. The difference in this version of that infamous relationship is that the bossman is an absentee landlord with a corporate, not a personal, identity whose "big house" is in a paneled board room in faraway Minneapolis or New York. Otherwise the analogy needs no explanation. The "cropper" is visited by the "field man" who supplies him with his essentials to make a crop (in this case, baby chicks, feed, and technical advice); the field man collects the harvest (eight-week-old chickens), measures the results (he weighs the chickens, and sets the price), and decides what the cropper's share ought to be. The cropper may even be forced to buy his supplies (his broiler equipment) from the company store. The corporate landlord keeps all the records. When results are totaled up, the poultry "cropper" often finds he has a bigger debt instead of a big payment, and is even more in thrall to his bossman than before.[27]

The poultry farmers have all the insecurities of an organization man and none of the fringe benefits. The farmers are not strictly employees of a corporation, and are therefore without retirement, medical benefits, a minimum wage protection. These farmers keep chicks in their houses only at the sufferance of the corporation. David H. Sloan, President of the South Carolina Farm Bureau Federation, states: "The poultry producer in most cases has invested everything he has in the property, poultry houses, and equipment. He is at the mercy of the processor because he must have birds to grow or go broke."[28] The grower also shares the psychological state of the sharecropper. The latter knew that he could be evicted if he complained; the grower knows that he can be cut off arbitrarily by the integrator and be left with no chickens to raise. A Georgia organizer for the National Farmers Organization used only mild hyperbole when he recently described the growers as "the last slaves to be freed in the South."

The Burn-Out

Pillsbury, Arkansas Valley Industries, and the other integrators argue that the grower benefits from the contract system and that the system itself has nothing to do with his penury. It is true that in the fifties, contract farming appeared to be a great opportunity for the farmers. Production was centered in the depressed, rural counties of five Southern states, where there were many unemployed white farmers with a little land and not much else. For many of these marginal farmers, raising chickens seemed to be the last chance to make money off their farms. The contracts promised to take all the risk out of chicken raising. The farmer on contract is somewhat protected from the fluctuations of the free market, but risks remain. Many growers have market related contracts and thus risk loss in a down market. They risk loss from condemnations which may not be their fault and from cutbacks during periods of overproduction; they risk loss through damage to or obsolescence of their equipment.

The integrators justify the growers' economic plight by pleading their own poverty. In the words of John Yarbrough, the militantly pro-integrator publisher of the news weekly the *Poultry Times*: "Any grower who believes his integrator is making money today is not acquainted with the economic facts of the broiler business."[29] The poultry industry was plagued with overproduction in 1970–1972 and the broiler divisions of many large integrators lost money. But on a five-year average, as mentioned earlier, the companies can average a 24 percent return on invested capital, according to a leading poultry consultant. (The cyclical nature of the business, rather than sustained low profits, has persuaded some conglomerates, Ralston-Purina for one, to get out of the business.) In any case, the losses of the broiler divisions of food conglomerates are not

what they seem. Current tax laws permit diversified companies to deduct losses of one operation from the profits
of unrelated or distantly related operations and substantially reduce their total tax load. An effort by
poultry growers to prohibit the use of farm production losses as deductions from nonfarm production operations in tax calculations failed to win support in
Senate hearings on corporation farming in 1968. Moreover, in periods of overproduction, large feed manufacturers like Ralston-Purina can make up in profits from
selling feed the losses they incur in processing chickens.

One indication of the integrators' financial strength
is that they frequently increase their investment in the
poultry industry during surplus crises. This was the
case with the turkey industry in 1961 and 1967. The
head of the Wisconsin Turkey Federation notes:

When a [conglomerate] goes into farming, profit should be
the motive. However, we have seen such companies enter
into or expand turkey operations during years where there
was little or no profit potential. This leads one to feel that
profit, for a specific year at least, is not the only motive.[30]

Overcapacity is precisely what keeps the poultry
farmer in peonage, for it robs him of any bargaining
power he might have. In the South, the growers have
a term for increases of production in a falling market.
They call it a "burn-out." Only the strongest independent growers survive, and they are far more vulnerable
than before. The Packers and Stockyard Administration
in 1967 accused the processors of using this strategy. It
reported that integrators use get-rich-quick advertising
campaigns to encourage farmers to build new facilities
to grow chickens, even in times of surplus.[31] Feed companies, for example, go into the chicken business primarily to create new markets for feed. They therefore
have a vested interest in a chicken surplus.

Chickens have to eat, whatever their price is in the
market. Therefore, while the farmer takes the brunt of
loss from low chicken prices, feed sales boom. Each
burn-out, however, leads to greater concentration of
market power in few economic units.

The farmers cannot match the financial staying power
of the integrators in a falling market. As their debts
increase, they become more dependent on the contrac-

tors. In order to meet mortgage payments and keep their farms, the farmers have to keep their chicken houses filled with birds even if they are losing money. In August, 1970, the Director of a Mississippi Marketing Association described the situation:

Most broiler farmers are small farmers and land owners. To get into the business, they had to mortgage their small farms and homes to build broiler houses. From this point on, they must have birds in their houses to make payments; they must have birds in their houses or they must leave home.[32]

The grower also suffers from the integrator's sleight of hand in accounting techniques. Large companies charge feed and sometimes chicks, produced by other divisions, to their broiler divisions at inflated or "puffed" prices. Since the farmer does not pay for feed and chickens, this may seem simply a matter between the integrator and the Internal Revenue Service. But when puffed prices result in paper losses for the broiler divisions, they work against the growers when they bargain for a new contract with the integrator.[33]

Self-Help

Whether or not the integrators are responsible, the fact is that when overproduction occurs, the grower, the weakest link in the industry, is forced to make most of the economic sacrifices. Lack of bargaining power, far more than market conditions, is the cause of his plight. This situation was recognized by the Packers and Stockyards Administration of USDA in 1967:

The problem in Southern broiler contracting is the weak bargaining position of the grower. He is ill-equipped to bargain vigorously and effectively with integrators.[34]

The relative defenselessness of the grower and the real incentives for irresponsible use of private economic power it creates provide an interesting test case for the Department of Agriculture and, on a broader level, for the possibilities for reform in the American political system. Should the growers bank on the objectivity of the federal government and look to it to protect their rights? Would Congress respond to their needs with

116   SOWING THE WIND

new legislation? Or should the growers dispense with
the old institutions and seek self-help through new institutions of their own making? It is clearly an offense to
democratic values that individual farmers should have
to confront alone the full force of corporate power, but
is the political system flexible enough to respond? Here
on the obscure stage of the chicken farm, one sees exaggerated in microcosm the plight of farm workers, consumers, textile workers, meat inspectors, and other
groups left exposed to irresponsible corporate power by
structural imbalances in the political and economic
system.

The federal agency with regulatory responsibility in
the area of chicken farming is USDA's Packers and
Stockyards Administration. In a strong report entitled
The Broiler Industry released in 1967, it first brought
the growers' situation to national attention. Based on
the uncompromising research of James D. Tuggle and
Everett Stoddard, the report described the inequities of
the contract system in merciless detail. Spurred by these
revelations, Secretary of Agriculture Freeman pledged
immediate investigation of any complaints of boycotting
or other retaliation by contractors against farmers who
joined cooperatives in an attempt to better their lot.[35]
He also promised new regulations for growers'
contracts.

The effect on the poultry industry was electric. The
large integrators directed a barrage of criticism at
Freeman and the Packers and Stockyards Administration. In September, 1967, in an attempt to gain industry-
wide support, Freeman promised that no new regulations protecting the growers would be put into effect
until they had been reviewed in advance by an advisory
committee which included integrators and growers.[36]
Thus began a long series of delay. Regulations giving
the grower a more equal voice in negotiating contracts
were not proposed until three years later in the fall of
1970. At the request of the National Broiler Council
and other integrator associations, they were then further
delayed. The regulations require:

(1) a written contract which includes all significant details,
including duration, termination and conditions, and payment terms;

(2) settlement sheets with all information necessary to compute payments due to the grower;
(3) condemnation and grading certificates;
(4) grouping or ranking sheets which show the grower's position vis-à-vis other growers during the settlement period.

The regulations seem modest enough, by the standards of any other industry, but they are seen as a fundamental threat to the free enterprise system by some integrator spokesmen. John Yarbrough of the *Poultry Times* called Assistant Secretary of Agriculture Richard Lyng a "pseudodictator" when he signed the *Federal Register* notice of the regulations on January 23, 1971. He quoted a poultryman: "If the Secretary of Agriculture can require all of the things contained in the new Packers and Stockyards regulations, we are living in the wrong country. This is just like Russia."[37] The regulations went into effect on June 1, 1971. Their effectiveness depends on their enforcement and, therefore, remains to be tested. Up to November, 1971, USDA had still initiated no formal proceedings against any integrator.

The growers have luckily not waited for USDA to equalize their bargaining terms with the conglomerates. Out of desperation, they have cast aside the separatist ideology of the family farmer and organized in self-defense. They recognized that the old clichés of individualism and economic independence, appropriate perhaps when an open market existed as a buffer between the farmer and the integrator, had now become luxuries they could not afford.

The efforts of farmers to organize against the integrators have a long and often violent history. They began in 1961 with the formation of the Northwest Poultry Growers Association in Arkansas. Its best known leader was Ellis Hale, who with his wife and four children, raised 200,000 broilers a year in Scott County, south of Fort Smith. His efforts to organize growers were at first discouraged, and then actively opposed by Arkansas Valley Industries, Ralston-Purina, and Tysons Foods, the largest integrators in the state. At first Hale was successful with his message that farmers should stop living off the depreciation of their investment and earn a fair return. But in the spring of

1962, the resistance of the integrators became more threatening. In May, when growers congregated at the Scott County Courthouse for one of Hale's meetings, they got an ominous reception. As the farmers arrived, they found that Arkansas Valley Industries had cars and trucks parked strategically on the square around the courthouse, covering all its approaches. Company officials were sitting in the vehicles taking down the names of the growers as they passed by. During the meeting, a company truck with no muffler gunned its motor near the courthouse door, drowning out Hale's words.

In August, Arkansas Valley Industries canceled its contracts with Hale and his father and brother, all of whom were members of the Northwest Poultry Growers Association. Ralston-Purina and Tysons Foods joined AVI in boycotting all growers who had joined the association. Because of the blacklisting, the Hales and dozens of other growers could no longer get chicks for their broiler houses and went bankrupt. The Hales filed a civil suit against the poultry companies in the hopes of recovering their losses, but when they could not put up the $10,000 necessary to prepare and present the case, their attorneys withdrew.[38]

After a lengthy investigation by the Packers and Stockyards Administration, the three integrators were ordered in 1968 to "cease and desist" their harassment of the growers. The order was subsequently overturned for lack of jurisdiction by the U.S. Circuit Court of Appeals in 1969. USDA has still not asked for legislation to give Packers and Stockyards jurisdiction in such cases. Hale lost everything.

The Arkansas case helped inspire new organizing efforts in other states. The holding action in Alabama in the spring of 1970 was organized by the National Farmers Organization, the most militant of the farm organizations which support the growers' demands for collective bargaining. The NFO strike was marred by violence on both sides. Night riders roamed the lonely claytop roads of northern Alabama, burning the chicken houses of striking and nonstriking growers alike. Company trucks were fired on, and there were fights on the picket lines. As one observer noted, there was "much violence, with neighbor turned against neighbor. The wounds will not heal completely during this generation."[39]

The striking farmers refused to accept checks from the integrators. They demanded higher contract payments and the right to monitor the weighing and inspection of their birds. From the beginning, the companies refused to negotiate with the farmers' representative. John Bagwell, the President of Spring Valley Foods in Cullman, Alabama, was asked by a reporter whether he would negotiate with the NFO. He gave a forthright response:

I'd rather be dead and in hell, than talk with W. O. Thomas [the NFO local President] . . . the day I talk to that bunch, I'll call the reporters to Cullman and have W. O. Thomas pull down his britches and I'll kiss him square on the ass.[40]

USDA, while officially an impartial observer of the strike, actually went to great lengths to discourage it. When eighty-seven USDA poultry inspectors refused to cross the NFO picket lines because of the violent atmosphere, the Inspector General investigated them, judged them to be AWOL, and deprived them of pay. All the inspectors received letters of reprimand from the Department. The Alabama Poultry Inspectors Local of the American Federation of Government Employees feels strongly that the investigation by the Office of the Inspector General was biased and unfair.[41] There are also charges that the Farmers Home Administration has made reprisals against striking growers. T. H. House of Addison, Alabama, who has an FHA mortgage on his farm, was told by local FHA representatives that his farm would be "a-changing hands" if he didn't take chickens from the integrators.[42]*

* USDA's intervention did give the strike a comic interlude. When the inspectors refused to cross the picket lines, the Consumer and Marketing Service was deluged with demands from the processors to keep inspection going. C&MS then made a nationwide appeal for volunteers to go to Alabama. GS 14's from C&MS Washington headquarters, men who had not seen the inside of a chicken plant for years and probably never wanted to see another one, were dispatched to Alabama in their coats and ties to sub for GS 7 inspectors. The crowning indignity came when the inspector-in-charge at Plant 6666 in Gadsden, Alabama, suspended two of these inspector-bureaucrats for incompetence.

The NFO holding action was temporarily stopped by an injunction on June 28, 1970, by the U.S. District Court for Northern Alabama. In July, 1971, nearly a year later, the U.S. Circuit Court of Appeals in New Orleans reversed the lower court, finding that the complaints of Ralston-Purina, Pillsbury, and twelve other integrators were only a "massive compilation of hearsay." The court held that "the procedures followed by the plaintiffs in this case cannot be sustained under any standard." This decision is cold comfort for the NFO. The picket lines have vanished and some growers have returned to the companies, but the nine-county local is holding on. John Bagwell, President of Spring Valley Foods, boasts: "They're whipped. We've broken them." He may be right. Many of the growers are in deep financial trouble. The lower court, in granting the preliminary injunction which broke the strike, required the fourteen corporations to put up only a $2,500 bond to compensate NFO members in the event that the injunction was found to be "improvident." NFO had asked for $1 million. Crawford Smith, one such grower, observes:

*

It's a hard row to hoe. All we're asking is fair wages for a fair day's work. . . . Seems like we just keep on losing ground.[43]

More recently, the American Agricultural Marketing Association, an affiliate of the American Farm Bureau Federation, has organized growers against the Maplewood Poultry Company in Belfast, Maine. The growers decided not to accept chicks after the integrator made contract changes which allegedly reduced the grower's income by 20 percent. The AAMA has asked the Packers and Stockyards Administration to investigate threats and intimidation against growers.

The growers have not as yet received much help from the Congressional arena. The Agricultural Fair Practices Act, better known as S.109, which was passed in 1967, in practice has proved a triumph of form over substance. It promised to protect the grower against unfair trade practices such as boycotts, blacklists, contract cutoffs, and harassment. In November, 1971, USDA filed its first suit against an integrator under the act. USDA charged that the Maplewood Poultry Company mentioned above threatened to boycott farmers who complained about its contracts. Responsibility for administering the act was recently transferred from the Farmers Cooperative Service to the Consumer and Marketing Service, a move which, by putting it in a primarily marketing agency, has left the act in a kind of bureaucratic limbo. The Consumer and Marketing Service has thus failed to give active support to investigation and prosecution under the act.[44] Claude Gifford, an editor of the *Farm Journal*, the leading farm magazine, recently accused USDA of being slow in pressing cases for farmers.[45]

Two other bills, S.2225, and a bill sponsored by Senator Walter Mondale (D.-Wisc.) go much further in defining and protecting the growers' rights at the bargaining table. They would make the failure of an integrator to recognize a bargaining association an unfair labor practice. These bills are now pending.

According to the National Broiler Council and other integrator spokesmen, these bills threaten the efficiency and lifeblood of the processing industry. On the contrary, the right to organize to protect occupational interests is a basic cornerstone of the free enterprise system. This kind of institution building is essential to give balance and fair play to the economic relationships of contract farming.

The integrators' attempt to invoke the ideology of economic independence and individuality to justify their attacks on growers' organizations is particularly ironic because it comes at a time when the integrators are trying to increase their own bargaining muscle through group action. Operating under the umbrella of the Capper-Volstead Act of 1922, Ralston-Purina and other integrators have formed the National Broiler Marketing Association which now controls 35–45 percent of the nation's broilers.[46] The Capper-Volstead Act was designed to allow small producers to legally collude in order to offset the power of large corporate buyers. It seems doubtful that its farmers wanted it to be used to allow large integrators and nonfarm processors to collude against the small farmer. Neither the Federal Trade Commission nor the Justice Department has challenged the legitimacy of the National Broiler Marketing Association. Both have long been indifferent to the impact of corporate concentration on the small farmer.

With the exception of the strong Packers and Stock-yards report in 1967, USDA has been at best lukewarm to the attempts of growers to organize in their self-defense. Assistant Secretary of Agriculture Richard Lyng recently gave bargaining associations the weakest possible endorsement: "We are not intrinsically opposed to bargaining associations."[47] He states that many farmers have become disillusioned with farm bargain-ing, and warns that the "rewards and incentives of the free market system must not be . . . unduly inhibited."[48] Lyng is strangely silent, however, on the free-market implications of collusion among the integrators.

One must conclude, therefore, that up to now USDA has failed this test of its responsiveness to the needs of small producers.* More help may be forthcoming in Congress now that the National Farmers Union and the American Farm Bureau Federation have joined forces to support a strong bargaining bill. NFO prefers to go it alone with its collective bargaining strategy without government interference. These groups may force USDA to re-evaluate its relationship to farm bargaining.

Defenders of the "corporate-integratee" system of agriculture, while conceding that low prices have pro-duced hard times for all branches of the poultry indus-try, argue that farmers and rural communities are still better off than if the integrators had not arrived on the scene. They make three basic points: (1) integrators allow farmers to stay on the farm which most of them would have left without the technical guidance and a stable market provided by the integrators; (2) integrators provide jobs off the farm in processing, dis-tribution, and marketing; (3) integrators are more effi-cient and therefore reduce prices for the consumer.

On the first point, it would be valuable to know more about the circumstances under which farmers become growers for an integrator, to see whether the alternative was in fact leaving farming altogether, and to see

---

* It is interesting to note that the Chilean government found it necessary to *take over* a Ralston-Purina subsidiary in 1970 because it was allegedly treating small chicken farmers unfairly.

whether total incomes in fact increased as a result of integration. In the integrated broiler industry of Northern Alabama, at least, it is abundantly clear that growers are making extremely low returns on their capital and labor. This experience suggests that collective bargaining and marketing associations are far more efficient than integration in protecting farm income. One problem is that even if the integrator does increase income for farmers in the short run, it tends to drive out small processors and other buyers for the farmers' commodities, creating a quasi-monopoly situation. In other words, vertical integration often leads to horizontal concentration. When this occurs, the farmer may find his contract price suddenly declining. Subsequently, if the integrator decides to shift its business elsewhere, in response to organizing efforts by farmers, for example, the growers are left in the lurch with no local markets for their chicken. Ralston-Purina's plans to move out of the contract chicken business create this threat in some Southern localities.

As for the off-the-farm jobs provided by the integrator, we need to know more about who gets these jobs, and what their wages and working conditions are. It is likely, however, that new bargaining institutions which keep ownership in the hands of farmers will have a more beneficial effect on the rural economy. This is true because small farms would keep profits in the area and at the same time avoid the effects of absentee ownership by integrators who may be more interested in low taxes than decent schools.

It cannot be assumed that lower costs to the consumer of a "corporate-integratee" produced commodity when they occur are the result of increased efficiency from integration alone. The big breakthroughs in lowering the costs of chicken production—e.g., improved feed conversions ratios—have taken place at the farm level. Of course, when one firm runs the whole vertical chain, it is possible that it could reduce consumer prices by eliminating the "waste" profit of a series of middlemen. However, no firm is going to give up increased profits just for the consumer's sake. For every middleman eliminated, who made perhaps a 5 percent profit, there is a service to be performed by the new firm's capital, on which it may earn a 10 percent return. If integration leads to significant market control, particularly when accompanied by horizontal concentration, higher prices for the consumer are the likely result. Unfortunately, corporate secrecy about the profits and losses of different operating divisions and products makes judgments about the relative efficiency of the integrators difficult.

For the individual chicken farmer, therefore, the lesson is clear. The integrated corporations have come to the South and the other poultry areas to stay. As the corporate state advances into rural America, the farmer will have to organize in self-defense. The alternative is the neo-feudalism of northern Alabama.

6

Hidden Ingredients

Federal regulation of meat and poultry is heavily biased toward the principle that what the consumer cannot see cannot hurt him. The plant inspector is primarily concerned with bruises, tumors, fecal contamination, enlarged livers, stray feathers—defects which he can see, touch, or smell. But of far greater potential danger to the consumer's health are the hidden contaminants: bacteria like salmonella and residues from the use of pesticides, nitrites, hormones, antibiotics, and other chemicals used in food production and processing.

Here the inspection failures are more often errors of omission than commission. Monitoring meat for chemical residues has traditionally been limited to spot checks for a few compounds, often with analytical equipment either too insensitive or too time-consuming to catch contaminated meat before it reaches the consumer. There is no regular monitoring of salmonella or other microbiological contaminants in meat and poultry plants in the United States. Yet at least thirty diseases, including brucellosis, hepatitis, trichinosis, and salmonellosis, are transmissible to man through meat, milk, poultry, eggs, and other foods of animal origin.

Changes in the technology of food processing have increased the risk of microbiological poisoning, as more fully processed foods are offered to the consumer and as the time span between processing and consumption continues to increase. The increased density of animal populations for both feeding and processing and the contamination of their environment have also increased the hazards. In the absence of microbial standards, strict adherence to the sanitation rules set out in the USDA *Inspectors Handbook* reduces the spread of bacteria within the processing plant. But as we have seen, the inspectors who apply these rules on the production lines are sometimes not backed up in USDA when the plant managers complain, and even if they do get cooperation from USDA and the processor, the speed with which they must work weakens this front line of consumer defense.

The hazards from chemical contaminants are both more serious and less easily controlled. With the possible exception of a few stores specializing in organically grown beef, it is virtually impossible to buy meat which is not contaminated to some degree with synthetic chemical residues. Between 80 and 90 percent of all beef and poultry produced in this country is grown on a diet of antibiotics and other drugs from birth to slaughter. Three-fourths of all cattle in the United States are fed stilbestrol and other growth-stimulating hormones. Pesticides enter the human food chain when meat animals eat contaminated feed and water or are directly sprayed to control parasites and insects.

Both the FDA and the USDA keep watch on the levels of chemicals in food but the technology of residue monitoring, as well as budget allocations for this task, is inadequate. For example, there are several highly poisonous chemicals which may be present in meat at levels too small to be discovered by present screening devices but too large to be safely consumed. Carcinogenic compounds, such as stilbestrol and nitrosamines, and the tetra-dioxin contaminant of the herbicide 2,4,5-T, a potent agent of birth defects in test animals, are three chemicals in this category.

The threat of chemical residues from pesticides, antibiotics, and hormones in meat and poultry is another side effect of the rapid application of chemical technology to agriculture. As with the use of pesticides on crops, the short-term effects on yields of hormones and antibiotics which increase the body weight of the animal are sometimes allowed to outweigh potential long-term hazards at the human end of the food chain.

The use of antibiotics and hormones has helped cause basic changes in cattle and poultry feeding practices.

The practice of cramming immense populations of live-stock into small areas is closely tied to the use of anti-biotics in feed. Cattle are now confined by the thousands in feedlots where they must stand shank to shank in a mire of manure. Tens of thousands of chickens are raised under one roof in cages in which three or four birds are stuffed together in a 12″ by 18″ space. Veteri-narians find that the incidence of respiratory diseases and other illnesses increases when animals are raised under such stressful conditions. Crowding also creates conditions favorable to the rapid spread of disease. While this feeding system may increase the efficiency of production to some extent, the farmer has to contend with increased fears of disease and epidemics in his animals. He therefore feeds them a substantial diet of antibiotics, tranquilizers, and other prophylactic drugs to suppress disease and relieve stress.

Corporate agriculture fears that its huge investments in feedlots and broiler houses would be threatened if discovery of unanticipated hazards to human health forced drastic restriction of the use of antibiotics and synthetic hormones. Their anxiety leads to tremendous pressures on the federal regulators and scientists who must evaluate the safety of agricultural chemicals. These pressures are doubly effective because the agen-cies which make the decision, FDA's Bureau of Veteri-nary Medicine and USDA's Consumer and Marketing Service, both have promoted the chemicalization of meat production. Questions about safety usually originate outside these agencies in the National Cancer Institute and other health agencies which have no direct voice in the decisions. For this reason, questions of safety in the use of animal drugs cannot be left to the experts in the federal agencies and laboratories on the assumption that objective science will prevail. The search for dan-gerous chemicals in meat leads into political thickets as dense as any in the Federal Trade Commission or the Interstate Commerce Commission.

Politics, for example, influence the question of which chemical residues are to be looked for in meat. Dr. James Stewart, until recently chief of chemical res-idue sampling at USDA, concedes this is often a politi-cal question. Money is given to the Agricultural

Research Service in a lump sum and allocated according to whatever residue has caused the biggest stir in
the media. When hormone pellets in chickens produced
a scare in 1956–1957, the number of animals checked
for stilbestrol and other growth-stimulating chemicals
greatly increased. In the mid-sixties, the possibility that
drug-resistant bacteria might result from the use of
antibiotics in feed caused alarms, and sampling for
antibiotic residues became the vogue. In 1970, since the
mercury scare, USDA has initiated sampling for heavy
metal residues, but planned to reduce monitoring of
antibiotics and hormones, until dissuaded by public and
Congressional criticism.*

In the past, the consumer has relied on scientists to
provide answers to the question: what level of chemical
residue in the food supply, when weighed against the
economic benefit of its use, is an acceptable risk? But
"acceptable risk" is ultimately a political judgment.
Evaluation of balance of risks and benefits should be
based on as complete and pertinent scientific data as possible, but decisions about how much risk the public is
willing to accept—e.g., weighing a potential cancer
hazard against an increase in the price of beef—must
be made by society and its political leaders. The chemical industry and the producers and processors of meat
know this and direct their paid advocates in the trade
associations accordingly. The consumer must also be
informed and represented if the hazards from meat's
hidden ingredients are to be kept to a minimum. It is
only when the condition of full and timely disclosure
of risks and benefits to the consumer is met that one
can justifiably speak of the level of safety the consumer wants and is willing to pay for.

Food Poisoning

The federal meat and poultry acts create a false sense
of security in the public mind. USDA, in its official

* Dr. Stewart, an authority on pesticides and other residues in meat,
resisted a planned cutback on monitoring for antibiotics and hormones. He apparently won the battle but lost the war. In the recent
reorganization by new inspection chief Kenneth McEnroe, he was
denied a planned promotion and assigned a new job with less
responsibility.

publications, advises consumers that the circular inspection mark with the word "Inspected for Wholesomeness" is the consumer's "guarantee of safety." The housewife who buys "USDA Inspected" meats may be forgiven, therefore, for believing she is buying a product free of disease-producing organisms. The USDA inspection sticker suggests that meat has gone through an inspection procedure which, with each successive step, leads to a safer product. In the case of bacteriological contamination—the presence on meat of disease-producing germs—the opposite may be the case.

In Poland and Denmark, countries with outstanding meat standards, every object which comes into regular contact with meat during processing is routinely checked for the presence of salmonella, staphyloccocus, hepatitis, and other bacteria. Meat handlers and inspectors are tested to eliminate human carriers. In this country, no effort is made at any stage from slaughter to retail sale to monitor and control microbiological contaminants in fresh meat and poultry. In the absence of these controls, meat and poultry may become *more* contaminated, not less, as they move through the stages of processing.

An inspector at a poultry plant in the South gives a startling description of indifference to bacteriological hazards:

During inspection, diseased and contaminated chicken parts drop into a belt which runs over a trough of water. Intestines, tumors, windpipes, fecal matter, and heads drop off into that trough. There are not enough spigots so employees wash their hands in the trough, then go back to handling chickens. I guess 40–50% of "ready to cook" chicken goes out in a highly contaminated form.[1]

Microbiological contamination most often occurs when the chicken's abdomen is opened and its viscera removed. Once fecal material is deposited on the skin, it is difficult, if not impossible, to remove.[2] After the bird has passed along the processing line, it goes into a "chiller," a large tub of ice water. This is the last stage before the chicken is packed for market:

Filthy feathers go directly into the chiller along with the bird . . . also fecal matter. The chiller is not supposed to be a washer but that's the way it's used. The bacteria count must be fantastic and the birds are absorbing 2 or 3 percent of that water.[3]

These conditions have been recognized by some sectors of the meat industry. The general manager of the Polo Food Products Company, which buys fresh poultry for its cooked products, reports that a continuing problem with the fowl he buys is the presence of tramp metal such as staples and pieces of equipment, screws, nuts and bolts, and excessive feathers, hair, and improperly eviscerated birds. According to the manager "this happens in many cases when a processor is trying to run a line too fast with not enough workers."[4]

These conditions are not typical of the industry as a whole, but indifference to contamination in clearly widespread. The General Accounting Office, in a November, 1971, report on sixty-five poultry plants accounting for one-fifth of the nation's poultry output, found gross contamination in thirty-five plants.

Ironically, the only person who checks bacteria counts in most chicken plants is a local health official who comes around once a year to sample tap water which goes into the chiller. Federally inspected poultry, therefore, may be potent carriers of bacteria to the marketplace.

The major causes of food poisoning are described in the chart below. The most common food-borne disease is salmonellosis, described by the National Academy of Sciences–National Research Council as "one of the most important communicable disease problems in the United States today," and "a potential threat" to every American.[5] Fifteen hundred species of bacteria compose the genus Salmonella. The victim of the disease experiences abdominal pain, diarrhea, nausea, and vomiting for from one to eight days. When the victim is very old or very young or debilitated by some other disease, it is frequently fatal. In the summer of 1970, twenty-five residents of a Baltimore nursing home died within forty-eight hours from salmonella infection caused by an unidentified contaminated food.

Salmonella is caused by an organism which abounds in nature, but is easily killed by normal cooking heat.

Consequently, most food poisoning occurs when food is inadequately cooked or is recontaminated by remaining for several hours in warm temperatures, or touched by hands, cutting instruments, or cutting boards which have previously come into contact with uncooked fowl or meat.

The National Communicable Disease Center estimates that 2 million Americans each year are afflicted with the disease at a probable cost of $300 million.[6] Even this figure may underestimate the hazard. The Task Force on Research Planning in Environmental Health Science, in its 1970 report to the National Institutes of Health, warned that present reporting of food-borne diseases is inadequate. The data is provided voluntarily and is, therefore, dependent on the interest of state health departments. In recent years, three states or less have reported almost all the cases of salmonellosis in the United States,[7] indicating that most states fail to make comprehensive reports. Accurate data on the prevalence of this food-borne disease, therefore, are simply not available. Most cases are never recognized, let alone reported. Sudden cases of nausea, diarrhea, headache, and fever are passed off as "twenty-four hour flu" when in fact they may have been caused by bacteria in unclean but appetizing food. The Task Force concludes:

Although reports from the National Communicable Disease Center have been of value, *the lack of adequate morbidity data is undoubtedly a major reason for the downgrading of the problem of food- and water-borne illness and for the lack of concern by decision-makers* (budget officials, health and welfare administrators, and political leaders) in seeking corrective action.[8]*

No one disputes that salmonellosis and other food-borne diseases are a serious problem, but there is controversy over whether they are a regulatory problem. USDA has tried to take its inspectors and the meat

* The Communicable Disease Center in a recent report stated: "Food poisoning in the United States is grossly underreported. In England and Wales, where food poisoning surveillance has been well developed, 705 outbreaks of food poisoning were recorded in 1967, whereas only 345 outbreaks of food poisoning were reported to NCDC for the same period. The estimated number of outbreaks for the United States proportionate to the population in England and Wales is over 2,800."[9]

Causes of Food Poisoning Reported in 1970

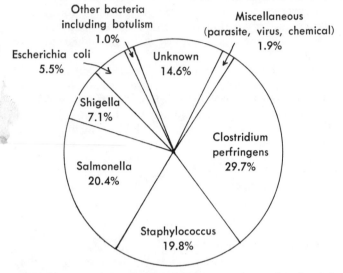

Other bacteria
including botulism
1.0%

Miscellaneous
(parasite, virus, chemical)
1.9%

Escherichia coli
5.5%

Unknown
14.6%

Shigella
7.1%

Clostridium
perfringens
29.7%

Salmonella
20.4%

Staphylococcus
19.8%

Clostridium perfringens—Most common source is reheated cooked meats; incubation period 8 to 24 hours; symptoms include diarrhea, abdominal cramps; symptoms usually gone after 8 hours.

Staphylococcus—Most common sources are custard and cream-filled bakery goods, also ham, tongue, processed meats, cheese, ice cream, potato salad, hollandaise sauce, chicken salad; incubation period 1 to 6 hours; symptoms include severe and sudden abdominal cramps, nausea, vomiting and diarrhea; recovery usually follows in 6 to 8 hours.

Salmonella—Most common sources are poultry, eggs and products containing dried eggs such as cake mixes; incubation period 8 to 24 hours; symptoms include nausea and vomiting followed by chills, high fever; symptoms may persist for two weeks; can be fatal to infants and elderly.

Shigella—Most common sources are milk and ice cream but may include any food contaminated by infected workers in food plant or by insects carrying bacteria; incubation period about 48 hours; symptoms include severe diarrhea, abdominal cramps, mild fever; symptoms usually last several days.

Escherichia coli—Most common sources include shellfish and sewage-contaminated water used in food processing; incubation period 6 to 24 hours; symptoms include cramps, diarrhea, nausea, vomiting; symptoms usually subside in 6 to 8 hours.   *Source: The New York Times.*

processors off the hook. Its publication *Agricultural Marketing*, speaking of salmonellosis, states:

Hardly ever is the villain inadequate inspection procedures or an error by an inspector in the packing plant. Rather the leading suspect is someone outside the plant, such as the retailer, the caterer or housewife who fails to follow a few basic rules in caring for meat or poultry.[10]

A study by the National Communicable Disease Center in Atlanta appears to support USDA. The study shows that, in a typical year of 124 outbreaks where the cause was known, only nine were caused by the food processor. In ninety-seven cases, the fault rested with food service establishments such as restaurants, schools, and nursing homes. The consumer at home was at fault in sixteen cases. The Communicable Disease Center warns, however, that "it is difficult to draw definite conclusions about patterns of food-borne illnesses from these data." It is far more complicated to trace microbiological contamination back to the processor than to the place where food is prepared.

The point is that the risks of serious illness from mishandling meat, poultry, and eggs are greater if the food is contaminated when it leaves the food processor. There is a strong presumption that poor sanitation in poultry slaughtering plants, careless handling of processed food, and exposure of meat to filthy equipment in meat plants, increase the incidence of food-borne diseases. Domestic fowl probably constitute the largest single reservoir of salmonella bacteria, according to the National Academy of Sciences.

The *New England Journal of Medicine* has reported that 50.8 percent of "U.S. Inspected" poultry in a survey was contaminated with salmonella while only 48.7 percent of uninspected poultry was contaminated. This seems to indicate that some clean chickens become contaminated in the slaughterhouse. In eleven of thirteen surveys of USDA inspected plants, public health doctors Arthur Wilder and Robert MacCready found high levels of salmonella present. They found that poultry products, both eggs and meat, are the commodities most often incriminated in outbreaks of the disease.[11] As much as 95 percent of the poultry from one USDA plant was found to be contaminated. The study concluded that:

It is obvious that the present federal inspection system for poultry cannot insure a pathogenic-free product. The consumer expects that a product processed under governmental supervision is free of disease-producing organisms and every effort should be made to produce a pathogen-free product.[12]

Contamination of beef in meat plants also warrants concern. The National Academy of Sciences has stated that the number of individual animals carrying salmonella is usually relatively small, but slaughtering procedures provide very effective means of spreading contamination from infected to clean animals.[13] Meat contaminants often originate in the slaughter operation from the soil and manure in cattle hides, spillage from the intestines, and the knives used to cut carcasses. Under presently approved USDA methods, carcasses being dressed on the kill floor are exposed to huge numbers of organisms.

Scrupulous sanitation is especially vital when the processor is the one with control over cooking. Ready to eat meat products are usually processed at temperatures sufficient to destroy bacteria present in the contaminated raw materials. Nonetheless, according to Dr. John Siliker of Siliker Laboratories: "The greatest potential danger lies in sliced sausage products, sliced bologna, luncheon meats, etc., that are consumed without further cooking. In many cases these products are sliced and packaged in areas that are in close proximity to raw meats, or in locations having air supplies in common with raw meat processing."[14] Siliker urges constant bacteriological surveillance of the processing environment. In a one-week period in August, 1971, Genoa salami produced by Armour and Hormel had to be recalled nationwide by USDA after twenty people became ill from staphylococcus bacteria found in the products.

Dr. Gilbert Wise, a meat specialist for the Consumer and Marketing Service, warns that the public health danger from this source of contamination is increasing: "The food chain is getting longer. We're introducing new handling procedures, new processing procedures and every time the product is manipulated, there is another chance for contamination. Heat-and-serve convenience foods, which do not require thorough cooking prior to consumption, as well as mass production and distribution, rapid processing cycles and new packaging in containers, have added to the urgency of development of microbial standards."[15]

Federal efforts to establish microbiological standards have floundered. In 1968, Rodney Leonard, then administrator of the Consumer and Marketing Service, proposed microbiological standards for meat processing. Leonard left the Department before they were implemented and action is still pending.

In the absence of microbiological monitoring, USDA's failure to enforce its present sanitation standards is an even more serious problem. The General Accounting Office, in its 1969 report on poultry inspection, presented a graphic example of this failure. On November 23, 1962, an inspector at a poultry plant which processed chickens to be used in meat pies reported the following violations: gravy used in the pies was often kept at temperatures up to 98° Fahrenheit for over five hours at a time, providing a perfect breeding ground for salmonella and other food poisoners; baskets and racks were filthy and crusted with food from previous days. Sixteen memos from USDA to plant management warning of these violations were ignored. On December 3, 1962, USDA finally threatened to withdraw inspection services if the problems continued, but took no action. In another visit on February 13, 1964, USDA inspectors turned up eighteen violations, but no action followed. Two years later, in 1966, another letter from the Consumer and Marketing Service warned the plant that its sanitation was a disgrace and gave it a deadline of December 3, 1966, to clean itself up. This deadline was then extended until March 17, 1967, although subsequent inspection showed that conditions remained about the same. The deadlines were again extended until finally, on November 3, 1967, the plant closed for relocation. This case and subsequent GAO reports showed that this five-year saga of noncompliance was not an isolated case.[16]

For the present, the housewife remains her family's last and perhaps only defense against these disease-carrying bacteria. The risks can and should be reduced through more rigorous inspection, the setting of maximum allowable microbiological levels, and the development of microbiological standards for use in processing plants, food service establishments, and other facilities where food is handled. To educate the consumer, the New Jersey Public Health Association has formally petitioned the Secretary of Agriculture to affix the following label to all raw meat and poultry:

Caution: Improper handling and inadequate cooking of this product may be hazardous to your health. Despite careful government inspection, some disease-producing organisms may be present. Consult your local health department for information on the safe handling and preparation of this product.

The Water Game

Of the hidden ingredients added to meat products, excess water has the greatest potential for direct consumer fraud. The General Accounting office estimates that a 1 percent increase in the weight of poultry from added water may cost the consumer $32 million a year.[17] Selling water as meat is obviously very profitable. And as a medium for bacteria and other contaminants, water threatens the consumer's health as well as his pocketbook.

Poultry absorbs moisture in two ways: when it is washed and chilled after evisceration, and by the deliberate addition of oil and water basting solutions by the processor. Some absorption of water in the production process is inevitable and desirable. The question is: how much? The chilling stage, where the birds are rotated in large tubs of ice water, is critical. In order to prevent the incubation and rapid growth of bacteria, the body heat of the poultry carcass must be rapidly reduced after slaughter. Chilling is designed to lower the internal temperature of poultry to 40° or lower, a temperature which stops the growth of most food-poisoning bacteria.

In the past, when chickens were chilled on ice, they did not absorb much water. But during the 1950s, equipment came into use which caused chickens to gain as much as 20 percent water by weight during processing. In 1960, the Consumer and Marketing Service responded to this problem by moisture tolerances for the various classes of poultry processed at federally inspected plants. Chickens shipped in "ice pack" cartons, the most common method, were allowed to absorb 12 percent moisture during processing. The standards were developed in accord with what C&MS felt was "good commercial practice" (i.e., the industry norm). In the 1960s, new developments in refrigeration made it possible to clean and chill birds adequately with considerably less water absorption, but the old C&MS standards remain in effect. As a result the washing and chilling operation acquired an ulterior motive: to put as much water into the birds as is legally possible.

One processing plant employee frankly admitted that the controls on his plant's chilling equipment were set to put as close to 12 percent moisture in the poultry as possible, despite the fact that the poultry could be adequately chilled and washed with 7 or 8 percent moisture absorption.[18] This extra 5% costs the consumer approximately $160 million a year. Attempts by plant managements to keep the moisture absorption at the legal maximum means that small variations in plant operation frequently push the moisture absorption over the legal limit.[19]

USDA has been frequently criticized for failure to enforce its moisture regulations. The General Accounting Office has charged that large amounts of waterlogged poultry are being shipped to the consumer. In 1967, for example, USDA allowed forty-four federal plants—accounting for over 13 percent of all interstate poultry—to stay in business despite exceeding moisture limits at least 20 percent of the time.[20] The GAO concluded that the Department's failure to act defrauded the consumer and encouraged managers of other plants to think that violations would go unpunished.

In the past the inspector in charge in a poultry plant took samples of slaughtered birds and reported the plant when it was out of compliance on 20 percent or more of processing days. The inspector reported to a regional moisture controller who then visited the plant to check its chilling procedures. The in-plant inspector did not have authority to retain the watered poultry nor to adjust the chilling machinery. This led to excessive delay in correcting violations.

In 1970, two years after the GAO first presented its complaints to the Consumer and Marketing Service, USDA proposed a change in its regulations to allow the inspectors in the plants to retain waterlogged poultry and to allow the plants to adjust the chilling machinery under inspector supervision. Any poultry exceeding 13 percent moisture is retained by the inspector until drained. Any poultry between 12 and 13 percent is suspect and retained if it exceeds 12 percent on more than one test. The new regulations were proposed on March 20, 1970, but their implementation was delayed another eight months by protests from the poultry industry.

In the past, USDA poultry officials justified their foot-dragging by arguing that excess water is drained from the birds during shipment and handling and that, therefore, the consumer is protected. However, protests from the poultry processors over the new moisture limits clearly show that the new limits, by reducing the weight of birds at the plant and therefore the price super-markets pay for them, can save the consumer money. Theodore Huisinga, Vice-President of the Willman Poultry Company in Minnesota, estimates that the new program will cost his plant between $30,000 and $40,000 a year. James Rooney of the Gopher Turkey Farm, also in Minnesota, warned that the new regulations would cost Minnesota turkey men $1 million to $2 million a year.[21]

The new regulations put additional pressure on the poultry inspector. Excess water in chicken is never discovered by the consumer. If the inspector does not control the poultry processor, he can water his birds with virtual impunity. Small changes in the water pressure or temperature of the chiller or even improper opening cuts in the birds can cause percentage gains in moisture absorption.

New regulations providing for injections of water in meat of 2 to 10 percent and basting fluid in poultry up to 6 percent will put even greater burdens on the meat and poultry inspector. These regulations, advocated by the processors, went into effect in January, 1971. Liquid injections are designed, according to the poultry industry, to inhibit dryness and make meat more tender and juicy. Unless carefully monitored, however, they can also bloat the meat or improve the meat's color so that consumers will not be able to tell whether it is stale.

The Federal Poultry Products Inspection Act and Federal Meat Inspection Act define an adulterated product as one having any substance "added or mixed or packed with the meat in order to increase its weight and size or reduce its quality or strength to make it seem of greater value than it is." USDA claims that the liquid injections will serve a beneficial purpose and therefore are permitted under the law. Such meat must include a bold statement that declares the amount of solution added and the common or usual name of each of its ingredients "stated in the order of predominance."[22] Strict enforcement of these standards is necessary to protect the consumer from buying oil as well as water for the price of meat.

USDA also permits the packers to sell added water at frankfurter prices. Under USDA regulations, the packers can add up to 10 percent water to cooked sausage products. As with chickens, the extra water is added during the chilling stage of processing. Using a generous rule of thumb, USDA assumes that typical meat contains four times as much water as protein. Therefore, if the average frankfurther has 11 percent protein, it will have 44 percent water. The packer can then add 10 percent more water, up to a level of 54 percent, before the frankfurter is considered adulterated.

In practice, however, the water added to this hotdog is closer to 15 percent than to 10 percent. Laboratory analysts for Consumer Reports discovered recently that the typical meat used in frankfurters has a natural water-protein ratio of 3.6:1, not 4:1. The natural amount of water in an average 11 percent protein hotdog is therefore 39.6 percent, not 44 percent. When the packers, using USDA's rule of thumb and 10 percent dispensation, market a frankfurter with 54 percent water, the consumer ends up buying 36 percent more water than the natural meat contained. This invisible inflation of the food dollar costs consumers millions of dollars each year.

Antibiotics and Microbial Pollution

Antibiotics, the heralded miracle drugs developed during World War II, are now more frequently used by farmers than by doctors. There is increasing concern that this use of antibiotics may jeopardize their effectiveness in human medicine, yet feedlot operators, chicken growers, and other intensive livestock producers claim that their operations are inextricably hooked on these drugs. This apparent conflict creates a highly charged risk-benefit decision for federal regulators. Nearly 80 percent of the meat, milk, and eggs consumed in the United States comes from animals fed medicated feed during all or part of their lives.[23] Antibiotics are fed to swine, chickens, and cattle from birth to slaughter as growth stimulants and to prevent disease. Doses of antibiotics between 4.5 and 11 ppm (parts per million) are supposed to make the animals gain weight faster than they would if they ate their feed without drugs. Higher doses, up to 50 ppm in feed, are used prophylactically to keep disease from gaining a foothold in a herd of animals.

Over half of the nation's annual antibiotic production goes to livestock and poultry. Antibiotic feed additives make up a rapidly growing $100 million industry, involving sixty companies. *Feedstuffs*, the leading weekly newspaper for agribusiness, has nearly as many drug ads as the *AMA Journal*. There is a difference in style, however. Where the *AMA Journal* has a reclining bikinied beauty hawking Ampicillin, *Feedstuffs* has a healthy hog with the caption "Protect 'em, push 'em all the way to market with Pfizer's Terramycin."

While the FDA must screen each antibiotic for safety and efficacy, farm use of these drugs is hardly controlled at all. A farmer can buy penicillin by the pound at his local feed store, yet he needs a prescription to buy one tablet for personal (human) use. Dr. William

B. Buck of the Iowa State University College of Veterinary Medicine told a 1967 National Academy of Sciences symposium:

> At present a farmer or any lay person can purchase many of these drugs in any quantity and without any restriction. Such persons can and do incorporate them into feed grain mixes for livestock at levels up to ten, perhaps twenty, times those recommended.[24]

Critics of the use of antibiotics in feed cite several potential health hazards: allergic and toxic effects of drug residues in drug sensitive persons; the development of hypersensitivity through frequent exposure to antibiotic residues; and most important, the development of drug resistant bacteria which may make some "miracle" drugs obsolete for human medicine.

If antibiotic residues occur in food, highly allergic people may become seriously ill, particularly with penicillin. Antibiotics may also upset the bacterial ecology of the stomach, intestines, and bowels and lead to digestive disturbances. Finally, small prolonged doses of antibiotics in food could lead to the development of drug resistance in man. Up to now, residues in meat appear insignificant, but those in eggs and milk have been high enough at times to cause allergic reactions. In 1969, for example, USDA randomly sampled 3,523 of 135 million animals slaughtered and found antibiotic residues in less than 1 percent of them. However, when 470 animals were tested after the government had received word that excessive residues might be present now, 130 contained illegal residues of up to 40 units of penicillin per pound.

FDA and USDA share responsibility for keeping antibiotics out of meat. FDA sets a safe level or tolerance for antibiotic residues in meat which USDA analysts then monitor. FDA is supposed to withhold approval of any antibiotic for which a practical method for detecting its residues in meat is lacking. Unfortunately, because the agency, FDA, which approves the analytical method is different from the agency, USDA, which must use it, conflicts develop. FDA sometimes approves an antibiotic before USDA has had time to validate it in practice. For example, the nitrofuran drugs, used as coccidiostats in poultry (*coccidia* are poultry parasites), were approved by FDA before a sensitive method of analysis was available to detect their residues.[25] This failure has become more serious as FDA now suspects that some of the nitrofurans are carcinogenic.[26] One reassuring factor, however, is that antibiotics are destroyed in the cooking of most food.

Of far greater concern for public health is the threat that the use of antibiotics on farm animals will cause harmful bacteria to become drug resistant. Bacteriologists have long known that bacteria can quickly become resistant to an antibiotic and hand the mutant gene down to the next generation.[27] Concern about this phenomenon increased in 1968 with a Japanese discovery that bacteria can "catch" resistance to antibiotics much as people "catch" germs. A harmless intestinal bacteria which becomes resistant to tetracyclines, for example, *can transfer* its resistance or R-factor to disease-causing bacteria that it bumps into. Moreover, certain bacteria, when exposed to one antibiotic, can develop and transfer resistance to other antibiotics with which they have never been in contact.

Danger arises when an individual becomes ill from one of these resistant bacteria populations. Doctors may discover too late that the antibiotic he customarily uses to treat the illness is no longer effective. Japanese doctors, during a 1968 epidemic of dysentery, found that the disease-carrying bacteria, shigellae, were resistant to not one but four different antibiotics.

The health implications of drug-resistant bacteria are ominous. Dr. David H. Smith, an antibiotic expert at Harvard University, reports that in one year at Boston's Children's Hospital twenty-four of twenty-six deaths due to bacterial disease were caused by drug-resistant bacteria. The *London Times* reported on April 4, 1969, that a total of thirty babies died of gastroenteritis over a three-month period in two hospitals in Manchester. A year earlier fifteen children died under similar circumstances in a hospital in Teeside. In both incidents, the deaths were caused by bacteria that failed to respond to antibiotics.[28]

There is no direct evidence connecting these cases of drug resistance with the use of antibiotics in feed.

It is important to note, however, that antibiotics used in feeds are often the same as those used to treat human diseases, including streptomycin, penicillin, and tetracycline. Moreover, bacteria carried by animals often cause human illness, notably salmonella. A British study found humans and pigs to be harboring the same spectrum of drug-resistant salmonellae during a particularly lengthy outbreak of salmonella in England in 1969.[29] It has also been demonstrated that farm workers who look after animals on antibiotic feed have more antibiotic resistant bacteria in their intestines than those who do not.[30]

Laboratory tests have clearly established that it is theoretically possible for the drug resistance of animal bacteria to be transferred to human germs. Whether such transfers take place *outside* the laboratory remains a matter of controversy. Nevertheless, the Swann Report, an assessment of the risks and benefits of animal drugs by a British committee of distinguished scientists and health experts, relied heavily on a case where antibiotics used in calves produced a drug-resistant salmonella germ. The germ was transferred from calves to farm workers to dairy cattle, which passed it along in their milk.

The Swann Report (named after the chairman of the Joint Committee on the Use of Antibiotics in Animal Husbandry and Veterinary Medicine) recommended sweeping restrictions on animal drugs to Parliament on November 20, 1969. The Report concluded that (a) an increase of bacteria showing transmittable antibiotic resistance has resulted from the use of antibiotics in farm livestock; (b) some enteric animal bacteria (e.g. salmonella typhimurium) can cause disease in man and animals and that, therefore, development of resistance to antibiotics in these bacteria may endanger life.

The report recommended that no antibiotic which has therapeutic value for man—such as penicillin or the tetracyclines—should be added to feed. Other antibiotics, such as nitrovin, virginiamycin, and zinc bacitracin, which are not used to treat human disease, can be substituted as growth promoters in feed. The Report also advised that other therapeutic antibiotics be sold only by prescription from a trained veterinarian. It

noted that farm workers who handle drug fed livestock
are becoming resistant to antibiotics at a faster rate
than the rest of the population. Because of these hazards, it finds "particularly indefensible" the practice of
giving antibiotics at subtherapeutic doses to simply
relieve stress in animals.

The Swann Report has been vigorously attacked by
scientists associated with the chemical and drug industry in this country. Dr. Robert White-Stevens, now
at Rutgers University but formerly with American
Cyanamid, calls the report "a desperate attempt to turn
the clock back. If the protein needs of man are to be
met by the year 2,000 then such obsolete procedures
will simply have to be abandoned and their adherents
will be dragged kicking and screaming into the twenty-
first century."[31] American drug companies have joined
with the British pharmaceutical industry in trying to
discredit the report in the United Kingdom. British
scientists have complained about a propaganda campaign designed to frighten the consumer and small
farmer with alarmist predictions about higher prices
and costs. They also criticize "distinguished men in the
feed antibiotic field from the U.S." for giving out misleading and irrelevant data to support the anti-Swann
cause.[32]

Nevertheless two successive British governments
have upheld the Swann recommendations, and in 1970
the U.S. Food and Drug Administration established a
Task Force on the Use of Antibiotics to review the
report. Compared to the British, FDA has been remarkably nonchalant in evaluating the potential hazards of
animal drugs. In September, 1967, Dr. C. D. Van Houweling, who is now Director of FDA's Bureau of
Veterinary Medicine, the nation's chief regulator of
animal drugs, warned that "FDA believes it is imprudent
to persist in such a widespread application [of anti-
biotics] without attempting a systematic understanding
of the consequences to the microbial environment of
man and nature."[33] But while sales of animal antibiotics
have increased well over 60 percent since this statement, FDA by December, 1971, had still failed to complete its evaluation.

The FDA Task Force did state in its interim conclusions that "it is a logical conclusion that the use of antibiotics in food animals, which results in development of resistant organisms and an increased reservoir of some bacteria in animals which can be transferred to human beings, may give rise to a human health hazard."[34] But bitter divisions among its members on the policy implications of this and other findings have delayed its final report. FDA Commissioner Charles Edwards has threatened to discharge the Task Force if it did not report by the end of 1971. Three points of controversy on the task force are findings by some members (1) that the use of antibiotics as growth stimulants makes treatment of sick animals more difficult, (2) that feed antibiotics prolong the carrier state of salmonella organisms in the animal, (3) that bacteria have the ability to transfer to one another resistance to several antibiotics after being exposed to only one antibiotic.[35]

In carrying out FDA's responsibilities, Dr. Van Houweling states: "the Bureau of Veterinary Medicine tries to strike a balance between safeguarding human health and meeting the needs of the livestock industry.[36] Spokesmen for the livestock industry and drug companies warn that intensive livestock production would be very expensive if not impossible without drugs, but critics of antibiotics have evidence that the need for drugs has been exaggerated, and that the farmer is often pressured into buying drugs he does not need. First, there is the question of diminishing returns. One of the three most prevalent poultry diseases, coccidiosis, shows increasing resistance to antibiotics. Dr. Whitehair and Dr. Pomeroy at a 1969 National Academy of Sciences symposium on animal feeds concluded, after a survey of animal infections, that even though the response to antibiotics is at times rather dramatic, "yet poultry diseases, enteric infections in pigs and calves, and mastitis in dairy cattle present a much greater problem today to both producers and public health officials than they did before the advent of antibiotics." [37] British veterinarians too are finding that "multiple resistant strains are common and in recent times it has become more difficult for veterinary surgeons to select a suitable drug for treating enteric bacterial disease of farm animals."

Second, drug companies use the same tactics as pesticide makers in making claims for the economic value of feed antibiotics to farmers. The latter give pesticides credit for increases in crop yield which frequently are the result of fertilizers, new seed strains, and other farm technology. The drug companies, pointing to the increased weight gain and quality of livestock since the introduction of antibiotics, neglect to mention the contributions, in the same period, of better breeds, better housing, conveyor belt feeding, and improved diet to animal growth.[38] Third, many scientists question the adequacy of the effectiveness of data supplied by the drug companies. Members of the federal antibiotics task force have noted that the data supporting the efficacy of antibiotics as a growth stimulant is often ten to fifteen years old and strongly recommend that the effectiveness of these drugs be reviewed "as promptly as possible."[39] Dr. David Smith has observed that "early experiments on antibiotic-induced growth promotion were not adequately controlled and were carried out before modern breeding and sanitation procedures became a part of animal production."[40] Antibiotics appear to be most effective as substitutes for sanitation when animals are crowded or improperly housed or nourished.[41] Antibiotics may also cause harm to the animal by upsetting the normal microorganism balance in his intestine. Just as a pesticide can make a new pest out of a previously harmless insect by upsetting the ecological balance of beneficial and pest insects, antibiotics in some cases release harmful bacteria from natural control by other microorganisms, thereby causing disease.[42]

On another level, farmers, like the typical consumer, have wasted millions of dollars buying combination antibiotics with bogus claims that they were doubly effective against disease. FDA has recently suspended the sale of over 1,000 antibiotic combinations because they were ineffective for their intended use.

While the FDA's experts may violently disagree in the overall assessment of antibiotic hazards, it does seem clear that the use of human antibiotics, such as penicillin and the tetracyclines as growth promoters and stress-relievers for livestock, poses an avoidable human hazard which the public should not tolerate, particularly when there are substitutes available which have no use in human medicine. The *New England Journal of Medicine*, in an editorial on the phenomenon of resistant microbes, gives an apt warning: "Man has succeeded in polluting his environment with an astonishing variety of noxious agents. The development of an antibiotic resistant microbial milieu might be a logical extension of this self-directed biologic warfare. . . ."[43]

Partial List of Common Animal Drugs

Hormones
1. Diethylstilbestrol
2. Hexoestrol
3. Progesterone
4. Testosterone Propionate
5. Estradiol Benzoate
6. Estradiol Monopalmitate
7. Dienestrol Diacetate
8. Medroxyprogesterone Acetate
9. Sodium Thyroxine
10. Prednisolone
11. Prednisone Acetate

Other Growth-promoting Substances
1. Arsanilic Acid
2. 3-Nitro-4-Hydroxyphenylarsonic Acid
3. Sodium Arsanilate
4. Methylthiouracil
5. Propylthiouracil
6. Arsenobenzene
7. Arsenosobenzene
8. Thiouracil

Coccidiostats
1. Acetyl-(p-nitrophenyl) Sulphanilimide
2. Amprolium Hydrochloride
3. Aklomide
4. Bithionol
5. Diaveridine
6. 3,5-Dinitrobenzamide
7. Methiotriazamine
8. Nitrofurazone
9. Nitrophenide
10. Nicarbazin

11. Pyrimethamine
12. Sulphadimidine Sodium
13. Sulphaguanidine
14. Sulphaquinoxaline
15. Zoalene (Methyldinitrobenzamide)
16. Alinitrozole
17. Ethopabate
18. Glycarbylamide
19. Nihydrazone
20. Trithiadol
21. Di-iodohydroxy Quinoline
22. Furaltodone
23. Furazolidine

Pesticides and PCB's

The Department of Agriculture shares with the FDA responsibility for detecting residues of pesticides in the food supply. The residue surveillance program in the Consumer and Marketing Service collects tissue samples from beef animals and poultry before they reach the retail shelf, while FDA tests for residues in all foods after they are offered for sale.[44]

The chief virtues of the USDA program are that it tries to catch contaminated meat before it reaches the consumer and that it promises an intensive scrutiny of meat products alone. FDA's market basket surveys of retail food, on the other hand, look at average pesticide intake from one's total diet, not the amount of pesticide contamination in a particular food. According to Dr. Virgil Wodicka, Director of FDA's Bureau of Food, Pesticides, and Product Safety, food is tested by making "composite samples of commodity groups." One result is that high levels of pesticide in individual samples such as meat products "tend to be leveled out by dilution of other substances of the same analytical sample, so that the overall (average) . . . would not necessarily reflect the presence of extreme samples."[45]

Listed in the table below are results of sampling for pesticide residues in meat for the years 1967–1969. These low levels of pesticide residues in meat are reassuring on the surface. Everyone appears to gain from these results: the consumer, worried about the long-term effect of pesticide residues on his health; the

PESTICIDE RESIDUES IN MEAT

Year	Residue Group	Number of Samples	Number of Positive Samples Above Allowable Limits
1967	Chlorinated Hydrocarbon Insecticides	2,785	47
1968	Chlorinated Hydrocarbon Insecticides	5,382	66
	Organophosphorus Insecticides	246	1
	Carbamate Insecticides	288	0
	2,4-D Herbicide	170	0
1969	Chlorinated Hydrocarbon Insecticides	5,368	45
	Organophosphorus Insecticides	282	1
	Carbamate Insecticides	237	0
	2,4-D Herbicide	240	1

Source: V. H. Berry, DVM, Chief, Planning Branch, Slaughter Inspection Division, CMS, USDA, August 13, 1970.

chemical companies fearing new restrictions on pesticides; the cattlemen and poultrymen who fear condemnation of their animals; the budgeteers in the Executive Office and appropriations committees fearful of public pressure for expanded pesticide monitoring; and the powerful marketing and commodity branches of USDA which do not want their promotional efforts for meat embarrassed by their colleagues in the pesticide regulatory branches. A closer look at these results, however, suggests strongly that they promise a good deal more than they deliver.

USDA's surveillance of pesticides in meat and poultry falls short in the following areas:

(1) The number of animals sampled for pesticides is too small to give valid statistical estimates of the extent of contamination or to identify local pesticide hotspots. In 1969, CMS's eight regional laboratories tested only 3,000 poultry carcasses out of over 2 billion chickens and turkeys slaughtered. Sampling on this scale allows for spot-checks which at best might identify major national trends in pesticide residues. Excessive pesti-

cide contamination of meat or poultry is often very localized, however, the result of negligence by farmers and processors in a single county or plant. Rodney Leonard, former Administrator of Consumer and Marketing Service, states that "the sampling they do isn't intended to locate particular birds with pesticides in them. It's more like sticking thermometers in rivers and lakes around the country and coming up with a national average water temperature."[46]

In October, 1969, Campbell Soup's packing plant at Worthington, Minnesota, discovered illegal amounts of heptachlor epoxide in turkeys stamped "inspected for wholesomeness by USDA." A crash testing program conducted in strict secrecy was launched by USDA. There was fear that turkey sales nationwide might have to be banned on the eve of Thanksgiving. It turned out that only 350,000 turkeys were affected, and all of these came from growers under contract to Arkansas Valley Industries. The growers had spread heptachlor epoxide on their turkey ranges to hold down chiggers, despite label warnings that livestock should not be exposed to it.* Some of the birds contained as much as seventeen parts per million of heptachlor (or thirty-four times the permissible level). If Campbell Soups had relied on USDA's official assurance of "wholesomeness" without checking on its own, the contaminated turkeys would have been routinely sold for Thanksgiving dinner.

(2) Some of the most dangerous pesticides are overlooked when USDA examines its meat samples. Many consumers have the mistaken impression that to look for one pesticide contaminant is to look for them all, but this is not the case. Until 1970, USDA never looked for mercury. Sampling for lead, cadmium, and other heavy metals is just getting under way in response to recent alarms. These oversights occur because USDA's residue samplers are crisis oriented. They rarely take the initiative in looking for new contaminants in meat. The same can be said for the whole profession of chemists. No American chemist thought to examine fish for mercury until a Norwegian exchange student at West-

---

* According to Burt Schorr of the *Wall Street Journal*, one Arkansas grower explained his misreading of the label: "Hell I ain't raising livestock; I'm raising turkeys."[47]

ern Ontario University in Canada showed them the way in 1970. Another chemical contaminant overlooked by USDA until 1971 is the polychlorinated biphenyls, commonly called PCB's.

(3) USDA permits the uses of some pesticides which may contaminate meat even though it lacks analytical technology to detect the chemicals in the food supply. USDA permits the use of the herbicide 2,4,5-T on pastures and rangeland where cattle graze. 2,4,5-T contains up to 1 ppm tetradioxin, a highly stable compound which causes birth defects in test animals and is highly poisonous to man (see Chapter 7). USDA's pesticide monitors report, however, that they lack instruments sensitive enough to measure dioxin regularly in meat.

(4) The secrecy with which USDA shrouds incidents of seizure gives the public a false sense of security about chemicals in meat and discourages public pressure for more effective chemical monitoring and controls. The PCB emergency in the summer of 1971 illustrates this point, as well as many other weaknesses of chemical surveillance.

PCB's (for polychlorinated biphenyls) are used in the form of a colorless, odorless liquid which is thicker and more syrupy than molasses and has the remarkable ability to withstand temperatures up to 1,600 degrees Fahrenheit. It is primarily used to conduct heat in transformers and other heat exchange equipment.

PCB's possess toxicological, chemical, and environmental properties strikingly similar to DDT. In fact, the compounds are so similar that some of the environmental damage attributed in the past to DDT is now thought to have been caused by PCB's.[48] Monsanto is the sole domestic manufacturer of PCB's (under the name Aroclor).

Like DDT and many other chlorinated hydrocarbons, PCB's are extremely persistent, pervasive, and toxic substances. They degrade even more slowly than DDT, and are water insoluble and fat soluble. Thus, PCB's accumulate and concentrate in bodily fat tissues. In addition to (and in part because of) their stability, PCB's are found virtually everywhere in the ecosystem. One researcher reports that in arctic lakes "rarely if ever visited by man," all of the fish analyzed contained measurable amounts of PCB; one lake trout had 12 ppm in its fat. Concentrations of up to 250 ppm have been found in human tissues. And random samples of milk from nursing mothers in California averaged over 2 ppm.

The incomplete scientific evidence on PCB's suggests that they constitute a significant human health hazard. Back in 1942, all 100 men in continual work contact with PCB's in one plant contracted chloracne, a skin disease. In 1968, cooking oil contaminated with PCB's caused an outbreak of skin disease affecting over 300 people in Japan, including nine pregnant women. Some miscarried, two of their babies were stillborn, and all showed symptoms of chlorobiphenyl poisoning. According to the rough calculations of Dr. Robert Risebrough, a PCB expert at Berkeley, consumption of 45 pounds of fish and/or poultry contaminated with PCB's at the FDA approved level of 5 ppm might produce the effects observed in Japan. There is evidence that the toxicity of PCB formulations may in fact be due to the presence of contaminants (called dibensofurans) similar to and only slightly less toxic than the dioxin contaminants of 2,4,5-T.

Because PCB's are primarily industrial chemicals, they have been exempt from the safety tests required of pesticides and food additives. FDA has never established a formal tolerance for PCB's in food. But after several incidents of massive PCB contamination of the food supply, FDA finally set a temporary "action level" of 5 ppm in flesh and 0.5 ppm in eggs, below which PCB residues were deemed safe. According to Dr. Robert Risebrough, the 5 ppm figure "is just a number. I'm sure FDA pulled it out of the air." And recent events strongly suggest that FDA does not even enforce these levels with any seriousness.

In 1971, a PCB accident led to the most widespread accident of food contamination in regulatory history. PCB's used as heat transfer fluid leaked into fish meal produced at a North Carolina plant between April 30 and mid-July. The meal was sold to sixty-five companies in twelve states for use, among other things, as an ingredient in feed for chickens, turkeys, hogs, and catfish. When Holly Farms, the nation's largest producer of broiler chickens, discovered in June that flocks fed this feed showed mortality about seven times the normal rate, FDA (responsible for inspection of shell eggs) and USDA (responsible for inspection of meat, poultry, and egg products) were faced with a full-scale food crisis. In the ensuing weeks, these agencies condemned many tons of fish meal, over 165,000 broilers, 250,000 pounds of turkeys, hundreds of thousands of eggs, several hundred thousand pounds of egg products, over 1,000 tons of catfish feed, and other assorted foodstuffs.

The PCB incident has several lessons. First, the peculiar division of inspection responsibilities between USDA and FDA can lead to a striking lack of coordination. For example, FDA never furnished USDA with a list of the subcontractees of the sixty-five firms which purchased the contaminated meal; thus USDA could not ensure that all possible sources of contamination of meat and poultry were closed off.

Second, many of these failures are chronic and derive, to a great extent, from the agencies' lack of adequate resources to deal simultaneously with more than one food emergency (a fact acknowledged privately but almost never publicly by many food inspection officials). Indeed, it is precisely *because* these agencies are so vulnerable to crisis and need more support and resources that their passion for secrecy and public complacency is so irresponsible. Throughout the PCB affair, the agencies never wavered from their Panglossian public information posture.

An egregious case in point occurred in August when FDA took samples from a suspect shipment of 60,000 eggs in North Carolina, releasing the shipment for trucking to a Washington, D.C. distributor. Five days later, when FDA completed its analysis of the sample, it found PCB levels in the sample four to five times the permissible concentration. FDA went to the distributor's warehouse, only to learn that the eggs had been sold to Washington area restaurants several days earlier. At this point, FDA threw up its hands and went on to other things. It made no effort to alert consumers to the danger so that they could destroy those contaminated eggs not yet consumed. The matter only became public when, over a week later, an outside investigator leaked it to the press. FDA, asked by the press to explain its performance, proceeded to systematically undermine the integrity of its own "action level," established in light of the chronic toxicity of PCB's, their concentration in human tissues, and their ubiquity in the ecosystem. One FDA spokesman told the press, "that much PCB is like a drop in a tank car." Another insisted that there was no real health problem due to the short-term exposure. "I'd hate everybody to start worrying about the eggs they eat."

It is precisely such perfunctory, complacent public assurances in the face of scientific uncertainty concerning PCB's that is bound to *increase* the alarm of consumers, for FDA is in effect requiring them to bear the risks of uncertainty.

These incidents of nondisclosure to the public are all too common. Not only do they—when they are ultimately brought to light—erode public confidence in food inspection agencies, but by inhibiting the public and Congress from learning of the magnitude of the threat of chemical contamination of the environment, these agencies dissuade the public from pressing for changes in public policy concerning food inspection and toxic substances.

Finally, effective regulation requires detailed information about the characteristics and location of chemical contamination of the food supply. This information is at present not available to the food agencies or even to Congress. For example, Monsanto, the sole manufacturer of PCB's, has continually and steadfastly refused to furnish Congressman Ryan with its production and sales data concerning PCB's. It regards such data as "extremely confidential" even though it has no competitors for this product. Monsanto states that it is willing to furnish the information to "responsible government agencies" but reserves the right to determine which are and are not "responsible." Legal authority to compel the disclosure to government agencies of all information for the protection of the public should be enacted.

Carcinogens in Meat: Who Gets the Benefit of the Doubt?

Almost 200 years ago, Sir Percival Potts, an English physician, discovered the relationship between exposure to soot and a high rate of scrotal cancer in chimney sweeps. This discovery marked the beginning of studies of the environmental causes of cancer.

In the late nineteenth and twentieth centuries the studies began to focus on man-made chemicals as causes of cancer. A leading cancer specialist, Dr. E. Boyland, now estimates that "not more than 5 percent of human cancer is due to viruses and less than 5 percent to radiation. Some 90 percent of cancer in man is therefore due to chemicals, but we do not know how much is due to endogenous carcinogens and how much to environmental factors."[49] An expert committee of the World Health Organization concluded in 1965 that at least half of all cancer in man is due to environmental factors. These scientists feel that a great deal of human cancer could be prevented by finding and removing chemical carcinogens from food, water, and other environmental sources.[50]

During the 1950s, when the breakthroughs in chemical technology achieved in World War II began to be applied to agriculture and food processing, concern mounted about the potential hazards for man and the environment of the chemical industry's rapidly proliferating products.[51] This concern led to a series of amendments to the Food, Drug, and Cosmetics Act of 1938—the Pesticides Amendment in 1954, the Food Additives Amendment in 1958, and the Color Additives Amendment in 1960—which aimed to place the burden of establishing safety of these chemicals on the chemical industry.

These laws make the government's safety decisions appear very straightforward. When judging food chemicals, FDA is to consider only whether the chemical is effective—i.e. whether it serves its intended purpose—and whether it is safe when used as directed.[52] The economic impact of the chemical on the food industry was ruled out, as are any benefits it may have.

In practice, however, these guidelines break down. For example, the Delaney Amendment, one of the 1958 amendments, states categorically that it is unsafe for a chemical that causes cancer to be added intentionally to food. But, as we shall see, exceptions to this rule permit some carcinogenic chemicals to appear in meat indirectly. Second, safety is a very relative concept, especially when one is trying to extrapolate hazards for man from reactions of test animals. The latitude for human judgment in estimating risk is very, very wide. Third, when hazards turn up, as they often do, *after* a chemical has become entrenched in the marketplace, the definition of safety often takes on political implications as the food lobbies maneuver to protect their investment. The regulators, in defining safety, often use code words such as "toxicological insignificance" and "no-effect levels" and "limits of analytical sensitivity" to mask the fact that benefits and industry reaction are being weighed unofficially against risks.

As a result, regulators are constantly making decisions which have the effect of determining whether small levels of carcinogenic chemicals (chemicals causing cancer in test animals) should be tolerated in food. These decisions are as politically hazardous for the regulator as they are potentially perilous for the public. To the sausage maker and the cattleman who uses the chemicals to make his hotdogs red and his steers grow faster, the risks may seem very remote and the benefits very palpable. To cancer specialists, however, the economic benefits may seem trivial and the risks—a possible increase in the incidence of cancer a decade or more after human exposure—often catastrophic. The consumer, if he knows about the carcinogenic residues at all—and often he doesn't—is simply confused and often a little frightened. No one wants to increase the risks of cancer, but does it really make sense to increase the price of beef or turn hotdogs gray because a chemical caused cancer in a mouse or a hamster?

These questions are made more complex because the consequences of a given decision are shrouded in mystery. One often does not know how much of the carcinogen is in the food, how much is dangerous to the consumer, or how many people might ultimately be affected by it.[53] Unlike botulism where an inspection failure leads rapidly to a readily diagnosed lethal disease, a carcinogen may wait years to strike and then leave no clue to its identity when it does. In other words, the regulator's decision usually has little or no feedback to tell him whether he has done the right thing. In the absence of confirming scientific data, politics often moves in.

No responsible critic expects the agencies to guarantee absolute safety. But many of the questions about the relative risks and benefits of food chemicals could be answered with more research and sharper residue detection methods. Unfortunately the agencies, influenced by consumer apathy (now diminishing), internal organizational conflicts, and pressures from the food and chemical industries and the budget cutters in the Office of Management and Budget, have often been slow to make this investment or require industry to make it. For example, Congress appropriated over $6 million more for meat and poultry inspection for fiscal 1972 than USDA requested, at a time when USDA laboratory officials, pleading poverty, were planning to cut back on chemical surveillance of meat.

It is up to Congress, not the food bureaucracy, to decide how much the public is willing to pay for safer food. If Congress is to set priorities responsibly, the public must be informed about the risks, costs, and benefits of food safety decisions. The next two sections provide an inside look at two of the most significant food safety issues facing FDA and USDA.

DES: Balancing the Risks of Hormones in Meat

Nearly three-fourths of the 40 million cattle slaughtered annually in the United States have been fattened with an artificial hormone banned as a threat to public health in Sweden, France, Australia, Argentina, and seventeen other nations. In addition, Sweden and Italy have banned the importation of cattle from the United States which have been fed this hormone. Known as DES, or diethylstilbestrol, it is mixed with feed to increase the efficiency with which cattle convert feed into pounds of beef. It is the only chemical widely used as an animal drug for which there is strong evidence that it causes cancer in *both* test animals and man.*

According to the Elanco Products Division of Eli Lilly, the chief producer of DES, cattle fed this hormone gain 10 to 13 percent more weight on 10 percent less feed than cattle without stilbestrol. It adds $90 million annually to the profits of cattle growers. The National Cattlemen's Association estimates that beef prices would increase up to 10 percent if DES were not used. (Some meatpackers and veterinarians claim that DES also makes beef watery and of lower quality, but experiments to date fail to support this charge.)

Since it was first approved for use in poultry in 1947, DES has caused concern because it causes cancer in several species of test animals, including cancer of the breast in mice, rats, and dogs, cancer of the testicles in mice, and cancer of the kidneys in hamsters.[54] Like many other known carcinogens, DES induces cancer only after a long latency period. Malignant tumors appear only after the average animal has been exposed to DES for one-third of its lifetime.

Until very recently, cattlemen took comfort in the fact that DES had not been shown to cause cancer in human beings. But in April, 1971, researchers at the Massachusetts General Hospital in Boston made a startling discovery which puts the risks of DES in a new light. In seven young women, they diagnosed adenocarcinoma of the vagina, an extremely rare cancer which heretofore had been virtually unknown in premenopausal women. Medical detectives, compiling exhaustive case histories on the girls, found one common factor in their backgrounds which seemed to explain this astonishing cluster of cases: between fifteen and twenty years ago, the mothers of each of the girls had been treated with stilbestrol during pregnancy to prevent miscarriage.** The victims had received DES *in utero*, as fetuses. The *New England Journal of Medicine*, in an

---

* It is not known whether DES is carcinogenic because of its estrogenic effect or because of some other property in this synthetic compound. It is imprudent, therefore, to compare DES levels in meat with levels of natural estrogens in the human body. Nor is it known whether DES or a metabolite is the proximate carcinogen.
** DES has also been used as a "morning after" contraceptive pill.

alarmed editorial, called this discovery "highly significant, of great scientific importance and serious social implications."[55] In the following months up to December, 1971, nearly sixty cases of adenocarcinoma have been diagnosed in girls in their late teens and early twenties.

In addition to the cancer risk, there is also the possibility that synthetic female hormones, such as DES, may upset the hormonal balance and induce sterility or feminine characteristics in men. Stockholm University's Dr. Allan Bane, a veterinary specialist with the United Nations Food and Agriculture Organization which has called for a worldwide ban on DES, cites cases in the United States where farmers who inhaled DES dust while mixing it with feed, developed female-like breasts and symptoms of sterility. There is also the famous case of the New York restaurant employee whose fondness for chicken necks led to startling changes in his anatomy. After the restaurant's patrons were served the wings, legs, and breasts, the man was given the leftover chicken necks for his supper in the kitchen. At that time, DES pellets were routinely implanted in the necks of chickens to speed growth. The man ate a multitude of necks and developed pronounced female characteristics. (DES implants in chickens were subsequently banned in 1959.) Such feminization, however, requires DES far in excess of amounts the average citizen would be exposed to.

It is the cancer hazard primarily which leads USDA to condemn all meat in which any residues of DES are detected.* Nevertheless citizens continue to be exposed. While the amount of DES getting into meat is the most urgent question and will be discussed at length, there is also the problem of the fate of the hormone after it is excreted from the animals in the feedlot. While little definitive information is known about DES after it

---

* The fact, cited by many cattlemen, that DES causes no apparent harm to cattle is irrelevant to considerations of risks to human health. As noted above, in animal experiments when ingestion of DES is begun early in life, the majority of tumors arise when the animals are old. Commercial cattle are slaughtered long before tumors have a chance to develop. If DES is present in the food supply, human beings will be exposed from birth onward, leaving ample time for cancer to occur.

leaves the steer, it is a highly persistent chemical and has been detected in water supplies downstream from feedlots. No present water treatment affects it.[56]

The discovery of DES-induced adenocarcinoma of the vagina created a political storm on Capitol Hill. USDA, caught by surprise, was swept up in a whirl of contradictions and blunders which ultimately damaged its credibility with the Congress and fueled pressure for a new independent food inspection agency. To understand USDA's role in this affair, one must first recognize that the discovery that DES caused cancer in man, as dramatic and poignant as it was, had technically little regulatory significance. DES has been known to cause cancer in test animals since 1940, and this alone was enough to ban it if it were getting into meat. Since 1958, the Delaney Amendment to the Federal Food, Drug, and Cosmetic Act has banned all food additives "found to induce cancer when ingested in man or animal" (21 U.S.C. § 348 (c) (3)). DES, although an animal drug, might also be classified as a "food additive," defined as "any substance the intended use of which may reasonably be expected to result directly or indirectly in its becoming a component or otherwise affecting the characteristics of any food" (21 U.S.C. § 321 (s)). On October 10, 1962, however, the Delaney Amendment was revised expressly to allow carcinogenic drugs to be given to animals raised for food provided that "no residue of the additive will be found (by methods prescribed or approved by the Secretary by regulations. . . .) in any edible portion of such animal after slaughter or in any food yielded by or derived from the living animal. . . ." (21 U.S.C. § 348 (c) (3), Supp. 1970).

DES was saved because USDA and FDA steadfastly maintained that no residues of DES could be found in meat. FDA required cattlemen to cease feeding DES at least forty-eight hours before slaughter. This supposedly is enough time for the hormone to pass through the animal's system and be excreted. While the withdrawal period depended largely on the voluntary cooperation of the cattlemen, top officials in FDA and USDA have always claimed it was highly effective.

Laboratory checks for DES in meat appeared to confirm this view. Since 1965, USDA has been collecting random samples of liver and muscle tissue from DES-fed cattle and analyzing them in USDA laboratories. In 1969, USDA detected DES in only three of the randomly selected cattle; in 1970, it detected only one. In May, 1971, shortly after the vaginal cancer cases had been reported in the press, Assistant Secretary of Agriculture Richard Lyng relied on these results when he issued a press release stating that "USDA's tests show that no red meat containing detectable levels of DES residues has reached the consumer." He further stated that no DES had been found in any samples checked the first five months of 1971.[57]

As an example of public relations overkill, Lyng's statement turned out to be something of a milestone in the annals of USDA press agentry. A cursory glance at how the DES safeguards really worked shows that Lyng was making a gigantic leap of faith with his unqualified assurances. First, there is the embarrassment of numbers. It is true that USDA detected DES in only one steer in 1970. What Lyng neglected to say was that of 31 million cattle slaughtered under federal inspection in 1970, USDA had tested only 192, or six one-thousandths of 1 percent, for DES (in 1968 and 1969, the number was 539 and 505 respectively). The tests had no statistical significance. Second, and more important, USDA's analytical method was grossly insensitive, so that many of the 191 cattle carcasses which were tested and found to be "free" of DES could in fact have contained potentially dangerous levels of the hormone.

It is fair to say that at the time of Lyng's statement, in April, 1971, seventeen years after DES was first approved for use in cattle, neither USDA nor FDA could make a serious estimate of how much DES was getting into the nation's beef. This result is an object lesson in the ways bureaucracy can silently evade the consumer protection mandates of Congress. The law has always required that the Secretary of HEW keep DES out of the feedlot unless the chemical and feed companies could provide evidence that no residue would remain in human food products derived from treated animals. The burden of proof was to be on the makers and users of DES. When DES was first approved for cattle in 1954, federal law required the Secretary to prevent its use if he had insufficient information to determine whether the drug was safe for its intended use (21 U.S.C. 355). The Federal Food, Drug, and Cosmetic Act, as amended in 1958, required all animal drug petitions to contain a "description of practicable methods for determining the quantity" of such chemicals in food (21 U.S.C. 348(b)). Further amendments in 1962 and 1969 confirmed these conditions and required the Secretary to make certain that directions for safe use, such as the forty-eight hour withdrawal period, were being followed in practice (21 U.S.C. 360b, Supp. 1970). But while there have been dozens of animal drug applications for new uses of DES in cattle and sheep feed since 1954, these safety conditions have been rarely, if ever, applied.

From 1954 to 1965, for example, FDA made no attempt to check meat regularly for DES residues, or even to develop a practical regulatory method for detecting it. When USDA finally began to look for DES in meat in 1965, it found itself in an embarrassing position.* The method of analysis submitted by the manufacturers of DES in 1954 and approved by FDA as the official method required by law turned out to be totally impractical for detecting DES in meat. FDA's method was a bioassay, in which tissues of DES-dosed animals are fed to immature female mice whose uterine weights then indicate whether DES is present. While this method could detect DES down to a level of two parts per billion (ppb) it was too time-consuming and lacking in specificity to be used in screening hundreds of samples.[59] Because the method was not practical, FDA, in approving DES, was in violation of law.

USDA, forced to improvise at government expense, developed a chemical method of analysis which was rapid and cheap but relatively insensitive. It could not

---

* While FDA approves the drugs, including the methods of analysis, USDA is in charge of actually checking for drug residues in meat. In the past FDA has often approved animal drugs without giving USDA a chance to see if the methods for detecting their residues were effective. This has been the case with DES, MGA, and other synthetic hormones. The fault here lies primarily with FDA's Bureau of Veterinary Medicine but the Consumer and Marketing Service, as its Administrator readily admits, has been weak in not using its power to refuse drugs which his agency lacks the techniques to detect.[58]

detect DES at levels below 10 ppb. This method, according to a top USDA chemist, was a "regulatory control chemist's nightmare."[60] Failure to develop a more sensitive analysis significantly increased the public's risk of exposure to carcinogenic residues in the 1960s. As far back as 1956, a symposium on medicated feed warned:

. . . it is obvious that the cancer-producing dose of this drug [in animals] approaches the infinitesimal. Claims that no appreciable quantities can be demonstrated in tissues of cattle to which it has been fed must therefore be carefully scrutinized as to the sensitivity and accuracy of the test methods.[61]

But it was not until April, 1971, that USDA developed a chemical capable of detecting DES in concentrations as low as 2 ppb, the level of sensitivity of FDA's official method of analysis.

Even at this sensitivity, the tests do not mean that DES-fed beef is safe. DES causes cancer in test mice when as little as 6.25 ppb are added to their diet.[62] This was the lowest level tested. The "no-effect" level of DES in test animals has still not been determined. Even if a "no-effect" level is found, FDA would reduce it by a factor of 100 before considering it a safe level for man. DES may be present in meat in amounts many times higher than any hypothetical safe level and still be below the 2 ppb detection threshold. A letter from the National Cancer Institute to Representative L. H. Fountain, Chairman of the House Intergovernmental Relations Subcommittee, on January 31, 1972, warned that "a safe level of DES by any conservative rule would therefore have to be a good deal below 6.25 ppb. But I understand that detection levels for DES are not sensitive below 2 ppb so that no direct measurement of DES in slaughtered animals could give assurance that the level was low enough." Other scientists challenge the concept of "safe levels" of substances such as DES. A 1970 report to the Surgeon General by an *ad hoc* committee of cancer specialists stated as accepted doctrine in the field of carcinogenesis that *no* level of exposure to a chemical carcinogen should be considered safe and warned that exposure to small doses of a carcinogen over a period of time usually results in a summation of or potentiation of effects.[63]

Many cancer specialists believe that the mechanism of carcinogenesis operates on a molecule-to-molecule basis. In recent hearings before the House Intergovernmental Relations Subcommittee, five cancer experts, including Dr. Roy Hertz of Rockefeller University, Umberto Saffiotti of the National Cancer Institute, Morton Lipsitt of the National Institute of Child Health and Development, and Arthur Herbst and Peter Greenwald, the physicians who discovered the link between vaginal cancer and DES, emphasized that no one knows how much of a carcinogen, taken for how short a time, can induce cancer. Perhaps, they said, one molecule in the 340 trillion molecules in a five-ounce serving of beef liver could do it.[64] A level of DES just below 2 ppb and therefore beyond detection could amount to nearly 2 million million (2,000,000,000,000) molecules in a pound of meat.

FDA's failure to develop more sensitive analytical procedures between 1954 and 1971 is all the more irresponsible because it had ample reason to suspect that cattlemen were not observing the forty-eight hour withdrawal period. Factors of profit and convenience made noncompliance likely. Within twelve hours after a farmer decides the price is right, his cattle are likely to be at the slaughterhouse. Moreover, taking cattle off DES, especially when they are jammed by the thousands into feedlots, is no simple task. Many cattle feedlots use elaborate feeding machines stocked with DES-supplemented feed. Cleaning out the machines and restocking them with pure feed for a short forty-eight hour period was simply too much trouble for many farmers.[65] In 1970, USDA became so alarmed at this situation that it informed FDA it would no longer concur in the approval of any animal drug where a withdrawal period was required to prevent contamination of meat.[66] Compliance was further crippled by FDA's failure, until 1971, to initiate criminal proceedings against cattlemen who shipped livestock with illegal residues.

The record shows, therefore, that FDA and USDA failed for over a decade to enforce effectively Congress's mandate to keep DES-contaminated meat out of consumers' hands. FDA's continued approval of new DES petitions when it knew that it lacked practical detection procedures and any real evidence that feeders were complying with procedures for safe use, was highly irresponsible. Events in 1971 have made the agency's willingness to expose the public to risks of a carcinogen seem even more inexcusable.

In April, 1971, USDA began using a new analytical method, gas liquid chromatography, which could detect DES down to 2 ppb. At the same time, it increased the number of animals sampled from 192 in 1970 to 6,000 projected for 1971. On August 31, Assistant Secretary Lyng wrote Senator William Proxmire that all samples in the new survey had proved negative for DES. The monthly reports USDA had been sending to the House Intergovernmental Relations Subcommittee since its March hearings said the same. At the time, both Proxmire and the committee were contemplating legislation to ban DES.

Unknown to Lyng, however, scientists at USDA's Beltsville laboratories were sitting on a bombshell about to blow up in the agency's face. Since July, they had begun to find alarming amounts of DES in cattle and sheep livers. By the end of August, DES had been detected in ten randomly selected animals, up to 15.4 ppb in cattle and 36.9 ppb in sheep. Acting apparently on his own initiative, USDA's chief of laboratory services, Dr. Harry Mussman, had instructed the Beltsville officials not to report the findings to Washington. Mussman's reason for concealing the residues had a familiar Catch 22 logic to it. No residues were to be reported, he said, until they had been confirmed by a second method of analysis. The catch was that no second method of analysis was available. This made it administratively impossible for any DES residues to be reported since April, 1971.

The DES data were kept secret until September 30, 1971 when Peter Schuck, a lawyer with Washington's Center for Study of Responsive Law, asked Dr. Kenneth McEnroe, USDA's meat inspection Chief, to confirm or deny rumors of the findings. McEnroe emphatically denied the rumors, then called Schuck up twenty-four hours later to apologize. To his shocked surprise, he found upon checking that the rumors were correct. David Hawkins, a lawyer with the Natural Resources Defense Council who had first learned of the DES data, now made the findings public in a letter to Secretary of Agriculture Clifford Hardin. An embarrassed Lyng then wrote Senator Proxmire apologizing for his Department's "inexcusable error" and promising a thorough investigation of this "gross malpractice."

By the end of 1971, DES had been detected in twenty-four carcasses of randomly selected cattle and sheep, six times the total for the previous two years. The voices calling for a ban on DES now swelled to a chorus. Senator Proxmire introduced a bill to ban DES outright and the National Resources Defense Council sued USDA and FDA for the same purpose. The House hearings on DES reconvened in November to hear a leading cancer specialist, Dr. Roy Hertz of Rockefeller University, testify that nothing short of a possible "famine situation" could now justify continued use of DES.

FDA and USDA are now weighing the costs of restricting DES against the increased evidence of risks. The federal courts and Congress may provide additional forums for the decision. While public opinion will force the agencies to take some action it appears they will be far more circumspect in restricting DES than they ever were in approving it.

FDA has three basic options. First, it can ban DES outright. In light of the residues found in meat in 1971, the 1962 amendment to the Food, Drug, and Cosmetic Act would appear to dictate this move. The Act granted animal drugs an exemption from the Delaney clause only on condition that their residues not appear in food. In 1971, DES was found in approximately 0.5 percent of the animals tested. If this rate of violation is representative of the cattle and sheep population as a whole, then some 200,000 animals with illegal residues of DES were probably marketed in 1971. It is reasonable to presume that the number would have been much higher if USDA's ability to detect DES did not stop at 2 ppb. The costs of banning DES is estimated at approximately $3.85 per person in additional meat costs each year.[67] However, increased demand for feed grain (drug free cattle would consume approximately 3 million more tons annually than DES-fed cattle) would reduce the impact of a DES ban on the farm economy as a whole and save $105 million in farm subsidies.[68]

Second, FDA could ban beef liver. DES accumulates in beef liver at ten times the rate in muscle tissue. Beef liver is a major poor people's food. It is therefore likely that inner city residents are consuming more DES than any other segment of the population. Such a ban would not solve the DES problem but would reduce the risks of human exposure.

Third, FDA and USDA could amend the directions for use of DES, forcing feeders to take cattle off DES further in advance of slaughter. The agencies have chosen this route. The withdrawal period has been increased from forty-eight hours to seven days and feeders are required to sign a statement of compliance. However the same incentives for non-compliance exist now that the limit has been increased to seven days. USDA will test only 6,000 of the 50 million cattle and sheep slaughtered in 1972. An individual feeder who falsely states that he has properly withdrawn his animals from DES has less than one chance in 8,000 of being caught. Voluntary compliance, in effect, is still the rule.

Throughout the history of DES regulation, FDA and USDA have given the producers' interest, rather than the consumer's health, the benefit of the doubt. They are doing so once again. Dismissing the DES contaminants found in 1971 as "isolated" and "toxicologically insignificant," they are gambling that no more will turn up in 1972.

Unfortunately there is little evidence that FDA and USDA have learned from their mistakes with DES. At least five other animal drugs with estrogenic-like activity have been approved by FDA without first providing USDA with a practical and sensitive method for detecting their residues. All of them are suspected carcinogens and one of them, dienestrol, has been linked to a case of vaginal cancer in one young woman (the woman's mother was given the drug during pregnancy). The bioassay, the same analytical method which proved so impractical for DES, is the "official" method of analysis for this hormone.[69]

The fate of DES will ultimately depend as much on the organizational politics of the agencies as on its merits as a carcinogen. With both USDA's Consumer and Marketing Service and FDA's Bureau of Veterinary Medicine, we are expecting agencies which to a significant degree provide services to agribusiness to exercise sophisticated public health functions without any direct decisional input from the National Cancer Institute or other public health bodies. The institutional bias runs far deeper than one or two individuals. There may well have been no attempt by subordinates to conceal the DES findings if their superiors had not so rashly committed the agency to an unqualified defense of USDA without first getting the facts.

One example of USDA's producer bias is the numerous booklets it puts out on feedlot management. The booklets give technical advice on feedlot layout and the use of DES in cattle feeding but none seen by this author discuss the potential health hazards of DES or means of complying with withdrawal periods. Technical advice and technological boosterism come naturally to the agency and are in perfect harmony with its overall mission; warnings do not.

The producer orientation of FDA's Bureau of Veterinary Medicine is more subtle and more important, in a policy sense, than USDA's. The BVM screens for safety and effectiveness the hundreds of animal drug petitions submitted by the drug and chemical industries every year. This work puts its staff in constant, daily contact with industry representatives trying to speed clearance of their petitions. This pressure has two primary effects: it makes the staff intimately familiar with the views of the company men, many of whom become first-name acquaintances; second, in the interest of conflict avoidance, the staff tends to identify efficiency with rapid approval of petitions.

Dr. Van Houweling, BVM's Director, appears on occasion to reflect this conditioning. In August, 1970, USDA refused to concur in BVM's approval of DES implants for use in the ears of beef cattle because USDA feared withdrawal periods would not be observed. Van Houweling chafed at the delay and rejected USDA's recommendation that he require the drug firms to demonstrate the practicality of withdrawal periods. On December 24, 1970, he finally recommended to FDA Commissioner Edwards that the practice of seeking USDA's concurrence be abandoned and that the DES implants be approved anyway (FDA was not required *by law* to seek USDA's approval in advance). Cooler heads prevailed, however. William Goodrich, FDA's general counsel, advised Edwards to turn down Van Houweling:

We must not be put in the position of being indifferent to the presence of illegal drug residues in food animals and unwilling to test the adequacy and realism of compliance with withdrawal restrictions imposed by approved labelling.[70]

Another explanation of BVM's rather casual attitude toward the human risks of animal drugs lies in the background and training of its toxicologists. Veterinary toxicologists are accustomed to anticipating acute effects of drugs on animals, not long-term effects on human beings. Moreover the recent advances in the sensitivity of analytical technology have taken many of the more traditional toxicologists by surprise. Despite new discoveries of residues from drugs with a "zero" tolerance (i.e., no residues permitted in food), many are still inclined to give the drug firm the benefit of the doubt. Now, more than ever, their failure to require adequate methods to detect the residues of drugs makes a mockery of the concept of "zero" tolerance.

Nitrites in Meat: Better Red than Dead?

Sodium nitrite is the chemical additive which gives hotdogs, corned beef, and other processed meats their fresh red color. Now, nearly a half century after they were first approved by USDA, nitrites are under fire as possible precursors to the development of carcinogenic chemicals in food and in the human body known as nitrosamines. In November, 1971, Norway's National Health Department banned the use of nitrites and nitrates as coloring agents in meat (effective 1973), after experiments showed that small doses, when combined with other ingredients, can cause cancer in animal organs.

USDA answers the nitrite critics with the argument: better red than dead. According to the Consumer and Marketing Service, nitrites not only serve a useful cosmetic function by making meat attractive to consumers, but they also protect the consumer from deadly botulism. Faced with this grim trade-off between a short- and long-term hazard, the government has opted for the status quo—and allows up to 200 ppm nitrite in cured meat.

If nitrites do in fact lead to carcinogenic residues in meat, the Delaney Amendment to the Food, Drug, and Cosmetics Act would appear to force the government's hand. This amendment requires FDA to ban all food additives which cause cancer in animals. Because of a peculiar twist in the law, however, this strict rule does not apply to nitrites. In a classic example of the overlapping functions which stultify food regulation, nitrites are exempt from the Delaney Amendment because USDA approved them as coloring agents under the Federal Meat Inspection Act before the Delaney Amendment was passed in 1958.[71] This means that nitrites have managed to bypass the safety tests FDA requires of other food additives. With the Delaney Amendment in abeyance, USDA is left free to weigh the risks and benefits of nitrites in an atmosphere of deepening scientific controversy. The importance of this decision is highlighted by the fact that cured meat, in which nitrites are used, accounts for approximately 33 percent (over 5 billion pounds) of the total meat products manufactured by federally inspected plants.[72]

Nitrites may be hazardous chemicals, both as direct poisons and as potential cancer-causing agents. Nitrates, while relatively harmless in themselves, create concern because they may be converted to nitrites through bacteriological action in foods and in the human stomach. Children are particularly vulnerable because their stomachs, being much less acidic than the stomachs of adults, have abundant bacteria which can reduce nitrate to nitrite and cause severe poisoning.[73] In 1965, several infants in West Germany died after eating spinach with a high nitrate content which was then converted to nitrite.*[74] Nitrates may also be converted to nitrites by bacteria in the air or in food once a food can or package is opened. While there are no reported cases of children being poisoned by legal levels of these additives in meat alone,[75] it is prudent for mothers to avoid baby foods containing processed meat, and other nitrate or nitrite laden food, such as spinach, especially after they have been opened for a time.

There are, however, many cases on record of death and serious illness from the misuse of sodium nitrite in food. Many of these cases occur because nitrite's white granules have been mistaken for sugar or salt. Dr. A. J. Lehman, former Director of FDA's Division of Pharmacology and Toxicology, has warned that "only a small margin of safety exists between the amount of nitrite that is safe and that which may be dangerous. The margin of safety is even more reduced when the smaller blood volume and the corresponding small quantity of hemoglobin in children is taken into account."[76] Dr. Lehman's statement was prompted by over a dozen cases of nitrite poisoning of children in 1955 and 1956. The children had eaten wieners and bologna which contained up to 5,000 ppm nitrites, far in excess of the permitted levels.[77]

Partly because nitrite levels are easily, if infrequently abused, the FDA has until recently treated them with great caution. Years ago, FDA classified nitrites as poisonous or deleterious substances and attempted to exclude them from *general* use in foods. The Supreme Court overruled this effort in the case *United States v. Lexington Mill and Elevator Company*. Arguing that the red color of meat helps the consumer judge its freshness, FDA did successfully rule that the use of nitrites in fresh meat (as opposed to cured meat) is deceptive and prohibited its use.

In the last few years, scientists have become aware of potential new hazards from nitrites which dwarf previous concerns. Animal experiments around the

---

* Barry Commoner, the well-known biologist at Washington University (St. Louis), has warned against excessive use of nitrogen fertilizers which may cause spinach to have nitrate levels of potential danger to small children.

world have conclusively shown that nitrites, through a synergistic reaction with other chemicals called secondary and tertiary amines, may be converted to cancer-causing substances called nitrosamines. About 80 percent of the nitrosamines tested have been found to cause cancer in a wide variety of species, including the rat, hamster, mouse, guinea pig, dog, and monkey.[78] Unlike many carcinogens which are organ-specific, nitrosamines attack many different organs of the animals, including the lungs, liver, oesophagus, and other sites. Up to now, no animal species has been found resistant to carcinogenesis by these agents.[79] According to Dr. William Lijinsky, a leading cancer researcher at the Oak Ridge National Laboratory, nitrosamines "are among the most potent carcinogens we know and are certainly the most widely acting group of carcinogens. They seem to be most effective in eliciting tumors when they are applied in small doses over a long period, rather than as large single doses."[80] These are exactly the conditions under which the meat consumer would be exposed to nitrosamines if they are formed by the interaction of nitrites and amines in the diet or human stomach.

While there have been no long-term studies of human beings exposed to nitrosamines, there is a strong presumption that they are carcinogenic for man. Dr. R. Preussmann of the German Cancer Research Center in Heidelberg states that the metabolism as well as the acute toxic effects of nitrosamines are similar or identical in man and experimental animals and concludes:

. . . I do not hesitate to say that N-nitroso compounds are carcinogens also in man with a probability being close to certainty. The opinions of Lijinsky and Epstein that nitros-amines and nitrosamides "seem to be a major class of carcinogens that are likely to be causally related to human cancer" is shared by many now. The widespread concern about carcinogenic N-nitroso compounds in the human environment is therefore justified."[81]

An FDA Status Report on the toxicology of nitrites and nitrosamines states that since nitrosamines "can induce tumors in a wide spectrum of experimental animals, including the nonhuman primate, these compounds may have a high potential for induction of neoplasia in man."[82] Of all the nitrosamines tested to date, dimethylnitrosamine (DMN) is the most biologically potent.

Nitrites are also suspect on other grounds. Dr. Hillel Shuval, Director of the environmental health laboratory at the Hadassah Medical School of Israel's Hebrew University, reported in October, 1971, that high levels of nitrite caused epileptic-like seizures in the brain activity of rats and, by passing through the placenta of pregnant rats, caused excessive deaths among their offspring. Dr. Samuel Epstein, an environmental toxicologist at Case Western Reserve Medical School, recently told the Senate Government Operations Committee that nitrites cause "point" mutations in microorganisms, another warning sign the human significance of which has not been determined.

When scientists learned that nitrosamines could be formed through the interaction of nitrites and secondary amines, they saw a danger of human exposure from two sources—the possible formation of nitrosamines in food and in the human stomach. Both dangers were strictly theoretical. No nitrosamines had been found in meat except in trace amounts at the threshold of detectability where analysis was very uncertain. In fact, before 1971, the possible formation of nitrosamines in the human stomach seemed more threatening. The preconditions for such a reaction were present. Man ingests secondary amines in his beer, wine, tobacco, cereals, certain medicines, and many other foods.[83] The interaction of nitrites and the amines is favored by the acid conditions which prevail in the mammalian stomach. This reaction has been established *in vitro* (test tubes) with gastric juice of cats, rabbits, dogs, and man, and it has been established *in vivo* (living systems) in cats, rats, and rabbits, species whose gastric juices are similar in pH to man. The presence of one nitrosamine, nitrosodiphenylamine, was found in the stomachs of thirty-one human subjects given a combination of nitrate and a secondary amine.[84]

Given these potential hazards, why have FDA and USDA been so reluctant to restrict the use of these additives? The answer is found in the way the agencies assess the burden of proof on the many unanswered questions about nitrites.

First, the interaction of nitrites and amines to form nitrosamines in human beings is still only a theoretical possibility, derived from animal tests. Moreover, nitrites and nitrates are absorbed rapidly by the stomach and therefore do not have much time for reaction.[85] Dr. Epstein and Dr. Lijinsky further noted in a January 1970 issue of *Nature*, that the individual occurrences of nitrites and secondary amines are not necessarily hazardous:

Both reactants must be present simultaneously in the stomach to form nitrosamine. Even so not all secondary amines react with nitrite to form nitrosamines in conditions prevailing in the mammalian stomach and not all nitrosamines are carcinogenic.

With this caveat in mind, the two scientists nevertheless conclude that the possibility of interaction raises a flag of warning on nitrites and suggests that a reduction in human exposure to nitrites and certain secondary amines may result in a decrease in the incidence of human cancer.[86]

Even if we accept the government's position (FDA Commissioner Charles Edwards, and Consumer and Marketing Service Chief Clayton Yeutter are the main government spokesmen in defense of nitrites) that formation of nitrosamine in the human stomach remains to be proved, there is still the problem of the possible formation of nitrosamines in meat products. Dr. Virgil Wodicka, Director of FDA's Bureau of Foods, stated flatly that "we could not permit the use of nitrites if it led to the formation of nitrosamines in food."[87] Until very recently, this possibility seemed very remote. The most sensitive analytical technology available (gas-liquid chromatography confirmed with a mass spectrometer) had not found nitrosamines in meat above 10 ppb, the threshold of detectability.

In August, 1971, a scientist at USDA's Eastern Regional Research Laboratory in Wyndmore, Pennsylvania, made a discovery which temporarily shattered the government's composure. In two of ten samples of hotdogs obtained from a local supermarket, he discovered dimethylnitrosamine (DNM) at 80 ppb and 48 ppb, respectively, the highest levels of DMN ever found in meat. DMN produces cancer of the liver in rats at 2 ppm, the lowest dietary levels ever tested, only twenty times greater than the level found in these hotdogs. No safe level of DMN has been established and it is the opinion of many scientists that any levels of DMN and certainly levels in excess of 10 ppb pose carcinogenic hazards for man.[88] Subsequent analysis of twenty-three samples from the same manufacturers turned up one additional weak positive.

These findings caused a great stir in USDA. Dr. Leo Friedman, Director of FDA's Division of Toxicology, and Dr. Harry Mussman, Director of USDA's Laboratory Services Division, both considered the levels "significant," and Mussman in a memo dated September 13, 1971, urged that the findings be announced in a press release. The release never left the Department of Agriculture, and the DMN findings were kept a closely held secret. Three months later, USDA did announce the Pennsylvania discovery, but in a very circuitous way. The press release stated reassuringly in the lead paragraphs that USDA had tested twenty samples of cured meat products for DMN since September 14 and all were negative. Then in the fine print below, it mentioned parenthetically that three positives had been found in ten samples tested before September 13. One explanation for the delay is that FDA's nitrosamine analysts apparently questioned the competence of USDA's August tests, while USDA stood behind them.

Nitrosamines have subsequently been found in many other meat products, including bacon (*after* frying) up to 106 ppb and in drippings up to 207 ppb, in dried beef and cured pork products up to 48 ppb, in ham up to 5 ppb, and in fish up to 26 ppb.[89] Since a limited sampling program for nitrosamines has only recently been inaugurated by USDA, these findings are strongly indicative of significant contamination of the food supply with highly carcinogenic nitrosamines.

Until more tests are run on retail hotdogs and other cured meat products and USDA and FDA resolve their differences over test methodology, the amount of DMN

and other nitrosamines in meat products will remain a
mystery. DMN has also been found in beef blood and
fish products, but at lower levels. The USDA findings
therefore add to the suspicion surrounding present uses
of nitrites. It is critically important to reduce human
exposure to nitrosamines to the maximum possible degree and to define the extent of human exposure to
nitrosamines in food.

The government's last line of defense on nitrites is its
contention that they protect the consumer from botulism. Botulism is extremely rare in meat (there has
never been a recorded case of human illness from
botulism in cured meat) and it is killed by cooking at
250°. Refrigeration keeps it from multiplying. Yet while
refrigeration and heat sterilization techniques have
improved greatly since 1925 when nitrites were first
approved, contamination by botulism is still theoretically
possible.

According to USDA scientists, nitrites damage the
spores of *Clostridium botulinum* when the meat is
cooked. If the bacteria subsequently break out of their
spores, they cannot grow and reproduce.[90] FDA scientists, on the other hand, play down nitrite's effect on
botulism. In a Status Report on the chemistry and
toxicology of nitrites dated August 28, 1970, FDA noted
that "sodium chloride is relied upon as the major preservative (in cured meat) and sodium nitrite is primarily a color fixative in fish and meats since nitrite is only
minimally effective as a bacteriostat."[91] When nitrite is
used without salt, it is not effective against botulism.[92]

If nitrite is in fact necessary to protect the consumer
from botulism, one wonders why USDA does not require
a minimum level in meat, a floor as well as a ceiling,
for the amount of nitrite in meat products varies widely.
The answer is that USDA lacks scientific data to justify
present levels of nitrite in hotdogs, bologna, canned
ham, and the other cured meats. Nitrites are now
permitted in meat up to 200 ppm. According to a USDA
report prepared forty-five years ago, USDA arrived at
this level in 1926 not by scientific assessment of potential human risk, but by simply taking the highest concentration of nitrite commonly found in hams after

curing and making it the standard.[93] This 200 ppm figure is far in excess of the amount necessary to control botulism, as indicated by studies by the American Meat Institute reported to FDA in February, 1972.

One thing is fairly clear. If there is a danger from botulism, it is greatest in lightly processed canned meats, which are expected to remain stable at room temperature. There appears to be no risk of botulism in bacon and hotdogs, which are both refrigerated and thoroughly cooked before eating.[94] The research which shows nitrite protecting against botulism was performed on canned meat, not hotdogs.[95] Nitrites may be needlessly used in other products as well. The FDA recently reported to Senator Abraham Ribicoff that "the regulated use of nitrite not to exceed 10 ppm in smoked, cured tuna would appear to serve only as a color fixative."

The use of nitrites in hotdogs and bacon may account for a large proportion of the total human ingestion of these chemicals. It creates needless risks for the consumer, especially since hotdogs are the most popular source of meat for children. Giant Foods, which has become the conscience of the supermarket industry under the guidance of its consumer advisor, Esther Peterson,* has recently developed a prototype for a non-nitrite hotdog which it soon hopes to market. The Maple Crest Sausage Company, which uses the brand name Shiloh Farms has marketed such a hotdog. If these companies can free their hotdogs of nitrite, why not Hormel and Oscar Mayer?

Consumers Union has recently called for a ban on nitrites in hotdogs, stating that "when reputable scientific researchers present strong evidence of hazard, the FDA should ban a questionable substance until the scientific issues are resolved." The National Health Department of Norway has announced that it will ban the use of nitrite to make meat red, beginning in 1973. If the meat processors want to continue to use it, they must, within one year, prove that nitrites are essential to protect against botulism in each meat product where the additive is used. This policy makes good sense. It

* This is the same Esther Peterson who lost her job as consumer advisor to the President to Betty Furness (see Chapter 1).

places the burden of proof on the meat processor where it belongs, and it ensures that nitrites if necessary will be kept at the essential minimum. The regulatory philosophy behind this policy has been expressed by the Medical Director of the Norwegian Health Department: "As long as there is doubt about a [chemical] substance and in addition it is not absolutely necessary as an additive, it is quite natural to forbid it. This is part of the work to reduce the number of chemical additives in Norwegian foodstuff."

USDA and FDA's response to the concern about nitrites appears to express a different scale of values. First, even if the American consumer wants to cut down on the amount of nitrite in his diet, his freedom of choice is undermined by a USDA policy which allows nitrite to be used in canned and smoked ham, bacon, and corned beef (in some cases) without notice on their labels. In justifying this practice, USDA contradicts itself. USDA claims it is not required to label color fixatives in standardized meat products (products for which a standardized list of ingredients is published in the *Federal Register*). In hearings before the House Subcommittee on Intergovernmental Operations, however, USDA justified the use of nitrite as a preservative against botulism. But there is *no* exemption for the labeling of preservatives.

USDA cannot have it both ways. If nitrite is used as a preservative, as well as a color fixative, it must be labeled. Moreover, since nitrite received prior sanction under the Meat Inspection Act only as a color fixative, its additional use as a preservative places it squarely within the reach of the Delaney Amendment.

The labeling loophole suggests rather vivid contrasts between the regulatory philosophy of food safety officials in this country and in Norway. Top administrators in USDA and FDA tend to define risks in terms of concrete human victims and place the burden of proof concerning the hazards of nitrites on the consumer, not the meat processor. Dr. Gilbert Goldhammer, consultant to the House Subcommittee on Intergovernmental Operations, states that his queries to FDA about the safety of nitrites were met with the retort "but you haven't shown me it's unsafe for man." An FDA official recently conceded that ". . . these suspicions [about nitrite] would make it impossible under present regulations for the Agency to approve the present level of nitrite if the compound had been discovered last week. But that is because you would not have the factor of human experience. Man is the most important experimental animal and nitrites have not been linked to cancer in all the years that man has been eating the chemical."[96]

The reference to human experience seems persuasive at first glance. If a substance we have been consuming for generations causes cancer, surely we would know about it by now. Unfortunately this is not the case. First, although millions may be exposed to a cancer-causing chemical, relatively few persons will actually develop clinical cancer. While the chemical causes irreversible and additive effects on cells, the proliferation of these cells into malignant tumors depends on many poorly understood factors, including genetic susceptibility, the extent of exposure to the carcinogen, the presence of other chemicals such as hormones or phenols which act as cancer growth promoters, the diet, age, and sex of the person, and the physical form and route of administration of the carcinogen, to mention only a few.[97] Therefore if a food additive did cause cancer, only a small fraction of those exposed may become ill and these may not be enough to cause a noticeable rise in the statistical incidence of cancer.

Second, even if the number of victims were very great, it would be very difficult for epidemiologists to track down a specific chemical such as nitrosamines as the cause. Except in very rare cases, as with DES, the tumor itself gives no clues. DES was discovered only because the type of tumor it produced in teenage girls was so extraordinarily rare that investigators suspected that some very specific common experience—treatment of their mothers with DES during pregnancy—was the cause. Dr. Epstein warns that "epidemiological techniques [statistical surveys of hospital records, etc.] are unlikely to detect weak carcinogens and other toxic agents unless there are sharp differentials in exposure of the general population, as with cigarette smoking. For widely dispersed agents, such as intentional or accidental food additives, to which the population at

large is generally exposed, human experience is unlikely
to provide any meaningful indication of safety or hazard."[98] These facts are known to FDA. References to
human experience by FDA therefore seem designed to
give false comfort to the layman.

A second tenet in FDA's and USDA's estimate of
risk on DES and nitrosamines, is that a little carcinogen
will not hurt you. Again, this seems plausible at first
glance. After all, the amounts of DES and nitrosamines
found in meat *are* very small, in parts per billion. Even
if we grant that high exposure to these chemicals may
be dangerous, it defies common sense that the microscopic amounts found in meat (amounts so small that
they were undetectable two years ago) are harmful.

This concept of "safe" levels of carcinogens is fundamental to the philosophy of safety evaluation which
prevails in FDA's and USDA's middle echelons.

Dr. Leo Friedman, Director of FDA's Division of
Toxicology, has described this concept in a recent
memorandum:

For every biologically active substance there usually is a
dose response relationship; there is always a threshold level
below which the substance does not exert any physiologically
significant effect and, therefore, for every substance there is
a "no-effect" level. The design of a safety evaluation study
is to determine a level at which there is no demonstrable
effect. This level, when divided by a suitable safety factor,
is then considered to be a safe level, in that there is a
practical certainty that no harm will result from the use
of the substance at that level.[99]

The view that there can be "safe" levels of carcinogens
in food was supported by a 1969 report of the Food
Protection Committee of the National Academy of
Sciences–National Research Council which set down
guidelines for permitting "toxicologically insignificant"
levels of cancer promoting substances in food.

The concept of "insignificant" exposures which Dr.
Virgil Wodicka, Director of FDA's Bureau of Food, and
FDA Commissioner Charles Edwards reportedly also
embrace, was sharply challenged by a committee of
eight scientists which evaluated the risks of chemical
carcinogens for the Surgeon General in 1970. This committee stated flatly that it is "impossible to establish

any absolutely safe level of exposure to a carcinogen for man." The committee further charged that the "safe level" concept of NAS-NRC's Food Protection Committee not only has "absolutely no validity" but also displays "a lack of understanding . . . of the irreversible and delayed toxic effects which occur in carcinogenesis."[100] Noting that the majority of human cancers are environmentally related and therefore potentially preventable, it urged that "every effort be made to control sources of carcinogenic contamination." It concluded with a ringing defense of the Delaney Amendment:

The principle of a zero tolerance for carcinogenic exposures should be retained in all areas of legislation presently covered by it and should be extended to cover other exposures as well. Only . . . where contamination of an environmental source by a carcinogen has been proven to be unavoidable should exceptions be made . . . [and then] only after the most extraordinary justification is presented. . . .

The Surgeon General's committee is supported by leading cancer specialists in government and universities. A recent report on "Chemical Carcinogenesis" in the *New England Journal of Medicine* noted that "the known carcinogens have not yet been effectively banned from our environment, and efforts must continue to educate populations and governments about their presence. In this regard, it should be remembered that weak carcinogenic exposures have irreversible and additive effects and cannot be dismissed lightly as standing 'below a threshold of action.' "*[101] In claiming to estimate "safe" levels for man, Dr. Friedman seems to confuse the threshold level in experimental animals with the threshold level in man, which may be very different. The former can be determined by laboratory experiments, the latter may always remain unknown.

* The author of the article, Dr. Hughes Ryser, notes that the irreversibility factor may sound discouraging to a person, like a heavy smoker, who has undergone severe carcinogenic exposure. However, the incidence of cancer for heavy smokers who stop is less than for those who do not. "This is due to the presence, in tobacco smoke, of both initiators (hydrocarbons) and promoters (phenols) [of carcinogenic growth]. Thus when both factors are removed, the irreversible effects of past initiation may remain unexpressed for the rest of a lifetime. This should encourage cigarette smokers of all vintages to kick the habit."

The Delaney Amendment "no residue" rule has come under attack lately. As residue analysis becomes more sensitive and more trace contaminants turn up in food, some scientists fear that most of the food supply would have to be banned if the Amendment were applied strictly. This is not the case. First, in the past FDA has ruled that the Amendment applies only to intentional additives over which we have some control, not to unintentional contaminants like DDT or other pesticides, by far the largest source of trace carcinogens in food. Second, only a very few food additives are carcinogenic. Of 150 "suspicious" chemicals tested by the National Cancer Institute in a recent study, less than 10 percent turned out to be carcinogenic. Most food additives remain safe under the Amendment. As long as cancer specialists remain convinced that there is no safe exposure level for carcinogenic substances in man, the principle of the Delaney Amendment remains sound.

The fact that the Surgeon General's Committee feels that food should be free of all avoidable carcinogenic chemicals while the National Academy of Science's Food Protection Committee feels there are "insignificant" levels of carcinogens which may be permitted needs some explanation. First let us look at the membership of the committees. The committee which reported to the Surgeon General was made up of eight scientists, four from the National Institutes of Health and four from the academic community. Its chairman was Dr. Umberto Saffiotti, Associate Scientific Director for Carcinogenesis of the National Cancer Institute. It was financed by government funds.

The NAS-NRC Food Protection Committee was made up of nine scientists, three of whom were employed by chemical companies and two by food companies. Its chairman was Dr. William J. Darby, a Vanderbilt University nutritionist who is also President of the Nutrition Foundation, an industry-financed research and educational institution.* The Food Protection Commit-

* In 1962–1963, Dr. Darby led the attack on Rachel Carson's *Silent Spring*. His views were widely distributed by the chemical industry. In 1962 and 1964, he received awards from the Nutrition Foundation, at a time when fifteen of seventeen members of its Board of Directors were industry representatives. For Dr. Darby's attack on Rachel Carson, see Chapter 10.

tee, although part of the National Academy of Sciences, is, according to an NAS pamphlet, "independently financed by grants from food, chemical, and packaging companies, commercial laboratories, and individuals."

The men on both committees are established scientists, but differences in their professional backgrounds perhaps unconsciously led them to different conceptions of risk. The industry-based majority on the Food Protection Committee came from a professional community whose *raison d'être* in part is their ability to persuade FDA that chemicals which their companies want to add to food are safe. Only a few may ever deliberately "cook the books" to mislead FDA, but the very nature of their task may instill a bias to give the chemical the benefit of the doubt.

The majority of the Saffiotti committee was made up of men actively engaged in research on the cause and prevention of cancer. They too may have a professional bias which leads them occasionally to err on the side of caution. They may well be less sensitive to the economic benefits of a food chemical than they are to its potential hazards.

The top administrators in FDA are caught somewhere in the middle. Some, like Dr. Virgil Wodicka, are former food industry executives (Hunt-Wesson), others have a government or university background. They are also subject to a number of extraneous pressures. Many food additive decisions become politically charged, as were those on cyclamates and monosodium glutamate. In those issues, two of President Nixon's key supporters in the business community, Don Kendall of Pepsi-Cola and Murphy of Campbell Soups, allegedly worked behind the scenes in the White House to influence FDA policy. There are presently rumors in FDA's lower echelons that the White House has instructed Commissioner Edwards to stand firm on DES. Whether or not this is true, the fact that many FDA scientists think it's true is significant.

Another vector of influence, is the appropriations committee. Congressman Jamie Whitten (D.-Miss.), Chairman of the House appropriations subcommittee which approves FDA's budget, is an avowed advocate of pesticides and has a rather naive "show me the victims"

attitude toward the potential hazards of chemical resi-
dues in food. With its control of the pursestrings,
Whitten's subcommittee has more leverage over FDA
than the more publicized investigating subcommittees of
Congressmen Paul Rogers (D.-Fla.) and L. H. Fountain
(D.-N.C.).

Finally, the organized daily pressure from the meat
and other food industries, their trade associations, and
research foundations, like waves against chalk cliffs,
may eventually erode the objectivity of most deter-
minedly independent administrators. In delicate decisions where risk is suspected but not proved, this
presence can make the difference. If the agency in
restricting a chemical errs on the side of caution, the
industry can quantify the error in terms of a dollar and
cents economic loss. If the agency in approving a
chemical errs on the side of risk, even the most out-
rageous result, for example a two or three thousand
increase in the number of cancer victims ten or fifteen
years later, will probably never be discovered, or if
discovered, could not be traced back to its decision.

Regulatory officials, therefore, need informed public
support if they are to keep the cancer risks of this and
future generations to a minimum. Unfortunately FDA
and USDA seem wedded to a public relations posture
whose motto is "ignorance is bliss." This view was well
summarized in testimony by FDA Commissioner
Edwards before the Senate Appropriations Committee
on May 13, 1971:

We can't deluge the public with scare items based on our
suspicions. We can't caution the public that there might be
something wrong with a product in rare instances or that
use of a product should be restricted, because public reaction
is always an over-reaction. The pendulum swings too far in
most cases, and consumers tend to boycott a product if any
doubts have been raised about it, even though we might
feel that continued use within certain limits is entirely
justified.*

* Edwards' fear of public hysteria was revealed on another occasion.
During Congressional hearings on DES, Edwards was asked why
FDA had not promptly warned young women whose mothers might
have taken DES during pregnancy that they should get a medical
examination. Edwards replied that the agency had to be careful "not
to create an emotional crisis on the part of American women. . . ."

Apart from the straw men created and destroyed by this statement—no one wants to deluge the public with "scare" items—its prejudice against an informed public has pernicious consequences for the regulatory system. Congress, not the food agencies, must decide how much risk the public will tolerate and how much money will be spent to make food safer. It is contradictory in the extreme for Commissioner Edwards and other officials in FDA and USDA to point to inadequate laboratory equipment and staff shortages to excuse their failures, when they keep the public in the dark about the potential hazards of food contaminants.

It is clearly time that decisions about DES, nitrosamines, and other carcinogens in food be taken away from the animal health specialists and service agencies of agribusiness in FDA and USDA. There are no panaceas to ease the burdens of such decisions, but the creation of an independent food safety agency,* combining the inspection functions of USDA and FDA, is one reform that has obvious merit. Second, the National Cancer Institute or other appropriate public health body should be given an equal voice in food or feed additive decisions which may increase human exposure to carcinogens. Such an agency will still have to act on incomplete information, but it will be less likely to make the burden of uncertainty fall on the consumer.

For the first time in his evolutionary history, man is being exposed in an exponential fashion to a large number of synthetic chemicals whose long-term effect is still largely conjecture. But while our knowledge of the effects of particular substances, such as nitrites, DES, and antibiotics is, to say the least, imperfect, we can no longer plead ignorance about the fact that we are taking significant risks in the increasing chemicalization of our technology. These risks are bound to increase geometrically as more substances are introduced, but the record suggests that our governmental institutions are not now capable of ensuring that benefits and costs are kept in some reasonable balance. In short, we are not masters of this technology. Our technological reach has exceeded our institutional grasp and the gap is widening all the time.

* See conclusion for discussion of this proposal.

While food and feed additives are important, the greatest source of chemical contaminants in man's environment is probably pesticides. In the second part of this study, the spotlight is on the risks, benefits, and regulatory politics of these chemicals, but the theme remains the same: how to keep safety criteria in step with escalating technological risk.

7

Six Mice in a Cage: Long-Term Hazards and 2,4,5-T

There is now little doubt that many diseases hitherto regarded as spontaneous, including cancer, birth defects, and mutations, are caused by environmental pollutants. This realization is heightened by the exponential increase in human exposure to new synthetic chemicals . . . which in general are inadequately characterized toxicologically and environmentally.

> —Dr. Samuel S. Epstein
> Environmental Toxicologist,
> Children's Cancer Research Foundation

Six mice in a cage! Twenty-five years of use without hurting anybody, and it all counts for nothing against six mice in a cage.

> —Plant physiologist at the
> Pesticides Regulations Division,
> commenting on the fact that the herbicide
> 2,4,5-T causes birth defects in test animals.

For federal regulators confronting the challenge of chemical technology, it is a short step from hormones, antibiotics, nitrites, and other hidden ingredients in meat and poultry to insecticides and herbicides, some of which get into food as hidden ingredients, others of

which remain hidden in the environment. The following chapters focus on the regulatory politics of pesticide control, the challenge of technological assessment
in the chemical field, and the corporate responsibility
and accountability of the pesticide makers. While
this study will be concerned throughout with the
economic benefits as well as the risks of these chemicals, it begins with first things first: the hazards of
pesticides to man. The next chapter will discuss the
hazards to farmers, farm workers, and others who
come into direct contact with acutely toxic pesticides.
This chapter will discuss the possible long-term hazards to the general population from chronic exposure
to pesticide contaminants in the environment. The
herbicide 2,4,5-T, the first pesticide to be restricted
because it may cause birth defects, is discussed as an
illustrative case.

At the 1971 annual meeting of the American Association for the Advancement of Science, a symposium
attempted to rank nineteen major environmental
stresses as to their potential risks for man and the
ecosystem. According to Dr. Howard Reiquan of the
Battelle Memorial Institute, who invented the rating
system, each environmental threat was scored according to the persistence, range, and complexity of its
hazards. At the top of the list stood pesticides with a
score of 140, followed by heavy metals such as mercury (90), carbon dioxide (75), sulphur dioxide (72),
air particulates (72), oil spills (48), waterborne industrial wastes (48), all the way down to noise with a
rating of only 4. The key characteristic of pesticides
which earned their high rating was the persistence and
omnipresence of their residues in food, water, and air.

These residues create long-term hazards for man,
chiefly in the form of potential impact on the incidence of birth defects, cancer, and mutations. While
there is no conclusive clinical evidence linking pesticides now in use to these effects, the fact that some
pesticides cause cancer and birth defects in experimental mammals has caused concern. As amazing as it
seems now, for the first two decades of heavy pesticide use in this country, federal regulators in FDA and
USDA were largely unaware that pesticides might

have these effects. They focused instead on acute toxicity, the short-term effects on man of extremely heavy exposure to pesticides from farm accidents, ingestion by children, and the like. These immediate poisoning effects were studied by traditional toxicologists who generally had little interest or competence in carcinogenesis or teratogenesis, the studies of the causes of cancer and birth defects respectively. Birth defects, cancer, and mutations were the province of different, nonconverging scientific disciplines, concerned with the long-term effects of chronic exposure to small doses of a chemical, not one-time instances of acute poisoning. These geneticists, microbiologists and teratologists were not involved in pesticide policy. A time-lag developed between toxicology and developments in these fields, which discouraged exploration of new routes to safety evaluation.

For the toxicologists charged with protecting the public against dangerous chemicals, the short-term hazards of acutely toxic pesticides such as the organophosphate parathion have one virtue—they are very difficult to ignore. Parathion poisoning affects a specific group of victims and it does not prolong the agony—its often fatal effects are immediate and therefore usually identifiable as to source. And, if caught in time, human illness caused by low doses of organophosphates is usually reversible.

The situation is very different for the long-term hazards of pesticides. Unlike parathion poisoning, cancer and birth defects are separated from their causes by time. Cancer, for example, may develop fifteen years or more after first exposure to a carcinogen; a chemically induced birth defect or mutation may not show up for months or years. Moreover, there is usually nothing in the tumor or birth defect itself to link it to a chemical or any specific cause. If pesticides did cause these effects, they could be identified only by extrapolations from tests on laboratory animals. Until the mid-sixties, pesticide regulators, guided by traditional toxicology, saw no need to ask the chemical industry to conduct such tests.

In 1969, the Secretary's Commission on Pesticides and their Relationship to Environmental Health (the

Mrak Commission), a panel of distinguished scientists appointed by the Secretary of Health, Education, and Welfare, surveyed the available research on the long-term effects of pesticides and concluded that important potential hazards had been overlooked. The Commission identified thirteen pesticides, including DDT, Aldrin, Dieldrin, and mirex, as potential carcinogens and seven pesticides, including 2,4,5-T, mercury fungicides, and Captan, as potential teratogens (causes of birth defects).

The impact of these reports was heightened by mounting evidence of human exposure to a wide variety of pesticide pollutants in the environment. The Mrak Commission noted that the individual is exposed to pesticide residues in the food and water he ingests and the air he breathes; that he may be further exposed to contaminants from aerosols and no-pest strips in his home; that factory and farm workers chronically inhale or absorb pesticides through their skin. The Commission found that in many instances pesticides account for the highest level of foreign material present in fatty tissue and perhaps in the liver of man.[1] The Mrak panel concluded:

To sum up, the field of pesticide toxicology exemplifies the absurdity of a situation in which 200 million Americans are undergoing life-long exposure, yet our knowledge of what is happening to them is at best fragmentary and for the most part indirect and inferential.[2]

These hazards have been neglected so long because they are usually traceable only in the laboratory, not in the environment. The complexity of the detective work necessary to detect a teratogenic or carcinogenic chemical is illustrated by the tragic incident which forced the government to re-evaluate chemical hazards in 1964.

Detection

Between 1957 and 1962, dozens of doctors in Western Europe were faced with the ultimate obstetrical horror: the birth of infants with alert and normal minds imprisoned in grotesquely misshapen bodies. These children were born without arms or legs, or with vestigial stumps where their limbs were supposed to be. For five years, as the number of children afflicted reached 5,000, the cause of these bizarre defects remained unknown despite a massive international investigation. Yet, ironically, if the children's trauma had not been so catastrophically unique, there would probably have been no investigation at all. Common birth defects, such as cleft palates, defective kidneys or other organs, and brain damage have many causes. In such cases doctors despair of isolating a specific cause for a specific defect in a child. But in this case the children were afflicted with malformations rarely seen. As with the rare vaginal tumors in the DES affair, a single common cause was highly likely.

The infants' doctors searched desperately for clues in their mothers' medical histories, diets, and habits. In 1962, alert investigators in West Germany found the common factor they were looking for: many of the mothers, it appeared, had taken a new sleeping pill containing the drug thalidomide during the first few weeks of pregnancy. The doctors did not know how the drug might affect the development of the fetus. All they had to go on was a statistical pattern in the mothers' medical histories. These first clues were followed up with a thorough study of all the mothers of these crippled children and with tests of the drug on animals.

The animal tests were somewhat disappointing. The drug did not cause birth defects in two species of test animals; it was a mild teratogen in some other species but only at relatively high doses, far higher than the mothers received (as it turned out, human beings were far more sensitive to the drug than the test animals). The statistical surveys were more conclusive: virtually all of the mothers investigated had taken thalidomide during the weeks of pregnancy when the fetus is developing its arms and legs.

Causality in the strict sense was still not established. Thalidomide's metabolic pathway to the fetus remained uncharted, but the statistical correlations could not be ignored. In the end, the doctors came to see thalidomide's grotesque deformities as a kind of blessing.

Given the inconclusiveness of the animal tests, if
thalidomide had caused a common and therefore un-
traceable birth defect it would now be considered one
of our safest drugs.[3]

Thalidomide showed that some synthetic chemicals
hitherto regarded as safe may increase the rate of
birth defects in the human population. It also rang the
tocsin around the world warning scientists about the
potential effects of other chemicals on birth defects and
cancer and mutations as well. Those hazards could no
longer be ignored. The President's Science Advisory
Committee in 1963 responded by recommending a
large-scale safety screening program for pesticides
and other industrial chemicals. This led the National
Cancer Institute to commission the Bionetics Laboratory, a private firm, to perform these tests in 1964.
The results of the tests, showing that pesticides could
cause cancer and birth defects in test animals, were
studied by the Mrak Commission in 1969, and led it to
recommend sweeping restrictions on a number of key
pesticides.

One year later, the warnings of the Mrak panel were
reiterated by another panel of scientists who linked the
occurrence of cancer to environmental pollutants, including pesticides. The Ad Hoc Committee on the
Evaluation of Chemical Carcinogens in the Environment reported to the Surgeon General in 1970:

The types of cancer in man that are due directly or indirectly to extrinsic [environmental] factors are thought to
account for a large percentage of the total cancer incidents.
During the past decade considerable progress has been made
in the detection of carcinogenic agents and the analysis of
their biological effects. . . . It is estimated, therefore, that
the majority of human cancers are potentially preventable.[4]

With birth defects, there are equivalent risks and opportunities for prevention. About one out of seven
pregnancies fails to produce a living child.[5] Approximately 250,000 children, nearly 6 percent of all live
births, are born each year with significant birth defects.
The National Foundation March of Dimes arrived at this
estimate in the late 1950s. Later studies, using more
sophisticated techniques, find an even higher incidence.

A recent study of 4,000 seemingly normal newborns in Madison, Wisconsin, showed that 14.1 percent had minor defects.[6] The social costs of birth defects are tragically high. The financial burden of one severely retarded child, computed on the basis of specialized training and custodial care alone, approximates $250,-000.[7] In the case of babies with thalidomide-like defects, the costs are very much higher, as much as $500,000 in many cases. (The manufacturers of thalidomide, after years of haggling during which they paid nothing, recently settled their account with the afflicted children for $10,000 each.)

The extent to which chemical contaminants and especially pesticide residues account for this toll is not known. Aside from mercury, which is used in some fungicides, no pesticide chemical has been conclusively linked to a human birth defect. Nevertheless, the teratogenicity panel of the Mrak Commission concluded:

Pesticides may represent an important potential teratogenic hazard. Therefore any teratogenic pesticide to which the population is exposed should be promptly identified so that appropriate precautions can be taken to prevent risk of human exposure.[8]

Even less is known about the effect of chemical residues from pesticides on human genes. A report of the genetic study section of the National Institutes of Health states:

There is reason to fear that some chemicals may constitute as important a risk as radiation, possibly a more serious one. Although knowledge of chemical mutagenesis in man is much less certain than that of radiation, a number of chemicals—some with widespread use—are known to induce genetic damage in some organisms. To consider only radiation hazards is to ignore what may be the submerged part of the iceberg.[9]

A mutation is defined as any inherited change in the genetic material. Geneticists stress that most such alterations are harmful or at best neutral. Dr. Barton Childs of Johns Hopkins University recently reported to the Conference on Evaluation of the Mutagenicity of Drugs and Other Chemical Agents that between 4 and 20 percent of all conceptions have chromosome abnormalities and that 20 percent of the patients admitted to the pediatric service of the university hospital had chronic diseases in which the action of the genes was primary or very significant. It is further estimated that approximately 25 percent of spontaneous abortions are associated with chromosome abnormalities.[10] The effects of increased mutation rates are likely to pass unnoticed, for they will be spread over many generations and probably be expressed as increased susceptibility to disease, notably leukemia and cancer, premature aging, increased infertility, and other ill-defined maladies.[11]

There is no present requirement for mutagenic testing of pesticides and few pesticides have been screened for mutagenic effects. DDT and DDVP, the active ingredients in the Shell No-Pest Strip, have been found to be mutagenic in bacterial systems, but the human relevance of these tests has not been established. DDVP does not appear to be mutagenic in mammalian species.[12] The FDA's Advisory Committee on Protocols for Safety Evaluations has recommended that all new chemicals to which man is exposed be tested for mutagenic effects. FDA has failed to adopt this advice to date. At present, until new evidence is available, the mutagenic potential of pesticides remains a mystery. But it is at least another warning that unnecessary human exposure to pesticide residues should be avoided.

These potential risks of pesticide-induced cancer, birth defects, or possible mutations pose a dilemma for federal regulators of chemical technology. How are they to predict which chemicals are potentially dangerous? What degree of proof is necessary to establish that a health hazard exists? Who has the burden of proof? The Mrak Commission put these problems in perspective. It concluded that in approving new pesticides we should not add to the existing burden of teratogens, mutagens, or carcinogens in the environment, but that if the additional hazard represented by the compound is "in all probability trivial," we have a responsibility "to weigh those benefits conferred by use of the compound against the hazard that its presence in the environment represents."[13] This task is made more difficult by the fact that the pesticide regulators must balance a concrete economic benefit against a potential and often immeasurable hazard.

The most celebrated case in which the benefits of a pesticide were publicly weighed against its long-term risks to man as a teratogen involved the herbicide 2,4,5-T. It reveals a great deal about the politics as well as the scientific dilemmas facing federal officials who exercise this responsibility.

2,4,5-T

In the summer of 1969, four newspapers in Saigon, South Vietnam, published stories, reports, and photographs of deformed children born to mothers allegedly exposed to weed-killing chemicals which were sprayed from American warplanes. Premier Thieu, fearful of the anti-American feeling which such reports aroused, promptly banned the newspapers. Reporters who tried to follow up the story were met with silence from American officials in Saigon; and the few medical personnel interviewed had no information about the effects of defoliants on human populations. There were no investigations of the reports of deformed children.*

In July of the same summer, an FDA official gave Anita Johnson, a student at Boston University Law School who was working as an intern with the Center for Study of Responsive Law, a heretofore undisclosed document which proved that some government officials in the Defense Department and other federal agencies knew a great deal about the potential danger of these chemicals. This report, given to her by a concerned government scientist, was prepared by the Bionetics Laboratory under contract with the National Cancer Institute. It revealed that the weed-killer 2,4,5-T (2,4,5-Trichlorophenoxyacetic acid) caused a high rate of birth defects in laboratory mice. It also labeled as "potentially dangerous" the herbicide 2,4-D which is often mixed with 2,4,5-T for use in Vietnam

---

* These reports have never been confirmed. The results of the Herbicide Assessment Commission's investigation of 2,4,5-T effects in Vietnam are discussed later in this chapter.

and on pastures, food crops, waterways, and suburban back-yards in the United States. In the next six months, as the facts about 2,4,5-T gradually emerged, this report created a credibility crisis in the scientific community for the Nixon Administration and federal pesticide regulators. More important, for the first time, the government's and private industry's failure to anticipate the long-term risks of pesticides was thoroughly discussed in Congress and in the press.

Herbicides are the fastest growing and most profitable branch of the pesticide industry. Sales have increased 271 percent between 1963 and 1969, double the rate of increase for all pesticides. It is estimated that annual herbicide use will cost $1.5 billion by 1975, a seven-fold increase in less than a decade. Yet very little is known about the impact of herbicides on the environment and human health.

2,4-D and 2,4,5-T belong to the family of polychlorinated phenolic compounds developed from chemical warfare research at Fort Dietrich, Maryland, during World War II. They are very sophisticated chemicals. When applied to a broadleaf plant, they quickly spread through the plant's system, causing its metabolism to accelerate at fantastic rates. The plant finally bursts open in a frenzy of growth. Although developed too late for military use, these herbicides were easily adapted for peacetime use to kill weeds on water, ditch-banks, forests, food crops, pastures, and back-yards.

2,4,5-T was first registered on March 2, 1948, by the Amchem Products Company of Ambler, Pennsylvania. By the end of the 1960s, it was being applied to approximately eight million acres annually. 2,4,5-T, therefore, was massively applied to American soil for nearly twenty years before anyone checked to see if it might cause birth defects, cancer, or other harm which did not immediately follow contact.

The Bionetics Laboratory studies of the long-term hazards of pesticides, commissioned in 1964 by the National Cancer Institute, should have provided an early warning of 2,4,5-T hazards, at least as far as its use in Vietnam was concerned. In the fall of 1966, the first test results were complete. In a contract report to the National Cancer Institute, Bionetics revealed that 2,4,5-T caused birth defects in laboratory mice. The Mrak Commission summarized these results three years later:

Tested more extensively than other pesticides, 2,4,5-T was clearly teratogenic as evidenced by statistically increased proportions of abnormal features . . . in particular, cleft palate and cystic kidneys were significantly more prevalent. . . . The incidence of fetuses with kidney anomalies was threefold that of the controls, even with the smallest dosage tested.[14]

This discovery came at a critical time for the manufacturers of 2,4,5-T, principally the Dow Chemical Company. Domestic herbicide sales had just begun to take off in the early 1960s. Most significant, a vast new market had opened up in Vietnam, where the Pentagon used 2,4,5-T as a defoliant. Specially adapted war planes spewed tons of 2,4,5-T and other herbicides over South Vietnam (often over populated areas) to remove ambush cover and disclose enemy troop movements. This use reached its peak in 1967, a year after the first Bionetics results were obtained. 2,4,5-T was ultimately sprayed on one-eighth of the total area of South Vietnam.[15]

The Bionetics discovery, coming so soon after the thalidomide tragedy, had alarming implications, for thousands of people in the United States and Vietnam were exposed daily to 2,4,5-T. Yet the knowledge of the herbicide's birth-defect risks had no immediate effect on policy. Instead of presenting the Bionetics results for review and comment by the scientific community, the government clamped a policy of strict secrecy on the report. No results were published, no outside scientific comment was solicited. In fact, the results were concealed from other birth-defect specialists and the rest of the scientific community for over three years. Key officials in the FDA in 1968 and in the USDA and Department of Defense early in 1969 were informed, however. In all this time, they took no steps whatever to minimize human exposure. As late as August, 1969, Dr. Samuel Epstein was initially rebuffed by the FDA when he sought the full Bionetics report for use by the teratogenicity panel of the Mrak Commission, an *official* committee specifically authorized to study pesticide hazards for the Secretary of HEW. It was finally made available when the chairman threatened to dissolve the panel and go home.[16]

There are many conflicting views as to why the Bionetics Report was suppressed. A former White House staffer suggested that the report, if released earlier, would have added fuel to the antiwar movement, already critical of the defoliation program in Vietnam. It might also have increased international criticism of the American government's use of chemical warfare in Vietnam. Scientists in the FDA conceded that the war might be a factor but felt that protests from the chemical industry, particularly Dow Chemical Company, were more influential.*

Dr. Edward Burger, deputy to Dr. Lee Dubridge, the President's Science Advisor in 1970, had another explanation for the delay which gives an additional insight into pesticide regulation. In retrospect, he condemned the delay but urged us to remember how unprecedented the Bionetics study was. He points out that the regulatory procedures for pesticides are designed to deal with industry test data, not outside studies financed by the government. There are standard operating procedures in the Pesticides Regulation Division for reviewing industry data but there were no official points of access to the regulatory process for independent research at this time.** As far as the pesticide regulators were concerned, the 2,4,5-T producers had met their burden of proof as to safety when the product was originally registered. In the absence of demonstrable victims of herbicide poisoning, they felt no need to require further data—even though the early tests focused only on *acute* toxicity, *i.e.*, the

* Questions by some scientists about the methodology of the Bionetics study did not offer a wholly credible reason for withholding the report. The most efficient way to test the report's scientific competence was to expose it to the rigor of scientific debate, not sequester it in the bureaucracy.
** The Environmental Protection Agency in January, 1972, with certain exceptions, opened its files of industry data to the public and requested comments from outside scientists.

herbicide's immediate effects as a poison, not on possible long-term effects such as birth defects. In other words, the report fell between the cracks of bureaucratic routines geared to short-term hazards and industry data.

The Ban

At the end of the summer of 1969, Anita Johnson took a step which ensured that the Bionetics findings would no longer remain hidden from the public. She made the report available to Professor Matthew Meselson, a leading geneticist at Harvard University who was interested in unconfirmed reports of an unusual number of birth defects in Vietnam, allegedly connected with chemical defoliation. Dr. Meselson had not previously heard of the Bionetics findings. He now tried to obtain a copy of the final report, but was told that it was "confidential and classified" and inaccessible to outsiders.[17] In this exclusion, Meselson was not alone. Dr. Fred Tschirlev, USDA's leading herbicide expert, had not heard of the report at this time, nor had key officials in the Food Toxicology Branch of the FDA.

In October, Dr. Meselson traveled to Washington and discussed the need for action to restrict 2,4,5-T with a number of government officials, particularly Dr. Lee Dubridge, the President's Science Advisor. On October 29, 1969, Dr. Dubridge finally brought the 2,4,5-T controversy into the open when he announced that the government would restrict federal use of the herbicide in populated areas and all uses on food crops. His action was prompted by the complaints and inquiries of a number of scientists, especially Dr. Meselson.

This action by Dubridge, apparently made with the support of the President but without prior approval from USDA or FDA, had two fatal weaknesses. First, because he erroneously estimated that "almost none (of 2,4,5-T) is used by home gardeners, or in residential areas," Dubridge did nothing to stop the sale of 2,4,5-T for use in residential back-yards, where pregnant women and small children were most likely to be exposed. Second, Dubridge soon found that his "ban" was totally ignored by FDA, USDA, and DOD.

When Dr. Dubridge tried to bring the agencies into line, he received a bitter lesson in bureaucratic politics. Without strong Presidential pressure, the old line departments were not likely to take orders from a science advisor; but when Dubridge leaned on his White House support, he fell on his face. The President decided not to buck the departments, and the October 29 ban fell apart.

On February 6, the Department of Agriculture found a face-saving reason for its inaction. It announced findings by Dow Chemical Company that the 2,4,5-T used in the Bionetics test was highly contaminated with an extremely toxic substance identified as 2,3,7,8-tetrachloro-dibenzo-p-dioxin (hereafter TCDD). Dow claimed that tests with a purer 2,4,5-T of its own make produced no adverse effects in test animals.

In retrospect it is remarkable that USDA used this discovery as justification for ignoring Dubridge's order, for TCDD, one of the most toxic substances known, is *invariably* found in 2,4,5-T. Even Dow's "purest" 2,4,5-T had up to 1 ppm TCDD.

TCDD is roughly 700 times as toxic as parathion in the female rat (a few drops of undiluted parathion on the human skin may be fatal) and over 10,000 times as toxic as parathion in the female guinea pig. In terms of its toxicity, TCDD is closer to nerve gas than to pesticides. It rivals the botulism toxin as a hazard to man.[18]

TCDD is also a powerful inducer of birth defects in test animals. In tests on chicks and hamsters, it proved to be 100,000 to 1,000,000 times more potent as a fetus deforming agent than thalidomide. The Surgeon General has described TCDD as a very potent teratogen in mice at dosages 10,000 to 300,000 times smaller than the "no-effect level" of 2,4,5-T.

Moreover, there was readily available clinical evidence that TCDD was harmful to human beings. Dow Chemical Company had been forced to close one of its plants in Midland Michigan, when TCDD caused a serious disfiguring skin disease known as chloracne in workers.[19] Most disturbing was what was *not* known about TCDD.

Even such basic facts as how persistent it was in the environment, whether it accumulated in human tissue like DDT, and how much was present in the various formulations of 2,4,5-T on the market remained a mystery. No safe level of human exposure to this compound had been determined.

Nevertheless, USDA seized on the "unknowns" of the mystery compound to give the chemical companies the benefit of the doubt. Until further tests were conducted, no efforts would be made to minimize human exposure. The burden of proof in challenging the safety of this chemical remained with the public.

In the meantime, the National Institute of Environmental Health Sciences (NIEHS) and FDA were carrying out experiments designed to replicate the Bionetics study and to determine whether "pure" 2,4,5-T—essentially free of TCDD—was itself teratogenic. In striking contrast to the Dow studies,[20] NIEHS found that 2,4,5-T (in the purest form available) produced birth defects and increased fetal toxicity in mice, rats, and hamsters.[21]

These tests proved highly embarrassing for USDA. On April 7, 1970, its representatives, relying on the Dow tests, had defended the safety of 2,4,5-T and opposed any restriction on its use in hearings before Senator Philip Hart's Subcommittee on Energy, Natural Resources and the Environment; on April 15, however, the Secretary of Agriculture was notified by the Surgeon General that the NIEHS studies had confirmed that 2,4,5-T is teratogenic. USDA then made an abrupt about-face. In a joint statement with the Secretary of HEW, the Secretary of Agriculture announced that he was immediately banning as an "imminent danger" to public health the use of liquid formulations of 2,4,5-T around the home and all uses in lakes, ponds, and ditch-banks. USDA, however, failed to ban the other 90% of 2,4,5-T's uses. As a result, 2,4,5-T could be freely used on food crops pending outcome of lengthy cancellation proceedings. Nearly two years later, in March, 1972, these proceedings still continue, while approximately 90 percent of 2,4,5-T sales remain unrestricted.

In the next two years, as the government was challenged by the chemical companies for going too far and

by environmentalists for not going far enough, 2,4,5-T
became the Dreyfus case of the pesticide industry. Judging from the bitter public debate by scientists on different sides of the issue, it was clear that much more was
at stake than the fate of a single herbicide. The federal
government's top scientific advisors and consultants were
pitted against one another on this issue.

Both the President's Science Advisor and the Surgeon
General of the United States had endorsed the limited
action against 2,4,5-T. On the other hand, Dr. Emil
Mrak, Chairman of the Secretary's Pesticide Advisory
Committee in HEW and a leading pesticide consultant,
told the National Agricultural Chemical Association at
its annual meeting in September, 1970, that "2,4,5-T
has been the victim of a panic-button operation."[22] Mrak
even proposed that a National Center for Reliable Information be established to investigate, among other
things, "any responsibilities or irresponsibilities that may
have been involved in this unfortunate occurrence."[23]
Mrak was supported by the Weed Science Society of
America, which has labeled the proposed ban "sensa-
tionalist" and "alarmist." On the other side, the American Association for the Advancement of Science, spurred
by Dr. Meselson, created a Herbicide Assessment Commission to study the impact of 2,4,5-T on the human
health and ecology of Vietnam. The commission supports restrictions of 2,4,5-T uses where human exposure
is likely.

The Philosophy of Risk

The significance of the 2,4,5-T case transcends its economic utility and possibly even its potential health effects. 2,4,5-T has become a battleground of opposing
philosophies about the relationship between technological risk and human safety. Arrayed on one side (with
some notable exceptions) are typically the technocrats
of agribusiness—the classical toxicologists, food tech-
nologists and agrichemical engineers—who are trained
to look for the short-term effects of pesticides both in
their impact on the human body and on the pests in
the fields. On the other side are typically the microbiologists and geneticists, the specialists in the causes

of cancer, birth defects, and mutations, who are professionally concerned with the long-term effects of chemical contaminants on human health.* At stake is the question of who is to set the standards upon which the safety of a pesticide (or any chemical) is to be judged.

When a question is raised about the safety of a pesticide, the traditional toxicologists have a predictable set of responses. They tend to argue that a pesticide should not be restricted until proven harmful in man and they place the burden of proof on consumers and environmentalists who object to a pesticide, not on the producer who markets it.

The traditionalists also tend to discredit the significance of animal tests as predictors of human hazards. Dr. Leon Golberg, who has been a member of the Mrak Commission and EPA's top advisory committee on pesticides, is a widely quoted spokesman for this view. Dr. Golberg stresses that the human significance of birth defects or cancer in animal tests is burdened with great uncertainty, and cites the extreme sensitivity of test animals to all kinds of non-specific stress in the laboratory. According to Golberg "it is safe to predict that, by appropriate choice of dose, concentration of solution, and frequency of administration of the subcutaneous route, any chemical agent can be shown to be a carcinogen in the rat and probably also in other species of laboratory rodent." Golberg points out that birth defects have been produced by feeding mice a diet of raisins for one day, transporting of mice by air on the 12th and 13th days of pregnancy, fasting, vitamin deficiency, and many other non-specific factors which cause stress on the pregnant female. "Even subcutaneous sodium chloride [table salt] is teratogenic in mice," he notes. Golberg further states:

On the other hand, should it happen that a chemical agent turns out negative in all the tests applied, it remains under suspicion until such time as someone can discover an organism, devise a route of administration or achieve a sufficiently heroic dose to produce some positive biological result, however bizarre. Thus there is an obvious premium on in-

---

* These categories are only rough approximations. Dr. Leon Golberg, for example, a well-known microbiologist at the Albany Medical College, is a leading defender of 2,4,5-T.

genuity and persistence. Carried to their logical conclusion, these considerations of carcinogenesis, teratogenesis, and mutagenesis strike at the very roots of technological advance in food production, processing, and distribution.[24]

Dr. Golberg, to a large degree, reflects the views of the Society of Toxicology and the Food Protection Committee of the National Academy of Science, the two chief establishment citadels of the traditionalist view of chemical hazards.

The Pesticide Regulation Division, for many years, has been a stronghold of this point of view, as expressed by Mr. T. T. McClure, a plant physiologist on PRD's herbicide staff. "Six mice in a cage," he complained when asked about the limited ban on 2,4,5-T, "twenty-five years of use without harming anybody and it all counts for nothing against six mice in a cage,"[25] Dr. E. A. Walker, head of PRD's herbicide staff, declared: "I never saw a case of 2,4,5-T hurting anybody." And then he pulled out a copy of his speech to the Northeastern Weed Control Conference which asked the rhetorical question: "What would happen to agriculture if herbicide use was discontinued? *Job* 31:40 has the answer: Let thistles grow instead of wheat and foul weeds instead of barley."[26]

These attitudes—where skepticism about laboratory test results is matched by complacency about a lack of documented victims—are strongly criticized by scientists who tend to be associated with the National Cancer Institute, the Environmental Mutagen Society, and the American Association for the Advancement of Science. These scientists find little cause for complacency in the fact that it is generally impossible to prove that pesticides which cause birth defects in test animals can produce similar effects in human beings. First, they stress the magnitude of the risk involved when one increases the burden of any teratogenic agent in the environment. It is estimated that one-third of the beds in children's hospitals today are occupied by congenitally defective individuals; congenital disease is the third most common cause of death in the newborn, accounting for 14 percent of all infant deaths.[27] Yet there is a paucity of data available on birth defect trends and causes. Nationwide statistics on birth defects are so inadequate that even an increase of several thousand deformities could probably go undetected. Nationally no attempt has been made to collect and evaluate all the data on birth defects that are presently available on birth certificates. After careful study of this problem, the writers of the Mrak Report concluded that "epidemiologic data on possible effects of pesticides on human reproduction and teratology are grossly inadequate."[28]

Even if an increase in the incidence of birth defects were detected, it would be virtually impossible to trace an observed defect back to a specific pesticide. A single birth defect may have several causes.[29] As the Mrak Report notes, any one teratogen may produce a variety of birth defects and any one birth defect may be produced by a variety of teratogens.[30]

Tracing observed defects to a specific cause is even more difficult when the defect occurs commonly. In the case of 2,4,5-T, the typical defects produced in test animals are kidney abnormalities, cleft palates, and skeletal anomalies, none of which is unusual in human beings. (2,4,5-T would not, of course, necessarily produce the same effects in man as in animals.) Had thalidomide produced such ordinary malformations, it may never have been implicated as a teratogen.

For these reasons, the Mrak Report states unequivocally that there is little hope that studies of hospital records, doctors' reports, and other epidemiological data could discover a pesticide which causes birth defects. It states that no major known human teratogen, such as X-rays, German measles, mercury, and thalidomide, has been discovered in this way.[31] Moreover, these surveys, even if effective, would still be retrospective, detecting a chemical only after its damage had been done. It is therefore irresponsible and unscientific to deduce the safety of a teratogenic pesticide from an absence of demonstrable human victims.

How then can regulators predict the birth defect potential of a pesticide? It would be neither moral nor practical to test large numbers of human beings with a pesticide found to cause birth defects in laboratory animals. We are therefore left with tests on animals as the only feasible method for screening chemicals for potentially harmful effects. One should not minimize the difficulty of drawing policy conclusions from these tests. Not only may the same chemical cause different effects in different animals, but the reaction becomes even more unpredictable when we compare animals to man. Ideally one would hope to select an animal species which metabolizes a chemical the same way that humans do, but this is not easily done. For example, dogs and monkeys are much closer to the human animal than rodents, but because of the latter's low cost and convenience as laboratory animals, rodents are the favorite experimental species.[32]

Despite these problems, the value of animal tests for anticipating hazards to man is widely recognized. The Surgeon General's Ad Hoc Committee on the Environmental Carcinogens reported in 1970:

Timely decision to exclude [chemical] materials from uses involving exposure to man, therefore, must be based solely on adequately conducted animal bioassays. Retrospective human evidence of risk must not be allowed to show itself before controlling action is taken.[33]

The Saffiotti committee was speaking specifically of carcinogens but the basis for its statement—the failure of other methods to detect carcinogens compounded by the latency period between exposure and human effect —also applies to teratogens.

The Mrak Commission concluded that "the use of currently registered pesticides to which humans are exposed and which are found to be teratogenic (fetus deforming) by suitable test procedures in one or more mammalian species should be immediately restricted to prevent risk of human exposure."[34] The National Foundation March of Dimes warns:

Nothing whatsoever of unknown toxicity should be introduced into the environment, either as a pesticide, herbicide, defoliant. . . . The teratogenic effect is the vital key. Any agent found to be . . . teratogenic in test animals should be excluded from public use.[35]

Controversy enters when regulators try to determine if human beings may be safely exposed to a pesticide which causes birth defects or cancer in these animal tests. Here fallacies abound. The most common fallacy, which was heavily promoted by soft drink manufacturers in the cyclamate case, is that all chemicals, even salt and pepper, may produce cancer or birth defects in test animals at the high doses commonly used in screening experiments. No human being, they complained, could possibly ingest a chemical in the amount the animals received.

This argument is very misleading. Dr. Golberg, who is often quoted by the chemical industry as a source for this view, directs his skepticism primarily to tests where chemicals are administered subcutaneously, through repeated injections under the skin.[36] The chemical companies neglect this qualification, and fail to mention that chemicals administered to the test animals orally, as human beings are likely to receive them, have given much more reliable results. The Bionetics Laboratory tested 140 pesticides in mice at the highest doses they could survive, administered both subcutaneously and orally, and found less than 10 percent to cause cancer. It screened 48 pesticides for birth defects in the same manner and found only seven to be teratogenic.[37] The tests, therefore, were highly selective. Even with maximally tolerated doses, they exonerated the great majority of chemicals tested.

The complaints about high doses are also misleading. As any textbook on teratology will show, it is a recognized procedure to give test animals doses of pesticides far higher than man would naturally receive.[38] The need for high dose levels derives from elementary statistics. Only a small number of animals are tested to indicate the effect of a pesticide on millions of people. Usually only fifty or so animals are tested per dose level of pesticide. Even if a given dose of pesticide produced equivalent effects in man and rats, it would be blind luck if a fifty-rat test discovered a teratogenic pesticide which affected only 1 in 100 pregnant women. Yet a pesticide with this impact would be a catastrophe. By using doses greatly in excess of expected human exposure, scientists increase the chance that a dangerous chemical will reveal itself in the limited test sample.

These dose levels also compensate for the fact that the test species may be either more or less sensitive than man to a given pesticide. Human beings were 60 times more sensitive to thalidomide than mice, 100 times more sensitive than rats, and 200 times more sensitive than dogs. It is perilous, therefore, to predict "safe" levels for man of a teratogenic chemical based on "no effect" levels of the chemical in animal tests.[39] 2,4,5-T may be a case in point. Almost all toxicity and teratogenic tests with 2,4,5-T have been conducted on rodents, although dogs, an animal much closer to man, are 5 times more sensitive to 2,4,5-T's toxic effects than rats or mice.[40]

Animal tests, to be sure, will never be able to tell us how many human beings, if any, will be affected by exposure to low doses of a teratogenic pesticide, but they do provide the best early warning system we have. Dr. Joshua Lederberg, a Nobel Prize winning geneticist at Stanford, warns the skeptics among the traditional toxicologists not to allow the scientific uncertainties about the human effects of chemical exposure to confuse the question of what constitutes a significant hazard. Lederberg warns:

We must not confuse "experimentally unmeasurable" with "insignificant" . . . . An additive that eventually caused one per thousand cases of bladder cancer after a decade of human exposure would be a catastrophe. But it would probably be unmeasurable with present methods of analysis. We have no recourse but to extrapolate from animal tests to the human situation.[41]

For these reasons, the manufacturer of a pesticide which causes cancer or birth defects in test animals must carry a heavy burden of proof in establishing its safety. As the Surgeon General's ad hoc committee on environmental carcinogens put it, "chemicals should be subject to scientific scrutiny rather than given individual rights; they must be considered potentially 'guilty' unless and until proven innocent."[42] But while at first glance they appear high scientific, the questions about the effects of chemical contaminants on human health, like so many other conflicts between technology and society, are really transscientific. For example, the 2,4,5-T case boils down to the public policy issue of weighing public health risks against economic benefits. The decision-maker, who must put the political, economic, social, medical, and scientific weights onto the scales, is in effect legislating risk levels for the public. In this delicate exercise, scientists are no more competent than anyone else. It is perhaps for this reason that Congress has made a political appointee, the Administrator of the Environmental Protection Administration, not a committee of the National Academy of Science, the final judge for all appeals on pesticide regulations.

It is no surprise, therefore, that the government's decision whether to lift, maintain, or extend the restrictions on 2,4,5-T took place in an adversary and often highly political setting. As we shall see, the 2,4,5-T debate provides a strong argument for the principle, expressed by a panel of the President's Science Advisory Committee in 1969, that "the public should not be asked to accept risks resulting from purely internal government decisions if, without endangering national security, the information can be made public and the decision can be reached after public discussion."[43]

The Outsiders vs. the Insiders

When the government delayed its decision on the fate of 2,4,5-T in 1970-71, more and more groups, both for and against the herbicide, entered the controversy. In December 1970, jurisdiction over the 2,4,5-T case was shifted from USDA to the new Environmental Protection Administration. By the summer of 1971, it had become the young agency's first crucial test.

In the past, pesticide policy decisions have been largely left up to the Pesticide Regulation Division and its science-advisory structure coordinated by the National Academy of Science. Since Rachel Carson, environmentalists have frequently questioned the confidentiality and objectivity of this advice. As the physicists Frank von Hippel and Joel Primack document in their book *The Politics of Technology*, the Federal Executive often used the science-advisory establishment to legitimize its decisions in the eyes of Congress and the public, while invoking the confidentiality of the advisory relationship as an excuse to conceal the technical bases for its decisions.[44]

Much of the drama and ultimate significance of the 2,4,5-T case is found in the efforts of environmentalists and outside scientists to break through this system and bring the weighing of public risks and benefits into the open. The first intervenor was a coalition of consumer and environmental groups who challenged in federal court USDA's refusal to take further action to restrict 2,4,5-T. On January 7, 1971, the Court of Appeals for the D.C. Circuit, in deciding the case of *Wellford vs. Ruckelshaus*, held that the Secretary of Agriculture in his denial had failed to assign sufficient importance to the risk of harm to human life. Specifically the court found that the government failed to consider the "risk of injury to farm workers or others who might be exposed to the chemical by virtue of its use on food crops." The court ordered EPA to reconsider the Secretary of Agriculture's refusal to suspend the uses of 2,4,5-T which risked human exposure.

On March 18, EPA announced that it would not suspend further uses of 2,4,5-T pending the decision of a science advisory panel convened to evaluate 2,4,5-T. This panel reported to William Ruckelshaus, Administrator of EPA, on May 7, 1971. In a surprise statement, the committee virtually gave 2,4,5-T a clean bill of health, even urging that the limited ban on 2,4,5-T around the home be lifted (the committee did concede that 2,4,5-T should be labeled "Do Not Use Around Pregnant Women"). The report was even more surprising because six weeks earlier, a panel of the President's Science Advisory Committee, having independently reviewed largely the same data, reported that there was a critical need for more information on the birth defect risks of 2,4,5-T, and on the extent of TCDD (dioxin) accumulation in food and the environment.[45] It therefore made no recommendations to remove existing restrictions on 2,4,5-T usage. As it turned out, the two committees differed less in their interpretation of the scientific data than on the political and moral question of whether the public should continue to be exposed to 2,4,5-T before the necessary additional experiments had been done.

The EPA advisory committee majority, put the following conditions on its recommendations: that residues of 2,4,5-T must be less than 0.1 ppm in food and drinking water; that future formulations of 2,4,5-T contain no more than 0.1 ppm of TCDD, but that existing stocks of 2,4,5-T with 0.5 ppm TCDD could be used up.[46]

The committee majority based its conclusions that 2,4,5-T is safe on two assumptions: that there exist some dosages of 2,4,5-T and TCDD, its dioxin contaminant, which do not produce deformities in animal fetuses and therefore are probably safe for man, and that it is "highly unlikely" and "virtually impossible" that residues above these "safe" levels could accumulate in the environment or human body, even when 2,4,5-T is used around the home, on water, and food crops. (Paradoxically the committee also recommended that research be undertaken immediately to remedy "existing deficiencies" in the data about possible accumulation of TCDD in food chains.)

In thus postulating the safety of 2,4,5-T, the committee majority was making a double leap of faith. First the committee discounted tests demonstrating that 2,4,5-T caused birth defects in test animals on the ground that the dosages used, circa 100 mg/kg, were too high. The committee then predicted that at some undefined lower level, 2,4,5-T would have no effect. The difficulty with this view is that it is just speculation. Virtually all the data available to the committee were derived from tests at the relatively high doses of 100 mg/kg or above. There was a critical shortage of experiments to show the effect of 2,4,5-T and TCDD at very low dose levels. In the few experiments where lower doses were used, the number of animals tested was too small to give a reliable estimate of the risk to the millions of persons potentially exposed to these chemicals.

The committee also ignored the possibility that human beings may be more sensitive to 2,4,5-T and TCDD than the rodents tested. In the opinion of Dr. Samuel Epstein, the claims by the committee that there are safe levels of 2,4,5-T are completely unsubstantiated.[47] Dr. Thomas Sterling, a statistician who was the lone dissenter to the committee report, notes that the data analyzed by the committee did not contain a *single* experiment on the effect of 2,4,5-T at very low doses. But despite this lack of reliable data, Sterling complained, the report "presumes to lecture the scientific community on the wisdom of instituting a 'permissible residue' of substances thought to be teratogenic."[48]

There is even less evidence to support the committee's speculation that TCDD does not accumulate in food chains. TCDD, as noted above, ranks second only to the botulism toxin as a poison.

The Herbicide Assessment Commission of the American Association for the Advancement of Science recently summarized the significance of TCDD as a potential hazard for man:

Its potential importance lies in the fact that it is exceedingly toxic, may be quite stable in the environment, and, being fat soluble, may be concentrated, as it moves up the food chain into the human diet.

The fact that residues of 2, 4, 5-T are relatively rare in food provides no assurance with regard to TCDD. Standard residue sampling devices which monitor pesticides in food are not sufficiently sensitive to detect TCDD at all levels at which it may be harmful. Neither the Slaughter Inspection Division of USDA nor the FDA's market basket survey check for TCDD in either beef or other foods. Production and application of 2,4,5-T in the United States continues to increase the burden of this highly toxic and virtually permanent contaminant in the environment. Moreover, 2,4,5-T also contains approximately 5 percent trichlorophenol impurities which, when burned, may produce more dioxins.[49] Dr. Sterling, in his minority report, concludes:

After recent experience with DDT and mercury, it would be reckless to leave such questions in abeyance while approving the unrestricted use of 2,4,5-T . . . . A great deal of damage may be created if the committee restores 2,4,5-T to its normal use while hoping that further research will justify our confidence in having made a correct guess.

The EPA advisory committee in effect gambled that future research would justify its contention that 2,4,5-T is safe. It may of course be right. The problem is that no one knows. In such uncertainty, the best reasonable men can do is to weigh the potential risks of the chemical against its present economic benefits. This, unfortunately, the committee failed to do. It did not consider any alternatives to present uses of 2,4,5-T (with the exception of some forest uses, 2,4,5-T has many substitutes) and neglected data prepared by USDA which show that the economic costs to domestic users of banning 2,5,5-T in 1969 would have been only $52 million, if other herbicides could still be used. This figure must be weighed against the incalculable costs to society if the herbicide increased the incidence of birth defects in the population.

The 2,4,5-T case may therefore be classified as low benefit–high risk. The use of 2,4,5-T for the growing of crops, especially rice, benefits a few farm industries by increasing the yield per acre of cultivated ground. Since there are many acres not now cultivated, no great hardship would result if 2,4,5-T were limited until doubts about its safety are settled.

Why did the EPA advisory committee fail so badly to produce a balanced report? For the answer, we must look at the way the committee was chosen. The scientific credentials of the committee are not in question. The problem is that no effort was made to ensure that the committee was not unduly biased either toward or against the pesticide industry's point of view or the environmentalists. The members were selected by USDA from a list of candidates prepared by the National Academy of Science. The members were screened for financial interests but the question of environmental or chemical industry biases never came up. As it turned out, all the members except Doctor Thomas Sterling, who wrote a scathing dissent, tended to come from one side of the philosophical divide about the long-term hazards described above. (Sterling apparently got on the committee because he had written a number of papers challenging the evidence linking cigarette smoking with cancer and USDA assumed that he would share the industry point of view on other issues as well.) Moreover, the list of witnesses who appeared before the committee is composed almost entirely of administrators, not active scientists. The committee chairmen declined to hear evidence from environmentalists, despite what one member recalls as a general agreement to hear environmentalist witnesses, as well as the petitioning manufacturers.

Despite the shortcomings of the report, it is highly likely that the committee's recommendations would have been accepted by EPA without review by any outside group but for a fortuitous circumstance. Here one must pause and recall the bureaucratic context in which EPA's decision was made.

At the time the 2,4,5-T case reached William Ruckelshaus's desk, his agency was barely six months old. It was still establishing its identity with environmentalists and the agricultural appropriations committees on Capitol Hill, which controlled its budget. Senator Ellender (D.-La.), chairman of the Senate Appropriations Committee, was a loud defender of 2,4,5-T, which is widely used by the sugar and rice farmers in his state. It is rumored among committee staffers that a major reason Ellender gave the agricultural subcommittee jurisdiction over EPA was to keep pesticide regulation out of the clutches of Senate environmentalists. Ruckelshaus would therefore have to pay serious political costs if he banned 2,4,5-T, particularly after it had been blessed by an official advisory committee.

Reinstatement of 2,4,5-T would alienate environmentalists, to be sure, but if Ruckelshaus took a tough stand on 2,4,5-T which he could not substantiate, precious credibility for his young organization among scientists and on Capitol Hill would be lost. He needed independent advice, but here was the rub. EPA's in-house pesticide review team, on which the administrator would have to lean heavily if he went against 2,4,5-T, was dominated by traditional toxicologists, holdovers from USDA and FDA, who were out of the same mold as the advisory committee majority. Dr. O. G. Fitzhugh, chairman of the group, failed to consult with other independent scientists in preparing his review of the committee report. He even failed to pass along to the Administrator briefs against 2,4,5-T previously prepared by environmentalists at EPA's request.

Similarly Ruckelshaus could expect little help from outsiders in advance of his decision. The advisory committee report, which would have aroused environmentalists and independent scientists, was traditionally kept confidential, to be revealed only after a decision, if at all. Few outsiders knew a major decision was imminent. Industry scientists, however, were on top of the issue. Earlier in the year, when EPA had asked for public comment on 2,4,5-T, the agency was deluged with replies. Chemical companies, public utilities (which use 2,4,5-T to clear rights of way), timber companies, paper mills, and a plethora of agribusiness interests presented several hundred lengthy briefs, prepared by staff scientists, arguing for the economic essentiality of 2,4,5-T. On the other side, to the best of this writer's knowledge, there were four comments from public interest groups and concerned citizens. There was not a single submission by a non-industry scientist or public health group. The reason is clear. The latter lack trade associations to sound the alarm when their interests are at stake and the money and staff resources to prepare a rapid response. Unlike the chemical companies, public interest groups cannot determine the priorities of their scientists. As a result, when Ruckelshaus weighs the risks and benefits of a pesticide decision, the benefits are frequently defined by the pressure of the pesticide's sponsors in agricultural and chemical industries.

Ruckelshaus would have had little choice but to clear 2,4,5-T, except for a chance occurrence. On July 14 the confidential advisory report was leaked to the staff of *Environment* magazine, who then circulated it to a group of environmentalists and independent scientists. The Committee for Environmental Information, publisher of *Environment*, and the Center for Study of Responsive Law then organized a press conference in Washington at which they severely criticized the advisory committee report. At the press conference, Dr. Samuel Epstein endorsed the critique and was supported by a number of prominent biologists, geneticists, and ecologists.* This group attacked the committee for its willingness to

* Barry Commoner, chairman of Scientist's Institute for Public Information; John Edsall, professor of biological chemistry, Harvard University; Arthur Galston, professor of biology, Yale University; Matthew Meselson, professor of biology, Harvard University; James Crow, professor of genetics, University of Wisconsin; and Jeremy Stone, director, Federation of American Scientists.

gamble on the safety of 2,4,5-T in the face of acknowledged uncertainty about TCDD's concentration and
persistence in the environment and human food chain,
its speculation about "no-effect" levels in the absence
of data on the effect of 2,4,5-T at low doses, its dismissal
of the Herbicide Assessment Commission's data showing
a circumstantial association between defoliation with
2,4,5-T and an increased incidence of birth defects in
sprayed areas of Vietnam, and its failure to make any
risk-benefit assessment.

The public criticism of the advisory committee report greatly increased William Ruckelshaus's freedom to
maneuver and shifted his political stakes. Alerted to the
report's weaknesses, EPA then consulted FDA scientists,
including its leading teratologists, who had not been consulted by the advisory committee. The FDA group
detailed major omissions in the report and recommended
that the present bans on 2,4,5-T remain in force. The
U.S. Surgeon General concurred. Buttressed by this
opinion, Ruckelshaus, on August 9, 1971, took the unprecedented step of rejecting the recommendations of
his advisory committee. Instead he ordered a public
hearing on the public risks and benefits of 2,4,5-T.

EPA officials were apparently surprised that scientists
could disagree among themselves to such an extent on
a highly technical subject. They concede that the criti-
cisms of the outsiders increased their options and made
it possible for them to seek independent advice. "I'm
glad the report was leaked," one official told *Science*
magazine. "After Daniel Ellsberg, isn't that a terrible
thing to say?"

The press conference represented the second major
effort of outside scientists to intervene in government
decision-making on 2,4,5-T. In 1970, Dr. Matthew
Meselson, after fruitless requests to the government for
a study of the ecological and human impact of the U.S.
defoliation and crop destruction programs in Vietnam,
took his case to the American Association for the Advancement of Science (AAAS). The AAAS took the
unprecedented step of funding a small Vietnam study
group out of its own limited resources. The findings of
this group, known as the Herbicide Assessment Comis-
sion, were made public in 1971 and were instrumental

in convincing the White House to phase out the defoliation program.

The 2,4,5-T case demonstrates the effectiveness of scientists taking an issue to Congress and the public when a governmental policy appears to endanger public health or welfare. At three key points—the release of the Bionetics report, the creation of the Herbicide Assessment Commission by the AAAS, and the attack on the Advisory Committee report—outside scientists intervened to force the government to reassess its pesticide policy. The physicists Frank von Hippel and Joel Primack, in discussing the role of scientists in the politics of technology, give a rationale for the outsiders:

In cases where government agencies are unwilling to inform Congress and the public of the possible undesirable consequences of their policies, Outsiders must try to fill the gap. . . . They enjoy a freedom of public expression which Insiders (scientists appointed by the Federal Executive to give confidential advice) usually do not feel that they have, and the Executive bureaucracy is often forced to listen and respond to arguments presented publicly which it refused to hear in private.[50]

But for all its sound and fury to date, the 2,4,5-T case is still technically a standoff. As of March 1972, the public hearing ordered by EPA has still not been convened.* In the meantime, 2,4,5-T's use on food crops, pasture land, and rights of way, accounting for 90% of its sales, continues unrestricted. Western ranchers are now pressing for Agent Orange, as the Vietnam defoliant is called, to be declared surplus so that they can buy it cheaply to kill sagebrush on their rangeland.

It has now been five years since 2,4,5-T was first suspected of causing fetal deformities. In all this period, the government regulatory machinery has taken no action to safeguard public health, except in response to external pressure generated by the release of secret reports. Reflecting on the 2,4,5-T case, Nicholas Wade of *Science* magazine stated:

---

* The delay was caused in part by Dow Chemical Company, which after requesting a public hearing in the spring of 1971, sued EPA in December 1971 to enjoin the hearing until the courts ruled on Dow's claim that EPA had acted capriciously and arbitrarily in rejecting the Advisory Committee report.

The history of the 2,4,5-T episode is cogent evidence of the shambles into which the official decision-making machinery has lapsed. At two crucial points—the springing of the suppressed Bionetics report and the exposé of the EPA Advisory Committee's whitewash—the intervention of outside scientists has been essential in keeping the government machinery on the rails and in motion. And only through by-passing the existing machinery of the Advisory Committee's report and the review of it by the EPA Office of Pesticides did Ruckelshaus and his aides arrive at the correct decision to maintain the existing restrictions. In short, the established machinery for protecting the public health has failed, and failed ignominiously.[51]

8

Big Bad John: Short-Term Hazards of Pesticides

We face a dilemma in deciding how to respond to the long-term hazards of pesticides. The effects of persistent pesticides such as DDT on fish and birds have been highly publicized and have led to increasing restrictions on their use. Similarly, animal studies linking pesticides to risks of cancer and birth defects have increased the public demand for controls over insecticides and herbicides which may leave persistent residues in food. While this concern is legitimate, it raises the question: what will be the consequences of shifting to shorter-acting pesticides?

Herein lies the dilemma. Most of the chemical substitutes for persistent pesticides are highly toxic contact poisons, where spillage on the skin or accidental ingestion may lead rapidly to death. These pesticides, the organophosphates and carbamates, account for over 90 percent of the known pesticide deaths in this country. While nationwide statistics on fatal poisonings are hard to come by, some local reports suggest the magnitude of the problem. For example, of 1,000 poisoning deaths subjected to a medico-legal investigation over a ten-year period in Dade County, Florida, 10 percent were due to pesticides and, in the under five-year group, pesticides were the leading cause of death, far exceeding deaths from all medications including aspirin.[1] At least twenty-five deaths from parathion alone are known to

have occurred in 1969–1971.[2] Of increasing concern
are the effects of "orange pickers' flu," the nausea, head-
aches, depression, and skin irritation which result from
chronic low level exposure of farm workers to these
poisons.

The replacement of persistent pesticides by organophosphates seems to many farm workers a very poor
trade. "While this may be a blessing for the birds and
fish, it's at the expense of the farm worker," asserts
Charles Farnsworth, a lawyer and pesticide specialist
for Cesar Chavez, head of the United Farm Workers
Organizing Committee. Dr. Philip Handler, President
of the National Academy of Sciences, made the same
point in an emotional address to the annual meeting of
the American Association for the Advancement of
Science in 1970:

The predicted death or blinding by parathion of dozens of
Americans last summer must rest on the consciences of
every car owner whose bumper sticker urged a total ban
on DDT.[3]

While Handler's prediction did not come true (there
were far more annual deaths from parathion in the early
1960s before the restrictions on DDT than in any year
afterwards), his remarks do highlight the fact that many
environmentalists, swept up in the battle to ban the
persistent pesticides, have tended to emphasize the
organophosphates' rapid breakdown characteristics without sufficient attention to the trade-offs in health hazards.

The psychology of anxiety is very interesting. While
there is nothing potential or vague about death or injury
from parathion, its risks have received relatively little
public exposure. There is far more controversy, polari-
zation, and rhetoric among scientists and environmentalists about the potential but unproven cancer and birth
defect risks from pesticides with persistent residues.
In the public at large, it is far easier to provoke anxiety
about hidden hazards such as radiation, cancer, or birth
defects than about proven hazards such as cigarette
smoking or organophosphate poisoning. The reason is
obvious. Cancer or birth defects induced by pesticide
contaminants seem to threaten us all, even our unborn
children. The fact they cannot be proven heightens their

insidious, subliminal character. On the other hand, only a few isolated groups of people are exposed to organophosphates, and these people, the migrant and farm workers who pick our apples, pears, and oranges, are perhaps this nation's most defenseless and silent minority, largely out of sight and out of mind.

As we shall see, there are other ways of coping with organophosphate hazards than rushing to embrace DDT. But to put the hazards in perspective before discussing alternatives, this chapter provides snapshots of the short-term hazards of pesticides to farm workers. There are about 400 different chemicals used for pest control. These are sold in approximately 50,000 different formulations. Discussed below are case histories of some of the more hazardous compounds.

Parathion

In July, 1970, a sixteen-year-old boy in North Carolina collapsed and died after walking barearmed and barefooted through his father's tobacco field. The cause of death was acute pesticide poisoning. The boy's arms and legs brushed against tobacco leaves which had been sprayed one day before with "Big Bad John," the trade name for an insecticide containing the poison parathion. A few weeks later at another farm in North Carolina's tobacco country, a boy fell into convulsions and died after playing barefoot on his front lawn. The cause of death was puzzling at first; then his parents remembered that *five weeks earlier*, a container of parathion had overturned on their way home from a farm supply store. They had washed out the trunk of the car near the spot where the boy died. While the cause of death has not been definitely confirmed, the dead boy displayed the classic symptoms of massive organophosphate poisoning.[4]

Before the summer of 1970, tobacco farmers controlled their pests with DDT and other chlorinated hydrocarbons, pesticides which are relatively safe to the touch. Now these pesticides are being phased out because of their long-term hazards to the environment. As a result, pesticide use has suddenly reached dramatic new levels of hazard. In North Carolina and in other cotton and tobacco regions of the nation, new substances hundreds of times more toxic than DDT are coming into general use. Parathion, the most popular substitute for DDT on cotton and tobacco, is an organophosphate insecticide. Unlike DDT it does not persist in the environment and does not accumulate in human tissue. It does have one drawback: when absorbed through the skin or ingested, it poisons rapidly by a devastating assault on the nervous system. A few drops of parathion concentrate on the skin will sicken a man and a few more will kill him.

Organophosphates belong to a class of chemicals developed as by-products of nerve gas research during World War II. They attack the nervous system by suppressing blood enzymes known as cholinesterases which help regulate the body's nerve impulses. Low level exposures create chronic eye irritations, nausea, cramps, depression, and chronic fatigue.[5] If exposure is stopped, the patient usually recovers. If enough of these enzymes are affected, a barrage of extraneous nerve impulses disrupts bodily functions and may eventually lead to death by suffocation following paralysis of the diaphragm. Organophosphates like parathion and Phosdrin are the biggest killer pesticides in this country. The long-term effects of chronic exposure to organophosphate poisoning remain unknown.

When a farm worker receives a lethal dose of a pesticide with the toxicity of parathion, his body becomes a poison carrier contaminating anything it touches. Dr. Lee Mizrahi of California's Salud Clinic describes this phenomenon: "I read in one reported case where a patient was sprayed and died within thirty minutes. The doctor who attended him then became critically ill and had to be hospitalized just from touching him. The ambulance driver who transported him became critically ill and had to be hospitalized, and the coroner who took care of the patient after he died became critically ill as well. The recommendations in our textbook are that when you see a person with organophosphate poisoning, put on gloves and a gown and treat them as if there's a really high degree of poison."

The accident toll indicates that many users lack the knowledge or the protective equipment to handle these pesticides with the caution they deserve. Accident prevention is hampered by the fact that pesticides still have a benign image for many rural people. Most Americans became acquainted with pesticides in the newsreels of World War II. Lice-ridden soldiers were filmed lining up in the streets of Naples to be fumigated with DDT. They would disappear in a cloud of dust and emerge smiling and obviously healthy. In the postwar years a familiar sight on summer evenings was the fogging machine moving up and down suburban streets as laughing children played hide and seek in a dense cloud of DDT mist. DDT, which won a Nobel prize as the scourge of malaria and a multitude of other insect-borne diseases, gave many people, unaware of its long-term hazards, a false sense of security about pesticides.

Unfortunately, the little boy who runs through the cloud from a DDT fogging machine is not learning to treat pesticides with respect. This attitude, if he lives in a rural community, may cost him his life. Not only attitudes but pesticide marketing practices are out of step with the accelerated risks of pesticides like parathion. These toxic substances are far more lethal than most drugs, yet in most areas they can still be bought at any farm supply store by anyone, whether or not he can read and write. This highly sophisticated technology is sold to semiliterate tobacco farmers who may still plow their postage stamp allotments with mules. Because of these pesticides' extreme toxicity, they are not registered for use around the home, but this rule is often not observed. In Florida street vendors have sold parathion granules in paper bags for roach control. In Puerto Rico, where parathion is the leading killer among poisons, it is freely sold in pharmacies, hardware stores, and groceries as a white powder which has been mistaken for sugar.[6]*

---

* As yet no quantitative analysis of the effect of parathion on the environment exists. However, the Ecological Investigations Branch of the Pesticide Regulations Division of the EPA has compiled a partial "Summary of Parathion Incidents." Noted cases include (1) three groups of citrus workers who after exposure to parathion-coated fruit experienced varying degrees of illness requiring hospitalization; (2) the death of eighty-one Colombians after eating bread contaminated with parathion; and (3) the death of seventeen Mexican children after eating sweet bread made with parathion-contaminated sugar.

Thimet

In the spring of 1970, over twenty children became violently ill with nausea and stomach cramps when their elementary school in Phoenix, Arizona, was doused by the spray of a lethal pesticide drifting from a nearby sugar-beet field.[7] The spray contained the organophosphate Thimet, the second most toxic of all pesticides in common use.[8] When the crop duster made his run, the wind was blowing about ten miles per hour from the field toward the school. The stench from the spray lingered in its hallways for several days. At first, Robert Rayburn, administrator of the state Pest Control Applicators Board, a regulatory body responsible for pesticide safety, maintained that none of the chemical had drifted from the sugar-beet field to the school. When he was confronted with the sick children, he remained unconcerned: "This is one of the hazards of living next to a field which must be sprayed to save crops. People should learn not to build houses next to fields in these areas."

What is remarkable about this incident is not the insensitivity of the state pest control official, but that a farmer can spray his field with a pesticide as toxic as Thimet on a windy day a few hundred yards from an elementary school and *break no law*. All the law requires is a one-quarter mile corridor between the area sprayed and the school. In this case the intervening distance was precisely that. The point is that methods of application, in this case aerial spraying, can be as important as basic toxicity in gauging the hazards of a pesticide.

Paraquat

This nitrogen compound, an herbicide, differs from Thimet and parathion in that it has a delayed effect. The Chevron Chemical Company, using billboards and radio spots, has heavily promoted the use of Paraquat on cotton and soybeans in the South. The ad campaign has been so successful that it alarmed professional crop dusters who had to apply it. Finding themselves deluged with requests from farmers for Paraquat, they wrote to the Civil Aeronautics Board asking for guidance in its use. The CAB responded in 1969 with an unprecedented warning: Paraquat, in small quantities, can have "a delayed and irreversible effect on the lungs. There is no known antidote at this time."[9] The pulmonary fibrosis caused by Paraquat develops gradually. By the time the victim realizes that his lungs are damaged, it is usually too late to save his life.[10]

The Paraquat label fails to mention that it has no antidote. According to an official at the National Communicable Disease Center, Chevron's claim that one has to drink Paraquat to get a toxic dose is not true.[11] Both the CDC and PRD (the Pesticide Regulation Division of the Environmental Protection Agency) warn that inhalation may be a hazard and have recommended that Paraquat only be used with masks, goggles, and protective clothing. These cautions are rarely followed.

The pesticide aerial applicators further note that many soybean fields are surrounded by tenant shacks, that some of these homes rely on open rain barrels and wells for water, and that often people are working in the fields while they are being sprayed. They question the discrepancy between the elaborate cautions the CAB suggests for aerial applicators for their own protection and the lack of concern by any federal agency for the people on the ground who may breathe Paraquat vapors or ingest it through their water supply after it is sprayed from the air.

TEPP

On a large California ranch in 1965, a group of Mexican-American workers were picking berries. None could read or understand English. A four-year-old boy and his three-year-old sister were playing around a spray rig while their mother worked in the field. The boy took the cap off a gallon can of tetraethylpyrophosphate (TEPP) left on the rig. The three-year-old put her finger in the can and licked it. She vomited immediately, became unconscious, and was dead on arrival at the nearby hospital. TEPP is the most deadly of all pesticides in common use. The estimated fatal dose for TEPP concentrate for an adult is one drop orally or one drop on the skin,[12] a toxicity which puts it in a class with nerve gas. When TEPP dust is applied in very still, hot weather, it forms a dust cloud which may settle over homes and pastures, forcing evacuation of people and cattle.[13]

Temik

The Mrak Commission reports a case of a woman who ate about four to six leaves of a mint plant growing near a plot being treated with an experimental pesticide. She developed a nearly fatal case of "fulminating intoxication." The mint she had eaten grew adjacent to roses whose roots had been treated with Temik, Union Carbide's trade name for the insecticide aldicarb.[14]

Temik is one of the most poisonous chemicals ever developed for general use in the United States. The only other insecticides with acute toxicity comparable to Temik in its technical form are the organophosphates TEPP and Thimet. Temik is a carbomate insecticide and, like parathion, inhibits the cholinesterase enzymes vital to nerve transmission. Technical Temik has an acute oral LD_{50} level* in rats of about one milligram per kilogram of body weight.[15] By comparison Methoxychlor, a DDT relative, has an LD_{50} level of 6,000 mg/kg.

Union Carbide envisions a potential market for Temik equivalent to that of the carbamate Sevin, which has sales approximating $80 million. Temik was sold commercially for the first time in 1970 to treat cotton in the Mississippi Delta. Union Carbide launched a major advertising campaign to promote Temik in 1971 and hopes to extend its use to potatoes, citrus fruits, and other crops.

Union Carbide has worked hard to insure that Temik can be safely used and has invested nearly $10 million in its development. The company bases its safety claims first on the fact that Temik is formulated as granules covered with a chemical coating which permits the

* The LD_{50} level is a common measure of a chemical's poisoning power. It refers to the quantity of a chemical which when administered in a single dose kills 50 percent of a group of test animals. While specific dose-response relationships are often very different for animals and man, pesticides which are highly toxic to the experimental animal are usually quite poisonous to man.

poison to be released gradually. The granules are planted two inches under the soil so that in normal use exposure to wildlife is eliminated. The aldicarb poison in Temik is absorbed by the roots of the cotton and gives the cotton plant a built-in or systemic insecticide for ten weeks or more. Moreover, Union Carbide has organized the most elaborate safety program ever developed for a pesticide, including a twenty-four-hour emergency telephone number for medical assistance and safety instruction, instruction of physicians and Poison Control Centers where Temik is used, and special courses in safe handling and emergency procedures for all regional distributors, warehousemen, and field personnel.[16]

Despite these precautions, lingering doubt about Temik's safety under field conditions caused the Pesticide Regulation Division to hold up its registration for over three years. Some leading scientists doubt whether it should ever have been registered. Dr. Robert Metcalf, an eminent toxicologist and author of a standard text in the field, states flatly that "the marketing of materials as hazardous as Temik is not in the best interests of the agricultural and pest control industries. Accidents are sure to occur and very unfavorable publicity and consequent legal actions will result."[17]

Dr. Frederick W. Plapp, an entomologist at Texas A&M University where some of the experimental work on Temik took place, also questions its safety: "When I first heard of Temik, I thought of it as an interesting curiosity, not a material that would eventually go into commercial use. I personally have never done any research with Temik. I feel that materials with such high toxicity are not safe to use even in the laboratory. As an entomologist I am distressed that the profession has acquiesced so supinely in the development of such a toxic chemical. I feel that we as a professional group should set limits on the toxicity to non target organisms of chemicals with which we deal. If we don't it will probably be done for us by society at large."[18]

There is much reason to doubt whether Temik can be used safely when produced in the millions of pounds Union Carbide envisions. The carbowax coating on the Temik granules can be dissolved by moisture.[19] Farm workers will be handling Temik in humid climates where sweat and rain may remove the coating. The LD_{50} level for formulated Temik with the carbowax intact is nearly 2,400 mg/kg but when the carbowax dissolves and releases the aldicarb poison, Temik's LD_{50} level drops calamitously to 1 mg/kg.[20] Temik is one of the few pesticides more toxic to mammals than to insects. It is at least five times as toxic to the laboratory rat as to houseflies.[21]

When Temik is used on thousands of farms instead of a few carefully monitored experimental areas, Union Carbide will almost certainly find it too expensive to enforce its present safety procedures. There are bound to be accidents. Dr. Barthell at the National Communicable Disease Center says that the 1971–1972 poisoning statistics should be watched closely.

Temik has stimulated a sense of euphoria in Union Carbide's Agricultural Chemical's group. Few products have ever had so much advance publicity or so much support from organizations such as the National Cotton Council. Richard Wellman, a Union Carbide executive and founder of Temik, is convinced of its safety: "Any pesticide used as directed is safe for the use it was intended. Once it has been established, it is not relevant to prove it is the safest."[22]

Fine Print

One must emphasize that these pesticides are commonly used by thousands of farmers exposing hundreds of thousands of farm workers. A recent survey of small farmers in Hawaii revealed that 46 percent regularly use Paraquat, 33 percent use parathion, and a full 18 percent use TEPP.[23] The pesticide makers and the federal government claim that even these deadly poisons are safe for general use if the label on the container prescribes a safe use. The motto "Stop: Read the Label" usually with the credit, "Courtesy of the National Agricultural Chemicals Association," can be found in most farm and gardening publications.

This motto projects the pesticide lobby's image of social responsibility. Its basic theme is that pesticide problems, if they exist, only arise through consumer misuse. For those who followed the struggle for automobile safety legislation, the motto has a familiar ring. As a scapegoat for consumer injuries, the nut behind the wheel has now been joined by the nut behind the spray can.

As protection against pesticide hazards, the label hardly satisfies the industry's obligation to public safety. First, four out of five pesticide accidents occur where "the nut behind the spray can" is less than five years old. Second, many studies have shown that few farmers or home owners read the label before using pesticides.[24] Even if the user does read the label, he may not understand it. A two-year study by the University of Illinois completed in 1971 found that "the average pesticide label is suitable only for those with at least 10 to 12.9 years of formal education."

The labels of some pesticides actually magnify their hazards. Smith-Douglas Farm Chemicals, a division of Borden, Inc., mixes parathion with Thiodan (Endosulfan) to make Thiodan-Parathion 3-2 Dust. The label contains the following "note to physicians":

Parathion is a cholinesterase inhibitor and treatment of poisoning should include use of atropine; Endosulfan produces central nervous system excitation which responds to the barbituric acid derivatives.

The problem here is that atropine, the antidote for parathion, may act as a stimulant, thereby aggravating the Endosulfan symptoms, while barbituric acid, the antidote for Endosulfan, acts as a depressant and aggravates parathion poisoning.[25] In medical terms, the antidote for Endosulfan is *contra-indicated* for parathion poisoning and possibly vice versa. The person poisoned by the Borden product will be getting a dose of both pesticides, but treatment for one may magnify the hazards of the other. Similarly the Pesticide Regulation Division allows Sevin-parathion mixtures, although a common antidote for parathion (2-PAM) should not be given in the presence of Sevin.

Some labels are so contradictory that they provoke laughter rather than outrage, as this excerpt from Congressional hearings in 1969 shows:

MR. JAMES NAUGHTON (Committee counsel): Mr.
Chairman, this is a labeling for concentrated insecti-
cide, fly and roach spray, manufactured by the Hysan
Products Co. of Chicago.

The cautions include the following statements:

Use in well ventilated rooms or areas only. Always
spray away from you. *Do not stay in room that has
been heavily treated. Avoid inhalation.*

On the other side, the directions for use start out
in this manner:

Close all doors, windows, and transoms. Spray with
a fine mist sprayer freely upwards in all directions
so the room is filled with the vapor. *If insects have
not dropped to the floor in 3 minutes, repeat spraying,* as quantity sprayed was insufficient. *After 10
minutes, doors and windows may be opened.*

CONGRESSMAN BENJAMIN ROSENTHAL: If there is anybody around to open them. [Laughter.]

REPRESENTATIVE L. H. FOUNTAIN: Any comment on that
particular label?

DR. HARRY HAYS (PRD Director): I have no comment.
I would have to study the label carefully.[26]

These examples help to explain why labels have been
ineffective in preventing the 75,000 pesticide poisonings which the National Product Safety Commission
estimates occur each year. This is only a rough estimate.
Until very recently there has been no nationwide
attempt to compile records on pesticide poisonings. The
Mrak Report in 1969 lamented that no federal agency
has a clear picture of pesticide hazards in America and
predicted that the actual number of accidents far
exceeds those reported. Some local studies support the
Mrak estimate. In Puerto Rico, for example, pesticides
are the leading cause of fatal poisonings.[27] According
to the California State Department of Health, the actual
pesticide injury rate among farm workers in California
is 150 per 1,000 workers, thirty-three times the average
injury-illness rate for all industry in the state. These
were injuries treated by doctors.

Other investigators, notably Dr. Wayland J. Hayes,
dispute the significance of these figures. Hayes estimates
that the mortality rate for pesticides is one per 1 million

in the United States. All of these estimates, however, are limited by the fact that in most areas pesticide poisoning is not a reportable disease under the law. Many doctors are reluctant to report cases of pesticide poisonings because of their fear that they may be involved in litigation if the patient decides to take action against the manufacturer or user of the chemical concerned.[28] Moreover, the Mrak Commission reports that between one-half and two-thirds of counties in the United States lack the facilities for death investigations necessary to definitely establish a pesticide as cause of death.[29]

None of these estimates take into account the subacute hazards which may result from chronic exposure. These effects may be far more subtle than direct poisoning upon ingestion. Researchers who compared two groups of homeowners, one spraying pesticides once a week or more, the other spraying less often, found that the heavy-use group had significantly reduced lung capacity, more asthma and chronic sinus inflammation, and twice as much chronic hay fever.[30] As we shall see, the long-term effects of chronic exposure to pesticides on the incidence of cancer, birth defects, and mutations remain unknown.

Until very recently, the Pesticides Regulation Division was egregiously nonchalant about investigating the accident records of the pesticides it regulates. This attitude was revealed in hearings before the House Intergovernmental Operation Subcommittee in 1969:

REPRESENTATIVE FOUNTAIN: Approximately how many reports do you receive annually on pesticide poisoning?

MR. DELLAVECHIA (PRD staff): Last year we investigated 151 accidents.

MR. NAUGHTON: You think the 150 poisoning reports or 175 that you receive annually is a fair share of the total number of pesticide poisonings?

DR. HAYS (PRD Director): I think it is a reasonable estimate. . . .

MR. NAUGHTON: The Poison Control Centers (set up by the Public Health Service) . . . receive . . . 5,000 reports of poisonings by pesticides annually, of which approximately 4,000 involved children under five.

The Poison Control people advise us that in their opinion the number of poisonings is actually eight to ten times greater . . . the number of pesticide poisoning is somewhere in the area of 50,000 annually.

MR. FOUNTAIN: It is obvious you weren't aware they receive about 5,000 reports a year.

DR. HAYS: That is correct.

MR. FOUNTAIN: How many of the 150 or so reports . . . you receive . . . involve human beings?

DR. HAYS: Of the 151, 52 of these involved humans (the other victims were cows, horses, and other farm animals).

EPA has now established an Ecological Investigations Branch (EIB) to monitor accident data. Unfortunately the EIB lacks the staff and funds to initiate a comprehensive program. EIB's three professionals rely on voluntary reports from hospitals and a clipping service as their only data sources. A limited number of the reported cases are then investigated.

The risk from the new generation of pesticides is greatest for the farm workers who pick vegetables and fruits sprayed by organophosphates and carbamates. This is a very vulnerable population. Many suffer from malnutrition, which increases their susceptibility to pesticide poisoning. Most have no union to bargain for their safety. These workers and the landowners who hire them are alarmingly ignorant about pesticide hazards. And this ignorance is often compounded by the landowner's refusal to comply with the few safety regulations which do exist.

The list of violations is tedious to relate. Farm workers in contact with pesticides have no place to wash their hands, recently sprayed fields are not marked with warning signs, waiting periods after spraying are not observed, medical care is not available. Farm workers commonly complain that they are sprayed from the air while working in the fields. Often their only warning is the approaching drone of a low flying plane. In a recent Colorado survey, half of the pilots responding indicated they had sprayed with workers in the field.[31]

While violations of safety standards threaten the health of farm workers, USDA continues to deliver huge agricultural subsidies to growers who regularly ignore health laws. On July 27, 1970, the California Rural Legal Assistance unsuccessfully petitioned USDA to cut off payments to thirty agricultural growers who received agricultural subsidies of $7 million in 1969, while allegedly violating these laws.

The migratory farm worker is the most powerless of all groups exposed to the dangers of pesticides. The first attempt to collect information on pesticide exposure in this group was in hearings before the Subcommittee on Migratory Labor of the Senate Subcommittee on Labor and Public Welfare in 1969.[32] The most pithy summary of these hearings was provided by C. C. Johnson, Chief of the Bureau of Consumer Protection and Environmental Health of H.E.W.:[33]

SENATOR WALTER MONDALE: But insofar as those most exposed to the danger of pesticides, the farm workers, there is no federal protection?

MR. JOHNSON: There is not, except that which is provided by the Federal Pesticide, Fungicide, and Genocide Act [*sic*].

The farm workers' lack of knowledge about pesticides to which they are daily exposed is abysmal. Cesar Chavez testified in the Senate hearings that pesticide safety agreements in United Farm Workers Organizing Committee (UFWOC) contracts were necessary to force growers to inform them what is being sprayed and when.[34] The 1969 California Community Pesticide Study reported:

Knowledge of Pesticides. Informants were asked, "Have you ever heard of parathion? If so, what have you heard?" Results have not yet been tabulated, but it looks as though an amazingly large number of farm workers have no knowledge of this toxic substance, including those who work in the very crops where it is used most extensively.

Informants were also asked if they had ever heard of DDT. In view of the extensive publicity which this pesticide has received in the past year in California, it is a revealing index of the insulation of agricultural workers that most had no knowledge of DDT.

In the early phases of the survey informants were asked
about two other agricultural chemicals which are widely
used in Tulare County, and which may have untoward
health effects: ammonium sulfate, a fertilizer, and 2,4-D, a
weed-killer and defoliant so toxic that it has come under
some criticism even in Viet Nam. It was felt there was no
useful purpose to be served by continuing these questions
after the first several hundred farm workers were virtually
unanimous in agreeing that they had never heard of these
substances.

The report concluded:

Agricultural workers are almost never informed about the
chemicals which have been used at the places of their employment; even when they themselves work as sprayers they
are frequently uninformed about the composition of the
mixtures they are using. Under these conditions, a precise
etiology of symptoms cannot be established. It appears,
however, that fungicides, fertilizers, weed-killers, and other
substances officially classified as "noninjurious" are widely
implicated.

Ignorance of pesticide hazards is just as great in other
countries. In a recent study of thirty-eight peasant
farmers in Guatemala who used parathion and other
pesticides, twenty-four were found to take no precautions at all. When asked what treatment they gave to
victims of pesticide poisoning, they cited lemon juice,
eggs, milk, lard, coffee with lemon, and salt water.[35]
Dr. Lee Mizrahi, of the Salud Clinic in Tulare County,
California, who serves as pediatrician for 4,000 farm
worker families, warns that farm workers have become
fatalistic about pesticide hazards. Many of his patients
apparently did not associate their symptoms with the
use of pesticides and those who did were inclined to
shrug them off. Some were quoted as saying, "Well,
this is just something that farm workers just have to
suffer with—it happens to everybody in the fields." Only
acute poisonings get medical attention; the workers put
up with the gradual effects because the economic pressure to remain in the fields is too great. Pesticide
symptoms in children are as frequently ignored as the
similar symptoms in adults.[36]
The following evidence on the effects of pesticides
is taken from reports and affidavits given by farm

laborers working in Colorado. It is unsettling to realize that the apples, oranges, pears, and apricots we enjoy were picked by human beings half-intoxicated by chemical spray:

There was a heavy "natural blush" on the plums—so heavy that it left a white (metallic-looking) residue on the hands.

This year there was a white powder on the cherries.

After one day and at the end of each following day he noticed a black residue built up on his hands. At the end of two weeks of picking pears, he could no longer wash the black out of his hands.

This man has also picked lemons. The spray on the trees was so heavy that the whole tree was white with spray. They couldn't tell the fruit from the leaves.

In pears, he noticed excess sneezing coming from the sinuses and unpleasant feeling in the sinuses that is almost painful. Slight burning sensation in the lungs. In plums, he felt all these things, only to a greater extent.

Apples: after picking for three or four days, the skin on her hands started to be eaten away. A lump and cramps in pit of stomach, nausea.

. . . he had to be taken to the hospital in Delta after a night of severe stomach cramps and pain, plus a sore throat. As mentioned before, his tonsils were swelling and he had bad earaches, since picking peaches in Palisade. Now after two days of apple picking, his tonsils became much worse again, then he got the stomach cramps. . . . The doctor told him some kind of poison had collected in his tonsils which had ruptured. The poison had been draining into his stomach and causing the cramps.

. . . two women were out in the field topping onions when a small plane flew over their heads—one woman said, "I thought, 'O that plane is flying so low' and then I saw a black cloud, and I smelled an awful smell, it made me sick. They sprayed . . . all over us and our food and everything. My son got so sick he couldn't work anymore or go to school the next day."[37]

When poisoning occurs, the victims have little hope of outside aid. Unfortunately agricultural workers are the pariahs of the workmen's compensation system. The political muscle of the farm lobbies has kept them outside the scope of most state acts. When states do extend coverage to farm workers, it is too often riddled with exceptions. Today farm workers, who number some 3.6 million, are the largest class of employees denied full protection from the economic hardships caused by on-the-job accidents and diseases.

Conclusion

The chemical industry has attempted to make the victims of parathion and other acutely toxic pesticides martyrs to the cause of saving DDT. This effort should not go unchallenged. Present patterns of use for both kinds of substances entail unacceptable risks, the one short-term to the farm worker, the other long-term to the public and environment.

The following steps will greatly reduce the hazards to farm workers:

(1) Congress should enact the Farm Workers Compensation Act (H.R. 11007) extending workmen's compensation to all agricultural workers. Compensation costs for pesticide poisoning under this Act should be charged not to the Environmental Protection Agency itself, but to the Pesticide Regulation Division within EPA, which reviews the labeling of economic poisons. This will allow Congress, in reviewing pesticide control appropriations, to see the costs of lax labeling practices and pressure PRD to strengthen its safety criteria.

(2) Congress should require all pesticides which bear the skull and crossbones on the label (the most toxic category) to be available by prescription only from EPA and applied under the supervision of a pesticide applicator licensed by EPA.

(3) The Federal Trade Commission should require all advertisements for pesticides with the skull and crossbones on their label to display the same symbol. Chemical companies promote parathion, Paraquat, and other dangerous pesticides with a style and tone appropriate for Wonder Bread or Wheaties. Parathion ads often use trade names such as Big Bad John and Big Daddy without mentioning the presence of parathion.

(4) Congress and EPA should create incentives to increase research to develop new and less harmful substitutes for DDT and other persistent pesticides. Just as new noncarcinogenic artificial sweeteners quickly

filled the vacuum left by the ban on cyclamates, the technological ingenuity of the chemical industry, if pressed, can meet the challenge of developing safe substitutes for DDT. The chemical industry has proven on numerous occasions that adversity in the form of safety standards is the mother of invention.

(5) USDA and EPA should instruct farmers in the use of nonchemical controls and "integrated" control (see Chapter 10) which will allow them to reduce pesticide use drastically without sacrificing yield. Farmers are already facing the spectre of diminishing returns from the use of organophosphates and other relatively new pesticides. The following chapter discusses the economic costs and benefits of pesticide use and shows that needless chemical overkill by farmers imperils not only farm workers but farm profits as well.

9

Diminishing Returns:
Pesticides and the Farmer

*Well, like I was pointing out, I started farming in
1953. At that time, I had better times than I've had
any year since. The first year I didn't spray at all. The
next year I didn't spray at all. The third year I
probably started spraying once, the next year maybe
twice and it seems that it's got progressively worse
till now it's almost an every two-week occurrence
that they have an airplane flying over your field. And
if it's not this bug, it's that bug and if not that
bug its another bug. . . .*

—*Jack Grimmer*
  California grower

*In pest control, . . . probably the overwhelming
problem in an agri-economy such as California [is
that] the grower is under constant pressure—either
internal [from] his own apprehensions or from
the pressures that he is under from the chemical
industry—to use insecticides. This is most ironic . . .
that the greatest direct victim of pesticide misuse
and overuse is the grower himself.*

—*Dr. Robert van den Bosch,*
  Entomologist at the University of California

Study of the unanticipated and still largely unmeasured
health effects of pesticides is properly the first step in
any social accounting of this technology. The second
step, and one that has received far less publicity, is an

assessment of the long-term economic consequences of pesticide use for the farmer. Pesticide chemicals have clearly played a major role in the development of present agricultural abundance. Yet their early success instilled a technological arrogance which led many farmers to abandon natural controls and rely exclusively on chemicals to protect their crops. In putting all their eggs in one technological basket, they perilously ignored the adaptability and genetic diversity of their insect enemies. There is now compelling evidence that the single strategy of chemical control has been an economic as well as environmental failure.

Although insecticide use increased nearly 150 percent between 1957 and 1967, there are now more insect species of pest status than ever before; many of the most harmful pests have developed resistance to chemicals; the use of ever more indiscriminately toxic pesticides has destroyed the pests' natural enemies; and the costs of pest control for many farmers have mushroomed to the point of diminishing returns. When Rachel Carson wrote *Silent Spring* in 1962, there were approximately 137 insect species which were resistant to one or more of the three basic insecticide classes: chlorinated hydrocarbons, organophosphates, and carbamates. By 1971, the number had increased to 250, including the bollworm, the boll weevil, the tobacco budworm, and other key crop destroyers, as well as 105 species which are vectors for malaria, elephantiasis, encephalitis, and other human disease.[1]

Resistant pests have destroyed the cotton industry in northeastern Mexico and threaten to overwhelm it in southern Texas, Guatemala, Nicaragua, and other parts of the world. The *Progressive Farmer*, hardly a journal to cry wolf at the pesticide peril, recently warned its readers that reduction of beneficial insects by insecticides has brought about a "serious increase in secondary cotton pests," with key pests "fast becoming immune to even the newest, more powerful insecticides."[2] Entomologists also predict disaster for tobacco production in the South if present pesticide practices continue. The Banks grass mite, formerly a minor pest which became destructive when pesticide treatments for another insect killed off its natural enemies, has developed resistance

to all known pesticides and threatens the entire feed
grain industry of western Texas, including allied industries such as feedlots.[3] The impact of pesticides on
honeybees and other natural pollinators has caused
severe economic loss to fruit growers and beekeepers
(in 1970, Congress found it necessary to indemnify the
latter).

The farmer's technological hubris has hastened the
obsolescence of his valuable chemical tools. Overwhelmed by the miracle drug promotional claims for
pesticides and looking only for immediate returns, he
has ignored the ecological impact of pesticides and
weakened the environment's natural defenses against
insect attack. The insect species' response to the chemical challenge makes pesticides a classic illustration of
what Barry Commoner calls the fourth law of ecology
—that there is no such thing as a free lunch. The law,
premised on the ecosphere as a connected whole, warns
that every gain is won at some cost, that every effect
is also a cause. The Dutch biologist C. J. Briejer raises
this admonition to a mystical level: "Life is a miracle
beyond our comprehension and we should reverence it
even when we have to struggle against it."

In a very fundamental sense, the proper use of pesticides depends on an understanding by both the farmer
and the environmentalist of the ecological principles
which govern a pesticide's impact on life in the fields
where it is applied. It is on this understanding that
their natural community of interest in avoiding the
overuse of pesticides can be developed. The most
instructive ecological lessons may be found in the
experiences of the cotton farmer, who applies over 40
percent of all farm insecticides used in the United
States (in the Deep South, the figure is nearer 70 percent). Control by pesticides is now his most expensive
cost input, and he has suffered the full gamut of
ecological boomerangs—pest resistance, pest resurgence, and pest trade-offs—from their misuse.

The Snow White Jungle

The cotton field with its snowy blossoms stretching row
on row seems a simple, almost antiseptic environment.

But to the entomologist or any close observer, it is a dense jungle teeming with life. Over 1,300 different species of insects have been identified in cotton and over 100 species of insects and spider mites are known to attack the cotton plant.[4] Damage from most of these pests is kept below economic thresholds by parasites, predators, and insect diseases. Predators of the boll-worm, for example, destroy as much as 40 percent of its eggs within twenty-four hours after they are laid.[5] There are usually only one or two key pests in any cotton area. In the San Joaquin Valley of California, the key pests are bollworms and lygus bugs. In the Deep South, the boll weevil is the traditional scourge. From a world viewpoint, the pink bollworm is the most destructive insect.

The population dynamics of pest and predator in the cotton field are always in a delicate balance. The cotton farmer, to be really efficient, must, therefore, be a highly skilled ecological engineer. Every intrusion in this environment stirs changes in the insect colonies, giving advantage to some and bringing disaster to others. Even a simple housekeeping measure—eliminating weeds from a field's borders—may have an earthquake impact on its insect world. These weeds, which the farmer considers as a pest and a nuisance, may be vital parts of the cotton ecosystem. Some weeds provide nourishment and refuge for beneficial insects, others harbor plant diseases and insect pests. If the farmer pulls the wrong weed, he may be in trouble.*

A minor pest may cross the economic threshold and do major damage because the moisture of the soil increases or decreases, because the nitrogen content of the plant is too high, because the crop is planted earlier or later than usual, or because the space between crop rows is changed. Genetic tampering with the plant to

---

* In California, the grape leafhopper became a major pest after herbicides were used to kill wild blackberries, a common weed around vineyards. Dr. R. L. Doutt, an entomologist at the University of California, discovered that the leafhopper's natural enemy, a tiny wasp, overwinters in blackberries. If a vineyard lacks blackberry bushes, the wasp seeks them out in other fields, often many miles away. When the grape leafhopper emerges in the spring, it often devours the tender grape leaves before its wasp enemy can return to control it. Blackberries are now planted around vineyards to keep the wasp within striking distance.

increase its yield or reduce processing costs may also undermine its defenses against insects. Early in this century, successful efforts to breed cotton with low levels of the pigment gossypol led to a boll weevil attack which plunged wide areas of the South into economic depression. Gossypol is present in small glands throughout the cotton plant. Because it is toxic to animals and costly to process, efforts were made to develop "glandless" cotton with low gossypol content. But when this cotton strain was developed it was devoured by pests, including many not previously recorded as enemies of cotton. Subsequent tests revealed that gossypol, the unwanted pigment, acts as a repellent to pests.[6] The Southern cornleaf blight, which devastated corn harvests throughout the South and Midwest in 1970 also illustrates the hazards of playing genetic roulette to improve yields without concern for pest problems.

The external influences on the insect world of the cotton field are legion but none compare with the explosive disruption of chemical pesticides. From planting time to harvest, cotton is subjected to a more intensive shower of chemicals than any other crop. In 1964, over half of the 143 million pounds of insecticides used on crops in the United States was applied to cotton. In California, the cotton farmer averages six treatments per acre at a cost between $35 and $100 per acre per year. In Central America and other cotton growing countries, the treatments may reach fifty or more. When the cotton seed is planted, the field may be already treated with pre-emergence herbicides and the seed itself coated with systemic insecticides such as American Cyanamid's Thimet. The latter pesticide is taken up into the plant's system to act as an insect preventive. As the plant matures, it may be treated every three or four days with parathion, toxaphene, DDT, Sevin, endrin and other pesticides, either singly or in combination. When it is ready for harvest, it may be sprayed with Paraquat or another desiccant to dry its stalks and make it easier to harvest.

The cotton insecticide miracle, as it is described in the agrichemical journals, has had the ironic result of allowing cotton yields to almost double since World

War II, at a time when cotton was in such surplus that acreage was constantly reduced to cut production. Much of this chemical technology has been hastily applied, with an eye for short term increase in yields, with no concern for the population dynamics in the insect world.

Even without pesticides to speed it up, the rapid evolutionary clock of pest species makes them incredibly adaptable. The cotton boll weevil, for most of this century, was the peculiar nemesis of the humid South. But in the early fifties, it suddenly appeared in the hot arid areas of the Southwest, defying predictions that it needed heavy summer rainfall to survive. In the Imperial Valley of California, a leafhopper species once was a serious pest only on sugar beets. Then it began to move into cotton after the sugar beets were harvested. A few years later, it began to feed on cotton even when sugar beets were present.[7] Dr. Briejer has called the insect world's adaptability "nature's most astonishing phenomenon. Nothing is impossible to it; the most impossible things commonly occur there. One who penetrates deeply into its mysteries is continually breathless with wonder. He knows that anything can happen and that the completely impossible often does."[8]

Above all it is their response to pesticides, which make insects the classic exemplars of Darwin's "survival of the fittest." Since 1948 when there were only twelve, the number of resistant species has jumped to nearly 250. The salt marsh sandfly, for example, developed resistance to dieldrin after only three applications of one pound per acre.[9] There are eighteen pests of cotton in the United States which have shown resistance to chlorinated hydrocarbons, eight of these are also resistant to organophosphates, and two pests, the cotton bollworm and the tobacco budworm, have shown resistance to all four classes of synthetic pesticides.[10]

The three cases below show how the response of insects to a crude unilateral chemical attack can overwhelm not only the individual farmer but an entire agricultural economy.

Mr. Hobe of Hobe Ranches has been a top cotton farmer in Madera County, California, for over twenty years. Between 1961 and 1965, the cotton from his fields, nourished by the bright sunshine and irrigation water of the San Joaquin Valley, averaged from 15 percent to 50 percent more pounds per acre than the average for his county. But in the fall of 1966, a sudden disaster struck his crop. Yields at his ranches plummeted to 389 pounds per acre in a year when even average farmers brought 700 pounds per acre to market. Making his loss more cruelly obvious were two cotton growers who farmed land adjacent to his ranches and who averaged in this year between 885 and 1,750 pounds per acre.[11] At first glance, it seemed that Hobe had only himself to blame. Unwittingly, by his own hand, he had unleashed an ecocatastrophe in his fields.

In April, 1966, he planted 163 acres of cotton on his three ranches. By mid-July, the cotton was progressing well and had a good set of bolls. Then one day, Hobe noticed some bollworms feeding on the buds and bolls of his cotton.

Like many farmers he visited his local pesticide supplier for advice. Without inspecting Hobe's fields, the supplier suggested that he try Azodrin, an exciting new organophosphate pesticide produced by Shell Chemical Company (an affiliate of Shell Oil). In mid-July, Hobe applied one quart of Azodrin to each of his 163 acres. The impact was startling. Insect life in the fields seemed to vanish. The broad spectrum pesticide Azodrin moved like wildfire through the insect colonies of the cotton fields, killing pest and predator alike, sweeping the field clean of insect life.

Ten days later, life suddenly returned. Incredulously, Hobe watched the eradicated bollworm stage a population explosion in his fields. Where there had been two or three worms before, there were now a dozen or more devouring the cotton bolls and causing them to drop to the ground. Thoroughly panicked, he saturated his land with multiple applications of more familiar pesticides—methylparathion, DDT, and toxaphene. This expense was futile, for the bollworms were out of control. In early September, Hobe surveyed his fields and found damage so extensive that further application of insecticides was pointless. For the first time in many years, he lost big money on his cotton crop.

The bollworm outbreak at Hobe Ranches is a classic example of how the use of pesticides in defiance of ecological principles can victimize the farmer. Mr. Hobe had applied the Azodrin in late July, the time when the cotton plant is at its peak in setting the bolls which hold the cotton. At approximately the same time, the bollworm moth was laying its eggs on the plant. The eggs hatched in three days and the larvae then fed on the fruiting parts of the plant for a period of eleven to fifteen days until the bolls dropped to the ground.[12]

Unfortunately for Mr. Hobe, the bollworm at this stage is peculiarly adapted to escape its destruction by Azodrin. The poison does not kill the bollworm eggs and it does not completely penetrate the cotton boll where the bollworm larvae are busily eating away the farmer's profits. The bollworm's natural enemies are not as fortunate. Tests conducted by Shell Chemical Company in 1964 and 1965 showed that Azodrin could cause a severe depression of the beneficial insect population for as long as thirty days.[13] With its natural predators apparently eliminated, Mr. Hobe's cotton field suddenly would become an Elysian Field for the bollworm. Its eggs could hatch in great numbers because the predators which usually ate them were dead. Once hatched, more of the young bollworms could survive because other insects which preyed on them or competed with them for food were gone. With all natural controls destroyed, the bollworm could then resurge in devastating numbers.*

The ecological boomerang which caused Mr. Hobe's loss is not unique to the San Joaquin Valley of California. It has happened on a vaster scale elsewhere in the United States and in many of the world's cotton grow-

* Whether this was the actual sequence of events in Hobe's fields is not certain without a more complete inventory of pest and beneficial insects at the time Azodrin was sprayed. So many bollworms could have been present that the absence of beneficial insects after spraying would make little difference. Dr. M. J. Sloan, spokesman for Shell Chemical, states that Mr. Hobe erred in allowing the pest infestation to get out of hand by waiting approximately thirty days to spray again after the initial Azodrin treatment. Hobe apparently had two choices. When he first saw the bollworms, he could have not sprayed at all, hoping enough beneficial insects were present to prevent economic loss, or he could have applied multiple treatments of Azodrin. The single treatment of Azodrin was disastrous. Shell claims that Azodrin is highly effective against the bollworm when correctly applied.

ing areas. Farmers in these widely scattered regions have a common source for their plight: the flagrant overuse of pesticides without regard for the ecological principles which govern insect life. At Hobe's Ranches misuse of pesticides led to pest resurgence, the sudden secondary onslaught of a pest species when all of its natural controls have been removed. Other problems which arise are the development of chemical-resistant pests and costly pest trade-offs where a nonpest suddenly becomes damaging after a pesticide destroys its natural enemies.

These phenomena are well known to farmers in the Canete Valley of Peru. The Canete Valley shelters about 35,000 acres of farmland in the mountains of Peru. During an eight-year period which ended in 1956, heavy use of synthetic organic pesticides had nearly ruinous results. Cotton is the valley's dominant crop. Before spraying began in 1949, there were seven species of insects which caused sufficient damage to be considered pests. The farmers had traditionally used hand collection of insects on damaged parts of the plant and simple inorganic compounds such as arsenicals for pest control. In 1949, the farmers began to use DDT, BHC, toxaphene, and other chlorinated hydrocarbons imported from the United States. The results were striking: average cotton yield climbed from 442 pounds per acre to 530 pounds. The farmers were delighted with these results. They did not notice that the chemicals were also nonselectively destroying the natural enemies of their seven pest species, as well as other insects capable of harming their cotton but kept under control by their own natural enemies. One man who did notice was Dr. Theodore Barducci, director of the Canete farmers' agricultural experiment station. A prophet without honor in his own country, he warned the farmers against exclusive use of these pesticides but found them "seduced by the promotional claims of the pesticide manufacturers."[14]

Before long, the farmers found themselves on a pesticide treadmill. Spraying had a temporary effect on destructive insects but a lingering effect on beneficial ones. Their fields were therefore quickly reinvaded by the seven original pest species and attacked for the first time by six additional species, which had never been pests before. Pesticide resistant strains of the aphid, boll weevil, and the Peruvian bollworm then began to emerge. As the effectiveness of the original pesticides declined, the farmers turned to other insecticides, including aldrin, endrin, and parathion, as well as mixtures of different pesticides. These chemicals were applied at increasing rates with decreasing intervals between applications. In some parts of the valley, fifteen and even twenty-five applications of insecticides were common.[15] Nevertheless, cotton yields steadily declined, until there was a disastrous crop failure in 1956. The total crop loss reached 50 percent and the harvest dropped to 254 pounds per acre.[16]

Fearing an economic disaster for the valley, the farmers joined with the government to forbid the use of synthetic organic pesticides without a special permit. The government also introduced predators and parasites, including parasitic wasps, to attack the pests. The farmers returned to using mineral insecticides such as lead and calcium arsenate. These insecticides, which kill by ingestion rather than contact, are less likely to destroy beneficial insects. They kill enough of the pest species to bring their population to a level which natural predators and parasites can control. By reducing their numbers instead of totally wiping out a pest species, these pesticides were also less likely to hasten resistance which occurs when all but a few resistant freaks of a pest population are destroyed. These measures were introduced in 1957. By 1958, cotton yields had returned to the former high levels.[17]

The disastrous escalator of chemical resistance, with its economic and social disruption, is graphically evident in the experience of the Mexican and Texas cotton farmers of the Lower Rio Grande Valley, first described by Dr. P. L. Adkisson, a leading entomologist at Texas A&M University.[18] The Rio Grande River runs between Texas and Mexico into the Gulf of Mexico. Its fertile semitropical valley is ideal for citrus, vegetables, grain sorghum, corn, and other crops, but cotton is a principal cash crop. The primary pest of Rio Grande cotton, until recently, was the dreaded boll weevil, which invaded the valley in the 1890s and caused crippling losses until arsenical dusts provided some control. The pink bollworm made its way to the valley in the 1920s. The farmers reduced it to a minor pest by timing planting and harvest dates to avoid periods when it is most active, and by destroying cotton stalks after harvest to deny it shelter in winter. Before World War II, the bollworm (a different species from the pink bollworm) and the tobacco budworm were also minor pests. A fifth pest, the cotton fleahopper, although present in great numbers, was kept under control with sulfur dust.

This is the cast of characters. In the last twenty years, they have played a destructive game of musical chairs in the Rio Grande Valley with pesticides calling the tune. One insect has replaced another in the seat of honor as primary pest, leaving much of the cotton industry of the valley in ruins.

The game began shortly after World War II when the introduction of chlorinated hydrocarbons had a spectacular impact on cotton production in the valley. Toxaphene, BHC, dieldrin, and endrin controlled the boll weevil effectively for the first time and cotton yields skyrocketed. These pesticides were not effective against the less serious pests, the tobacco budworm and the bollworm. Toxaphene and dieldrin did kill their natural enemies, however, threatening to make them major pests. To counter this threat, DDT, which was not effective against the boll weevil but deadly for the bollworm and the tobacco budworm, was then added to the mixture.

In the late fifties, the first sign that the growers' hasty switch to exclusive pesticide control may have had hidden costs appeared. The boll weevil became resistant to the chlorinated hydrocarbons and the growers switched to organophosphates, particularly methyl parathion. Between 1960 and 1962, the scene shifted again. The bollworm and the tobacco budworm became resistant to DDT and then to carbamates such as Sevin as well. The doses of parathion which controlled the boll weevil had little effect on these pests. The pest picture therefore turned upside down, with the bollworm and the tobacco budworm becoming major pests while the boll weevil became secondary. Trading challenge with response, the cotton farmers in the valley tripled and quadrupled the doses of methyl parathion to control the new primary pests. This effort succeeded, but at considerable costs. Yields remained high but profits declined.

Five years later, in 1968, the farmers made a frightening discovery. The tobacco budworm began showing signs that it had developed resistance to the organophosphates, the last weapon in the farmer's pesticide arsenal. The farmers increased their spraying up to eighteen applications but still suffered great losses in yield. Tests at Texas A&M University by Dr. Adkisson showed that doses of parathion, which killed all of a test population of budworms in 1967, killed less than 50 percent in 1968.[19] After surveying the situation, Dr. Adkisson told a group of growers that if they wanted to stay in the cotton business, they would have to stop relying exclusively on chemical poisons.[20]

Those warnings had little effect. By 1970 the tobacco budworm population in much of Texas had reached the highest populations ever recorded. Resistance in the cotton bollworm is expected to follow the budworm pattern. With no substitute chemicals available, it may be only a matter of time before chemical control procedures fail completely.

Across the Rio Grande, the onslaught of the budworm struck Mexican farmers with the fury of a Biblical plague, leaving much of the cotton country around Tampico and Matamoros in the desolation of severe economic depression. The tobacco budworm increased its resistance to parathion in the Tampico area from 31-fold in 1968 to 169-fold in 1969. Yields plummeted and by 1970 the farmers had virtually ceased to plant cotton. In the Matamoros-Reynosa area of the Lower Rio Grande Valley, where cotton production declined from 710,000 acres in 1960 to 1,200 acres by 1970, and in the Tampico-Mante area, where planted acreage declined from 500,000 to less than 1,200 acres, the cotton industry literally disappeared.

In August, 1970, a USDA official from Brownsville, Texas, visited the area and reported that 70 percent of its cleared land was no longer in cultivation. Of the thirty cotton gins in the area, ten had been dismantled and moved to the West Coast and the rest were boarded up. Farmers found it impossible to borrow money to continue farming. In the town of El Mante, formerly a thriving agricultural marketplace, nearly 30 percent of the stores were vacant.

In retrospect, it is clear that the farmers of the Lower Rio Grande Valley sowed the winds of their destruction when they decided to rely exclusively on regularly scheduled applications of broad spectrum insecticides to control their pest problems. Ultimately, the chemicals were no match for the genetic diversity of the insects.[21]

As the experience of the farmers in the San Joaquin, Canete, and Rio Grande Valleys shows, cotton pesticides in many parts of the world have reached the point of diminishing returns. The response of insects to chemical attack has placed pest control in a state of crisis which can have serious economic, social, and political consequences. Up to now, the chemical companies have managed to ignore this problem. In light of the wasteland produced by parathion in the Rio Grande Valley, the following comment by the Stauffer Chemical Company seems astonishingly smug:

In recent years the seriousness of tobacco budworm and resistant bollworm outbreaks in cotton have brought about rather revolutionary changes in the concept of phosphate poison use. Here we have resorted to the instant mass kill of all insects in the target area by using Ethyl and Methyl Parathion at rather high rates as the infestation dictates. Initially this aroused some ire over the hazards involved and the resulting unbalanced predatorial insect ratio. *Fantastic control and practical economics have since quelled this misapprehension. . . .*[22] (Emphasis added)

A different view is held by Dr. Roy Smith and Dr. Harold Reynolds, two University of California entomologists who are among the most widely recognized cotton ecologists in the world. They describe the use of pesticides without regard for the complexity of the cotton ecosystem as the *basic* cause of worsening cotton pest problems over the past ten to fifteen years.[23]

The problem is being recognized elsewhere in the world of agribusiness. *Agricultural Science Review*, a staid journal of USDA's Cooperative State Research Service, which has rather uncritically promoted pesticides in the past, recently made a startling about-face. In California, it reported, "the untimely, ill-advised, and even indiscriminate use of chemicals applied largely because of uncertainty, has placed cotton production in a serious position." It warns that "production costs have spiraled and pest problems have been triggered to a point where efficient insect control is now in jeopardy in many areas of the state. If current attitudes and control practices continue, there is every reason to believe that the situation will worsen. In fact, the pest control problem seriously threatens the entire cotton industry in California."[24] In Louisiana, cotton pests are becoming resistant faster than substitute pesticides can be found, and the situation has reached a critical stage. Dr. Leo D. Newsom of Louisiana State University, in a paper for a conference on the Ecological Aspects of International Development, reported that certain populations of insects in his state's cotton belt can no longer be controlled satisfactorily with any currently available pesticide.[25] In Colombia, extravagant use of parathion has led to impending resistance and the unleashing of secondary pests which portend a grim future for cotton pest control in that country.[26]

The situation is similar in Central America where individual farmers, in desperation, have resorted to up to fifty treatments of parathion to a field in a single season. There have been serious side effects. Residues turned up in beef and milk. There are also hundreds of cases of insecticide poisoning in man, with many deaths reported.[27] In Guatemala and Nicaragua, where cotton earns over 30 percent of export dollars, American pesticide practices have led to pest outbreaks which, according to Smith and Reynolds, may soon result in a major crop failure, an economic disaster in these countries if it occurs. They conclude that "the misuse of pesticides and the resulting aggravated insect infestations have been the major cause of the declining yields in Central America. It is no exaggeration to say that pest control which leads to an economic calamity may topple a government."[28] The results of one attempt to measure the effectiveness of pesticides by Guatemala are summa-

ECONOMIC SUMMARY OF COTTON, FINCA AFRICA*
Costs and Returns per Manzana (= 1.7 acres)

	Experimental Field	Commercial Field
Yield, total seed cotton (= cotton seed + ginned or lint cotton)	1500 lb.	1800 lb.
Yield, lint cotton	500 lb.	600 lb.
Yield, seed	1000 lb.	1200 lb.
Value of ginned cotton, at $0.28/lb.	$ 140	$ 168
Value of cotton seed, at $0.02/lb.	20	24
Total value (return per manzana)	$ 160	$ 192
Production costs (based on Nicaragua data) (excluding insecticides)	$ 110	$ 110
Insecticides (cost to Monsanto Chemical Co.)		62
Total costs per manzana	$ 110	$ 172
I. Net return per manzana	+ $ 50	+ $ 20
Production costs (based on Nicaragua data) (excluding insecticides)	$ 110	$ 110
Insecticides (cost to grower)		95
Total costs per manzana	$ 110	$ 205
II. Net return (or loss) per manzana	+ $ 50	− $ 13
Production costs (based on Ray Smith's estimates in Guatemala) (excluding insecticides)	$ 200	$ 200
Insecticides (cost to grower)		95
Total costs per manzana	$ 200	$ 295
III. Net loss per manzana	− $ 40	− $ 103

* The figures on production costs are tentative, since data on real production costs are not yet available. For this reason we have used several different cost figures which were available to us. Regardless of the variation in cost figures, the experimental field shows a better cost/return ratio.

Source: *Center for the Biology of Natural Systems Notes*, vol. 4, no. 1 (1971).

rized in the table above. The experimental fields were unsprayed. The commercial fields were sprayed as usual with organophosphates by their owners. In all cases the experimental field, although it produced less, was economically more successful than the commercial field.

The Farmer's Plight

As these cases suggest, the farmer is often the greatest single victim of pesticide abuse. Misuse of pesticides not only threatens his health but increases his cost of production and may actually reduce his yield in the long run. Unfortunately, pesticide critics tend to view the use of chemicals by farmers only in terms of a conflict between private property rights—the right of the farmer to exploit his land as he sees fit—and the public interest in avoiding fish kills, food contamination, destruction of wildlife, and the other harmful fallout from the misuse of pesticides on private land. They hold the farmer responsible as one who willingly pollutes to increase his profits. This view of the farmer makes two assumptions: that present patterns of pesticide use are profitable for the farmer, and that the farmer could stop their use if he would only try.

The picture is not so simple. The farmer, in fact, is often a pawn of economic and corporate forces which put him on a costly pesticide treadmill. He is forced to walk the treadmill, even when it has brought the use of pesticides to the point of diminishing returns on many of his crops. Environmentalists, therefore, in making the farmer a scapegoat for pesticide pollution, have not only misplaced blame; they have turned off a potentially powerful ally in the cause of pesticide reform.

For over twenty years, the agribusiness establishment has conditioned the farmer, through economic incentives and propaganda directed by the chemical industry, to embrace pesticides with little thought for their ecological impact. The sudden availability of pesticides after World War II coincided with a farm policy which was a pesticide salesman's dream. Controls were placed on acreage, not production. The farmer poured technology into his remaining land to increase his yields. In

1950, for example, the average yield of corn per acre was 40 bushels; by 1960, it was over 60 bushels. As a result, the total resources devoted to agriculture did not decline as much as expected: an increase in nitrogen, fertilizer, pesticides, and machinery helped offset the decrease in land and labor.[29] The new chemicals offered one of the cheapest ways to increase yields. The cotton allotment program, in particular, helped addict the farmer's land to increasing doses of chemicals by encouraging him to substitute pesticides for inputs of land and labor.

Once initiated to the uses of agricultural chemistry, the farmer abandoned cultural controls such as crop rotation, field sanitation, and adjustment of planting and harvest dates to avoid peaks in a pest population. It served as a tranquilizer, relieving his anxiety and feeling of helplessness before the elements. In this emotional state, he was easy prey for the pesticide maker. Unfortunately, the farmer tends to seek advice on pest control from chemical salesmen with a vested interest in exploiting his ignorance. He often has nowhere else to turn.

The technological breakthrough in chemical control of pests after World War II burst onto the agricultural scene without a professional technocracy to guide and control its use. Literally overnight, some of the most toxic and ecologically disruptive chemicals known to science were placed in the hands of farmers, agribusiness salesmen, and federal farm advisors almost totally unaware of their genetic and ecological implications.[30] Choosing a chemical to control a pest—in terms of its effectiveness, its proper dose level, and possible side-effects—parallels the complexity and risks of prescribing a drug for human disease. Yet often the farmer's only available advisor is the agrichemical company fieldman, often motivated by sales quotas and commissions to promote excessive pesticide use by confirming the farmer's worst fears. As a consequence, a great many farmers use pesticides with the blind faith of a purchaser of patent medicines, often with similar therapeutic results. According to Professor Robert van den Bosch, Chairman of the University of California's Division of Biological Control:

. . . a highly developed technology utilizing complex techniques and highly toxic ecologically disruptive materials came to rely in great measure on salesmen for its implementation. It takes little imagination to envisage the chaotic state of medicine, were the diagnosis of illness and its treatment, particularly through the use of drugs and medicines, the responsibility of the pharmaceutical-house salesman. Yet this is the case in plant protection.[31]

Manufacturers can be quite frank about their sales approach, as demonstrated by a recent address by R. H. Wellman of Union Carbide to the Western Agricultural Chemicals Association on the responsibility of pesticide distributors:

The distributor must maintain and continually improve an aggressive knowledgeable sales force who SELL products. The order takers and price salesmen are not the type on which the distributor can rely for both profit and volume. Nor do they make up the kind of sales force for which the manufacturer is justified in providing adequate suggested margins on his products.[32]

Another basic cause of the farmer's excessive and self-destructive use of pesticides is often overlooked: the fact that most pesticides are ecologically crude, killing pests and beneficial insects alike. Professor van den Bosch, a pioneer in the application of ecological principles to pest control, has frequently criticized this limitation of pesticides:

The modern insecticide is ecologically crude because nowhere in its synthesis, development, or utilization is serious consideration given to the essentially ecological nature of insect control. The materials are devised to kill the widest possible insect spectra, and thereby capture the widest possible markets. In practice this is the way they are used, the environment be damned! And quite ironically, . . . the pocketbook of the user too![33]

While these features of pesticides give farmers and environmentalists a joint interest in pesticide reform, in practice the chemical industry has found it easy to drive a wedge between them. Pointing to a few strident critics who would casually ban all pesticides, the companies have convinced the farmer that any control threatens all chemicals and that therefore the farmer and the agrichemical industry must stand or fall together. The reformers often encourage this unholy alliance by appearing to attack the basic concept of chemical controls, failing to recognize that pesticides, when used as ecologically selective tools, are often necessary in helping to maintain the balance of some insect populations. Environmentalists should direct their attack, not at the pesticides *per se*, but at the ways in which they are synthesized, developed, and marketed.

The Shell Game

To understand how reckless promotion may harm the farmer, let us look again at the use of Azodrin in California's San Joaquin Valley in 1967. The Azodrin case is more than just another example of pest resurgence after overkill by a toxic organophosphate. It is a classic example of how pesticide marketing practices in defiance of ecological principles victimize the farmer.

The Azodrin story begins in the early 1960s when Shell's salesmen in California discovered there was a large potential market in the San Joaquin Valley for a new insecticide to kill the lygus bug, an insect which feeds on the buds and bolls of cotton. Azodrin was field tested by Shell for this purpose and found to be effective. It was registered for use in California by the State Department of Agriculture in 1965. But while Shell was preparing a massive sales campaign to introduce Azodrin to the California farmer, entomologists at the University of California made a disturbing discovery.* Their tests showed that while Azodrin did destroy the lygus bug, its use in many cases left the farmer worse off than he was before.

There were several reasons for this. The cotton plant, in the early season, has many buds which never grow into bolls and many bolls which never ripen.[34] Its capacity to set mature bolls depends upon its present fruit load and general physiology, and growing condi-

* These entomologists evaluate all new insecticides registered for use in California and make recommendations for safety and efficacy. Unlike PRD, they do not accept data compiled by the chemical industry alone. Their recommendations are based on their own experiments.

tions. It will shed the excess bolls even if no insects are present.[35] Except at very high infestations, the lygus bug appears to attack the surplus buds and bolls, which would never develop cotton anyway. Even when large numbers of lygus migrate from cut alfalfa fields, they may stay in cotton only a few days and move on. As a pest of San Joaquin Valley cotton, therefore, the lygus bug appears to have been frequently overrated.[36]

The use of Azodrin to kill the lygus bug was not only often unnecessary but potentially harmful: early season treatment of cotton with Azodrin not only kills the lygus bug, but also ladybugs, greenlace wings, pirate bugs, and other insects which prey on the eggs and larvae of the bollworm. (Azodrin turned out to be one of the most highly destructive materials to beneficial insects ever tested.[37]) The result is often a bollworm plague like the one which decimated Mr. Hobe's cotton.

University of California entomologists also investigated the possibility of using Azodrin for cotton bollworm control in 1965. Test plots receiving two full treatments of Azodrin and a partial third, were compared to a control plot, which received no treatment. All the plots had relatively light bollworm infestations when the test began in August. By October, the amount of damaged cotton in the Azodrin treated plot was significantly higher than in the control plots.[38] The scientists' conclusion was that the devastating effect of Azodrin on the natural enemies of the bollworm actually increased the bollworm populations in the treated fields.

Shell Chemical Company was aware of these results. Dr. P. L. Leigh, a University of California entomologist and one of the authors of the Experiment Station report which raised the questions about Azodrin, obtained his results from tests conducted jointly by the University of California and Shell Chemical Company. Dr. Robert van den Bosch presented the results to Shell representatives at a seminar given at the Shell Research Center in Modesto, California in 1966, at which time he expressly warned them of Azodrin's dangers for cotton farmers.[39]

Relying on other tests which the company claimed contradicted van den Bosch, Shell simply ignored his

warnings in its sales campaigns.* Apparently, it did not
inform its salesmen of the University of California tests.
Its district sales representative in Madera County where
Mr. Hobe has his farm stated that he knew of no such
tests, that as far as he knew, beneficial insects were
relatively unimportant in cotton pest control, and that
in any case they would "be back in there probably the
next day or the following day" under favorable conditions.[40] (In fact Azodrin may suppress beneficial
insects for as long as thirty days.)

In 1967, Shell gave Azodrin the largest promotion in
California pesticide history. The cotton counties of California were saturated with radio, TV, and billboard ads
praising Azodrin as a breakthrough in cotton insect
control. Shell also suggested that the farmers apply
Azodrin as prophylactic sprays on a fixed schedule
basis, regardless of the number of pests in the fields.
"If you are part of the trend toward a regular spray
schedule," said one Shell ad, "you'll find that Azodrin
can take over so completely that cotton bollworms, pink
bollworms, loopers, lygus, and mites can't get established in cotton." These "calendar" applications have
long been condemned by ecologists as a wasteful practice which hastens pest resistance and environmental
pollution.[41] This insured that Azodrin would frequently
be applied to pest populations which were either noninjurious or only marginally so (where the costs of
application exceeded the potential loss from the pests).
Shell was assisted by the Kern County Agricultural
Chemical Association, an organization of pesticide distributors which sent newsletters to growers in the San
Joaquin Valley claiming that Azodrin would increase
cotton yield by up to 280 pounds an acre.

By the end of 1967, the sales campaign was a phe-
nomenal success. There were approximately 1 million
acre applications of Azodrin in its first year—the great-

* The problem with Azodrin and other organophosphates is the
delicate timing required to make them effective. Their use in late
July and early August has led to aggravated pest problems and repeated use during peak bloom has at times reduced yields substantially.
Farmers in 1967 were not adequately informed of these risks. Shell
now recognizes these problems and recommends that Azodrin users
observe a cut-off period (twenty-one days after first bloom) to
minimize harm to beneficial insects.

est initial acceptance of any pesticide in California history.[42] Whether it helped the farmer is another question. The farmers of the San Joaquin Valley had to regain through increased yields their multimillion dollar investment in Azodrin. According to Professor van den Bosch, "the bulk of the evidence would seem to indicate that no outstanding benefit occurred, since the 1967 cotton yield in the San Joaquin Valley was one of the lowest of the past decade."[43]

The cotton committee at the University of California's Agricultural Experiment Station makes recommendations on pesticides to California farmers. Feeling strongly that the misuse of Azodrin was hooking the farmer to a costly pesticide treadmill, the committee took an unprecedented step. Usually when a chemical is found lacking in some respect, it is simply left out of the committee's official recommendations. In 1968, however, after reviewing the Azodrin case, it explicitly warned in its Cotton Pest Control Bulletin that "the organophosphorous materials (Azodrin and methylparathion) have had a severe impact on the natural enemies of the bollworm, and their use may lead to further outbreaks of this and other pests."[44]

These subtleties were lost on the California farmer. Buffeted by Shell's promotional campaign, he bought Azodrin in record quantity and seemed unaffected by the warnings from the University of California entomologists. The aggressive sales campaign successfully muffled the efforts of the Agricultural Experiment Station to communicate its research findings.

This is not surprising. Advice is readily available from the field representatives of chemical companies. Approximately 600 pesticide salesmen practice their trade in California. The cost of this sales apparatus, which is passed on to the farmer and the consumer, has been estimated at roughly $25 million per year.[45] The grower is often suspicious of the more sophisticated approach to pest control urged by university entomologists. One frustrated entomologist notes:

. . . the grower and the [pesticide] dealer are members of the same community—church, Rotary, and country club— and many growers think that everybody from the university

community (especially Berkeley) is some kind of radical
kook.[46]

This situation is not limited to California. A study by the
Agricultural Experiment Station at Iowa State in 1966
showed that farmers in that state placed greater trust
in chemical dealers than on the agricultural extension
service for information on pesticides.[47]

The conflict of interest in the advice the farmer
receives extends beyond pesticides. Gullible farmers are
also victimized by salesmen promoting fertilizers and
other agricultural chemicals. When the southern corn
leaf blight panicked farmers in the Deep South and
Midwest in the summer of 1970, chemical salesmen
planted rumors that heavy applications of lime or liquid
nitrogen would reduce the blight in 1971. While nitrogen does help to break down corn debris in which the
blight fungus takes refuge in winter, it gives little or
no protection to the farmer. Infected corn debris is
spread over 60 million acres in the United States and
corn blight spores are capable of blowing a hundred
miles or more to infect corn. Lime also had no effect
on the blight resistance of corn in 1970. Dr. M. C. Shurtleff, a plant pathologist at the University of Illinois and
an expert on the corn leaf blight, recently chided chemical salesmen for trying to exploit the farmer's anxiety
about the blight:

These rumors [that lime and nitrogen curb the blight] were
spread largely by aggressive salesmen "trying to make a
fast buck" . . . The only ones who win with rumors like this
are the salesmen and the companies they represent.[48]

While the overuse of fertilizers may have less serious
ecological consequences than with pesticides, their
cause is often the same: the farmers' ignorance about
the chemicals they use, an ignorance enhanced and
exploited by the patent medicine psychology of chemical salesmanship.

One might expect that the Extension Service, with
its $285 million budget (total funds from federal, state,
and county sources) and 6,000 county agents might
act as a buffer between the farmer and the chemical
companies. As we shall see in the next chapter some

Extension Agents do try to play this role. They examine the farmer's fields and encourage him to spray only when pest infestations demand it. Even so, they are often outgunned by the pesticide sales force. Most do not even try to compete. In many areas, county agents have abdicated their pesticide advisory function to the chemical salesmen. Many others are unabashed pitchmen for the chemical industry. One example is John J. Durkin, an extension specialist in entomology, who edits a bi-weekly newsletter for New Mexico farmers which regularly promotes the use of toxaphene and other chlorinated hydrocarbons, and criticizes USDA's efforts to restrict their use.[49] This pro-pesticide bias is not accidental. Extension agents and specialists are pressured by the sales representatives of the chemical industry in the same way that doctors are bombarded by the pharamaceutical houses.

The training of these advisors to the farmer is obsolete for modern pest problems. In the past they have had little or no ecological training. A professor of biology at New Mexico State University recently sized up this situation:

They are committed by twenty years' experience—their life's work, really—to a certain point of view. Secretary Hardin can restate policy all he wants to from Washington, and President Nixon can reorganize anything he likes. At the local level nothing's going to change because the same people are going to be doing the job, and they're not equipped to do it any other way than the way they're doing it now.[50]

Acts of God?

If a farmer does feel that a pesticide has damaged his crops because the claims for it have been overstated or misrepresented, he will have a hard time gaining redress in the courts. Mr. Hobe is a case in point. Because his single application of Azodrin was followed so quickly by a bollworm outbreak, he concluded that his loss in yield was the fault of Azodrin. He sued Shell Chemical Company but lost the case. (It is now on appeal.) The defense argued that the bollworm devastation was a natural event, an act of God, and that poor farming practices may have contributed to the loss in yield. In any case, Hobe freely assumed all risks when he decided to use Azodrin.[51]

In a similar case, *Banducci* v. *F.M.C. Corporation*,[52] a farmer claimed that use of the organophosphate Bidrin to control the lygus bug led to a bollworm outbreak which reduced his yield. As in the Hobe case, the contention was that the organophosphate had stimulated the bollworm explosion by killing its natural enemies. Banducci lost as well, the court finding that the bollworms were a natural occurrence and that Banducci had been incompetent as a farmer.

As we shall see in discussing federal registration of pesticides, the farmer's ability to make his case is hindered by omissions in federal law. Neither the label nor the advertisements for a pesticide are required to warn the farmer of its potential impact on beneficial insects, especially the possibility of pest resurgence or secondary outbreaks. If in most cases, federal pesticide regulations ignore the ecological aftereffects of pesticides, it is only natural that courts will too.

When the pesticide manufacturer or his agent fails to give adequate warning, he should be held accountable, either on the basis of negligence or strict liability. This step would force the chemical companies to professionalize their field agents, ensuring that they understand the ecological risks of their products. At the same time, it would give the farmer freedom of choice to reduce his economic risks and to restrict the use of pesticides to situations of real need, thereby minimizing the poisoning of farm workers and the environment.

Until the chemical companies, the extension service, the regulatory agencies, and the courts gain some ecological sensitivity with regard to pesticides, the farmer will continue to suffer needlessly. Not only will he suffer economic loss, but when he seeks compensation in the courts, he will either be ridiculed as an inept farmer, pitied as a target of the wrath of God, or chastised for not knowing what the agribusiness establishment has deliberately kept him from knowing—that pesticides may do him harm as well as good.

Neither the farmer, the consumer, nor the environmentalist can tolerate much longer the ecological insults from the overuse of pesticides. Either independently or through farm organizations like the National Farmers Union, the National Farmers Organization, or the Grange, farmers could join together with environmentalists to support legal action groups which can operate on the state and local level as a watchdog on the chemical industry. These legal action arms could bring test cases to force the chemical companies to compensate the farmer victimized by a pesticide, and they could advocate greater safety and ecological sensitivity for pesticides before regulatory bodies. As a first step, however, they could sponsor demonstration projects to instruct farmers in the relative costs and benefits of pesticides. As we shall see in the next chapter, there are many ways in which the farmer so instructed can greatly reduce his use of chemicals without sacrificing yield.

10

Pesticides in the Balance: Containment Versus Seek and Destroy

The current vicious, hysterical propaganda campaign against [pesticides], being promoted today by fear-provoking, irresponsible environmentalists, had its genesis in the best-selling, half-science, half-fiction novel "Silent Spring," published in 1962. . . .
If the use of pesticides in the U.S.A. were to be completely banned, crop losses would probably soar to 50 percent, and food prices would increase four-fold to five-fold. Who then would provide for the food needs of the low income groups? Certainly not the privileged environmentalists.
> *—Dr. Norman E. Borlaug*
> *Winner of the 1970*
> *Nobel Peace Prize for his work in developing new wheat strains, in an address before a U.S. conference in Rome, November 8, 1971.*

The evidence is abundant that with the single strategy of chemical control we not only have saturated the environment with deadly poisons that endanger a wide spectrum of living organisms, including man himself, but that we have begun to disrupt seriously the economic stability of the farming community, with disaster approaching if we follow our present course.
> *—Sen. Gaylord Nelson,*
> *In an address to the Senate upon introduction of a bill to stimulate research on alternatives to pesticides, 1971.*

Technology assessment, the attempt to find reliable yardsticks to measure the total impact of man's technical tools on his environment, is now a fashionable discipline, yet it has rarely been applied to pesticides. More often than not, those who have tried have suffered for their pains. When *Silent Spring* became a best seller in 1962–1963, its critics on the whole failed to debate Rachel Carson on the merits of her argument about the risks and benefits of pesticides. Instead, the chemical industry counterattacked with a platoon of scientists who, on the lecture circuit and in professional and trade journals, fired off skillful rebuttals to statements Rachel Carson never made. It was not American science's finest hour.*

Dr. William J. Darby, Chairman of the Biochemistry Department at Vanderbilt and a leading establishment scientist (Vice-Chairman of the Mrak Commission and Chairman of the Food Protection Committee of the National Academy of Sciences), charged in *Chemical and Engineering News* that, according to Rachel Carson, "it is neither wise nor responsible to use pesticides in the control of insect-borne diseases."[1] In fact, as a cursory reading of *Silent Spring* shows, Carson did not condemn all uses of pesticides in vector control; she tried, instead, to warn public officials, for the sake of public health, to weigh more cautiously the risks as well as the benefits of these spray programs.

For example, she criticized the strategy of chemical overkill in the mosquito abatement program, particularly the futile eradication efforts, because she feared such massive, repeated spraying would hasten the development of insects resistant to pesticides, which could then no longer protect human health in an emergency. Her warning has recently been vindicated in many parts of the world. In Guatemala, some twelve years after the start of a malaria eradication program based on intensive use of insecticides, the malarial mosquitoes have become resistant. The incidence of the disease is higher

* For a critique of the critics of *Silent Spring*, see the famous review by Lamont C. Cole, Professor of Ecology at Cornell, in the *Scientific American*, December, 1962. For a fascinating account of the entire *Silent Spring* controversy, see Frank Graham's *Since Silent Spring*, pp. 1–93.

than it was before the campaign and the levels of DDT in mothers' milk are higher in Guatemala than has been reported anywhere in the world.[2] From California, in 1971, came the chilling news that the encephalitis vector mosquito, *Culex tarsalis*, has become resistant to virtually all insecticides, leaving the public largely defenseless in the event of an outbreak of this disease.

Another member of the chemical industry's *Silent Spring* "truth squad" was Robert White-Stevens, then an assistant director of research at American Cyanamid and now a professor of biology at Rutgers. White-Stevens gave several dozen lectures in 1962–1963 in which he charged that Rachel Carson, in seeking to ban all pesticides, was promoting world famine, the victims of which, he predicted, would haunt her conscience. *Silent Spring*, of course, does not condemn all pesticides. It condemns instead the tubular vision which allowed pesticides to be crudely thrust into the environment without concern for their complex and often subtle impact on life beyond the target species.

Ten years after *Silent Spring*, when the hazards of chemical overkill are far more documented than in Rachel Carson's time, efforts to initiate serious assessment of the risks and benefits of pesticides are still sidetracked by the straw men and prophecies of doom thrown up by the chemical industry. Thus Robert White-Stevens in 1970 warned that any restriction on pesticides is a potential threat to the nation's food supply: "If the farms of America should fail, our people will have nowhere to turn for food, and our industry, our economy, our society, our defense, and our national integrity would shrink and collapse."[3]

Similarly Dr. Norman E. Borlaug, the Nobel laureate regarded as the father of the Green Revolution,* regards the efforts to restrict DDT in this country as the first step in a conspiracy to ban all pesticides: "DDT is only the first of the dominoes. But it is the toughest to knock out because of its excellent known contributions and safety records. As soon as DDT is successfully banned, there will be a push for the banning of all chlorinated

---

* The Green Revolution refers to the increase in grain production in Mexico, India, Pakistan, and other developing countries through the introduction of new seed strains.

hydrocarbons, then, in order, the organic phosphates and carbamate insecticides." Borlaug predicts that once pesticides are banned, crop production will plummet 50 percent, followed by famine in developing countries which would blindly join in a worldwide ban on pesticides.[4] It is important to note that these predictions, based on the banning of all pesticides, are used to counter restrictions of even one such chemical. Such is the magic of the domino theory.

Such prophecies of doom, based as they are on a specious all-or-nothing dichotomy, beg the questions environmentalists ask. They cloud the real issues of the relative costs and benefits of pesticides and their alternatives. Dr. Borlaug, for example, calls the Environmental Defense Fund "hysterical lobbyists" who, in trying to save the world from chemical poisoning from DDT, would condemn it to death from starvation. He fails to point out that EDF's position on DDT is based on a careful analysis of its risks and benefits for *this* country, where DDT residues are high and insect-borne disease is relatively low, and where more environmentally benign substitutes for control of insect vectors are available at a price we can afford to pay. The risk-benefit calculation is very different for Ceylon or India where human misery from malaria and other insect-borne diseases may outweigh DDT's harm to the environment and where financially practical alternatives are lacking for vector control and crop protection.

EDF is not trying to ban DDT throughout the world and it does not rule out the use of DDT in insect-borne disease outbreaks in this country if and when it is the most effective tool for the job. Dr. Borlaug fails to explain, by the way, why other nations with different risk-benefit ratios, will slavishly follow this nation's lead in banning DDT; other nations have frequently ignored U.S. bans on pesticides such as thallium sulfate, on drugs, on food additives such as cyclamates, and of course on liquor, during Prohibition.

Responsible use of pesticides requires careful consideration of complex and often subtle trade-offs, for which Dr. Borlaug's apocalyptic vision is extremely inappropriate. What Dr. Borlaug ignores is that the overuse of many pesticides not only concentrates potentially dan-

gerous residues in the food chain but, by contributing
to pest resistance and the destruction of natural controls,
actually hastens the obsolescence of the valuable chemical tools he wants to protect. On this point, Dr. Perry
Adkisson, head of entomology at Texas A&M, warned a
Senate Committee in September, 1971, that the continued development of insecticide-resistant insects
"threatens to render obsolete much of present pest control technology. If new methods of pest control are not
developed, then entire agricultural industries may
severely decline, or even disappear."[5] To paraphrase
Dr. Borlaug, who then will feed the hungry poor?

It is heartening to note that some farmers, driven by
the inexorable logic of diminishing returns, are beginning to weigh the benefits and costs of pesticides in a
more sophisticated fashion than the agribusiness
technocrats who claim to speak in their name. In doing
so, they are learning that farmers have been widely over-
sold on pesticides and that spraying can be reduced up
to 50 percent and more on many crops, if they use
presently available alternatives to unilateral chemical
controls.

Randall "Buck" Fawcett has a dairy and alfalfa
farm in Los Banos, California. Alfalfa is a major
source of feed for livestock, and is the nation's fourth
largest crop in acreage. It is a prime habitat for beneficial insects which help control pests, not only on
alfalfa, but on many other crops. But often they never
get the chance, for they are devastated by the four
million pounds of pesticides applied to alfalfa annually.[6] In the past, when armyworms invaded his alfalfa,
Fawcett faced a dilemma. He feared a loss in yield but
he was reluctant to use pesticides for control. He fed
the alfalfa to his dairy cows and he feared that residues
might turn up in his milk. Fawcett noticed, however,
that in some years pesticides were not necessary: "A
grower will tend to panic when he sees armyworms in-
vading his alfalfa fields. Yet with the proper balance
of parasitic insects in those fields, nature will take care
of the worms in four to five days if the grower will just
wait. And in those few days the worms aren't going to
do that much damage."[7]

The problem is in knowing if the necessary number

of insect parasites or predators is there. For this technical advice, Fawcett hired a consulting entomologist. For a fixed fee the entomologist visited his fields, checked on the levels of beneficial insects, and recommended control when necessary. With this help, Fawcett has found it necessary to apply pesticides only *once* in the past five years to his alfalfa, corn, walnut, and citrus crops.

Cotton farmers in Graham County, Arizona, have applied the same principles of insect management with excellent results. Until 1969 they sprayed 12,500 acres of cotton regularly on a preventive basis—that is, they sprayed according to dates on a calendar, not according to the number of insects in their fields. In 1968, the farmers spent $199,000 for pesticides, and still found, as one farmer noted, that they "were getting eaten up." In 1969, the farmers formed a committee to find an alternative to wholesale spraying. They decided to employ high school students as field checkers or cotton "scouts" to monitor the number of pests at different stages of the crop year. The scouts were trained by the extension service at the University of Arizona to identify the pink bollworm and other pests. With this help, the farmers were able to spray on a need basis, only when pest numbers reached a predetermined danger threshold. Using this method, the farmers controlled the pests on their 12,500 cotton acres at a cost of only $37,000,[8] including the costs of the scouts. The clear implication of these figures to the farmers was that pesticide marketers have been overselling them in the past.

As a result, Graham County's three main pesticide sellers have suffered sharp declines in sales. One has all but abandoned pesticides and is relying on feed sales for most of its revenue. Jack Wooley, president of the Arizona Agricultural Chemicals Association, complains that farmers now think the pesticide company field checkers are biased and condemns the University of Arizona for engaging "in competition with free enterprise, going up there and promoting this."[9] In fact, the university extension service acted only as a consultant and trainer of the scouts.

Scout programs are now under way in Mississippi,

Arkansas, and many other states. James Brazzell, chief of the methods development branch of USDA's Plant Protection Division, believes that putting pesticide use on a need basis through the scout system has great potential for avoiding ecological disruption: "I believe that you can get savings on pesticides of anywhere from 25 percent to 75 percent, though it's difficult to cite any general figure because every field is a different story and every season is different."[10]

The cases above are not isolated examples. Many farmers are finding it is possible, within the limits of present technology, to reduce dramatically current levels of insecticide use without drastic reductions in yield. Dr. F. R. Lawson, former Director of the Biological Control of Insects Laboratory, has stated that "there are probably very few crops where the amount of insecticide now used could not be reduced by at least half with a proportional reduction in cost and pollution."[11] Apples, one of the most heavily sprayed of all crops, are a case in point. In some states, nearly 50 percent of the total growing costs for apples are spent for pest control. In Michigan in 1971, an average 20 pounds per acre of chemicals were sprayed on apples, including ten applications with fungicides, six to eight with insecticides, and two to three with acaricides. In Indiana, however, farmers have initiated a simple monitoring system for the codling moth which has reduced the pesticide load by half. This system will now be tested on a larger scale, with the expectation that it will be applicable to other regions.[12]

Similarly, studies for the Scientists Institute for Public Information have shown that if farmers in North Carolina took the drastic step of forgoing pesticides altogether on flue-cured tobacco, they would be better off than they are now. This prediction is based on the growing trend toward pest resistance of the budworm and pest resurgence from the destruction of beneficial insects by broad spectrum pesticides.[13] If instead of total abstinence they sprayed judiciously only in the event of a severe outbreak, they would be still better off.

On bananas in Honduras, the establishment of realistic economic thresholds for pest numbers and the proper timing of treatments has increased the effectiveness of natural enemies and reduced pesticide costs by nearly one-half. In California, Dr. van den Bosch estimates that the overuse of insecticides on cotton in the San Joaquin Valley is costing growers over 5 percent of the total value of the crop, over and above losses which would occur with no chemical controls at all. An integrated control program, where cautious use of pesticides is supplemented with full exploitation of natural controls, would increase the growers net return by 8 percent.[14] As these examples show, when the benefits and hazards of exclusive pesticide controls are weighed against more environmentally benign alternatives, the farmer may have much to gain. Unfortunately, as we have seen, most farmers do not have the guidance necessary to make a rational decision as to when to use and when not to use pesticides. The data for this kind of an analysis is still largely uncollected; in fact, we know almost as little about the marginal benefits of pesticide inputs in farming as we know about their hazards. The Mrak Report concluded: "A full cost-benefit appraisal of pesticides in the American economy or in agriculture has not been made."[15] Such a study is extremely challenging, for it must proceed on two levels: the level of macroanalysis as described by the Mrak Report above, where destruction of wildlife and damage to the health of farm workers and the general public must be taken into account—factors which are difficult to quantify; and the level of microanalysis, where costs and benefits are weighed for a given crop on a given farm.

At the macro level, chemical industry spokesmen are very concrete about the benefits of pesticides. A shibboleth of the industry is the statement that withdrawal of pesticides would produce a drastic 30 percent decline in productivity, accompanied by a 50 percent to 75 percent rise in food prices. Where do these figures come from? Industry representatives point to USDA as the source, but Dr. Velmar Davis, chief of the Production Resources Branch of the USDA Economic Research Service, disclaims responsibility for these estimates:

That 30 percent figure was kicking around the USDA long before we began working on pesticides. It's misleading and shouldn't be used. I'm not concerned whether it's accurate—which I doubt with current production techniques and diverted cropland—but that it's an example of an "all-or-nothing" policy on pesticides. We are not going to ban all pesticides because the impact could be substantial—although we don't yet have the data to calculate how great. Meanwhile, I'm confident we can reduce the present use of persistent pesticides with only moderate increases in production costs.

Dr. Davis and a five-man Pesticides Group are responsible for USDA economic evaluations of pesticides. These economists are exemplary in their dedication to dispassionate analysis and the public interest. Unfortunately, their influence often does not reach the upper echelons in USDA, where officials such as Under Secretary Phil Campbell are still freely using the "30 percent figure" to mislead the public.

The Pesticides Group has not, however, had much time to discredit such calculations. Given the controversy that has long swirled around the alleged harms and advantages of pesticides, it is incredible that the first governmental group designed to provide a rational economic evaluation of pesticides was funded only in 1965. Even at that late date, Dr. Davis recalls, "pesticide economics was almost a completely unknown field." The Pesticides Group found a vacuum of data, lacking even the most elementary information such as amounts and kinds of pesticides used in agriculture.

In 1970, the Pesticides Group published its first economic report, a study of the cost of replacing the organochlorines (DDT family) with less persistent insecticides on the four major crops of use—cotton, corn, tobacco, and peanuts. They found that:

The usage of most of [the organochlorine] insecticides could be selectively restricted over a period of two to three years with *only modest increases in costs to farmers*. More than three-fourths of the 72 million pounds of organochlorines used by farmers on the four crops in 1966 could have been replaced by other insecticides without affecting production. However, costs for insect control on these crops would have increased $2.23 an acre treated, a total of nearly $27 million. This was about 0.3 percent of their 1966 farm value.[16]

The additional costs would have been much lower but the report failed to consider biological controls, integrated control, or other methods of reducing total pesticide use.

The Pesticides Group plans to make a comprehensive cost-benefit study in the future—though only for farm use of pesticides (there is virtually no information on nonfarm use). But as of 1971, the benefits and costs of pesticides even in the most narrow sense of their marginal effect on the farmer's profits (disregarding *external* diseconomies), remain unmeasured in agriculture.

On what then do USDA and the chemical companies base their claims for pesticides? One answer is that uncertainties in the methods used to evaluate pesticide benefits allow them to interpret the results as they choose.

For example, one method involves comparing production figures before and after the use of pesticides from the same farms or regions over a period of years. USDA and the pesticide companies, using this method, attribute the large increases in crop yield achieved by American farmers since the early fifties to pesticides. But they do not distinguish the contribution of increased use of machinery, fertilizers, better crop strains, and other changes. Indeed, the deductive logic of the numbers game can cut both ways: at least one standard textbook on economic entomology (Metcalf and Flint) estimates that percentage crop losses to insects in 1936 and 1957 were *virtually identical*, although synthetic organic insecticides had come into widespread use in the interval.[17]

This startling figure and indeed the whole cost-benefit calculus for pesticides must be understood in the context of a national farm policy which has institutionalized incentives for pesticide proliferation. A program of land retirement, linked to subsidy payments, was introduced in the fifties as a means of limiting farm production to avoid surpluses and maintain farm prices. This policy limits the number of acres the farmer farms, not the number of bushels he grows. The system therefore encourages the farmer to use the most sophisticated mechanical and chemical technology to increase the yields from his remaining acres. Between 1949 and 1968, harvested acreage declined by 16 percent but yield per acre increased by 77 percent. The farmer, therefore, has largely defeated efforts to limit production, while abandoning cultural practices such as crop diversity and rotation which helped to discourage pests. For example, if maximum yields were not the primary objective, cotton could be brought to maturity early enough to preclude the development of large pink bollworm populations.[18]

Because he must constantly increase his yield or perish, the farmer quickly adopts any technology which will increase his productivity in the short run. But in doing so, he may be increasing his crops' susceptibility to pests. New seed strains may increase his yields but be more vulnerable to insect attack. He adopts expensive mechanical harvesters and other equipment ($35,000 for some cotton pickers, $11,000 for large tractors), which, because they are often not transferable from one crop to another, force him to plant the same crop over more and more contiguous acres, eliminating the crop diversity necessary for a healthy balance of pest and predator insects.

These efforts have been accompanied by heavy applications of pesticides to control the pest outbreaks which result. As a result, between 1950 and 1967, the amount of pesticides used per farm unit increased by 138 percent.[19] For example, the use of aldrin, a chlorinated hydrocarbon, as a soil insecticide allowed farmers to grow corn contiguously on the same land instead of rotating crops to prevent buildup of corn rootworm. Today the rootworm has become resistant to aldrin. Rootworm damage has increased beyond previous levels and the costs of using alternative pesticides to maintain production have skyrocketed.

J. C. Headley, a professor of agricultural economics at the University of Missouri and a specialist in the cost-benefit analysis of pesticides, warned a USDA symposium on pesticide economics in 1970 that the national policy of land withdrawal, embodied in the Agricultural Act of 1970, had weakened the natural ability of the biological system to control pests and overtaxed the system's capacity to dispose of chemicals safely.[20] He estimates that a modest increase in cropland would permit large reductions in pesticide use without affecting production. Nationwide, he found that *insecticide use can be reduced by more than 6 percent for each 1 percent increase in land use.** The substitution of cropland for insecticides would have the greatest effect in the Southeast, the South Plains, and the Delta regions. Headley found that each acre of cropland returned to production in the South would allow farmers to decrease total pesticide use by 3,257 ounces, with production remaining constant.[21] If cropland were increased 12 percent, the nation could enjoy the same food output with 80 percent less pesticides.

The overuse of pesticides is therefore closely tied to national farm policy. The accelerating pace of farm land retirement, for this and many other reasons, is a source of concern for environmentalists. Legislative reforms which would divorce subsidy payments from maximization of yields and encourage diversified agriculture in localized areas to provide a proper habitat for beneficial insects would help immensely to free growers from the pesticide treadmill.

Changes in consumer attitudes are also necessary to reduce the economic impact on the farmer of limiting pesticides. The consumers' preference for aesthetically perfect fruits and vegetables forces the farmer to adopt "cosmetic" control programs which exacerbate pest problems without affecting the quality or quantity of the crop. For example, orange groves are sprayed to control citrus thrips which cause a scarring on the outer surface of orange peels. Although the scarring has no effect on quality, consumers avoid oranges with these blemishes. Grading and marketability standards now institutionalize the consumer's cosmetic preferences. As a result, he runs the risk of increased residues from the pesticides required to produce this unnecessarily perfect orange.[22]

Containment Versus Seek and Destroy

It is clear that public policy should discourage excessive pesticide use, particularly when its long-term costs

---

* Pesticide pollution is only one of the side effects of this national land policy. In a subsequent report, we will discuss the other diseconomies of cropland reduction, including the removal of surplus farm labor from the farms to the cities, the incentives it gives to the corporatization of agriculture, and its effect on the small farmer.

remain largely unknown. As Dr. Lawson has said, "It makes very little sense to continue increasing the number of pests that attack our crops, the incidence and severity of their outbreaks, and the level of resistance to insecticides, if there is any other alternative."[23] USDA should approach pesticides from the angle of minimum application, not maximum production.

The pest control strategy of "integrated control" is the most promising means to this end. With this system, farmers do not rely exclusively on chemicals to sterilize their fields of all insect life, but use a variety of biological, cultural, mechanical, and chemical controls to manipulate insect populations until they reach a healthy pest-predator balance. They use pesticides only after other measures fail to prevent crop damage and then only use pesticides which are most specific for the pest in the smallest possible amounts. Dr. R. F. Smith, one of the pioneers of integrated control, describes it as "an ecological approach to the control of harmful insects. It derives its uniqueness from the fullest practical utilization of existing mortality and suppressive factors in the environment. Its strategy is one of management and containment, rather than seek and destroy."[24] The "economic threshold" is a key concept in this system. It is defined as the density of pest population at which control measures are necessary to keep the pests from expanding and causing economic injury to crops.

Louis Ruud, who directs a consulting service in entomology for California farmers, explains the system as it works in an orchard:

We will visit the orchard once a week during the growing season charting the changes in pest populations—both destructive and beneficial. If a population of a given insect starts to climb, we will closely watch it. . . . Just by experience in dealing with insect populations in various crops, we have established what we call an economic threshold for various species—that is the point beyond which we believe an increase in populations will cause the grower to lose part of his crop. If the numbers are approaching the threshold and there are not enough natural enemies to bring it back below the threshold, *then* we recommend treatment.[25] (Emphasis added)

When spraying is necessary, the consulting entomologist recommends a soft insecticide which will have the least disruptive effect on the insect ecosystem. He neither sells nor applies the chemical—he simply writes a prescription for it.

The strategy of integrated control evolved out of necessity, when the unilateral strategy of chemical control began to fail. Ecologists and many entomologists had long embraced the ecological approach to pest control but they had little influence until evidence began to accumulate on the harmful side effects of pesticides for public health and the farmers' profits. As far as integrated control is concerned, the economic threat is really the key.

One of the earliest successful experiments with this method occurred in California in the early 1950s. The spotted alfalfa aphid, which invaded California from the Southwest, became resistant to most available insecticides and was causing staggering losses to the alfalfa industry. A multidiscipline team, including entomologists, plant breeders, agronomists, and extension specialists, was mobilized at the University of California to try to save the industry. Pooling their talents and resources, they pieced together an integrated control system with the immediate goal of understanding the alfalfa ecosystem and the role of the alfalfa aphid in it. The scientists used the full arsenal of pest control techniques: they evaluated the impact of the aphid's native natural enemies, imported new parasites and predators, determined a valid economic threshold, selected aphid-resistant alfalfa varieties, studied the aphid's seasonal activity patterns and developed cultural practices to exploit them, and perfected the timing and amounts of selective pesticides.

The program was implemented in 1958 with spectacular effect. Losses to the aphid dropped initially from $10 million to $2 million and then still lower as aphid-resistant alfalfa strains came into use. The alfalfa industry was saved and today the spotted alfalfa aphid remains a minor pest.

Despite such successful experiments, integrated control has still not found wide acceptance among farmers.

It is held back in part by educational and research failures in the Department of Agriculture. To use this system, the grower needs a lot of handholding by skilled advisors. After years of pesticide propaganda, it challenges common sense that the best way to deal with pests *may* be to leave them alone.

Chemical pesticides, with their quick catastrophic biological effects, are easy to understand. By comparison, biological and integrated controls are often slow to show results, and they may be so complex in their interactions that even entomologists find it difficult to explain exactly what is happening. As one leading entomologist has noted, "withdrawing a crop from hard pesticide use is somewhat analogous to a drug-addicted person withdrawing from his chemical dependence. The crop, like the patient, often looks its worst before it is to revive."[26]

In the past, the Federal Extension Service and agricultural experiment stations at land-grant colleges have largely failed to help farmers make rational judgments about the costs and benefits of pesticides and their alternatives. While this is still the case in many areas—a group of Iowa farmers recently complained that their extension agent used government stamped stationery to announce pest control meetings which turned out to be sales talks by chemical company men—there are some hopeful signs that USDA is finally waking up to its responsibility. The Extension Service, under the direction of Assistant Administrator Raymond C. Scott, has trained 628 scouts to assist growers in ten cotton states. Cotton scouting in Texas's Pecos and Reeves counties in 1971 reduced pesticide costs from $0.04 per pound of cotton lint to $0.015 per pound. Insect-scouted farms in Arkansas averaged 200 more pounds of cotton yield than farms in the same area not scouted for insects.[27] These are still demonstration projects limited to only one crop but USDA plans to expand this program in 1972. The National Science Foundation is now sponsoring more ambitious integrated control demonstration projects at North Carolina State and other universities.

Another barrier to integrated control has been the narrow specialization of entomologists and other agricultural scientists. As late as 1968, only one paper out of 397 presented at the annual meeting of the Entomological Society of America dealt with integrated control. What is needed is a new professional armed with the knowledge of modern entomology, plant science, toxicology, and industrial chemistry. With this synthesis of expertise, entomology may become, as the eminent entomologist Dr. H. T. Reynolds predicts, "the most dynamic of all sciences. . . . We try to put all of these [disciplines] together, and we think it is dynamic and certainly fascinating."[28]

Demonstration projects, guided by such advisors, are desperately needed on a much larger scale to show farmers how to optimize cost-benefit ratios in pest control with present technology and knowledge. Unfortunately, USDA has decided to oppose S. 1794, Senator Gaylord Nelson's 1971 bill to increase funding for such pilot field projects. As an incentive to farmers, the bill would indemnify farmers who suffered losses as a result of experiments with integrated controls. In a joint statement with the National Science Foundation, USDA stated that integrated control could not be approached on a grower-to-grower basis but only on a limited regional basis. It also noted that integrated control for the boll weevil would destroy a third of the remaining DDT market and expressed concern about the "legal, marketing, and economic problems" which might result from such projects.[29] As this statement suggests, the Nixon Administration's attitude toward pesticide alternatives has been at best ambivalent. In 1971, the White House impounded $1 million specifically allocated by Congress for nonchemical pest control research.[30]

If integrated control is to succeed, there will also have to be structural reforms in the synthesis and marketing of pesticides. At the present time, ecological pest control is hobbled by the fact that, for economic reassons, there are few chemicals so specific for a pest that they can be applied without upsetting biological controls. Without more selective pesticides and biological controls, integrated control will fail. Since *Silent Spring*, USDA has gradually increased its research on nonchemical means of pest control. In fiscal year 1972, over half of USDA's pesticide research budget of $82 million will go to studies of nonchemical controls. This sum is put in perspective when one realizes that a chemical company may spend up to $9 million in development costs for just one pesticide. These relatively small federal funds have serious consequences. First, at the period of critical need, universities are reducing the number of graduate students in entomology because there are no jobs open. Second, there are strong economic indicators that only government can provide non-chemical research.

A chemical company's total investment in a pesticide that reaches the market ranges between $6 and $10 million. This enormous investment and risk have the following results. First, manufacturers do not attempt to develop selective pesticides which would limit their killing power to only specific target pests, and, therefore, keep ecological disruptions to a minimum. Selective pesticides cost more to develop than broad spectrum ones. Extensive screening is required to find the pest or pests that are particularly susceptible to them. Selective pesticides are also less profitable because their market is limited to a few susceptible pests.[31] From the company point of view, the more varieties of organisms a pesticide kills, the better return on investments. As a result, all pesticides come out pretty much alike: toxic to a broad range of organisms.

Because pesticides *are* so much alike, many cannot be sold on their individual merits any more than can detergents; like detergents they must be pushed with heavy advertising and high pressure salesmanship. Such practices slide easily into promotion of pesticides for unsuitable purposes (such as arsenicals for home use) and outright deception.

In contrast, biological controls provide few incentives to dishonesty; in fact, they provide few incentives of any kind, except to the farmer and the public. Biological controls are not and, with a few exceptions, may never be profitable to industry. Government will have to pursue this alternative if it is to be developed.

Consider, for example, a project to control biologically an imported pest such as a scale insect on citrus fruits. Already more than thirty-two species of parasites have been introduced to control California scale insects.[32] In searching for a parasite to control a new scale insect, entomologists must first identify the pest and, if possible, determine where it comes from. If they are lucky enough to discover the pest's homeland, they must then go out and collect the pest and its parasites and predators. This is not an easy task, for in its homeland, the pest insect may be so thoroughly controlled by these natural enemies that it is virtually impossible to find. Having gotten this far, the entomologists must then breed the pest's natural enemies in large numbers and test them to make sure they will not harm other insects. Finally, the day comes when the entomologists turn the natural enemies loose. If they are lucky (90 percent of completed scale insect projects have been successful), within a year or two the natural enemies will have spread over the entire area of release. Compared to chemicals, such biological control projects are very cheap. They have cost as little as $1,000 to $5,000 with a maximum so far of $150,000.[33]

It is obvious why these projects are unattractive to the chemical industry. If a private company were to invest even as little as $150,000 in finding predators or parasites to control a pest, it almost certainly would not recover its investment. Competitors could seize much of the potential market since the company could patent neither the research nor the predators and parasites themselves. Nor could the company prevent the spread of predators and parasites to growers who had not paid for them. Finally, it could not expect continuing sales if the predators and parasites succeeded. In a few cases where a pest can be controlled only by repeated release of natural enemies, such biological control might conceivably be profitable, but hardly as profitable as chemicals.

Other forms of biological control are equally unrewarding to the agrichemical industry. For example, when researchers discovered that Hessian fly damage to wheat can be largely avoided by postponing spring planting until after the flies have emerged from winter hibernation and starved, this knowledge was free to any grower who wanted to use it. Also free is the knowledge that lygus bugs, which prey on cotton in California, are so fond of alfalfa that if a grower plants a strip in his cotton field, the bugs will congregate in the

alfalfa and stay out of the cotton. Insect diseases, like
Bacillus thuringiensis, are marketed on a limited scale
but, like insect predators and parasites, they are difficult
or impossible to patent and find only a small market,
due to their specificity. Disease research, therefore, cannot attract much business capital. As a National
Agricultural Chemicals Association spokesman commented, "There really is not much biological control in
industry research; they would research themselves right
out of the market."[34]

If private industry is not developing biological controls, what about research at universities? In the past,
the pesticides industry has paid for the bulk of pest
control research at universities; consequently, research
emphasized chemical control. Many university entomologists became propagandists for chemicals because of
their dependence on the chemical industry for graduate
student fellowships, consultantships, research expenses,
and attractive staff positions for their graduates.[35] In
the last year, this dependence has weakened as USDA,
the National Science Foundation, and private foundations such as Ford have put up more money for nonchemical research. The "ecological" entomology as
practiced by Drs. van den Bosch, Reynolds, and Smith
of the University of California is exciting to students.
What they need is more opportunities to practice their
trade in the fields.

The chemical industry has a very different view of
what is needed. According to Dr. Roy Hansberry, a
Shell Chemical Company scientist who is a leading
spokesman for the pesticide industry, the taxpayers are
being bilked in paying for research on biological controls: "The world is already hungry. In ten years we
may be short of some kinds of food in the U.S. I hope
that time will not be hastened by the entomologists in
state and federal service spending too much time on
esoteric approaches while largely ignoring the cheaper
and more effective insecticides we in industry will continue to introduce every year."[36] Hansberry points out
that biological and other nonchemical controls have not
worked on a large scale on the most important insect
pest such as the boll weevil.

Hansberry's skepticism has some merit. The success

of some biological projects has been exaggerated. For example, of 520 predator species imported into the United States, only about twenty have provided significant control of some of the most destructive pests on key crops.[37] On the other hand, Dr. Paul DeBach, at the University of California at Riverside, keeps a global score sheet on biological projects against 223 kinds of pests and has tallied complete or substantial control in about half, in sixty-six countries. Many of the problems with biological controls might now be resolved if the government had not failed so miserably for so long to support adequately biological research.

Before World War II, the various research divisions of the Agricultural Research Service performed some of the finest biological control research in the world, and made the results quickly available to growers. After World War II, these divisions continued their excellent work on the breeding of resistant crop varieties. Then, overnight, succumbing to the infatuation with chemicals stimulated by DDT, they largely abandoned their efforts. Even when problems of chemical controls became blatant in the early fifties, the ARS research divisions were notoriously slow to return to biological and other nonchemical alternatives, which only the government can provide.

The most progressive of the USDA research projects in biological control has been the Entomological Research Division, headed by Dr. Edward Knipling. Dr. Knipling saw the handwriting on the wall for chemicals as early as the mid-1950s; he gradually reduced the chemical research of the Division from about 67 percent of the budget in 1955, to 16 percent of its current $18 million budget.

In the late 1950s, Dr. Knipling won world attention with the first eradication program that achieved real success without harmful side effects. The screwworm fly, a major cattle pest that was costing farmers $120 million a year, was eradicated from the Florida peninsula and later from Texas. Knipling mass-bred and sterilized male flies, then released them to breed with wild female flies. Since female screwworm flies mate only once, the sterile males bred the wild flies out of existence.

There are now many other exciting success stories in the use of nonchemical controls. Insect and disease resistant varieties of wheat, corn, alfalfa, and potatoes have been developed. In some cases, aphid lions have been as effective against the bollworm as chemicals;[38] parasitic wasps released on alfalfa have controlled the pea aphid; a flea beetle, discovered by a USDA entomologist in Argentina, has a healthy appetite for the alligator weed, a pest which chokes the rivers and canals of the southern United States. Another promising approach is to turn the insect's sex urge against itself with sex attractants. Female insects produce chemicals called pheromones that attract males for mating. USDA has produced synthetic chemicals based on the chemical structure of the natural attractant. A USDA laboratory in Hawaii put the chemical on cardboard squares saturated with a poison and achieved eradication of the oriental fruit fly from isolated areas.[39] Another method is to saturate an area with the attractants to confuse male insects who cannot distinguish the synthetic attractors from the real thing. As a result, the females are not mated within their short life cycles.

When these cases are discussed, Dr. Hansberry and other critics of biological controls reply that their significance is limited because pests on no major crop have been controlled by these methods alone. The fact is that the unilateralist approach to pest control, whether with biological controls or pesticides, is bound to fail. What the critics ignore is that the ecological approach of integrated control, according to Dr. van den Bosch and Dr. F. R. Lawson, can reduce pesticide use by up to 50 percent, even with the nonchemical controls now available. For this to happen, however, there must be a third force of independent advisors to stand between the farmer and the pesticide salesman. The national farm organizations have a major but still unrealized role to play in informing their members of the profit potential in realistically appraising the costs and benefits of pesticides. In recent months, the *Farm Journal*, the *Progressive Farmer* and the *California Farm Bureau Monthly* have featured articles on integrated control and the hazards of overuse of pesticides.

This is a highly significant development. Without the

cooperation of farmers, pesticide reform efforts are an exercise in futility. Environmentalists, working alone, may succeed in picking off a particularly dangerous pesticide now and then, but there are always new products, often more hazardous, to take their place. The names may change but the amounts the farmers spray remain the same. In seeking to reach the farmers, environmentalists have erred in focusing so exclusively on environmental threats. As one Iowa farmer said in a recent interview, "I love the birds, but I love my farm better." The farmers have not been told enough about their economic stake in responsible pesticide use.

Here the environmentalists' biggest ally is the astonishing adaptability of the pests themselves. In 1962, Rachel Carson entitled her chapter on insect resistance to chemicals "The Rumblings of an Avalanche." In 1971, for many farmers on many major crops, the avalanche has arrived or is on the way, and integrated control is the only option left.

I I

The Ant Warriors and the Federal Pesticide Campaign

*On September 2, (1970) at about 10 a.m., I was
sitting under an oak tree eating scuppernongs at our
little place in the country when I heard a pitter-patter
on the leaves above and noticed yellow flakes
falling over me. A low-flying plane had flown over
shortly before . . . but I had given no credence to
local rumor that [it] was actually broadcasting poison.
This . . . chlorinated hydrocarbon is washed into
our pond from which we eat fish, and into our
well. . . . The poisoned insects which were thick atop
my lawnmower that afternoon were eaten by the
chickens which furnish eggs for our table.*

*It seems to me that the U.S. Constitution, in the
Fourth Amendment, guaranteeing "The right of the
people to be secure in their persons" should [protect]
anyone who wants to sit under his tree and eat
without having poison thrown into his food.*

> —Reaction of a citizen in
> Forsyth, Georgia, to the
> fire ant eradication program

In the spring of 1968, the Poor People's Campaign was
camped out on the steps of the Department of Agriculture lobbying for hunger relief in Mississippi. Up the
street on Capitol Hill, the Agricultural Appropriations

Subcommittee of the Senate was holding hearings. A member of the Mississippi legislature testified before a hushed chamber: "I know from personal experience, and I hope none of you ever have to experience it, how bad this problem is." Senator Russell of Georgia replied: "Yes, the Department of Agriculture just doesn't have the enthusiasm for this program which they have for a number of others which I don't think are as important."[1] The object of all this concern was not hungry children, but the imported fire ant which builds unsightly mounds in Southern pastures.

Every three or four years, since 1957, the Department of Agriculture has launched a final campaign to wipe out the fire ant, and every year the fire ant responds by either holding its own or extending its range. This tiny red insect with a painful sting entered this country from South America about 1918. Originally confined to Mobile, Alabama, it is now spread over part of nine Southern states, building high, hard mounds which sometimes interfere with hay and mowing operations. Occasionally the ants, if disturbed, sting laborers, picnickers, and school children. But despite its fearful name, the ant is not a major public health or economic problem. A report by the General Accounting Office made this assessment in 1965 and the National Research Council affirmed it in 1967. Public health officials in Southern states rank the fire ant below the mosquito, the sand fly, stable flies, midges, and stinging caterpillars as a human nuisance. The National Research Council found that "the frequency and intensity of the fire ant sting is no greater than of the stings of bees or wasps."[2] There is little evidence that the ant harms plants, birds, or wildlife. There have been no published papers on imported fire ants as destroyers of quail or livestock, despite scare stories to the contrary circulated through the South by advocates of eradication.[3] The diet of the ant consists primarily of insects, not plant material.[4] In its Argentine homeland, the fire ant is considered beneficial to agriculture because of its attacks on harmful insects.[5] In this country, the fire ant eats destructive insects like boll weevils, sugarcane borers, and cutworms. *Yet this minor pest has been the target of this nation's longest and most expensive*

federal pesticide campaign. To understand how this
came about one must take a plunge into the gothic
Americana of the Deep South, but first, it is helpful to
grasp the dimensions of the federal effort at pest control, of which the fire ant is only one episode.

Chemical warfare against the fire ant is almost
entirely supported by public funds, 50 percent federal
and 50 percent state. Similar federal efforts either to
control or to eradicate insects have been directed
against the gypsy moth, spruce budworm, the screwworm, the range caterpillar, and many others.

Multimillion dollar programs like these, conducted
in every part of the country, have made the federal
government the nation's most enthusiastic promoter
and user of pesticides. Despite the dubious effectiveness of some, and the clearly disastrous results of
others, these programs return as regularly as the sea-
sons, largely outside the pale of public notice or control,
often without critical evaluation by those who run
them.

Agencies within USDA conduct most of these programs; among them are the Plant Pest Control Division
of the Agricultural Research Service, the Agricultural
Stabilization and Conservation Service, the Forest
Service, and others. Agencies of the Department of
Interior, such as the Fish and Wildlife Service, as well
as the Army Corps of Engineers of the Defense Department have programs of their own. Finally, both the
USDA and the Department of Interior permit private
companies such as lumber companies and utilities to
spray public lands for their own benefit.

The programs include not only insect control but
forest improvement (the Forest Service in 1969–1970
sprayed 577,000 pounds of 2,4-D over 213,000 acres
and 182,000 pounds of 2,4,5-T over 61,000 acres of
national forest land to kill hardwoods and promote
pure stands of commercially valuable pines); *range
improvement* (the Agricultural Stabilization and Conservation Service sprayed more than 2 million acres
[half of them in Texas] in 1967 with Silvex, 2,4-D, and
2,4,5-T to increase the ratio of grass to brush on open
range land); *watershed improvement* (the Forest Service and other agencies use herbicides to defoliate water-

sheds in arid areas of the Southwest to increase runoff water for irrigation; these herbicides act selectively against weeds and brush which supposedly suck up valuable water); *aquatic weed control* (the Army Corps of Engineers and the Department of Interior use herbicides, Amitrole, and arsenicals to control the water hyacinth, the alligator weed, and other weeds which clog reservoirs, streams, and canals). Federal agencies also supervise or approve spraying on rights of way for public utilities, spraying for malaria and encephalitis control, weed control on federal highways, and other areas.

When added to regular agricultural use of pesticides, these government programs ensure that virtually no corner of the United States remains untouched by pesticide chemicals. Although conducted mainly on public land, by public agencies, and usually with public money, most serve private interests, including loggers, cattlemen, farmers, utilities, and the pesticide industry. These interests, together with their government and Congressional allies, form a powerful coalition to confront the citizen concerned about the hazards of the programs.

Each program in the federal pesticide campaign has a two-fold risk: that it may threaten wildlife, water purity, or human health; and that it may be ineffective and therefore waste federal funds. Some programs like the release of sterilized insects to eradicate the screwworm in the Southwest have been outstanding successes; many others are in dire need of critical evaluation by objective analysts. The use of herbicides for range and watershed improvement or aquatic weed control *may* contaminate streams, lakes, and rivers, accelerate erosion of arid land, and still yield no demonstrable economic benefit.[6] Forest programs to control the spruce budworm or the gypsy moth may be ineffective because the cultivation of pure stands of a desired tree by eliminating "parasite wood" (noncommercial species) has robbed the forest of natural controls[7] or because the pesticide is improperly applied. A recent study of forest insect control showed that 95 percent of the droplets sprayed from conventional equipment are too large to affect the target insects[8] but that smaller droplets may drift for miles, endangering wildlife far outside the target area.[9]

Many of these programs lead to a greater volume of pesticide use than would occur if the free market were operating. Stockmen who benefit from the controversial predator control program operated by the Department of Interior privately admit that they would not pay equivalent sums of their own money to control the prairie dog and the coyote on their lands. The same has traditionally been true for farmers with fire ant infestations.

The risk-benefit calculations for these programs are, therefore, very subtle and complex. Unfortunately, federal pest control operates in a political and bureaucratic milieu designed to shield it from serious critical evaluation. The federal regulatory officials concerned with responsible use of pesticides exercise little influence over these programs. Until November, 1970, the Pesticide Regulation Division, which must approve uses of pesticides, uneasily coexisted in the same department with more powerful agencies, such as the Forest Service and the Plant Pest Control Division of the Agricultural Research Service, which have a vested interest in pesticide spraying. PRD, an agency without an organized constituency except among the pesticide producers themselves, was up against agencies with grass-roots strength in the agricultural and timber industries. PRD lacked the power in either the office of the Secretary of Agriculture or the farm committees on Capitol Hill to rein in the pest control efforts of these agencies. The move of PRD to the Environmental Protection Agency relieves the conflict of interest inherent in having agencies in the same department regulate and promote pesticides, but it has no substantial effect on the federal pest control programs themselves. The attack on the fire ant and the other hardy perennials of federal pest control remains in the agribusiness network of USDA and the Congressional farm committees.

The Ant War

The fire ant issue dramatically illustrates the principle that with federal pest control the *politics* of ecology is far more important than its *science*. It is a fascinating case to show environmentalists how local politics, the power of appropriation subcommittees, and organizational rigidity in the federal bureaucracy interact to shape national priorities on pesticides.

In 1962, Rachel Carson described the fire ant campaign as "an outstanding example of an ill-conceived, badly executed, and thoroughly detrimental experiment in the mass control of insects, an experiment so expensive in dollars, in destruction of animal life, and in loss of public confidence in the Agriculture Department, that it is incomprehensible that any funds should still be devoted to it."[10] At that time the program cost $2 million a year. In 1969, USDA and the Southern Plant Board jointly approved a twelve-year program to treat 126 million fire ant infested acres, this time at the cost of $238 million,[11] almost $20 million annually. In 1971, USDA backed away at least temporarily from this grandiose plan but intended to spend $7 million on 7 million acres in 1971 to test its feasibility. The point is clear: nearly a decade after *Silent Spring*, the ant war is still hot.

Since 1962, the fire ant program has been repudiated by every official panel which has investigated it. The General Accounting Office, the Department of Interior, the Department of Health, Education, and Welfare, the National Research Council, and the Federal Water Quality Administration have condemned it as wasteful and potentially hazardous. The Bureau of the Budget has twice tried to cut it out of the budget and Presidents have refused to spend the funds appropriated by Congress. But while the fire ant warriors have lost all the scientific debates, they have successfully worked behind the scenes to sustain and usually to increase their appropriations every year since 1957. More than anything else, the fire ant program is a monument to the power which key Congressmen on strategic committees can exercise over environmental policy.

The origins of the fire ant program were suspicious from the start. USDA's 1957 bulletin *Insecticide Recommendations . . . for the Control of Insects Attacking Crops and Livestock* did not even mention the fire ant as a significant pest. But in the same year USDA launched a massive media campaign which portrayed the insect as a despoiler of Southern agriculture, a killer of birds, livestock, and even man. USDA even produced a movie depicting the horror of the fire ant's sting.[12] (There is one substantiated report of death due to allergic shock from the sting.) Beginning in 1957, the Plant Pest Control Division of the Agricultural Research Service received $2.4 million annually to eradicate the imported fire ant. In a joint program with state officials they sprayed thousands of acres with heptachlor and dieldrin at 2 pounds per acre. By 1960, when 2.5 million acres had been treated, the destruction of wildlife from these highly persistent and toxic pesticides had created a national outcry. Wild turkeys, bobwhite quail, raccoons, opossums, and even cattle died. FDA complained because this use of heptachlor and dieldrin created unsafe residues in milk and other foods.

In 1963, yielding to these pressures, USDA substituted mirex (a less toxic but still persistent pesticide) for heptachlor and continued the program. Eradication (i.e., permanent elimination) remained the goal despite the fact that the fire ant had continued to expand its range and density.

In 1964, the excesses of the fire ant program brought down the wrath of the government's watchdog, the General Accounting Office. In a characteristically understated report, the GAO accused USDA of disregarding scientific opinion which minimized the threat of the fire ant and of wasting federal funds:

Although since inception of the program in the fall of 1957 through June 30, 1963 . . . total cost of the eradication program had been about 24.7 million dollars . . . there had not been a net reduction in the number of acres infested with the ant. On the contrary, there had been a net increase of about 11 million acres in the land reported to be infested with the ant. According to the Agriculture Research Service, about 25.6 million acres of infested land remained to be treated as of June 30, 1963.[13]

The GAO found that mirex did not prevent reinfestation. Immature colonies escaped the poison because they did not have adult ants to carry the bait into the nest. Heavy rainfall immediately after treatment renders the bait ineffective in any case and skips of twenty feet in the aerial application of the bait allow colonies to survive in between and rapidly reinfest the area.[14] In addition, GAO researchers found no evidence of the extensive crop damage on which USDA based its original decision to pursue the fire ant. A consensus of entomologists at three universities in the heavily infested states of Alabama, Louisiana, and Mississippi found that the ant did not significantly damage crops or livestock but fed primarily on insects.[15]

The GAO report impressed officials in the Bureau of the Budget, which began to press USDA to cut the program. The Agricultural Research Service, which directed the ant war, reluctantly agreed. In March, 1965, two months after the GAO Report, Dr. George W. Irving, Administrator of ARS, and his deputy Dr. Robert J. Anderson went before Jamie Whitten's (D.-Miss.) House Appropriations Subcommittee on Agriculture with a budget which, for the first time in seven years, had no funds for fire ant control. Irving stated that of all the federal pest control efforts, the fire ant program could be cut "with the least damage to the nation's agricultural production." The original goal of eradication, he concluded, "no longer seems feasible."[16]

Jamie Whitten's response was scornful: "How many other situations have you walked off and left, allowing the insect hazards to spread unrestricted without any substitute means of solving the problem?"[17] Whitten then gave ARS the benefit of the doubt and put the blame on the Bureau of the Budget. Anderson at first refused to take this escape route but, under continuing pressure from Whitten, he began to waver. One of his assistants conceded that the budget cut had come from outside the Department and Anderson himself then became eloquent on the menace of the fire ant (he showed pictures of mounds 24 inches high, spoke of people allergic to the sting and noted ominously that one pig had died from a fire ant attack).[18] Whitten, triumphant, was then magnanimous: "Thank you, Dr. Anderson. We know of . . . the problems you have when you are here to justify a budget from the Bureau of the Budget."[19] At no point did Whitten acknowledge the existence of the GAO Report released two

months before. USDA's loyalty to the program, not the
merits of the program, was the issue. In the end, he
single-handedly resurrected the ant war and gave it
$3 million to spend in fiscal year 1966.

In the budget for fiscal year 1967, President Johnson
again eliminated the program. But Whitten again
restored it, and increased funding to $5 million a year.
President Johnson retaliated by freezing $2 million of
these funds. At this point, at the urging of the Bureau
of the Budget, USDA went outside the Department to
seek an objective evaluation of the program. Dr. Irving,
Administrator of the Agricultural Research Service,
commissioned a report by the National Research Council on the fire ant. Completed in 1967, the Report
concluded that "eradication is not now biologically and
technically feasible,"[20] and that the fire ant causes no
significant harm to land values, agriculture production,
or health. Armed with this report the ARS went back
to Congressman Whitten and asked, not for the elimination of the program, but for a substantial decrease in
its budget. Whitten ignored the National Research
Council report and criticized the agency for refusing to
spend all the funds he appropriated:

MR. WHITTEN: You know the committee put the
    needed funds in here, but the Department has been
    dragging its feet coming up with one excuse after
    another not to go ahead with this program. . . . What
    did the Congress tell you last year?
DR. ANDERSON: They told us to get on with the program.
MR. WHITTEN: And you did not pay any attention to
    it?[21]

At this point, in a rare moment for appropriations
hearings, where records are usually scrubbed clean of
such incidents, Whitten directly threatened Anderson.

MR. WHITTEN: We realize we cannot make you go
    ahead with the program, but if you are not going to
    do what the Congress says to do, maybe we ought to
    cut down the money *at your level*. Doctor, *I am
    serious!* (Emphasis added)
DR. ANDERSON: I understand.[22]

The committee swept aside the Administration's effort to cut $2 million from fire ant control and appropriated $6.4 million for the program. The enormity of this sum is revealed when one notes that the total spending for registration and enforcement activities under the Federal Insecticide, Fungicide, and Rodenticide Act in Fiscal Year 1969 was approximately half this amount. In other words, killing this single insect had a higher priority than screening the other 45,000 pesticide products on the market for hazards to human health and wildlife.

The strain on Anderson and the other USDA officials who had to confront Whitten was considerable. For three years in a row, they had to go before his committee and ask him to either eliminate or cut back a program he obviously cherished. So great is the power of an appropriations subcommittee chairman that he is capable of reducing the personal staff of an administrator who crosses him, of killing his pet programs, and otherwise disrupting his agency's plans. Anderson knew that not only his own job, but the personnel levels and priorities of the whole agency were at stake.

Congressman Whitten was not the only fire ant warrior facing USDA officials on Capitol Hill. Equally as devoted to the program was Senator Spessard Holland (D.-Fla.), Whitten's counterpart on the Senate Appropriations Committee. Holland comes from Florida's panhandle district, which is heavily infested with the ants. In 1967, Holland criticized then Secretary of Agriculture Orville Freeman for having a negative attitude toward the program. When Freeman replied that his technical people had real doubts about the program's practicality, Holland ordered him to quit stalling and come up with a plan for eradication. In 1968, after Whitten defied the Bureau of the Budget in giving $5 million for the program, Holland's committee complained that not enough attention was being given to the program and upped the recommendation to $8 million.[23]

In 1970, the Executive Branch made an about-face on the fire ant and ceased trying to cut the program. USDA asked Whitten for a $2 million increase, making the fire ant budget for Fiscal Year 1971 hit $7.6 million, the highest in the history of the program.[24] It also prepared a proposal for a $200 million program to eradicate the fire ant totally by 1982.

Hazards

The fire ant program, obviously, has more than enough political strength to counter the governmental and scientific investigators who have condemned it on its merits as wasteful and impractical. Before looking more closely at the political forces which sustain it, it is important to note that the ant war may be far more costly to the public than the dollar sum of its appropriation.

Mirex, the pesticide used to kill the fire ant, is a chlorinated hydrocarbon. It is mixed with corncob grits and soybean oil to form a bait for the fire ant. But while its acute toxicity is relatively low, far less than the heptachlor it replaced, it does have some disturbing qualities. Mirex breaks down rapidly when left in the open (often within forty-eight hours) but it is extremely stable in the fatty tissues of animals that ingest it. Like DDT, mirex residues become increasingly concentrated as they move up the food chain, reaching their highest concentrations in fish, birds, and man. A study of pesticide residues in 500 samples of oysters and shellfish from estuaries on the Atlantic, Gulf, and Pacific Coasts discloses that mirex is already the fourth most abundant pesticide residue, exceeded only by DDT, endrin, and toxaphene.[25] An extensive survey of large vertebrates collected in the vicinity of Savannah, Georgia, and St. Petersburg, Florida, showed that mirex was present in dosages from trace amounts up to 4 ppm in *all* samples.[26] Since private use of mirex is negligible, the fire ant program is clearly responsible for these residues.

The fact that these residues are accumulating is a cause for concern but until 1968, USDA was confident that they did no harm. There had been complaints from fishermen that millions of shrimp and blue crabs had died along the Atlantic Coast after the area was doused with mirex but laboratory tests on shellfish continued to find mirex harmless. In 1969, chemists at the Department of Interior's Gulf Breeze, Florida, Laboratory repeated the experiments, but this time they observed the shellfish for ten days rather than the standard ninety-six hours. They discovered that a tiny 0.1 part per billion of mirex in sea water killed 11 percent of shrimp tested. Fifty percent of the shrimp died after three weeks. Gulf Breeze Laboratory also reported delayed lethal effects on crabs.[27] There is no conclusive evidence yet, however, that mirex causes these effects outside the laboratory. Whether other animals which store mirex residues in their bodies will suffer harm is not yet known. The Council on Environmental Quality, which advises the President on environmental questions, sent this warning to the Secretary of Agriculture on March 18, 1971:

The persistence of mirex and its concentration in the food chain, laboratory tests indicating adverse effects on a variety of species, and the current incomplete state of knowledge concerning the fate of mirex residues in the environment all lead to the conclusion that there is a significant possibility that serious adverse effects will occur in the future.

Of more concern is mirex's unknown potential for causing harm to man. The answer given to this question depends heavily on the time frame in which it is considered. The Department of Agriculture, looking at mirex from the very short-term point of view, notes correctly that single doses even of fairly large amounts are unlikely to poison anyone immediately. But when one considers potential long-term hazards, it becomes irresponsible as well as inaccurate to say categorically that mirex is safe.

In 1969, the Mrak Commission reported that mirex was one of a small number of pesticides found to cause tumors in test animals. It placed mirex in category B, the classification for potentially carcinogenic compounds, and strongly recommended that human exposure to these compounds "be minimized":

Use of these pesticides [should] be restricted to those purposes for which there are . . . advantages to human health which outweigh the potential hazards of carcinogenicity.[28]

In addition to being a potential carcinogen, tests by Dr. Gaines and Dr. Kimbrough at the FDA Toxicology Lab in Chamblee, Georgia, found mirex to cause birth defects in test animals. When fed to pregnant rats at 25 ppm, mirex passed through the placenta of the mother and reduced the number of offspring. It also caused cataracts in the suckling pups. Mirex was excreted through the mother's milk and stored in their livers.[29]

Officials at the National Communicable Disease Center were so concerned by this study that they sent a telegram to the Food and Drug Administration's pesticide branch informing them of the results. In response to this telegram, Dr. Thomas Harris, then Director of the Division of Pesticide Registration for the FDA, wrote the USDA recommending that the following warning be put on the label of mirex:

Due to the possibility of these effects [the birth defects caused by mirex in rats] also occurring in the human female, we recommend that all manufacturers and formulators of mirex be advised of these potential dangers in exposing women of childbearing age.[30]

The FDA recommended that mirex be labeled: "Women of Childbearing Age Should Not be Employed In The Manufacture or Formulation of Mirex Because of Possible Adverse Effects of the Chemical on the Developing Foetus."

It is not known whether mirex will produce the same effects in man that it has produced in test animals, but leading scientists in the field of cancer research and the study of birth defects now warn that any exposure to such a chemical is an unnecessary risk.[31] A blue ribbon panel of cancer specialists reported to the Surgeon General of the United States in April, 1970, that "any substance which is shown conclusively to cause tumors in animals should be considered carcinogenic and therefore a potential cancer hazard for man."[32] The Committee further notes that exposure to small doses of a carcinogen over a period of time usually results in an accumulation of effects. It unequivocally warns:

It is essential to recognize that no level of exposure to a carcinogenic substance, however low it may be, can be established to be a "safe level" for man.[33]

HEW, in its comments on USDA's Environmental Impact Statement on the fire ant program, concluded "that the margin between the dose levels at which mirex shows serious ill effects on laboratory animals and the current tolerance levels for mirex in foods has become alarmingly narrow."

It is for these reasons that officials at every level of government have questioned the safety of the fire ant program. In a letter to the Secretary of Agriculture, then Secretary of Interior Walter Hickel, who banned the use of mirex in national parks, said:

We are concerned that the Department of Agriculture's proposed twelve-year campaign to eradicate the fire ant in the Southern United States may represent a threat to the environment of far greater consequence than the problems now created by the insect itself. Consequently, we cannot support your program as proposed.[34]

The program has been condemned by the Federal Water Control Administration and by the President's Council on Environmental Quality.

On March 18, 1971, the Environmental Protection Agency issued notices of cancellation on mirex, stating there is a "substantial question" about the safety of continued use of the pesticide. Allied Chemical appealed the order and requested a full scientific review. In the meantime the program will go on undisturbed.

Politics

The fire ant undeniably has a nasty, if rarely applied, sting; it is a bona fide nuisance. But do these disadvantages outweigh the risks to animal and human life from pelting Southern real estate with millions of pounds of these compounds? The fire ant's sting, compared to that of other insects, is not a significant hazard. Between 1950–1959, *all* species of ants accounted for only four of the 460 reported fatalities from venomous insects. Bees accounted for 124 deaths, wasps for 69, yellow jackets for 22. No one has proposed that the government eliminate these insects.[35] There is also the threat of economic loss to farmers if mirex residues turn up in fish, milk, and eggs in appreciable amounts. Given mirex's carcinogenic potential, FDA would then be forced to condemn these foods. Moreover, if aerial warfare against the ant is stopped, EPA professionals could control the ant by treating individual mounds on farms and homesteads at a cost estimated by the National Research Council to be not more than $1.50 per acre.

The question remains: why are Jamie Whitten and his allies in the Senate so devoted to fire ant eradication? Some observers feel that Whitten's ego now ties him to the program. He fought Rachel Carson and then the budget cutters in the federal government for years and now refuses to back down. Others see significance in the fact that Allied Chemical makes mirex baits in Prairie, Mississippi. The plant, however, has only fifteen employees. The $1 million annual sales of mirex are a tiny fraction of Allied Chemical's $1.24 billion annual sales business. Mirex, therefore, hardly seems worth a major political payoff.[36]

Whitten's staff gives a more prosaic explanation of the Congressman's interest: constituency pressure. While the fire ant is not a major issue in Whitten's district, it is among farmers elsewhere in the South, especially in Mississippi and Georgia. But while farmers in the Deep South do complain about the fire ant, there is much ambiguity in their response. Dr. Mulhern, Deputy Administrator of ARS, cited in the 1969 hearings results of a survey by county agents of farmer attitudes toward fire ant control. This confidential report, prepared in 1968, has never been released, but it makes interesting reading. While Mulhern gives the impression that the survey supports eradication, it is in fact a very ambivalent document. Its author seems to have had one eye on the Bureau of the Budget and the other on Jamie Whitten. The report's summary on page 1 states:

Imported fire ants represent a serious and a growing problem for both farmers and nonfarmers in the heavily infested areas. . . . It seems beyond doubt that the fire ant does reduce yields, damage equipment, and otherwise raise the cost of producing hay and pasture. . . . It appears to be a significant pest of cattle.

The report's conclusion on page 24 states:

We conclude that the imported fire ant ranks well down on the list of insect pests affecting agriculture. The judgment is reinforced by the reported lack of enthusiasm for private treatments [by farmers] to control the ants, the overwhelming agreement that neither farm laborers nor custom operators receive premiums for working on infested farms, and the model opinion that land values are not affected by the presence of the fire ants.[37]

More revealing is the remarkable indifference of farmers to the fire ant menace: over 80 percent of the county agents surveyed found that fewer than half of the farmers in infested areas bothered to control the fire ant on their farms. Even when the Georgia Department of Agriculture made free mirex available to farmers, there were few takers.[38]

As these facts suggest, there is reason to doubt the spontaneity of pressure by the average farmer for fire ant control. The program *does* have genuine support among Southern farm bureaucrats, however, for reasons which have little to do with the threat of the fire ant.

The prime movers in the fire ant campaign have been the commissioners of agriculture in the Southern states. These commissioners are powerful men in Southern politics. They sit astride the flow of agricultural subsidies and benefits which amount to the largest source of outside capital for many impoverished Southern counties. They also control substantial patronage. The Southern commissioners have long been the most vocal lobbyists on Capitol Hill for fire ant control. Since 1967, USDA has not made a move on the program without consulting the Southern commissioners in advance.

Nowhere is the fire ant program more entrenched in local politics than in the state of Georgia. Phil Campbell, the Georgia Commissioner, made eradication a personal crusade during the sixties when the Budget Bureau was challenging the program. Campbell is now

the Under Secretary of Agriculture. As chief propa-
gandist for fire ant control, he described the fire ant
as a "people pest" and warned legislators that if they
did not vote funds to stamp out the ant, the people of
Georgia would rise up and stamp them out.[39] In 1968,
a biologist at Emory University publicly complained
that the information put out by Campbell's office was
"a very skillful piece of propaganda, creating a fear
and revulsion of the fire ants."[40]

In fact, Campbell had a genuine interest in supporting the program but it had little to do with killing ants.
Funds for fire ant control were the largest item in his
Department's budget. In 1965, for example, Campbell
received $850,000 to kill ants, well over half of all
funds appropriated for his Department. The funds
could not be spent unless they were matched by federal
grants. However, this inconvenience forced Campbell
to carry his propaganda campaign across state lines.
Nineteen sixty-five was the year when Dr. R. J. Anderson of the Agriculture Research Service went before
Whitten's subcommittee and requested no more funds
for fire ant control. Without federal funds, Campbell
would have to turn back his money to the state. Campbell, therefore, visited Whitten to protest ARS's action
and Whitten obliged by restoring the program.

An obscure but significant point here is that the
fire ant program was not a line-item in Campbell's
Departmental budget but was appropriated by the
Georgia assembly as general funds. In 1970, Tommy
Irvin, who took over as commissioner of agriculture
when Campbell went to Washington to become USDA's
number two man, startled Georgia legislators by
revealing that "in the past, maybe as high as 25 to 30
percent of some year's appropriations for fire ants were
not used for fire ants."[41] He stated that control efforts
spanning ten years and costing $5 million in state
funds were "wasted" and promised that in the future,
fire ant money would not be used for other things.

The import of Irvin's revelation was that Campbell
had been using fire ant money as a slush fund for
other projects in his department. Between 1965 and
1969, Campbell was frequently mentioned as a potential gubernatorial candidate and was widely thought to

be using his position as agricultural commissioner to build a political empire in the state. Scare stories about the fire ant brought him the funds he needed for other purposes. As a reporter for the *Atlanta Constitution* observed upon hearing Irvin's speech: "I have heard of men building empires over broken bodies, but Phil is first to try to build one on dead ants."

Georgia environmentalists fighting mirex spraying regard the fearful image of the fire ant instilled in the minds of rural people by Campbell's propaganda as their biggest barrier. A description of the fire ant in this genre was recently released by the Southern Association of Information Officers of State Departments of Agriculture, with which Campbell was and is closely associated. This "gluttonous ant," says a press release, "indiscriminately gobbles insects and spiders," dispatching them with its "cobra-like sting":

From fort-like mounds up to a yard high and only a few feet apart, the ants send out armies of some 100,000 foragers per mound, driven by an insatiable lust for the oily juices of anything alive.[42]

The fire ant remains a fixture of Georgia farm politics. In February, 1971, a joint appropriations committee of the Georgia legislature debated whether to continue the program and invited experts pro and con from around the nation to testify. The session turned into an undignified version of the Scopes Monkey Trial. The chamber was packed with sober, well-dressed, rational men from the Audubon Society, the Sierra Club, the American Medical Association, university faculties, and public interest groups on one side and little boys with fresh fire ant stings, leathery rustics from the Georgia hinterlands, and virtually all the members of the appropriations committees on the other. The rational men got murdered.

The tone of debate was set by Rep. Dorsey Matthews of Moultrie, Georgia, Chairman of the House Agriculture Committee. He held a jar of fire ants in one hand and gestured toward a mangled potato on the table. The potato, he said, had been "ridiculed" by fire ants. He then gave a gavel-pounding, ranting speech, the *pièce de résistance* of which was a letter he had received from a "world famous doctor from down here in Buena Vista, Georgia." Waving the letter like a flag, the chairman said the doctor had advised him that fire ants were the real cause of scarlet fever, cancer, Bright's disease, and another ailment which he said he could not pronounce and besides, he did not know what it was anyway. He was assisted by "Buck" Ross, the Mississippi Commissioner of Agriculture, who stated that he knew of at least a dozen people killed in his state by the fire ant.

The rational men of the opposition could not begin to match this performance. Their statements were ponderous with facts and esoteric terminology. When a representative of the American Medical Association pointed out that mirex caused cancer in laboratory rats, Dorsey Matthews replied: "Doctor, that don't bother me. Nobody eats rats in my district. Besides we got too many rats anyhow."

The testimony about the potential long-term hazards of mirex bombardments on the Georgia countryside did impress urban legislators, but they traded away opposition to fire ant control in return for rural votes for a local option rapid transit tax in Atlanta. Conservationists were left out in the cold.

The organizational politics behind the fire ant program in the Deep South is reinforced by organizational interests in USDA. When an agency is assigned a program the size of the fire ant campaign, it significantly expands its share of bureaucratic turf. More staff is hired, more office space is allocated, new field offices may be opened, new constituencies are cemented, and careers are staked on the success of the program. This has been the case with the Plant Protection Division of the Agricultural Research Service, which has received as much as half its budget for fighting ants over the last five years. While its leaders may have had momentary doubts about the program in the mid-1960s, officials down the line have given it strong support. Their devotion reflects the fact that the agency gets many internal rewards from the program which are entirely independent of its success in killing ants.

For example, according to officials in the Bureau of the Budget, the ant war is the major justification for maintaining the methods improvement lab in Gulfport, a prime vacation spa on the Gulf Coast and considered a choice assignment for Plant Protection Division personnel. When the fire ant program began to fail, these vested interests made it very difficult for the agency to give it up. As a general principle, when a government program appears wasteful and futile, and its agency remains doggedly devoted to it, it is well to stop analyzing its merits and look more closely—there will usually be intimate organizational interests which keep it alive.

The Plant Protection Division, with its close ties to the House and Senate farm committees, is a striking illustration of a Washington subgovernment. To a significant extent, Donald Shepard, Director of the Division, and Francis J. Mulhern, Deputy Administrator for Regulation and Control in the Agricultural Research Service, act independently of the Council on Environmental Quality and the Bureau of the Budget in setting federal priorities for pest control. One former Bureau examiner of the USDA budget relates that frequently USDA would use the fire ant program as a stalking horse in the appropriations committees to help avoid budget cuts. The Department would acquiesce in cuts for the fire ant program, but resist cuts for other programs with less political strength—knowing that friends on the committees would restore the fire ant funds.

This examiner, who has now left the Bureau, was very critical of lack of professional integrity of some ARS scientists. He points out that the ARS scientists have an obligation to the public to tell the technical truth, even when it goes against their organizational interest; frequently they do not. In one case, to his personal knowledge, ARS officials deliberately falsified estimates given to Congress on the number of acres infested with fire ants in several Southern states. A scientist at the University of Massachusetts puts the problem of science professionalism in the agency in perspective:

You have to understand that the guys supervising these programs today got their training back in the forties and early fifties, when pesticides were the thing. But since they've been in government all this time, rather than at the universities where they would be subject to criticism from their colleagues, they just haven't changed their views. So now they're kind of a government unto themselves.[43]

This is not an isolated case of the subversion of science by the fire ant program. Frank Graham reports that state entomologists in Georgia wrote to Senator Richard Russell in an attempt to get a Fish and Wildlife biologist transferred from the state after he had questioned the program. Similar retaliation was taken against biologists in Alabama and Florida.[44] This kind of intimidation is still occurring. Dr. Denzel Ferguson, a zoologist at Mississippi State University, became critical of the fire ant effort after participating in an evaluation of the program's feasibility. After he had voiced his doubts in professional circles, he received a visit from a high university official who warned him that the fire ant was a very sensitive political issue. The message was clear: the university might suffer funding reversals in the state legislature if one of its faculty criticized the program. Professor Ferguson, nevertheless, established CLEAN, a group of Mississippi environmentalists. It joined the Environmental Defense Fund and the National Wildlife Federation in legal action to stop the program. His courage cost Professor Ferguson his job at Mississippi State, and he has now left the state.

Conclusion

In 1971, the National Wildlife Federation, the Environmental Defense Fund, and CLEAN were denied their request for an injunction against the spraying of mirex in the 1971 season. The only chance to stop the program now is in the White House, which could freeze its funds. Seven million dollars for fire ant control in 1971 makes for an embarrassing item in President Nixon's austerity budget, but he will probably continue to support the program. The fire ant campaign has become a hostage of the Southern Strategy. In 1968, in a speech in Atlanta, Georgia, Nixon promised to continue the ant war if elected, and Phil Campbell is just down the street to make sure he does not renege.

William Ruckelshaus, the able Administrator of the Environmental Protection Agency, acknowledged in September, 1971, that the fire ant issue is a severe challenge for his young agency. His proposal to cancel the registration of mirex earned him a rebuke from the floor of the House by Congressman Whitten, who described Ruckelshaus as a dangerously powerful man. The National Academy of Sciences, for the second time in five years, has been asked to nominate a panel of experts to evaluate the fire ant program. EPA will hold a public hearing in early 1972, after which Ruckelshaus will have to decide whether to bar mirex. Ruckelshaus's aides predict that the mirex decision will provoke a political crisis on Capitol Hill which will test the integrity of the agency.

To see what Ruckelshaus is up against, one should look at the transcript of the most recent fire ant hearings before the House Agriculture Committee in 1971. Robert Poage (D.-Tex.), Chairman of the Committee, questioned Dr. Ned Bayley, Director of USDA's Office of Science and Education, on the nature of the fire ant menace. At Bayley's side was Phil Campbell, the Under Secretary of Agriculture.

Congressman Poage sought to prove that the fire ant is an ecological hazard, at least as threatening to wildlife as mirex. He opened the questioning by asking Bayley: "All right. Now, what do fire ants do? Do they kill birds and small animals?"

As noted earlier, there is practically no scientific evidence that the fire ant is harmful to birds, livestock, or other animals.[45] Knowing this, USDA prefers to justify eradication of the fire ant as a *human* nuisance, although in fact it is no more hazardous to human beings than yellow jackets, wasps, or bees. Bayley started off by trying to set Poage straight on this point.

DR. BAYLEY: "Fire ants are very vicious and predacious, but the main problem of the fire ant is on human beings and the way they attack them."

This was not the answer Poage wanted: "I asked you a question. I asked you if fire ants kill small animals, if they kill birds or young chickens."

DR. BAYLEY: "They have been known to kill small animals, yes sir, but I just wanted to point out that the more serious problem is what they do to human beings."

THE CHAIRMAN: "All right. Now, there are some people who are more interested in what they do to the animals and birds than what they do to human beings, and I am asking you some questions as to what they do to those small animals."

At this point, Mr. Campbell came to Bayley's rescue.

MR. CAMPBELL: "Mr. Chairman, there is a veterinarian in my home State of Georgia named Dr. Shingler of Ashburn. He wrote me a letter . . . he had been out on three different farms where newborn calves had been killed by the fire ants."

THE CHAIRMAN: "Yes, and it is not simply that they have been known to do it. They do it regularly, don't they?"

MR. CAMPBELL, now warming to the theme, replied: "They also have killed some people."

THE CHAIRMAN: "Yes, they have killed some people and they are regularly killing small animals, aren't they?"

MR. CAMPBELL: "Yes sir, they are."

Chairman Page now turned back to Dr. Bayley: "I want to know if Dr. Bayley agrees with what you [Campbell] said. If you don't, I want it in the record that you do not."

DR. BAYLEY: "I have no objections to what Mr. Campbell has said."

THE CHAIRMAN: "Well, is it the truth? I didn't ask you to object or not to object, but is it correct?"

DR. BAYLEY: "Yes."

THE CHAIRMAN: "All right."

Dr. Bayley, now in full retreat, jettisoned his scientific scruples and even upstaged Campbell by suggesting that the fire ant is an amphibious threat, deadly by land and by sea.

DR. BAYLEY: ". . . I was trying to emphasize that this is much more important on humans, but I see the point you are trying to make and I have no problem with it at all. I can also point out that there is research data indicating that about four of these ants can kill a fish if he eats them. . . . I have no difficulty at all in agreeing with Mr. Campbell."

Environmentalists, like foreign affairs analysts, tend to use rational models of decision-making to explain policy outcomes, and just as often, they are betrayed by them. As Bayley's contortions before the House Agriculture Committee poignantly show, the fire ant program is entrenched in the bureaucratic and organizational politics of the agricultural establishment and more facts and scientific testimony will not budge it. Environmentalists would be advised to focus their energies on political organization and lobbying on the floor of the House and Senate. They should juxtapose the hazards and waste of the ant war against the need for rural economic development, cancer research, pollution control, and other national priorities. Finally, they cannot allow themselves to forget that environmental action is inextricably linked to reform of the electoral process and seniority system. If they continue to limit their efforts to rational debate on the merits of the program, the Dorsey Matthews will get them every time.

One barrier to effective action by environmentalists in fire ant politics is the suppression of relevant data by the agencies responsible for the program. The county agent report and the National Research Council study were at various times suppressed by the Department of Agriculture where they could have heavily influenced public and Congressional opinion. The problem of secrecy in pesticide regulation will be discussed in the next chapter.

12

Freedom of Suppression:
Pesticides and
Official Secrecy

Knowledge will forever govern ignorance.
And a people who mean to be their own
governors must arm themselves with the
power knowledge gives. A popular govern-
ment without popular information, or the
means of acquiring it, is but the prologue
to a farce or tragedy, or perhaps both.

James Madison

In Washington's regulatory agencies, information, especially timely information, is the currency of power.
The fact is illustrated in the reply of a leading Washington lawyer when asked how he prevailed on behalf
of his clients: "I get my information a few hours ahead
of the rest." The industry lobbyist derives his influence
from his superior intelligence apparatus. From routine
visits to an agency and leaks from carefully cultivated
contacts, he anticipates agency action and turns it to his
advantage. By contrast, most citizens learn about an
agency's plans only at their public stage, when a decision or proposal is announced in the *Federal Register*
or to the press. At this point, the opportunity for influence by the public is often very limited. It is at the
stage of inner council discussions, draft reports, and

interim choices by an agency's lower echelons that the real decisions are often made.

The advantages of early access were illustrated by Shell Chemical Company's successful maneuvering in the Pesticide Regulation Division in the sixties. On January 22, 1963, the Shell Chemical Company applied to the Pesticide Regulation Division for permission to sell a new household pesticide, Shell 20 percent Vapona Insecticide Resin Strip, an early version of the now famous No-Pest Strip. It was a plastic ribbon encased in a gold cardboard cage and impregnated with DDVP, an organophosphate insecticide. When hung from the ceiling of one's home, it promised to emit DDVP vapor in amounts sufficient to kill flies for up to three months. Shell's application went to the desk of Dr. Thomas von Sumter, a pharmacologist in PRD, who examined its label to see if it would be safe to use as directed. He decided that the Vapona Strip with its proposed label was not safe—and in February, he informed Shell that to obtain approval, the label must include the word Poison, with a skull and crossbones.[1]

These facts—that Shell had proposed a new pesticide for home use, that it killed flies through continuous pollution of the atmosphere of the home, and that PRD had initially denied Shell permission to market it—were not public information. In fact, few scientists outside the government and no consumer groups had heard of the Vapona Strip.

Shell responded to Sumter's denial by dispatching several representatives to Washington on March 6 to see Dr. John S. Leary, then Chief of PRD's Pharmacology Section. After talks with Shell, Dr. Leary overruled Sumter and withdrew PRD's objection. Leary held that while liquid DDVP was in a "highly toxic" category requiring the "Poison" label, DDVP in its Vapona form was eighty- to one hundred-fold less toxic and therefore exempt from the warning. The "highly toxic" category applies only to acute toxicity, not to long-term effects from chronic inhalation for which there had been no tests at all. On March 7, he issued registration no. 201–136 to the Vapona Strip, which was then widely sold throughout the United States.[2]

In 1964 and 1965, PRD received complaints from

the U.S. Public Health Service and California health officials who objected to the continuous exposure of infants and the infirm to any household pesticide where convenience, rather than health, dictates its use.* There was special concern that the Shell Vapona Strip was a respiratory hazard to infants and elderly persons and that it could deposit residues on food prepared in the home. In November, 1965, an ad hoc committee of the Public Health Service voted 6 to 2 to oppose continued registration of the Vapona Strips.[3] In October, 1966, one year later, Dr. Harry Hays, administrator of PRD, belatedly responded to these complaints by appointing a committee of medical experts to review vaporizing pesticides and other pesticide problems. A key document considered by the committee was a six-page memo from Dr. John Leary to Hays which discounted the Public Health Service report and urged continued registration of the strips. Hays accepted Leary's advice, despite the fact that he had been informed several weeks earlier of Leary's intention to resign to accept a position with Shell Chemical Company.[4]** The Vapona Strip went on to become the nation's largest selling pesticide consumer product.

All of the proceedings regarding the safety of the No-Pest Strip were veiled from public view. The Public Health Service Ad Hoc Committee Report was never made public. No minutes were kept by Dr. Hays's committee of experts. No further opinion was solicited by outside scientists. PRD still refused as of April, 1971, to make the safety data in its No Pest file available for independent review.

As this case shows, the federal pesticide agency enjoys great discretionary power over the programs it administers. The Federal Insecticide, Fungicide, and Rodenticide Act (FIFRA), which directs pesticide control officials, is basically a blueprint which sketches the agency's structure and states its goals. It leaves individual officials a wide freedom of choice in applying these goals to concrete cases. They can delay registration of a

* The scientists were concerned that there had been no tests to indicate the hazards of long-term chronic inhalation of DDVP vapors.
** According to a spokesman for Shell Chemical Company, Dr. Leary informed the committee that he was joining Shell.

pesticide by requesting additional tests for safety or accept the company's safety assurances without scrutiny; they can apply the effectiveness criteria narrowly (the pesticide need only show that it kills the target insect) or broadly (the pesticide in killing the target insect, must not kill so many beneficial insects that it reduces yield); they can decide which portion of the law to enforce or not to enforce; they can decide to recall a dangerous pesticide immediately or allow a company to sell all products already in marketing channels if it promises not to produce any more.[5]

In terms of impact on the public, the power not to act is often greater than the power to act. For example, PRD waited twenty years after passage of FIFRA to use its power to suspend pesticides found imminently hazardous to public health. This behavior, as Professor Kenneth Culp Davis points out, is not uncommon. In any regulatory agency, the inaction decisions, the choice to do nothing or to do nothing now, are ten to twenty times as frequent as action decisions:

Discretion is exercised not merely in final dispositions of cases or problems but in each interim step; and interim choices are far more numerous than the final ones. Discretion is not limited to substantive choices but extends to procedures, methods, forms, timing, degrees of emphasis, and many other subsidiary factors.[6]

These facts, the bureaucrat's freedom to choose and the value of inside information in helping outsiders influence that choice, are the cornerstones of the lobbyists' profession in Washington. For the special interests which form an agency's regulatory constituency, information gathering has become a science. In the case of the chemical industry in USDA and food and drug manufacturers in FDA, lobbyists have been able to develop highly efficient intelligence networks. The stakes are high. If a lobbyist learns of impending administrative action against his client, he can give him time to prepare for the change or he may be able to arrange that the action is not taken at all. If he succeeds, often only he, his client, and a small number of officials know that the action was ever considered in the first place. Access also tells him which official is friendly and which is not, and guides him in pressing for the ouster of officials judged unsympathetic or unreasonable.

As a result of pressure from regulated interests, many agencies have developed an information policy with a double standard—one for citizens and one for special interest groups. In the Department of Agriculture, the chemical industry is treated in accordance with the principle that, "with certain exceptions, the records of the Department are freely available for public inspection."[7] For the average citizen, however, the principle is turned on its head, and officials guard information with all the hauteur of a citizen above suspicion. As Dr. George Irving, Administrator of the Agricultural Research Service, candidly states: "The information in our files . . . is prepared for use by Government personnel. . . . It is not made available to any person outside the Government, except for the few documents specified. . . ."[8]

The double standard reflects the pattern of preferential access which lobbyists, trade associations such as National Agricultural Chemical Association, and corporations such as Shell have established in the Pesticide Regulation Division over the years. They develop institutions of privileged access such as advisory councils, cultivate the agency's key officials with countless dinners, conventions, and awards,[9] and often succeed in cajoling, compromising, or intimidating enough agency personnel to give them entry to the early decision process long before its public surfacing.

This interlocking chain of influence which includes an agency's regulatory clientele, its allies in the agency, and sympathizers on key Congressional committees has often been called a subgovernment. The impact of its superior access to information has been described by Nicholas Johnson, who as administrator of the Maritime Administration and later a commissioner of the FCC, has matched wits with Washington's most entrenched subgovernments:

On those rare occasions when pro-consumer action *is* proposed in an agency, the subgovernment moves in to block it. With its superior intelligence-gathering apparatus, leaks, and regular agency watching, members of the subgovernment can anticipate potential agency action that is either adverse to their interests, or that can be turned to their advantage. Calls are made, visits are arranged, studies are done and released, Congressmen are made to be interested, the full-page ads appear. Who is surprised any longer to have a lobbyist come to his office to discuss the contents of a staff document the Commissioners have not yet seen—or that is supposedly under confidential consideration? This is how things work in Washington—the point is that the public has no one to represent their interests in this swamp.[10]

The relationship between free access to information and responsible government is very direct. Excessive and discriminatory secrecy by federal agencies seriously blocks the citizen's understanding and ability to participate in government. It was with these truths in mind that Congress passed the Freedom of Information Act (FOIA) in 1966. According to a 1967 Attorney General's Memorandum, Congress intended that "disclosure be the general rule, not the exception, and that individuals have equal rights of access; that the burden be on the Government to justify the withholding of a document, not on the person who requests it; that individuals improperly denied access to documents have a right to seek injunctive relief in the courts, that there be a change in Government policy and attitude."[11]

The FOIA has not lived up to this broad promise. One problem is that the act expects of public officials an obedience to the unenforceable. If a public officer ignores the act, the citizen must engage the agency in court, the only recourse afforded by the act. Those who can afford legal challenge are those with special interests who need the FOIA least of all. Examination of court records establishes this point. In the first two years of FOIA, forty cases were brought under the act. Thirty-seven of these involved corporations or private parties seeking information for some private claim or benefit. Only three cases involved a demand by the public at large for information.[12] Most surprising of all, no member of the media, which should be the prime beneficiary of the FOIA, had initiated a single court action under the act. In practice, therefore, the attitudes of agency personnel determined whether FOIA was to be a pathway or roadblock for citizen access.

The broad discretion in the act has allowed each

agency to create its own "common law" in interpreting it. In doing so, they have developed a maze of confusing and contradictory regulations. Information which is claimed to be exempt from disclosure in one agency is freely given in another (for example, records of advisory council meetings—USDA-no, National Highway Safety Bureau-yes). In some agencies all requests must be in writing and all interviews cleared in advance, and strict records of all interviews required; in others information is freely given over the phone in an informal way.

No agency has so successfully forged the FOIA into a shield against the citizen's right to know as the Department of Agriculture. For two years a Task Force sponsored by the Center for Study of Responsive Law tested the defenses of secrecy in the Department and found them formidable. This struggle is a rueful lesson for the citizen who seeks to find out what his government is doing. Discussed below are the strategies of evasion employed by USDA and the Pesticide Regulation Division in concealing the facts about federal regulation of pesticides.

At first the Task Force anticipated little difficulty in carrying out its study. Before beginning, its director requested and was granted an interview with Secretary of Agriculture Clifford Hardin in June, 1969, to explain the study's purpose. Anticipating an informal talk with the Secretary in his office, he was surprised on the day of the appointment when one of Hardin's aides directed him to a large conference room down the hall. There, to his astonishment, he found fifteen of the Department's highest ranking notables grimly awaiting the Secretary's arrival. The quiet interview, it turned out, was regarded by USDA as a "visit of state." The Secretary appeared diffident and a little confused. It was difficult to hear his views because a covey of officious aides, notably the Inspector General Nathaniel Kossack, rushed to intercept all questions thrown his way. Secretary Hardin did graciously say that he expected the study to be "extremely valuable" in helping the Department assess its role in pesticide regulation, feeding the hungry, civil rights, meat inspection, and the other areas under investigation. He instructed the Inspector General to be the Task Force's liaison with the Department.

The Task Force was further reassured by a rather naive faith in the rights guaranteed by the Freedom of Information Act of 1967 (15 U.S. Code 552, 80 Revised Statutes 250). As discussed above, this act purported to make disclosure of information the rule, with exceptions only in special categories such as defense secrets, trade secrets, intra-agency memoranda, and investigatory files. If an agency illegally refused to divulge information, the citizen could sue the agency and his suit would "take precedence on the docket over all other causes . . . and expedited in every way."

This era of good feeling between the Task Force and the Department lasted just two days. On the third, Julian Houston, a Task Force member working on civil rights enforcement, was apprehended by one of Kossack's aides while waiting to interview an official in the Farmers Home Administration and taken directly to the office of the Inspector General. Kossack verbally charged Houston with "going through" the files in a USDA office. After a ten minute harangue, he abruptly dropped these charges and switched to a new tactic: hearty, avuncular charm. It was all just a misunderstanding, he said; the whole matter was really the fault of a nervous secretary. Kossack ended this incredible conversation by offering Houston a job with USDA.

Nathaniel E. Kossack obviously took his job as "liaison" very seriously. A former FBI agent, Kossack had come to USDA from the Department of Justice where he was the top civil servant in the Criminal Division (where Houston's stick-carrot treatment is a well-known interrogation tactic). Forced to resign in 1969 after a celebrated run-in with his new boss, Assistant Attorney General Will Wilson, Kossack was eager to prove himself in his new job. A tough cop with a deep suspicion of outsiders, Kossack saw his role as a watchdog to keep information from leaking out which might embarrass the Secretary. USDA is one of the few departments with its own internal police force. The Office of Inspector General was established in 1962, in response

to the Billie Sol Estes scandal. It performs highly confidential audits on all USDA activities and reports
directly to the Secretary.

With Kossack in command, access proved to be a
problem throughout USDA, but nowhere was the door
shut tighter than in the Pesticide Regulation Division of
the Agricultural Research Service. Secretary Hardin in
the June meeting requested that the Task Force prepare
written requests for all documents and give them to the
Inspector General. Kossack would, in turn, gather the
material. Responding to the Secretary's request, the
major part of June was spent preparing requests for
PRD files. Key information was in the registration and
enforcement files which allowed one to evaluate the
safety screening of new pesticides and the agency's success in removing dangerous pesticides from the market.
By talking with a number of persons the Task Force
determined that, of the files desired, only two parts of
the files sought could properly be called exempt from
disclosure under the Freedom of Information Act. The
first was the manufacturer's formula for each pesticide,
a trade secret under the Act; the second related to investigations of violations presently pending. The first
presented no problem, for the formula was separated
from other information and placed in an envelope
marked "Confidential," which could be easily removed
from the file folder. The Task Force expected, therefore,
that most of the information it desired would be legally
available.

The list was presented to Kossack in person on June
30, 1969, and began a long struggle which was ultimately to end in the federal courts in 1970 and 1971.
Much of the day-to-day confrontation took place
between Kossack, PRD officials, and two Task Force
members, Joe Tom Easley, a tall tireless Texan with
an easy manner and a nimble wit, and Bernard Nevas,
a Harvard law student, the son of a wealthy, prominent
New York lawyer, whose cool detachment and ironic
style nicely balanced Easley's charm. One attribute they
shared equally: the ability to ask and ask again.

After glancing over the list of information requests,
Kossack immediately called in Deputy Administrator of

the Agricultural Research Service, Frank A. Mangham. Mangham was told to "handle" the requests. Mangham whisked Easley and Nevas to his office and assured them that the information would be gathered as soon as possible. He then introduced Dr. Harry Hays, the head of PRD. Hays quickly glanced over the list, frowned, and stated that he was sorry but he was not sure that *any* of the items could be provided. To Mangham, Hays expressed concern that the study would "disrupt" his operations. Mangham gently told Hays that the Secretary had favored the study and that Hays should cooperate as best he could. Hays reluctantly agreed to look over the list and make a careful determination on each item. He would, in the meantime, arrange a series of "briefings" with his staff so that the Task Force could learn how PRD went about its business. The briefings were to begin the following day.

The first briefings came off exactly as scheduled. Like most formal briefings, they were uninformative and contrived, enlivened only by some insistent questioning by Nevas and Easley. When they returned to PRD for the second of the series the following day, they were taken directly to Hays who curtly stated that there would be no more briefings and that he was denying access to everything on the list. When they protested and pointed to the Freedom of Information Act, he blithely said it "didn't apply." PRD, he said, had been "investigated enough." When we pressed him for more specific reasons for his blanket denial, he retorted, "I just don't think we can stand this probing into the files."

What were the secrets the Task Force had asked to see? Among other things it wanted to examine safety data submitted by pesticide manufacturers, accident records for specific pesticides, and enforcement data on pesticides found to be dangerous after already going on to the market. Hays withheld all of this. On a request to see what action PRD had taken against violators of the law, Hays said, "We are not going to let out minor violations of the [Federal Insecticide, Fungicide, and Rodenticide]. I don't think that is what the law requires." As the meeting ended, Hays gratuitously remarked that the Task Force would, of course, want to drop its study because there could not be an investigation without this information.

Rebuffed by Hays, the Task Force filed a second written request with Hays's superiors.

With industry lobbyists so frequently, freely, and conspicuously visiting PRD staff, Dr. Hays could not deny interviews. He did, however, attempt to limit the information from his staff by ordering them not to give away documents without his written approval, and to file a memorandum with him after any conversation with a member of the Task Force. This order was also secret but several PRD employees nonetheless angrily complained to Task Force members that they regarded the memo requirement as intimidation. It was also discriminatory, since it did not apply to the visitors from industry. Many of the PRD employees interviewed were therefore very guarded in their remarks. One actually called in his secretary to take down an entire hourlong interview in shorthand. Another employee at the close of an interview nervously asked to be reminded of the subjects discussed so he could "satisfy Hays that I didn't spill the beans on anything."

Hays also made sure he knew exactly whom the Task Force interviewed. All interviews were subject to clearance in advance by Hays, or one of his division chiefs.

Lowell Miller, Assistant Director of PRD for Enforcement, immediately dispensed with this requirement, giving carte blanche to see any Enforcement Branch personnel we chose. But Easley and Nevas were astonished when they first went in to "clear" appointments with Dr. Hays: one by one Dr. Hays *personally* telephoned the individuals they asked to see and made the appointments. The Director of an important and overworked agency apparently had nothing better to do than act as appointments secretary for a couple of visiting students. Mr. Alford, the head of the registration section, was even less cooperative than his Chief. While the latter at least made appointments promptly, Mr. Alford always insisted on at least a day's delay. Many PRD employees interpreted these "personal" appointments as further intimidation—especially as neither industry representatives nor even the press required such clearance.

The Library Saga

Hays did not limit himself to refusing documents and intimidating employees. He also indulged in direct harassment in a series of events the Task Force came to call the Library Saga, an epic in three parts.

Part I: Given its inability to obtain PRD documents and its limited access to PRD staff, the Task Force determined to make diligent use of the PRD library, which contains a large collection of journals on entomology and toxicology, as well as industry publications and some of the basic PRD documents which had been denied.

The library, whose door opened onto PRD's main corridor, appeared to be available to the general public. When Easley asked the assistant librarian if he could examine the books, she granted permission without a second thought. He then spent several hours studying PRD's Inspector's Manual, the PRD Operating Manual, and a notebook of PR Memoranda—the last two items specified in the FOIA as available to the public but so far denied by Hays.

Returning to the library several days later, Nevas and Easley found these volumes missing from the shelves and asked the head librarian for them. She explained awkwardly that Hays had told her not to let them see the items and had ordered them removed—the Inspector's Manual to Enforcement Chief Miller's office, and the PR Memoranda to Registration Chief Alford's office. Nevas and Easley then walked down the hall to Miller's office and told him what had happened. Miller was dumbfounded. He called Hays and, after some argument, persuaded Hays to allow them to see the Inspector's Manual. Hays remained adamant on the PR Memoranda. (Dr. Irving, Administrator of the Agricultural Research Service and Hay's superior, overruled him three weeks later, presumably because the violation of the FOIA in denying this item would have been too blatant.)

Part II: Shortly after this incident, Nevas and Easley returned to PRD to find further changes at the library. First of all, the library door which had formerly opened onto the corridor now stood closed with a hand-lettered

sign tacked to it: "Enter through room ———," two
doors down. Following this new sign, they passed
through two offices, until they ran into the assistant
librarian who explained that the PRD had instituted a
new rule: all library visitors must be cleared with Dr.
Hays. Nonetheless, she permitted Nevas and Easley to
enter the library while she attempted to track down
Dr. Hays.

After browsing a few minutes, Easley suddenly
noticed that two large volumes published by Shell
Chemical Company which he had examined earlier
were now missing. Searching the shelves more carefully,
they discovered that the library had been swept clean
of all Shell publications, although the library had many
books and reports from other pesticide manufacturers.
Even more mysterious, all records of Shell publications
had been removed from the card catalogue.

At this point, Dr. Hays came rushing in, flushed and
obviously out of breath: "What are you doing here?
May I help you?" Easley replied, "Just browsing," and
asked about the missing Shell manuals. Hays became
flustered and stared intently at the shelves as if looking
for the missing volumes. Apparently he had ordered the
Shell publications removed because of the Task Force's
interest in possible conflict-of-interest questions regarding PRD's handling of the Shell No Pest Strip. Finally,
Nevas asked him if the new library entrance and procedures were meant to shut them out. Hays replied,
"No,—just as long as you don't look in any of the files."
(The answer was puzzling as there were no files kept
in the library.) After staring at the shelves a moment
longer, Hays suddenly rushed out of the room.

Part III: In early August, two other members of the
Task Force, wishing to use a pesticides reference, asked
Dr. Hays's secretary for permission to use the PRD
library. She referred them to Mr. Alford, Chief of Registration. Although he had never met these students
before, Mr. Alford was hostile from the start. He
demanded angrily to know why they wanted to use the
library and what they were doing looking into pesticides. After some argument, he refused them permission to enter the library, adding, however, that if they
made a formal request for some specific item in the

library, it "would be considered." Since despite all their troubles Nevas and Easley had never actually been denied access to the library, Mr. Alford's arbitrary refusal appeared to be pure harassment.

PRD vs. Time *magazine*

Perhaps the high point in PRD's comedy of evasions occurred towards the end of August, when relations with PRD were beginning to lose even surface civility. As part of a planned cover story on Ralph Nader, *Time* magazine decided to do a profile on one of the "Raiders" in action. The magazine selected Joe Tom Easley of the pesticides team and assigned a reporter, Douglass Lea, to follow him around for several days.

On the second day, he had an interview scheduled with Enforcement Chief Lowell Miller; Easley telephoned him, asking permission to bring Mr. Lea along. Mr. Miller readily agreed. When they arrived for the interview, however, Mr. Miller sheepishly informed them that Inspector General Kossack had forbidden him to admit reporters.

Easley and Lea went immediately to the Inspector General's office, where Lea and Kossack commenced a heated argument, with Lea speaking Miltonesque periods about freedom of the press and Kossack defending the virtues of secrecy with Baconesque epigrams. Reminded that a *Life* reporter had conducted an identical study a month earlier,* Kossack replied that the USDA had instituted a new "policy" on reporters. To support his position, Kossack marched Easley and Lea

---

* The *Life* interview produced another insight into Kossask's view of his watchdog role: Jack Newfield, on assignment from *Life*, accompanied Julian Houston and Jim Fallows, two Task Force members, on an interviewing mission at the Farmers Home Administration. The interviewee, picked at random from a list of civil rights compliance officials in the Department, turned out to be extraordinarily timid, rambling, and (apparently) uninformed. His main point during the interview was how much his large family depended on his job. The interview was an embarrassing and untypical experience which all concerned decided to forget. Later Kossack indirectly chided us for "setting the Department up." The implication was that we had sought out an incompetent for the Newfield interview in order to discredit the Department. In fact, the man's terrified performance was probably caused by the close monitoring of interviews which Kossack had imposed.

down to the office of USDA Director of Information, Harold Lewis.

Lea then engaged Lewis in more debate over his discriminatory treatment, but Lewis remained adamant: policy did not permit reporters to accompany Task Force members in PRD, and that was that. As to who had instituted this "policy" and when, he refused to answer.

Perhaps the most revealing episode involving PRD's arbitrary information policy occurred nearly nine months later when the Task Force was finally granted access to the "master registration card file," an index to information regarding the registration of new pesticide uses. Polly Roberts, a Task Force member who joined the Task Force from the Massachusetts Audubon Society, visited PRD on March 5, 1970, excited at the prospect of seeing these "sensitive" files so long denied.

Dr. Hays met her and ushered her downstairs to the filing area, remarking en route (although he had never met her before) that her presence was an "unfortunate situation," and that to make the best of it, "the clerks and other personnel downstairs have been instructed not to answer any of your questions as such information would be beyond their expertise." He then introduced her to Mr. Bussey, chief of filing operations, who conducted her to the room containing the master files. To her amazement, these heretofore secret files contained the manufacturers' names and the brand names of pesticides, arranged in the chronological order by which products had been registered. That was all! Thinking there had been some mistake, she returned to Mr. Bussey's office. Following is the record of her conversation:

ROBERTS: Do you have any records of nonagricultural pesticide use? [She was researching the use of pesticides around the home.]

BUSSEY: No, such information is contained only in the jackets [folders on individual pesticides]. Why do you want to know all this? What do you want to do with it?

ROBERTS: I want to know by what safety criteria certain pesticides have been registered.

BUSSEY: But why do you want to know?

ROBERTS: Because I am interested and the information is supposed to be public. I would like to see the jackets for certain pesticides.

BUSSEY: You don't seem to understand. Certain "public" information is really confidential.

ROBERTS: But I thought confidential information was kept in sealed envelopes in the jackets.

BUSSEY: The envelopes are *not* sealed.

ROBERTS: But they can still easily be removed, can't they?

BUSSEY: You don't seem to understand. The jackets contain company correspondence, which might refer to the confidential information. It would be too much work for our staff to read through all the correspondence to remove references to confidential information. [The "contamination" tactic—intermixing exempt and nonexempt information in the same file—is a familiar "ploy" of government secrecy. A registration staff officer informed us that confidential information, outside the special envelope, is referred to only by code letters or numbers.]

ROBERTS: Well, if *we* can't see the jackets, who can?

BUSSEY: Representatives of the manufacturers, and anyone else whom Dr. Hays approves.

ROBERTS: Whom does Dr. Hays approve?

BUSSEY: That's up to him.*

Remedies

Professor Kenneth Culp Davis, after surveying the patterns of official secrecy in the regulatory agencies, concluded:

The goal should be to close the gap between what the agency and its staff know about its laws and policy and

---

* Fortunately, not all USDA employees adopted the attitude of Hays, Kossack, and Lewis. Within PRD, many employees cooperated with the Task Force to a degree which, under the Hays information blackout, amounted to real personal courage. One PRD staff member who did his best to facilitate access is Lowell E. Miller, formerly Assistant Director of PRD for Enforcement, and Acting Director of PRD, now assistant to the Commissioner of Pesticides in EPA. Public servants such as Miller do a great deal to restore the citizen's legitimate right to respect his government.

what an outsider can know. The gap can probably never be completely closed but the effort should always continue.[13]

In USDA, as the incidents above demonstrate, the gap is very wide and no effort is being made to close it.

The Freedom of Information Act was little help against the capricious secrecy of PRD's director, Harry Hays. Hays and his superiors in the Agricultural Research Service treated the exemptions from disclosure permitted by the Act as if they were taffy in a taffy pull. Listed below are their most common evasion tactics:

(1) The "*contamination technique*": PRD takes items of unclassified material that may prove embarrassing and combines them with several items of classified information. Result: the whole sum is classified. PRD claimed that pesticide formulas were so intermixed with the safety data which must be filed by pesticide makers that the entire registration file must be closed. Independent scientists are, therefore, not permitted to judge the adequacy of the safety claims a manufacturer makes for his pesticide.

(2) *Trade secrets*: the formula of a pesticide, where it gives a company a competitive advantage, is properly exempt under the Act. PRD, however, applies the exemption to virtually all information which a company does not want disclosed. Correspondence between PRD and pesticide makers was denied because it might contain references to trade secrets. In fact, much of the information classified as trade secrets, including many pesticide formulas, is common knowledge within the industry. The only group not familiar with it is the public.

(3) *Specificity*: a typical tactic of many agencies is to delay replying to an information request for several weeks, then state that the request was not specific enough. USDA, for example, waited four months after we initially appealed Hays's refusals to tell the Task Force that its request was too general, in spite of the fact that it requested the Shell No Pest Strip file by its actual serial number. Because USDA will not make available its file indices, the requests had to be somewhat general.

(4) *Search fees*: even if the agency concedes that information is public, it may impose arbitrarily high fees for collecting it. USDA stated that it would cost $91,840 and take 1.6 years to prepare its registration files for public view.[14]

(5) *Investigation files*: a common tactic is for an agency to open a file involving the investigation of violations of a federal law or regulation and then conceal all information about a firm or product by dropping in into the file.

(6) *The "working paper"*: here information is withheld from the public but not insiders on the grounds that information is incomplete or in preliminary form. The President's Science Advisory Committee used this tactic with their report on 2,4,5-T. A draft of the report was finished in August, 1970, and released, with a few changes, in May, 1971. Industry defenders of 2,4,5-T made reference to the report for over eight months before it was made available to the public.

The Task Force eventually challenged USDA's denials in federal court. In *Wellford* v. *Hardin*, USDC, DC, Civil No. 740-70 (August 5, 1970), Judge June Green of the U.S. District Court for the District of Columbia found that the Department had circumvented the Freedom of Information Act in making secrecy the rule rather than the exception and held:

(1) It is a violation of the Act to withhold from the public the means for requesting specific records (i.e. the indices to the registration and enforcement files) when lack of specificity is given as the reason for refusing to grant an information request;

(2) It is a violation of the Act to withhold documents on the grounds that parts are exempt and parts are nonexempt. This ruling curbs USDA's use of the "contamination" tactic.

As noted earlier, Judge Northrop of the U.S. District Court in Baltimore, in a case involving denial of meat inspection information by the Department, restricted the "investigatory file" exemption and also held, with regard to the Act's requirement that records requested be "identifiable," that information on an issue is "identifiable" (sufficiently specific) even when the records are disbursed in more than one location in the agency.

USDA had withheld information on pesticide accidents on the grounds that it was scattered in both enforcement and registration files.

These cases are a step toward freer information in the regulatory agencies, but a small step only. Despite the Act's stipulation that such cases are to take precedence on the court's calendars, they may take six months or more to come to a decision. Then there is always the possibility of appeal. If public participation in agency decision-making is to increase, there must be immediate changes in the implementation of the Freedom of Information Act:

(1) Each agency should reply to a request for information within seven working days. If more time is needed, a notice should be sent to the requester informing him of the date when the information will be available, and the reason for the delay.

(2) If information is denied, the denial should state the exemption being claimed, why it is applicable in this case, and an outline of appeal procedures available.

(3) A central file of all denials and the reasons for them should be maintained for public inspection.

(4) Agencies should organize filing systems so that exempt and nonexempt information can be easily segregated on request.

(5) Each agency should establish a one-step appeal procedure with final action within ten days of the filing of the appeal.

(6) Specific procedures should be developed for taking corrective action when federal officials resort to harassment techniques or other actions contrary to the Act.

(7) Congress is not exercising effective supervision over the way the Act is being observed in the agencies. There have been no Congressional hearings since the Act was passed.

Now that the Pesticide Regulation Division has been shifted to the Environmental Protection Agency, citizens' access to pesticide decision-making may improve. Pesticide regulators continue to work out of the same drab offices in USDA's South Building but the atmosphere has changed. PRD is now off limits to Inspector General Kossack; Harry Hays has been deposed; and the oppressive fear of reprisal which embarrassed interviews with PRD's staff has now subsided. William Ruckelshaus, Administrator of EPA, acknowledges that environmentalists, farm workers, and the like are legitimate constituents of the pesticide agency, and promises to end some of the worst features of discriminatory treatment of citizens vis-à-vis industry.

But while there is hope for the new regime, one must beware of slippage back to the patterns of the old. PRD's personnel remain largely the same as it was under Harry Hays, and many still share his outlook. Alford is the new Director of PRD but has not yet indicated what his information policy will be. Now that all environment related regulation is centered on one agency, EPA is being subjected to the most intense barrage of industry advocacy ever witnessed in Washington. Without strong leadership from PRD's director and the administrator of EPA, and perhaps in spite of it, PRD will resume its practice of making better deals with industry than it does with the public.

13

The Enforcement Labyrinth

Major consumer and environmental protection laws typically result from a crisis—a mine disaster, an oil spillage, the discovery of a new pesticide residue in food and water—which commands momentarily the attention and anxiety of the public. This crisis energy is a very perishable commodity. For those who wish to stem the tide of public concern, the best defense, obviously, is time.

The pattern is classic. The concerned public relieves its fears by pressuring for a dramatic gesture from the government, while representatives of the affected industries quietly prepare devices to absorb the pressures. Typically they take the form of enforcement procedures, where exasperating technicality and labyrinthine delay mask federal inaction in a camouflage of tedium—until the public tumult subsides.

Nowhere has this pattern been more visible than in pesticide policy. When environmentalists mobilize to get a pesticide banned or restricted, they rarely leave energy in reserve for monitoring enforcement. The Congressman who gained headlines informing the public of a hazard often finds it politically unrewarding to badger bureaucrats for enforcement after the hazard has become old news. Very often, the constituencies mobilized by the original event tend to equate enactment of a program (or an official promise to do so) with solution of the problem, and move on to other causes.

It is here, in the vacuum left by the activists' departure, that the affected commercial interests go to work. Their aim is to ensure that the corridors of correction will be as winding and endless as the corridors of violation.[1] Because the agency's critics lack the resources to monitor implementation, months and years may pass before the gap between enforcement and official promises is noticed. Then a new crisis occurs and the cycle begins anew.

Federal Communications Commissioner Nicholas Johnson described this pattern for the Senate Subcommittee on Administrative Practice and Procedure:

Something happens which requires government action, and the matter comes to the attention of the public. A proceeding is undertaken to deal with the question. The public believes something will be done—but now accepts the fact that it will take time. Then the pressure starts—on those who have been handed the job of investigation and reform. Corporate interests that will be adversely affected move to delay, to water down, to remove "dangerous" people, and then finally to participate in the final whitewash. They hope the public will forget its original outrage until the process is next repeated. They generally do.[2]

The Federal Insecticide, Fungicide, and Rodenticide Act,* with its designed-in tiers of delay, its petty sanctions, its exasperating vaguenesses and omissions, provides endless opportunities for the maneuverings Johnson describes. These legal weaknesses were often reinforced and exploited by the Pesticide Regulation Division while it was part of the Department of Agriculture. Some of these flaws will be reduced now that pesticide regulation has been transferred to the Environmental Protection Agency, but others will require more fundamental reforms. The basic flaws in legislation, which often made enforcement procedures a sham in the past, remain.

The Sham Ban: The DDT Case

The chasm between public promises and official performance on DDT is deep and surprisingly little explored. It is the paradigm of the federal govern-

* Hereafter referred to as FIFRA.

ment's ability to counter public clamor for environmental protection with the gossamer weaponry of the press release. On November 20, 1969, the Nixon Administration with great fanfare announced that USDA, in the first step toward a total ban, had cancelled DDT for use on tobacco, shade trees, in households, and with certain exceptions, in aquatic areas.* Reaction to these initiatives by USDA was swift and laudatory. The *New York Times* praised the Nixon Administration for "taking a giant step forward in reducing the menace to all living creatures of the long-lasting poisons that have been used with such careless and ignorant abandon for many years."[3] Thirty days later, with no fanfare, the leading manufacturers and marketers of DDT appealed this ban and set in motion a stately procession of administrative delays. Two years later, in January, 1972, DDT's use on many major crops, including cotton (which accounts for 70 percent of DDT sales) remained untouched by government action.

DDT has been the primary target of pesticide critics because it has been the most widely used pesticide and because its residues are the most ubiquitous in the environment. DDT is inherently uncontrollable: once released into the environment, it is carried by air and water from the site of application to all parts of the world (including the polar ice cap and the depths of the most remote oceans); it is persistent, retaining its poisoning power for many years after release; it is accumulated in the fatty tissues of man and animals (DDT has been found in mothers' milk up to 25 ppm in Guatemala),[4] becoming more concentrated as it passes up the food chain where one organism becomes food for another. DDT has been established as a carcinogen and an inducer of fetal mortality in test animals.[5] It has also contributed to the reproductive failure in raptorial birds, including the bald eagle, the peregrine falcon, and the brown pelican.[6] Finally, it is an ecologically crude pesticide, killing pest and beneficial insect alike, and hastening the development of resistance and secondary outbreaks among pests.

---

* In June, 1972, EPA banned 99 percent of *domestic* DDT use effective December 31, 1972. Exceptions were made for public health uses, green peppers, onions, and sweet potatos in storage.

Four governmental committees which have studied DDT in depth between 1963 and 1969 have all recommended that its use be phased out. In 1963, the President's Science Advisory Committee declared that "elimination of persistent toxic pesticides should be the goal." In 1969, the Mrak Commission recommended that all uses of DDT not essential to public health be eliminated by December, 1971.

DDT is the most thoroughly studied chemical ever released in the environment, yet now that the federal government has been goaded into action by public pressure and the courts, it is giving DDT the pomp and ceremony of another full-scale scientific review, before it decides on further restrictions. The result is that while the public feels that the DDT battle has been won by the environmentalists, in fact, it has just begun. The chemical industry, taking full advantage of the cumbersome appeal procedures it helped to build into the Federal Insecticide, Fungicide, and Rodenticide Act, can delay effective restriction of DDT for many months and perhaps years to come.

At first glance, there is an apparent paradox in the often emotional* defense of DDT by the pesticide industry. DDT has been slowly dying from "natural" causes for several years and is no longer a mainstay of profits for the chemical industry. The amount of DDT used in this country has declined from 79 million pounds in 1959 to approximately 12 million pounds in 1970, largely because of a reduction in cotton acreage, the growing resistance of many insects to DDT, and public pressure in such states as Florida, Arizona, Michigan, and Wisconsin.[7] Over 80 percent of DDT produced in the United States is now exported. The making of DDT

---

* The DDT fight has unleashed a virulent form of the pesticide "McCarthyism" first directed at Rachel Carson. Dr. Max Sobelman of the Montrose Chemical Corporation of California charges DDT critics with being anticapitalistic; Louis McLean of Velsicol Chemical Corporation suggests they are "preoccupied with the subject of sexual potency." Dr. Wayland Hayes, Professor of Biochemistry, Vanderbilt University, suggests that they are aiding the machinations of foreign agents; Dr. White-Stevens, Professor of Biology, Rutgers University, charges that they may be responsible for the death of millions for malaria, and *Barrons* has accused them of plotting world famine—despite the fact that banning DDT in the U.S. will have no legal effect on overseas shipments and that DDT critics make an exception for use of DDT to control epidemics.[9]

has become a $20 million industry spread over basically five companies with domestic sales—the only sales affected by proposed federal action—of only $3.5 million.[8] It is entirely possible that the legal costs incurred by the companies in defending DDT will soon match their profits from selling it.

The fact is that DDT is more important as a symbol than a product. The preface to a 400-page defense of DDT prepared by its producers states that they are resisting the attacks on DDT because the attacks are the "opening guns against all pesticides and against science and technology."[10] DDT, which actually won a Nobel Prize for its role as a malaria fighter, enjoys a special reverence as the father of modern insecticides. In defending it, the industry sees itself defending the concept of progress against a plague of Luddites who would dismantle the technological advances of organic pesticides on which, in their view, "in no small measure the improvement of Western man's life has been [based]."[11] Dr. Charles Wurster, who has led the attack on DDT for the Environmental Defense Fund, also acknowledges DDT's symbolic power:

If the environmentalists win on DDT, they will achieve and probably retain in other environmental issues, a level of authority they have never had before. In a sense, then, much more is at stake than DDT.[12]

The DDT case is a classic illustration of how a federal law can be used by the interests it supposedly regulates to exhaust their opponents. Although the pesticide industry has largely lost the scientific debate on the cost-benefit merits of DDT use in this country, it is now capitalizing on the extraordinary opportunities for delay in federal enforcement procedures. In order to see how these procedures have become a defense of "business as usual" by industry, it is instructive to examine the stages of DDT's "elimination" step by step.

First, one must recognize that no pesticide is banned altogether, only certain *uses* are banned. DDT is approved for over 300 uses, and each one is entitled to the full scope of administrative and legal due process. Since November, 1969, the Pesticide Regulation Division has canceled approximately sixty uses of DDT.

The key point here is that the uses of DDT have been canceled, not suspended. While the term "cancellation" sounds very final, in effect it achieves no ban at all if a pesticide maker objects to it. Cancellation allows the accused product to continue to be sold while administrative and legal proceedings take place. Suspension, while it sounds more tentative, in fact removes the product from the marketplace while its case is being heard. As we shall see, suspension, which requires a finding of "imminent hazard," is rarely used.

The travail of cancellation, where statutory deadlines alone can consume over 300 days, began for DDT in November, 1969, when the Pesticide Regulation Division canceled the registration of four of its uses. Under the law, DDT manufacturers had thirty days to appeal and request the appointment of a science advisory committee or a public hearing. When the appeal was made by several DDT makers, USDA then delayed seven months in naming the advisory committee. While there is a thirty-day deadline for the companies to request the committee, and a sixty-day deadline for the committee to report once it has convened, there is no deadline compelling the government to name the committee members within a specified time. This loophole permits an indefinite delay.[13]

An advisory committee is given sixty days to finish its report. PRD then has ninety days within which to issue an order confirming or denying the committee's recommendation. After the order is made, the companies have sixty days in which to file an objection and to request a public hearing. Here the stately procession of deadlines pauses and another hiatus occurs. There is no deadline within which PRD must call a public hearing. Again a delay of several months could and often does occur. After the public hearing is held, PRD has ninety days within which to issue a final order.

At this point, administrative due process has consumed 310 days of deadlines and an indeterminate additional period of discretionary delays permitted the government under loopholes in the law. During all of this time, the product suspected of causing harm continues to be marketed as before the "ban."

This elaborate process, however, may be only a skir-

mish along the way to the ultimate outcome. At this
point, even if the company has failed in two hearings
and three agency decisions to win its case, it may simply shift the fight to another arena. It may now challenge PRD's final ruling in the courts, where the wheels
of due process also grind wondrously slow. At no time
in the history of Anglo-American jurisprudence has a
defendant ever enjoyed the elaborate assurances of justice routinely accorded to pesticide manufacturers by
FIFRA.

In the DDT case, four DDT producers withdrew
their request for a science advisory committee in July,
1970, but one, the Lebanon Company, then requested a
public hearing. After further months of delay, this
request also was withdrawn, and the use of DDT on
tobacco, shade trees, aquatic areas, and in households
was finally banned. The effect of this completed cancellation on the companies' DDT sales may be more
apparent than real. When a specific use of a pesticide
is banned, it may remain on the shelf for sale in its
original container. *Only the label is changed, to delete
the prohibited use.* There is no reason to expect that a
farmer accustomed to using a pesticide in container X
to spray his elm tree or his tobacco patch will cease
because container X has a few words changed in its
label to forbid its use on shade trees. Home owners will
probably continue to use DDT inside the house unless
the manufacturers abandon home use packaging, and
farmers may continue to use DDT on tobacco, a prohibited use, under pretense of buying it for cotton, a
permitted use.

Furthermore, cancellation applies only to products
manufactured after the effective date of the ban. Products in warehouses and on the store shelf can continue
to be sold as before. If the DDT makers have used the
delay to stockpile the chemical by inflating production,
the ban will remain ineffective for many more months.
In August, 1970, a USDA spokesman charged that
Lebanon and other DDT sellers had exploited administrative delays for exactly this purpose.

In the cancellation of DDT uses on tobacco and the
other three uses mentioned above, the federal government took the initiative. When the push for cancella-

tion comes from outside the government, bureaucratic inertia is added to FIFRA's delays to create a truly formidable barrier to action. On October 1, 1969, the Environmental Defense Fund filed a petition with the Secretary of Agriculture requesting cancellation and suspension of all uses of DDT. For six months, the Secretary ignored the petition. EDF then went into federal court and got a ruling ordering the Secretary to respond to the petition with a statement of reasons. The Secretary then notified EDF that he had refused to cancel the DDT uses. EDF subsequently challenged this refusal in court. On January 7, 1971, Judge David Bazelon for the U.S. District Court for the District of Columbia ordered EPA (responsibility for pesticide regulation had been shifted to the new agency from USDA in November, 1970) to cancel all remaining uses of DDT and to reconsider its failure to suspend these uses.[14]

On January 15, EPA canceled the remaining uses. Montrose Chemical Company then asked for a science advisory committee to weigh the evidence for and against cancellation and the administrative treadmill creaked into motion once again. Other DDT makers and formulators opted for a public hearing. On the other question, suspension, EPA, in January, 1971, asked for public comments on what it should do. After reviewing hundreds of documents, it decided on March 18 that it would stick with the cancellation route and not suspend.

The public hearing began on August 17, 1971.* Three days a week for six months, lawyers from the Environmental Defense Fund and the Environmental Protection Agency, acting as prosecutors, and lawyers for

---

* One moment of comic relief occurred in January, 1972, when the defense counsel for DDT was cross-examining Dr. Samuel Epstein. Epstein had just finished reviewing several scientific papers showing the effects of DDT on tumors in mice and rats. In an attempt to discredit the tests, the lawyer asked Epstein if it were not true that the animals were given unrealistically high doses. Epstein replied that the tests showing tumor growth were properly conducted. Then the lawyer triumphantly held up one paper: "Look at this test. The animals were given absurdly high doses. Surely they have no human significance." Epstein answered, "I quite agree." Puzzled, the lawyer looked at the paper more carefully. Its title: "The *Anti*-Cancer Effects of DDT." To his horror the lawyer saw that his prize exhibit of poor laboratory technique was the one experiment heralded by industry as evidence that DDT could cure tumors, not cause them.

Montrose Chemical Company and USDA acting for the defense, have met in a government hearing room in Arlington, Virginia, to carry on the most protracted inquiry into an environmental problem ever conducted by the federal government. Before it is over, the hearing will span ninety days of formal proceedings, examine over one hundred scientists, and amass approximately 12,000 pages of oral testimony, most of which will never be read.

Meanwhile in another arena, the science advisory committee requested by Montrose has considered the same questions before the public hearing and concluded that (a) DDT is not an imminent hazard to human health, (b) DDT is "an imminent hazard to human welfare in terms of maintaining healthy desirable flora and fauna in man's environment," and (c) DDT should be rapidly curtailed with the goal of virtual elimination, but the decision whether suspension or gradual reduction is the best course of action should be left up to the Administrator of EPA.

Neither the committee recommendation nor the recommendation which emerges from the public hearing is binding on William Ruckelshaus, Administrator of EPA. As noted above, the decision will probably be ultimately made *de novo* after political negotiations between Ruckelshaus and the White House. Even if Ruckelshaus eventually agrees to suspend more uses of DDT, the pesticide companies may then appeal his decision in the Court of Appeals, with the prospect of additional months of delay. In the meantime, it is business as usual for the DDT sellers.

EPA, in justifying its refusal to *suspend* the uses of DDT, notes that cancellation has been successfully completed against nonessential uses of DDT. The problem is that EPA, following the lead of USDA, exempts from this category the use of DDT on cotton, which accounts for over 70 percent of all current domestic use. In fact, after years of decline, DDT threatens to become once again a growth industry. In 1970, 12 million pounds of DDT were used to control the bollworm and about two dozen other pests of cotton, citrus, soybeans, and peanuts. In 1971, the figure had climbed to 16 million pounds.

Through the alchemy of enforcement procedures, the *New York Times*'s "giant step forward" has now been reduced to a marching in place. A final irony is the fact that even if the federal government does get tough on DDT, its action will only affect DDT sold in interstate commerce. In the big cotton states of the South and West, it may be profitable for DDT makers to set up shop and sell their wares to local farmers only. Unless the state acts to ban DDT, this action is entirely legal. In addition, DDT will continue to be exported in huge quantities to South America and other lands abroad, from which the winds and tides will carry its residues back to our shores. Some of these overseas uses—fighting malaria and other insect-borne diseases, are vital; but many more are wasteful, and leave peasant farmers on the treadmill of diminishing returns. It is little wonder that DDT fighters occasionally show signs of battle fatigue.

Science Advisory Committees

The cancellation process is too unwieldy for effective control of hazardous chemicals. The fact that a potentially hazardous product continues to be sold during proceedings gives the pesticide industry almost irresistible incentives for delay. Several plans for streamlining this process have been suggested. Many critics focus on the science advisory panels as major sources of needless delay.

The scientific panels have been criticized by environmentalists for their secrecy and their lack of objectivity. The panel members are nominated by the National Academy of Sciences and selected by EPA. Traditionally the National Academy has a poor record in anticipating pesticide hazards. Its report *Pest Control and Wildlife Relationships* published in 1962 and heralded by chemical companies as a refutation of *Silent Spring* was panned by leading environmentalists. The *Atlantic Naturalist* described the report as unscientific and "written in the style of a trained public relations official of industry out to placate some segments of the public that were causing trouble."[15] The *Jensen Report on Persistent Pesticides,* another NAS-NRC production, while stronger, failed to recommend any concrete restrictions on the use of DDT, dieldrin, and aldrin. Its research panels, with some notable exceptions, are frequently staffed with scientists well known for their ties to the chemical industry either as consultants or as grant recipients. In cancellation proceedings, the NAS does not supervise the advisory panels it helps select. The panel reports do not go through the clearance and review procedures of regular NAS studies, and therefore are even more vulnerable to industry influence. The panel reports directly to the EPA's administrator. Their meetings are closed to the public but open to government officials and the pesticide industry.

Nevertheless, the panels have proved useful, particularly to the harassed staff of EPA's administrator who need advice which is independent of PRD and the companies. Standards of objectivity and professionalism on the advisory panels may improve now that EPA, not USDA, is selecting their members. The following changes will further improve their performance and reduce delay:

(1) William Ruckelshaus has recently promised to make the advisory panel reports available to the public before, not after, he makes a decision. He should go even further and open the selection procedures and records and transcripts of the panel to public participation. If either side in a dispute feels the panel is unbalanced, it should have the right to request additional appointments.

(2) The time allowed for the panel to be appointed, meet, and report should be cut in half.

(3) At present, only the pesticide company can request a public hearing if a panel recommendation unfavorable to its interests is adopted by EPA. Environmentalists should be given the same privilege.

(4) EPA should have the right to refuse to call an advisory panel when it has reason to believe that the request is frivolous and aimed primarily at delay.

Preventive Detention and the Imminent Hazard Clause

When EPA moves against a pesticide along the cancellation route even with an improved science advisory system, enforcement will often become a sponge which soaks up public concern before it can affect the pesticide companies. EPA, however, has discretion to avoid the incentives for delay in cancellation by using the other weapon in the enforcement arsenal, the suspension power.

The difference between suspension of a hazardous pesticide and cancellation is, for practical purposes, the difference between banning the pesticide and no ban at all. A valid suspension order requires removal of a pesticide or herbicide from the market immediately. Suspension, in effect, holds the suspected product in "preventive detention" while its fate is being determined by administrative and scientific tribunals. FIFRA authorizes the administrator of EPA to use the suspension power when he finds such action is necessary to prevent an "imminent hazard" to the public. Unfortunately, this key phrase is nowhere defined in the act.

In the past, USDA lawyers, with casuistical fervor, so narrowly defined the meaning of "imminent" that FIFRA's suspension clause has become a dead letter. Public harm from a pesticide was not "imminent" unless (a) the harm threatened to happen immediately; and (b) it produced demonstrable victims. The bizarre consequences of this interpretation were illustrated in testimony before the Senate Subcommittee on Energy, Natural Resources, and the Environment in 1970:

MR. BECKWIT (Committee Counsel): If the evidence were absolutely clear that whenever we applied 2,4,5-T to food crops [and] those crops were eaten, we stood, say a 75 percent chance of a birth defect, do you feel that use of [2,4,5-T] on food crops would constitute an imminent hazard to health . . . ?

DR. BYERLY (USDA Official): We do not now have authority, in my opinion, not clear authority, to act in such a case.

According to USDA lawyers, the few months that may ensue between the application of a poison to a crop and the consumption of the poison on food destroys the "imminence" of the hazard. USDA contended in effect that a time bomb is not an imminent hazard.

This interpretation has created the largest single

hurdle in the way of swift federal response to pesticide hazards. From 1947 through 1970, the Pesticide Regulation Division invoked the suspension power only two times—against mercury fungicides and against some uses of 2,4,5-T. (USDA ordered the Aeroseal Company to stop selling its vapona strips, but technically, this was not suspension because the Aeroseal product had never been registered.)

On February 18, 1970, the Secretary of Agriculture found "imminent hazard" in the continued use of mercury fungicides and invoked Section 4c of FIFRA to suspend their use immediately. The suspension was triggered by an incident in August, 1969. A farmer in Alamogordo, New Mexico, fed waste grain to his hogs. The grain had been treated with an organic mercury fungicide. In mid-September one of the hogs was slaughtered and the pork was eaten for about three and one-half months. Then in December and January the farmer's children began to fall sick; today two of the children remain comatose, having suffered irreparable brain damage, and the other is making only slow progress towards recovery.

After USDA acted, the Nor-Am Company, a fungicide producer, obtained a District Court preliminary injunction against the suspension, and on appeal, the Court of Appeals affirmed the preliminary injunction. The Court held that the suspension was "arbitrary and capricious" and charged USDA with reacting to the New Mexico incident with "emotionalism." USDA's past failure to suspend other equally dangerous pesticides made its action against mercury appear capricious. The Department successfully appealed the decision to the full Court of Appeals.

In April, 1970, as we have seen, USDA also invoked the suspension power against some uses of 2,4,5-T. It suspended 2,4,5-T around the home and in aquatic areas, but refused to suspend its use on food and brush control. EPA must now decide whether it is rational to rule that this substance and its contaminants are imminently hazardous when inhaled but not when eaten. EPA's current definition of "imminent hazard" was stated on March 18, 1971 in its "Reasons Under-

lying the Registration Decisions Concerning Products
Containing DDT, 2,4,5-T, Aldrin and Dieldrin."

. . . This Agency will find that an imminent hazard to the
public exists when the evidence is sufficient to show that
continued registration of an economic poison poses a significant threat of danger to health, or otherwise creates a
hazardous situation to the public, that should be corrected
immediately to prevent serious injury and which cannot be
permitted to continue during the pendency of administrative
proceedings. An "imminent hazard" may be declared at any
point in a chain of events which may ultimately result in
harm to the public. It is not necessary that the final anticipated injury actually have occurred prior to a determination
that an "imminent hazard" exists. In this connection, significant injury or potential injury to plants or animals alone
could justify a finding of imminent hazard to the public from
the use of an economic poison. . . .

Congress should expand EPA's power to hold a dangerous product in preventive detention until doubts about
its safety have been resolved. First, EPA should have
the power to suspend temporarily a product for ninety
days, with the understanding that if the manufacturer
has not satisfied a burden of proof as to its safety
within this period, the suspension becomes permanent.
This measure would give the companies a strong incentive to sponsor the necessary safety research.

Second, EPA should recognize that the long delays of
cancellation increase the gravity of risk for a potentially
dangerous pesticide. The risks from continued sale of a
suspicious product may not seem "imminent" when cancellation is expected to reach the point of decision in
two or three months; the risks should be seen in a
different light when cancellation allows the product to
continue to be sold for a year or more. On March 18,
1971, EPA did not find the danger of residues in food
from 2,4,5-T and its contaminants to pose a "significant
threat" of human harm during the time necessary for
cancellation proceedings; ten months later, the proceedings had still not reached the public hearing stage,
with many months of further delay likely. The danger
that 2,4,5-T contaminants in the environment can cause
human hazards "during the pendency of administrative

proceedings" increases as the months go by. The hazards of continued use of 2,4,5-T on food crops may now indeed seem "imminent" enough to warrant suspension.

Third, the term "imminent hazard" should be defined to show that it encompasses serious long-term hazards, such as cancer or birth defects, whose human victims may not become stricken for months or years after exposure. Any teratogenic or carcinogenic pesticide found to leave residues in food should be subject to suspension as an "imminent hazard" even though case histories of specific victims cannot be produced. When the residues are suspected but not conclusively proved (e.g. because of inadequate analytical methods), suspension is still warranted when cancellation proceedings seem likely to drag on for months or years.

The Thallium Case: (1) Recall and Infanticide

It is a rule of regulatory agencies that they betray the public trust less by what they do than by what they fail to do. PRD's notorious reluctance to require companies to recall from the marketplace pesticides it has banned as a danger to public health is such a case. Twenty years elapsed before PRD initiated its first action to recall a dangerous pesticide, although it has had such authority since 1947. This pattern has held true even when, as in the case of thallium sulfate, the banned product was a proven killer of small children. Thallium sulfate is an extremely toxic rodenticide which can cause loss of hair, paralysis, brain damage, and death, in even very small amounts. Over the protest of the Public Health Service, PRD for many years allowed thallium pellets to be placed on the floors of homes to kill rodents, where they were very accessible to children. In 1962–1963, 400 cases of poisoned children were recorded. In 1965, PRD issued a final cancellation of the registration of thallium for home use, without protest from its manufacturer.

Three years later, in 1968, the General Accounting Office created a sensation when it reported that its agents had been able to buy thallium in 20 percent of the Washington-area stores it surveyed. An investigation revealed that PRD, after announcing the thallium ban, had neglected to find out the quantities and location of products already in the marketplace and had failed to seize or recall the banned products. When asked to justify PRD's failure to act, Dr. Hays admitted that PRD had deliberately left them on the market:

We did not make any attempt to withdraw the materials from the market on the premise . . . that the cancellation would in itself prevent the continued proliferation and thus a phasing out, dilution and finally disappearance [of the products].

Under cross-examination, PRD officials conceded that they did not keep a record of the number of thallium deaths and were not aware that over thirty children had been poisoned by the thallium sulfate left on retail shelves after the ban. In 1968 alone, there were at least 20 cases reported, and in 1969, nine more children fell victim to this product which might have properly been called an "infanticide." As a result of the Fountain Hearings, PRD surveyed 101 Washington-area stores in August, 1969, and found thallium in three—an impressive dilution perhaps, but hardly reassuring when one remembers that thallium had been banned four years before.

PRD has been hampered in removing dangerous products from the market by a glaring weakness in FIFRA. This weakness was illustrated in August, 1967, when PRD inspectors picked up a sample of the pesticide toxaphene in a formulation produced by the Agricultural Chemical Service Company in Montgomery, Alabama. Lab tests revealed that the product contained not only toxaphene but a deadly additional ingredient not on the label: methyl parathion. The sample was then destroyed. But what happened to the misbranded toxaphene at other retail outlets PRD did not visit?

Here is the rub. PRD does not have authority to issue blanket stop-sale orders to the hundreds and perhaps thousands of other retail outlets selling hazardous or ineffective products. Under FIFRA, PRD needs a separate federal court order for each store where the dangerous product is sold before it can initiate seizure. This gap in enforcement powers was acknowledged by

PRD officials in 1969 in testimony before the House Subcommittee on Intergovernmental Operations:

MR. NAUGHTON (Committee Counsel): ... in 1966 and prior thereto, is it correct that your normal procedure when your inspectors found a sample of a product which was in violation of the act and which might be dangerous and potentially harmful in a retail establishment, the procedure followed was to seize the product in that particular retail establishment and if this was one of 50,000 retail establishments which had received that potentially harmful product it would be seized at one establishment and remain for sale without interference by ARS at 49,999 other establishments?

My question is, can any of you at this table recall a single instance in twenty years where you went to the records of the manufacturer of a dangerous product to find out where additional supplies of that product were located for sale so that you could take it off the market completely?

DR. ANDERSON: We do not recall any instance where we went directly to the records of the company.

In an attempt to remedy this situation, Lowell Miller, then PRD's enforcement chief, instituted a procedure for voluntary recall in 1967. Under this procedure, PRD writes to the maker of the pesticide it wants banned and requests that the company write a letter to its retail outlets asking them to stop selling the product. While this is better than doing nothing at all, it still has serious limitations. First, there is delay of weeks while USDA notifies the company and the company notifies the retailer. Second, the pesticide maker may be very vague about where all of its products are being sold. The Shell No Pest Strip, for example, is sold in 300,000 retail outlets. Third, the retailer may with impunity refuse to comply with the company's request and continue to sell the banned product as long as he can get it.

Enforcement officials need authority to issue an effective stop-sale order to all sellers of a dangerous pesticide, with civil and criminal penalties for those

who violate it. Civil penalties, the most practical and
easily imposed sanction, are especially important.

*The Thallium Case: (2) Eagles and Penalties for
Misuse*

On May 27, 1971, Assistant Secretary of Interior
Nathaniel P. Reed held a press conference to announce
that at least twenty-five bald and golden eagles had
been poisoned by Wyoming ranchers since May 1. He
estimated that only 800 pairs of these majestic birds
remain in the United States. The eagles were killed
when they fed on carcasses which ranchers had baited
with poison to kill coyotes. Their deaths are all the
more tragic because they were needless: they were
caused by a poison banned by the federal government
for private use nearly six years ago.

Thallium, the poison used to bait the carcasses, was
banned for all uses except by government officials and
professional exterminators in 1965. These officials were
permitted to use it for rat and mice control, but they
were *not* authorized to use thallium for predator control.
In this case, a manufacturer of thallium sent the pesticide in its technical form to Wyoming where it was to
be prepared for use by these officials. It then got into
the hands of the ranchers.

Although thallium's registration clearly states that it
is not to be used by individual ranchers for predator
control or, any other purpose, the ranchers were subject
to no legal sanctions under the Federal Insecticide,
Fungicide, and Rodenticide Act. (It is, of course, against
federal law to kill an eagle intentionally but intent is
very hard to prove when eagles die from feeding on
carcasses ostensibly baited for coyotes.) Remarkably
under present federal laws, *there are no penalties for an
individual who misuses a pesticide in defiance of its
label.* Federal law controls what goes on the label of a
pesticide, but not what happens to the pesticide after it
is sold.

The death of the eagles in Wyoming forcefully illustrates the fact that as long as a pesticide remains on
the market for even the most limited use, individuals

will obtain it and use it in prohibited ways, as long as there are no penalties for misuse. This glaring weakness in federal government procedures must be eliminated. The federal government should be enabled to levy civil and criminal penalties against anyone who uses a pesticide in a manner not consistent with its label. In addition, pesticides like thallium should be put in a restricted use category to be applied only by professional applicators licensed by EPA.

Testing

The fact that environmentalists must perform the labors of Sisyphus to get a dangerous pesticide off the market once it's been approved highlights the need for careful premarket screening for pesticide hazards. Here the record shows that PRD has often failed its trust. There has been first a failure of concept—effectiveness and safety are very narrowly construed—and second a failure of performance—the testing is done either by scientists on the company payroll or by "independent" testing labs which depend on industry goodwill for their contracts.

Until recently, as we have seen in discussing 2,4,5-T, industry tests for adverse effects of new pesticides upon human beings have been astonishingly narrow in concept. For many years, PRD was content to focus on the immediate dangers to those people who come into direct contact with the pesticide. It relied on rough measures of acute toxicity such as the LD_{50}, the dose of the pesticides which kills 50 percent of experimental animals. It neglected the potential long-term hazards of pesticides. PRD approved the widespread use of the herbicide 2,4,5-T for twenty years before opening up a mother rat to see if it could cause birth defects. As a result of reports from the Bionetics Laboratory and the Mrak Commission and because of pressure generated by the 2,4,5-T controversy, PRD is now requiring teratogenic and carcinogenic testing on a number of basic pesticide chemicals. PRD does not yet require testing of pesticides for mutagenic effects in mammalian systems but pressure is building in the scientific community to force PRD's hand.

PRD has also been negligent in focusing on the ingestion or absorption of pesticides but overlooking the possibility of inhalation. The long-term hazards of chronic inhalation of pesticide vaporizers and Vapona strips have not been adequately reviewed, according to the Mrak Commission, the American Medical Association, the Public Health Service, and other medical groups. The lungs are peculiarly vulnerable to pesticide poisoning.

While EPA may be criticized for not requiring more safety tests from industry, one must also question the competence and impartiality of the narrow tests which are conducted. Few people realize the extent to which the safety analysis of pesticides has become a closed system for insiders only. Before a pesticide is presented to PRD, its maker, through its own labs, or through contracts with independent testing laboratories, arranges and pays for the testing necessary to satisfy safety criteria. Before reaching PRD, therefore, a pesticide's safety data passes through two sieves, each of which is likely to sift out data which proves embarrassing to the short-term profit considerations of the pesticide maker.

First the commercial laboratory which wishes to retain its industry contracts has incentives to choose a testing methodology which will reveal the least negative characteristics of a pesticide. A pesticide company has a clear incentive to avoid a laboratory which is embarrassingly thorough in its tests. The second sifting of test results occurs when the testing laboratory reports to the company. The company, not the laboratory or PRD, decides which data to submit in support of its pesticide.

The conflict of interest in the present testing system must be eliminated. Dr. Samuel Epstein, a leading environmental toxicologist at Boston's Children's Hospital, observes:

The present system of direct, closed-contract negotiations between manufacturing industries and commercial and other testing laboratories is open to abuse, creates obvious mutual constraints, and is thus contrary to consumer, and long-term industrial interests.[16]

The opportunities for abuse are obvious, for EPA's pesticide staff conducts only a paper review of industry data. The Pesticide Regulation Division has been criticized for accepting at face value testing data which is shallow and incomplete. PRD rarely conducts independent tests of its own and does not regularly solicit comments from outside scientists. As one PRD staffer commented in an interview in August, 1969, "a manufacturer runs the test he wants to run, selects the test results which are most favorable to him, and sends them to us. Rarely if ever will we ask him to submit additional data."

The Public Health Service and FDA have also criticized PRD's handling of industry tests. Dr. Thomas Harris, former head of the Division for Pesticide Registration of FDA before its functions were shifted to EPA, reported in an interview that he frequently requested former PRD Director Harry Hays to ask the manufacturer to run more tests and submit more data but found Hays very reluctant to go back to the company.

In 1964, the Public Health Service objected to the registration of the insecticide Dibrom for the following reasons: first, 100 percent of persons exposed to a 10 percent concentration of Dibrom suffered skin damage, yet PRD allowed the caution on Dibrom's label to read: This preparation *may* cause skin damage; second, malathion increased the potency of Dibrom eight-fold but PRD failed to require a warning that the two pesticides not be used together. After criticizing the tests for failing to measure the concentration of Dibrom in the air, for in one test using only one rat to measure acute dermal effects, and for furnishing no information on the concentration of Dibrom in food crops, the Public Health Service concluded:

In summary, most of the studies submitted lack any semblance of scientific rigor. In addition, chronic animal studies are lacking, observations on the health of occupational workers are not reported, and there are no laboratory experiments on higher animals. Furthermore there are no reproductive studies to determine teratogenicity or mutagenicity. The studies submitted [by Chevron Oil Company] are incomplete, unsophisticated, and unsatisfactory. . . .[17]

Despite this objection, Dibrom was duly registered by PRD in 1965 and put into mass circulation. By the end of 1971, Dibrom had still not be relabeled and the tests to which the Public Health Service objected six years ago are just now being reviewed.

With the removal of Dr. Hays and the shift of PRD to EPA, scrutiny of test data may improve. PRD now requires twice as much documentation of safety factors as it did five years ago and the costs to industry of conducting the necessary safety tests has helped reduce the number of new products developed.

Nevertheless, the problem of biased and incomplete safety data will not be solved until the direct connection between the pesticide industry and the testing laboratories is broken. If experimental screening of new pesticides were assigned to certified laboratories by a committee of independent scientists or by a federal agency, the conflicts of interest which now disguise the harmful side effects of pesticides would largely vanish. The Administrator of EPA should be made responsible for conducting all tests on pesticides submitted for registration. The Administrator could then assign testing to government laboratories or to independent or chemical company labs certified by EPA. The costs would still be charged to the registrant, and there would be no need for duplication of present laboratory facilities. Third-party testing would help put the chemical profession back in control of chemical analysis.

Two other measures which would improve the efficiency of premarket screening of pesticide hazards are presently being thwarted by the House Agriculture Committee. Section 3(c)(2) of the Committee's amendment to FIFRA should be amended to read: The pesticide application, and all supporting information, except that found by the Administrator of EPA to be a trade secret, shall be made available to the public by the Administrator at the time he receives it. Any supplemental information required by the Administrator also shall be made available to the public. At the time the Administrator registers a pesticide under the Act, he shall make available to the public all other scientific and other information which was submitted to him or which he consulted in connection with his decision.

Material submitted in support of an application for registration should be available *before* a decision is made so that the public will be aware of what is occurring and have an opportunity to make intelligent and relevant comments on the claims made for an economic poison. Otherwise the only information available to the Environmental Protection Agency may be that provided by the applicant itself, information which is not likely to be wholly unbiased.

Full disclosure of the data upon which the Administrator relied in reaching his decision, as well as material which was available to him, is necessary to facilitate appropriate judicial review of his decision.

Section 3(c)(5) of the House Agriculture Committee bill should be further amended to delete the sentence: "The Administrator shall not make any lack of essentiality a criterion for denying registration of any pesticide." On the contrary, the Administrator should be *required* to make lack of essentiality a criterion for denying registration of a pesticide. Essentiality should remain a criterion, if not the decisive one, in the assessment of costs and benefits which is necessary in determining whether or not to register. Such matters as essentiality, or the availability of alternatives to the substance to be registered, are critical in deciding whether the environment or the public needs yet another pesticide.

Section 3(c)(6) should be amended to provide the public the same right to appeal from a decision to permit registration of a pesticide as the applicant for registration has to appeal from a refusal. The section presently affords only the applicant the right to judicial review. This is unfair to the public which should have the same rights with respect to all registration decisions as do the pesticide companies.

Finally the House bill provides for an *indemnity* when a pesticide is suspended or canceled, thereby unfairly placing the burden of financial loss upon EPA and ultimately the taxpayer—rather than upon manufacturers and heavy users of those pesticides. This unique indemnity provision is inconsistent with the standard practice in comparable situations, such as with recall of products containing cyclamates, automobiles, soups and other products, in which manufacturers, retailers, or users have properly borne the risk. This indemnity provision also discourages self-policing of the pesticide industry by removing an otherwise important deterrent to promotion and sale of a pesticide whose safety and potential environmental harm are known to be suspect.

14

Conclusion

Specific remedies for many of the problems discussed in this study have been recommended in the chapters above. In closing, I want to discuss briefly four recommendations which flow from the main themes of this report.

(1) Food Safety Agency

The most common remedy for ailing regulatory agencies is a change in scenery. The Pesticides Regulation Division has now been moved out of USDA and into a hopeful new agency whose primary emphasis will be protecting the environment, not agribusiness. Food inspection, however, remains embarrassed by departmental conflicts of interests and overlapping jurisdictions in USDA and FDA, where the goal of protecting public health competes with services to agribusiness. Meat inspection and chemical monitoring in USDA, and the food inspection functions of FDA, should be transferred to a new food safety agency. Alternatively, the Senate Commerce Committee is now considering a bill to establish an independent "consumer safety agency" which could include food inspection among its functions. Either of these proposals is vastly preferable to the present system, whose failures are described in chapters 3, 4, and 6.

(2) Consumer Advocacy Agency

Reorganizations are laudable and necessary steps, but by themselves they will do little to increase the influence of unrepresented interests on decisions involving meat and pesticides. As the Center for Law and Social Policy stated in a recent report, a constituency, to be effective, needs organized advocacy:

It needs representatives or advocates to channel the constituency's general views into positions on particular regulatory questions, to make proposals, to refute arguments offered by industry representatives, to understand whether a particular measure adopted by an agency is substantial or a sham, to see that the regulators' public promises are kept. Without advocates to represent its views, a broad public constituency may not be able to convert its political power—its intensely and widely held views or interests—into triumph in the regulatory process.

Wherever it is located, a regulatory agency will be heavily lobbied by special interest groups. The agency's integrity depends on finding ways to give the consumer's interest equivalent representation. A promising approach is the proposed Consumer Protection Agency now being considered by the Senate. The CPA would be limited to advocacy of the consumer's interest before the courts, Congress, and federal and state agencies. It should be outside the Executive Office. As past Presidential consumer advisors have shown, a really vigorous consumer advocate needs some insulation from the President and the President needs some insulation from him. In order to keep the CPA as free as possible from the network of lobbyists and special interest pressures, it should have no regulatory powers whatsoever. It would, in addition to advocacy, develop critical information of value to the consumer and perform a powerful investigatory and disclosure function.

In the past, whenever major consumer legislation has been passed, the watchword of the affected interest group has been, "let the consumer have the substance, just give us the procedure." The substantive rights of consumer laws become hoaxes when their exercise is subverted by delay, preferential access, and secrecy. The CPA's lawyers, by keeping procedures in harmony with substance through advocacy in the agencies, would be taking a giant step in the direction of effective consumer rights.

356   SOWING THE WIND

(3) Institutions to Support Science "Outsiders"

The case studies of pesticides and food additives in this book have shown that small groups of independent scientists can provide the public with an early warning system and the information to defend itself against ill-conceived and risky government policies. Unfortunately, the Insiders, the confidential advisors who sometimes give short-sighted policy the veneer of expertise, outnumber the Outsiders by a factor of at least ten.[1] The outside scientists, frequently employed by universities, lack the resources to respond rapidly to science regulatory issues. Foundations, universities, and Congress should follow the lead of the American Association for the Advancement of Science, whose Herbicide Assessment Commission is a model of the way to help independent scientists take the time to assess government policies. If they do not, the Executive Branch, when challenged by citizens' groups, will continue to reply as it did at various times on the ABM, SST, and C-5A issues: "Here are our advisors! Where are yours?"[2]

(4) Defense of Professional Integrity

There is growing pressure on professional societies to take steps to protect the professional integrity of their members when they come into conflict with the profit interests of corporate or government employers. The National Association of Federal Veterinarians is planning to establish an ombudsman to defend its members in conflicts with USDA. The American Chemical Society has recently been attacked by some of its members for alleged indifference to the ethical conflicts its members sometimes face as employees of chemical companies. The chemist or engineer with several advanced degrees has far less job security than the average blue-collar worker and often less freedom to follow his conscience. The societies of engineers, chemists, and other professionals in technical disciplines should establish standing grievance committees to investigate and expose (and perhaps eventually blacklist) companies who put pressure upon scientists to compromise their professional standards.

Notes

CHAPTER 1

1. Statement of Ralph Nader before Subcommittee on Agricultural Research and General Legislation of the Committee on Agriculture and Forestry, U.S. Senate, 90th Congress, 1st Session, November 1, 1967, p. 142.
2. *Government Rejected Consumer Items*, Hearings before a Subcommittee of the Committee on Government Operations, House of Representatives, 90th Congress, 2nd Session, April 2, 3, 1968, p. 88.
3. Dr. W. L. Ingalls, paper presented to the 87th annual meeting of American Veterinary Medical Association, August 21–24, 1950. Hearings before Subcommittee on Livestock and Grains of the Committee on Agriculture, House of Representatives, 90th Congress, 2nd Session, February, 1968.
4. Gabriel Kolko, *The Triumph of Conservatism* (New York, 1963), pp. 98f.
5. Claude G. Bowers, *Beveridge and the Progressive Era* (Cambridge, 1932), p. 227.
6. *Ibid.*, p. 230.
7. House of Representatives Report No. 653 on Federal Meat Inspection Act (1967), p. 4.
8. Ralph Nader, "Watch That Hamburger," *New Republic*, August 19, 1967, p. 15.
9. *Meat Inspection*, Hearings before the Subcommittee on Agricultural Research and General Legislation of the Committee on Agriculture and Forestry, U.S. Senate, 90th Congress, 1st Session, November 1967, p. 92.
10. *Ibid.*, p. 182. Statement of Leslie Orear, Director of Publications, United Packinghouse Food and Allied Workers, AFL-CIO, who helped expose unsanitary meat conditions in Chicago.
11. Ralph Nader, "Watch That Hamburger," *loc. cit.*, p. 15.
12. *Meat Inspection*, p. 168.
13. *Ibid.*
14. Interview with Nick Kotz, January, 1971.
15. Interview with John Califano, January, 1971.
16. *Des Moines Register*, November 2, 1967.
17. Interview with Nick Kotz, January, 1971.
18. Interview with Ralph Nader, December, 1970.

CHAPTER 2

1. Statement to Congressman Benjamin Rosenthal, August 13, 1969.
2. Summary Minutes of the Technical Subcommittee of National Food Inspection Advisory Committee, March 3, 1970, p. 2.
3. *Boston Globe*, August 24, 1969.
4. *Boston Globe*, October 6, 1969.
5. *Boston Globe*, October 22, 1969.
6. *Boston Globe*, October 15, 1969.
7. The only exception is for plants which clearly endanger public health.
8. Letter of July 25, co-signed by Congressman Thomas Foley and Congressman Graham Purcell.
9. Report to the Committee on Agriculture of the House of Representatives and Committee on Agriculture and Forestry of the Senate with Respect to State and Federal Inspection Operations and the Slaughter Preparation, Storing and Handling of Meat and Food Products as Required by the Wholesome Meat Act–Public Law 90–201. Dated December 15, 1967, Report for Calendar Year 1969, and Report for Calendar Year 1970, by the Secretary of Agriculture.
10. John Rothschild, "Washington's Other Crime Problem," *Washington Monthly*, August, 1970.
11. *Ibid.*

CHAPTER 3

1. "Criteria for on the job inspection," CP (CPPS) (Instruction 923-1), Exhibit B, Consumer and Marketing Service, USDA, November 28, 1969.
2. Confidential communication from a Consumer and Marketing Service official, January, 1971.
3. Confidential communication from a federal inspector, October 23, 1970.
4. U.S. General Accounting Office Report to the Congress, *Weak Enforcement of Federal Sanitation Standards at Meat Plants by the Consumer and Marketing Service*, B-163450, by the Comptroller General of the U.S., June 24, 1970.
5. *Ibid.*, p. 11.
6. *Ibid.*
7. U.S. General Accounting Office Report to the Congress, *Enforcement of Sanitation, Facilities and Moisture Requirements at Federally Inspected Poultry Plants*, B-163450, by the Comptroller General of the United States, September 1969, pp. 7–8.
8. U.S. General Accounting Office Report to the Congress, *Consumer and Marketing Service's Enforcement of Federal Sanitation Standards at Poultry Plants Continues to Be Weak*, B-163450, by the Comptroller General of the United States, November 16, 1971, p. 16.
9. *Weak Enforcement*, pp. 2–3.
10. *Ibid.*, p. 28.

11. Much of the evidence presented in the following pages comes from confidential but verified communications with federal inspectors. In most cases, their identity cannot be disclosed without jeopardizing their jobs. When these reports arrive, they are checked for accuracy with other inspectors or other meat inspection personnel from the same area. These inspectors are obviously not a random sample; the inspectors' fear of reprisal if they speak out makes them difficult subjects for conventional sampling techniques. We contacted, directly or indirectly, approximately 5 percent of the federal inspection corps.

12. *Poultry Inspector's Handbook*, USDA, Consumer and Marketing Service, Poultry Division, Washington, D.C., p. 40.

13. *Ibid.*, p. 42.

14. *Ibid.*, p. 43.

15. Letter to Mr. Barnard Sacks, Assistant Director, Civil Division, U.S. General Accounting Office, September 3, 1970.

16. Affidavit of ———— (Inspector B), March 3, 1971.

17. *Washington Post*, October 3, 1970, p. B-1.

18. Confidential communication from poultry inspector in Wisconsin, October 21, 1970.

19. Confidential communication from a USDA meat inspection official, February, 1971.

20. Report of the Special Task Force on Reorganization of the Consumer Protection Programs, Alfred Bernard and Philip J. May, August 25, 1970.

21. *Ibid.*, p. 3.

22. Establishing a Department of Consumer Affairs, Hearings, Subcommittee on Executive Reorganization, Committee on Government Operations, U.S. Senate, 91st Congress, 1st Session, 1969, p. 381.

23. *Ibid.*

24. *Ibid.*

25. Interview with Don Russell, Assistant to Director of Consumer and Marketing Service, July 6, 1970.

26. *Los Angeles Times*, February 26, 1970.

27. *Weak Enforcement, op. cit.*

CHAPTER 4

1. Secretary's memorandum No. 1532, revised USDA, Office of the Secretary, Washington, D.C., June 16, 1969.

2. *Organizing Federal Consumer Activities*, Hearings, Committee on Government Operations, House, 91st Congress, 1st Session, 1969, p. 137.

3. *New York Times*, January 26, 1970.

4. Personal communication to Ralph Nader from D. Arnold Bendick, Research Associate, Michigan State University, College of Natural Science and College of Agriculture and Natural Resources, February 2, 1970.

5. Milt Dunk, "This Is the Way It Is . . . Ralph Nader Challenges Poultry Industry," *Poultry Tribune*, March, 1970.

6. B. R. Burmester and R. L. Whitter, *An Outline of the Dis-*

eases of the Avian Leukosis Complex, Agricultural Research Service, USDA, 1966.

7. *Avian Leukosis Viruses—Lack of Association with Human Cancers*, Report of the Surgeon General of the United States to the Secretary of Agriculture, February 3, 1970.

8. Martin Sevoian, "Current Status of the Avian Leukosis Complex," *Agricultural Science Review*, Vol. 8, No. 203 (1970).

9. See the proposal for consumer relevance statements which follows.

10. *Federal Register*, October 3, 1970, pp. 15,600–15,601.

11. *Ibid.*

12. 9CFR 319.180.

13. Memorandum from R. H. Alsmeyer, Head, Standards Group, to W. J. Minor, Acting Director, Technical Services Division, USDA, November 29, 1968.

14. Home and Garden Bulletin, USDA, No. 72, 1964.

15. *Feedstuffs*, December 26, 1970, p. 34.

16. R. H. Alsmeyer, *op. cit.*

17. Statement of L. Blaine Liljenquist, President and General Manager of the Western States Meat Packers Associations, Inc. (WSMPA) at USDA Public Hearings on Fat Content of Cooked Sausage, June 18, 1969, USDA, Washington, D.C.

18. Statement of Edward Berlin, at USDA Public Hearings on Fat Content of Cooked Sausage, June 18, 1969.

19. *Federal Register*, Vol. 34, p. 7823.

20. Interview with Edward Berlin. See also Brief of the Consumer Federation of America to the Secretary of Agriculture submitted by Edward Berlin in the Matter of Compositional and Labeling Requirements for Certain Sausage Products—Proposed Amendment of 9CFR 317.8 (c) (40).

21. *Consumer Preference Evaluation of Frankfurters of Varying Fat Content*, Peryam and Kroll Research Corporation, Chicago, Ill., 1969, p. 7.

22. L. Blaine Liljenquist, *op. cit.*

23. Public Hearings on Fat Content of Cooked Sausage, June 18, 1969, USDA, Washington, D.C., p. 13.

24. *Washington Post*, July 10, 1969.

25. Affidavit of Rodney Leonard in *Wellford v. Hardin*, United States District Court for the District of Maryland Civil Action No. 21551.

CHAPTER 5

1. Robert Troy, "Alabama Farmers on Strike," *South Today*, November, 1970, p. 4.

2. Letter of George Haefner, Operations Manager, Pillsbury Company, to Ralph Meadows, Poultry Producers Association, Montgomery, Alabama, October 10, 1968.

3. *Corporation Farming*, Hearings before the Subcommittee on Monopoly of the Select Committee on Small Business, U.S. Senate 90th Congress, Second Session on the Effects of Corporation Farming, Small Business, Great Plains and Upper

Midwest, Omaha, Nebraska, May 20 and 21, 1968, Eau Claire, Wisconsin, July 22, 1968.

4. *Corporation Farming, op. cit.* Statement of Nebraska Grange, Albert J. Ebers, Seward, Nebraska, p. 165.

5. *Feedstuffs*, December 12, 1970, p. 4.

6. William E. Cathcart, "Changes in the Poultry Meat Industry and Projections for the Decade," *Poultry and Egg Situation*, April, 1970, USDA Economic Research Service, p. 10.

7. *Ibid.*, p. 19.

8. James C. Finlayson, Consultant to the Pillsbury Company, quoted in *Feedstuffs*, January 23, 1971, p. 6.

9. William E. Cathcart, *op. cit.*, p. 19.

10. *Feedstuffs*, November 7, 1970.

11. *Corporation Farming, op. cit.*, p. 247.

12. *Ibid.*

13. *Ibid.*

14. *The Broiler Industry, An Economic Study of Structure, Practices and Problems*, Packers and Stockyards Administration, USDA, 1967, p. 4.

15. Robert Troy, *op. cit.*, p. 4.

16. *Ibid.*

17. Dr. Randall E. Torgerson, "A Vision of Broiler Bargaining in the Future," *Feedstuffs*, December 26, 1970, p. 29.

18. *The Broiler Industry, op. cit.*, p. 21.

19. *Cost and Returns: Commercial Broiler Farms*, Georgia, 1969, Economic Research Service, USDA, June, 1970.

20. Wilson Lee and Morris White, "Typical Cash Flow Budgets for Contract Broiler Growers," Cooperative Extension Service, Auburn University, 1970.

21. *Agricultural Marketing and Bargaining Act*, Hearings. Senate Committee on Agriculture and Forestry, 91st Congress, 1st Session, November 20 and December 9, 1969, p. 85.

22. Lee and White, *op. cit.*, Table 6.

23. Daryl Natz, "Take Good Look at Production Costs, Broiler Firms Advised," *Feedstuffs*, January 23, 1971, p. 82.

24. *The Broiler Industry, op cit.*, p. 61.

25. Letter to USDA Hearing Clerk on 9CFR Part 201, August, 1970.

26. *The Broiler Industry, op cit.*, p. 47.

27. Many observers of the poultry industry in the Deep South have remarked on the analogy to sharecroppers. See Robert Troy's excellent article in *South Today, op. cit.*

28. Letter to USDA Hearing Clerk, *op. cit.*

29. *The Poultry Times*, Northeast-Midwest Edition, April 21, 1971, p. 14.

30. *Corporation Farming, op. cit.*, p. 285.

31. *The Broiler Industry, op. cit.*, p. 45.

32. Letter to USDA Hearing Clerk, *op. cit.*

33. *The Broiler Industry, op. cit.*, p. 4.

34. *Ibid.*, p. 63.

35. *Corporation Farming, op. cit.*, p. 285.

36. *The Broiler Industry, op. cit.*, p. 45.

37. *Poultry Times*, Southeastern, March 17, 1971, p. 14.

38. Dr. Randall E. Torgerson, *Producer Power at the Bargaining Table*, p. 10.
39. *Feedstuffs*, December 12, 1970, p. 4.
40. Quoted to Robert Troy, *South Today, op. cit.*
41. Letter from Ed Harrison to Ralph Nader, October 21, 1970.
42. Robert Troy, *op. cit.*
43. *New York Times*, November 21, 1970.
44. *Feedstuffs*, December 26, 1970, p. 30.
45. *Feedstuffs*, January 23, 1971, p. 64.
46. Dr. Randall Torgerson, "A Vision of Broiler Bargaining in the Future," *Feedstuffs*, December 26, 1970.
47. *Feedstuffs*, January 23, 1970, p. 64.
48. *Ibid.*

CHAPTER 6

1. Confidential communication from a federal inspector, November 23, 1970.
2. *Poultry Meat*, February, 1971, p. 19.
3. Confidential communication, *op. cit.*
4. *Poultry Meat, op. cit.*
5. *Report on Salmonella*, National Academy of Sciences–National Research Council (1969), p. 14.
6. Report by the National Communicable Disease Center, Foodborne Outbreaks, Annual Summary, 1968.
7. *Man's Health and Environment—Some Research Needs*, Report of the Task Force on Research Planning in Environmental Health Science, U.S. Department of Health, Education, and Welfare (1970), p. 46.
8. *Ibid.*
9. Report by the National Communicable Disease Center, *op. cit.*
10. *Agricultural Marketing*, July, 1970, p. 10.
11. Arthur N. Wilder and Robert A. MacCready, "Isolation of Salmonella from Poultry," *New England Journal of Medicine*, June 30, 1966.
12. *Wholesome Poultry Products Act*, hearings, Committee on Agriculture and Forestry, U.S. Senate, July 2, 1968, p. 279.
13. *Report on Salmonella, op. cit.*, p. 11.
14. Dr. John Siliker, Siliker Laboratories, speech to the American Meat Institute, September 18, 1967.
15. Staff interview, 1970.
16. See GAO reports 1969–1971.
17. U.S. General Accounting Office Report to the Congress, *Enforcement of Sanitary, Facility and Moisture Requirements at Federally Inspected Poultry Plants*, Consumer and Marketing Service, Department of Agriculture B-163450, by the Comptroller General of the U.S., September 10, 1969, p. 26.
18. This information was supplied by Mark Wynn, Instructor of Political Science, Wisconsin State University, Whitewater, Wisconsin.
19. U.S. General Accounting Office Report to the Congress, *op. cit.* p. 25.

20. *Ibid.*
21. Letters in USDA hearing clerk's office.
22. *Federal Register*, October 8, 1970.
23. *Albuquerque Journal*, June 5, 1970, p. A-9.
24. Dr. William B. Buck, *The Use of Drugs in Animal Feeds*, Publication 1679, National Academy of Sciences, 1969, p. 215.
25. Statement of Dr. Harry Mussman, Consumer and Marketing Service, USDA, before the Subcommittee on Intergovernmental Relations of the House Committee on Government Operations, March, 1971.
26. Hearings before the Subcommittee on Intergovernmental Relations, House Committee on Government Operations, *op. cit.*
27. Lawrence C. Harold, D.V.M., and Robert A. Baldwin, D.V.M., "Ecological Effects of Antibiotics," *FDA Papers*, February, 1967.
28. E. C. Moorehouse, "Transferrable Drug Resistance in Enterobacteria Isolated from Urban Infants," *British Medical Journal* (1969), Vol. 2, pp. 405–07.
29. E. S. Anderson and Naomi Datta, "Resistance to Penicillins and its Transfer in Entero-bacteriacae," *Lancet* (February 20, 1965), pp. 407–09.
30. *The Use of Drugs in Animal Feeds*, National Academy of Sciences.
31. *Washington Post*, June 14, 1970.
32. *Feedstuffs*, December 12, 1970, p. 58.
33. C. D. Van Houweling, "Drugs in Animal Feed," *FDA Papers* (September, 1967).
34. Statement of Dr. Charles C. Edwards, Commissioner of Food and Drugs, Public Health Service, Department of Health, Education and Welfare before the Subcommittee on Intergovernmental Relations, House Committee on Government Operations, March 16, 1971.
35. *Food Chemical News* (December 13, 1971), p. 20.
36. *Feedstuffs*, June 6, 1970.
37. C. K. Whitehair and B. S. Pomeroy, "Veterinary Medical Basis for the Use of Antibiotics in Feeds," *The Use of Drugs in Animal Feeds*, *op. cit.*, p. 50.
38. Dr. G. D. Rosen, "Observations on the Swann Report and Its Consequences," *Feedstuffs*, December 12, 1970.
39. Statement of Dr. Charles C. Edwards, *op. cit.*
40. David Smith, "Antibiotics in Agriculture and the Health of Man," *FDA Papers* (September, 1968), pp. 10–12.
41. M. E. Coats and G. F. Harrison, "Observations on the Growth Promoting Effects of Procaine Penicillin and Zinc Baitracia on Chicks in Different Environments," *J. Sci. Ed. Agri.* (March, 1969).
42. Barbara AuClair and Carol Farkas, "The Use of Antibiotics in Animal Feeds," (unpublished).
43. *New England Journal of Medicine*, Vol. 281, No. 12, September 18, 1969, p. 677.
44. P. E. Corneliussen, "Residues in Food and Feed," *Pesticide Monitoring Journal*, Vol. 2, No. 4, March, 1969.
45. Statement of Dr. Virgil Wodicka before the Senate Sub-

364   SOWING THE WIND

of the Committee on Commerce, September 29, 1970.

46. *Wall Street Journal*, November 28, 1969, p. 4.
47. *Ibid.*
48. *Science*, Vol. 170, December 18, 1970, p. 1314.
49. E. Boyland, "The Correlation of Experimental Carcinogenesis and Cancer in Man," in *Experimental Tumor Research* (E. Homberger and S. Karger, editors), Basel, 1969, pp. 222–34.
50. *Ibid.*
51. Leo Friedman, "Drugs, Food Additives, and Pesticides in Relation to Environmental Cancer in Man: Historical Perspectives," in *Regulation of Food Additives and Medicated Animal Feeds*, Hearings before a Subcommittee of the Committee on Government Operations, U.S. House of Representatives (March, 1971), p. 388.
52. *Regulation of Food Additives and Medicated Animal Feeds*, pp. 543–44.
53. Friedman, *op. cit.*
54. Dr. Roy Hertz, "Prepared Statement on Diethystilbestrol," January 17, 1960 (unpublished), in files of National Cancer Institute.
55. Arthur Herbst, *et al.*, "Adenocarcinoma of the Vagina, Association of Maternal Stilbestrol Therapy with Tumor Appearance in Young Women," *New England Journal of Medicine*, April 22, 1971; Alexander Langmuir, "New Environmental Facts in Congenital Disease," editorial in the *New England Journal of Medicine*, April 22, 1971.
56. David Zwick, *Water Wasteland* (New York: Grossman Publishers, 1971).
57. USDA Press Release.
58. Memorandum to Kenneth McEnroe, Deputy Administrator, Meat and Poultry Inspection Program, in *Regulation of Food Additives and Medicated Animal Feeds*, p. 421.
59. Anthony Malanoski, "Regulatory Control of Hormone Residues by Chemical Analysis," *Journal of the Association of Official Analytical Chemists*, Vol. 53, March, 1970.
60. *Ibid.*
61. Granville Knight, *et al.*, "Possible Cancer Hazard Presented by Feeding Diethylstilbestrol to Cattle," in *Symposium on Medicated Feed*, New York, 1956.
62. George Gass, Tom Coats, and Nora Graham, "Carcinogenic Dose-Response Curve to Oral Diethylstilbestrol," *Journal of National Cancer Institute*, Vol. 33, No. 6 (December, 1964), pp. 971–77.
63. *Evaluation of Chemical Carcinogens*, Report to the Surgeon General, U.S. Public Health Service, April 22, 1970, in *Chemicals and the Future of Man*, hearings, Subcommittee on Executive Reorganization and Government Research, Committee on Government Operations, U.S. Senate (April, 1971), p. 180.
64. Hearings before the Subcommittee on Intergovernmental Operations, Committee on Government Operations, U.S. House of Representatives, November, 1971.

65. *Washington Post*, September 20, 1970; *Feedstuffs*, December 12, 1970, p. 41.
66. *Feedstuffs*, April 3, 1971, p. 52.
67. *Regulation of Food Additives and Medicated Animal Feeds*, p. 446.
68. *Ibid.*, pp. 453, 458.
69. *Ibid.*, p. 434.
70. *Ibid.*, p. 489.
71. Committee Report on H.R. 13254 (Food Additives Amendment of 1958), Committee on Interstate and Foreign Commerce, U.S. House of Representatives, July 28, 1958.
72. Review of the Chemistry and Toxicology of Nitrates, and Nitroso Compounds (Nitrosamines) as of August 28, 1970, Bureau of Foods and Pesticides, FDA, Department of HEW.
73. D. W. Fassett, Publication 1354, National Academy of Sciences, National Research Council, p. 251.
74. *Ibid.*
75. Statement of Dr. William Lijinsky, Eppley Institute, University of Nebraska, before the Intergovernmental Relations Subcommittee of the Committee on Government Operations, U.S. House of Representatives, March 16, 1971.
76. Dr. A. J. Lehman, "Nitrates and Nitrites in Meat Products," Association of Food and Drug Officials of the United States, Vol. XXII, No. 3, July, 1958.
77. *Regulation of Food Additives and Medicated Animal Feeds*, Hearings, Intergovernmental Relations Subcommittee, Committee on Government Operations, U.S. House of Representatives (March, 1971), pp. 215ff.
78. P. N. Magee, "Toxicity of Nitrosamines: Their Possible Human Health Hazards," *Fd. Cosmet. Toxicol.*, Vol. 9 (1971).
79. R. Preussmann, "On the Significance of N-nitroso Compounds as Carcinogens," Institute of Experimental Toxicology and Chemotherapy, German Cancer Research Center, Heidelberg (1971), unpublished.
80. Statement of Dr. William Lijinsky, *op. cit.*
81. Preussmann, *op. cit.*
82. *Regulation of Food Additives . . .*, p. 608.
83. William Lijinsky and Samuel Epstein, "Nitrosamines as Environmental Carcinogens," *Nature*, Vol. 225, No. 5227, January 3, 1970.
84. P. N. Magee, *op. cit.*
85. Communication by FDA to Subcommittee on Executive Reorganization and Government Research, Committee on Government Operations, U.S. Senate, May, 1971.
86. Lijinsky and Epstein, *op. cit.*
87. *Regulation of Food Additives . . .*, *op. cit.*, p. 541.
88. Review of the Chemistry . . . of Nitrites . . . , *op. cit.*; Preussmann, *op. cit.*
89. Joint USDA-HEW Press Release, February 5, 1972; *Regulation of Food Additives . . .*, p. 619.
90. *Regulation of Food Additives . . .*, *op. cit.*, p. 236.
91. Review of the Chemistry . . . of Nitrites . . . , *op. cit.*

92. "The History and Use of Nitrates and Nitrites," *Meat Science Review*, Vol. 5, No. 2 (January, 1971), p. 6.
93. *Ibid.*, p. 3.
94. R. Greenberg, *et al.*, *Appl. Microbiol.*, 14:789 (1966); *Regulation of Food Additives* . . . , p. 236.
95. G. M. Dack, *Food Poisoning* (Chicago, 1956), pp. 102–103.
96. *Regulation of Food Additives* . . . , p. 262.
97. *Ibid.*
98. *Chemicals and the Future of Man*, *op. cit.*, p. 54.
99. Memorandum from Dr. Leo Friedman to Dr. Virgil Wodicka, December 17, 1971.
100. *Evaluation of Chemical Carcinogens*, Report to the Surgeon General, USPHS, by the Ad Hoc Committee on the Evaluation of Low Levels of Environmental Carcinogens, National Cancer Institute, April 22, 1970.
101. Hughes Ryser, "Chemical Carcinogenesis," *New England Journal of Medicine*, Vol. 285, No. 13 (September 23, 1971), p. 721–734.

CHAPTER 7

1. *Report of the Secretary's Commission on Pesticides and their Relationship to Environmental Health* (the Mrak Report), USDHEW (December, 1969), p. 248.
2. The Mrak Report, p. 236.
3. Statement of Robert L. Brent, *Chemicals and the Future of Man*, Hearings before the Subcommittee on Executive Reorganization and Government Research of the Committee on Government Operations, United States Senate, April 6 and 7, 1971, p. 165.
4. "Evaluation of Environmental Carcinogens," Report to the Surgeon General, USPHS, April 22, 1970. Ad Hoc Committee on the Evaluation of Low Levels of Environmental Chemical Carcinogens, National Cancer Institute.
5. O. Warburton and F. C. Fraser, "Spontaneous Abortion Risk in Man," *Amer. J. Human Genet.*, Vol. 16, No. 1 (1964).
6. *Medical World News*, January 22, 1971, p. 54.
7. M. W. Oberle, "Lead Poisoning: A Preventable Childhood Disease of the Slums," *Science*, Vol. 165 (1969), pp. 991–992.
8. The Mrak Report, p. 657.
9. J. F. Crow, "Chemical Risk to Future Generations," *Science and Citizen* (June–July, 1968), pp. 113–117.
10. H. V. Malling, "Chemical Mutagens as a Possible Genetic Hazard in Human Populations," *Chemicals and the Future of Man*, p. 257.
11. Crow, *op. cit.*
12. Statement of Shell Chemical Co., *Chemicals and the Future of Man*, p. 267.
13. The Mrak Report, p. 262.
14. *Ibid.*, p. 666.
15. U.S. Military Assistance Command–Vietnam Reports; see also "Warfare with Herbicides in Vietnam" by Arthur Galston in

the collection *Patient Earth*, edited by John Harte and Robert Socolow (New York, 1971).

16. Dr. Samuel S. Epstein, "Teratological Hazards Due to Phenoxy Herbicides and Dioxin Contaminants," presented at The First International Meeting of the Society of Engineering Science, Tel Aviv, Israel, June, 1972.

17.

ACUTE ORAL TOXICITY

LD_{50}* levels in milligrams per kilogram of bodyweight

	Rat	Guinea Pig
2,4,5-T (pure)	500	380
DDT	150–800	400
parathion	1.7 (male)–30 (female)	9.3 (male)–32 (female)
TCDD	.022 (male)–.045 (female)	.0006

Source: Dow Chemical Company.

* LD_{50}=the amount of a toxic agent which kills 50 percent of the test animals to which it is administered under the conditions of the experiment.

Julius E. Johnson, Symposium, "Possible Health Implications of Widespread Use of Herbicides," American Institute of Biological Sciences, Bloomington, Indiana, August 26, 1970, p. 24.

18. Dr. Jesse Steinfeld, Testimony before Subcommittee on Energy, Natural Resources and the Environment, U.S. Senate, April 15, 1970.

19. K. H. Schultz, "Clinical Picture and Etiology of Chloracne," article in Hearings before Subcommittee on Energy, Natural Resources and the Environment, April 7 and 15, 1970, p. 336.

20. Dow did find that 2,4,5-T caused skeletal defects at 24 mg/kg but claimed they did not fit within the definition of a birth defect. The World Health Organization's definition of a teratogen clearly includes these defects. Dow appears to be playing a game of semantics to disguise the regulatory significance of its findings.

21. D. K. Courtney and J. A. Moore, *Toxicol. Appl. Pharmacol.*, Vol. 20, p. 396, 1971.

22. *Chemical and Engineering News*, September, 1970.

23. *Ibid.*

24. L. Golberg, "Trace Chemical Contaminants in Food: Potential for Harm," *Fd. Cosmet. Toxicol.*, Vol. 9, pp. 65–80. (Pergamon Press, 1971. Printed in Great Britain.)

25. Interview by Agribusiness Task Force, for the Center for Study of Responsive Law, 1970.

26. *Ibid.*

27. "Advisory Committee on Protocols for Safety Evaluations," FDA (December 1, 1969), *Toxicol. Appl. Pharmacol.*, Vol. 16, pp. 264–296, 1970.

28. The Mrak Report, p. 674.

29. Robert Brent, "Medicolegal Aspects of Teratology," in *Chemicals and the Future of Man*, p. 128.

30. The Mrak Report, p. 659.
31. *Ibid.*, p. 661.
32. T. D. Sterling, "Difficulty of Evaluating the Toxicity and Teratogenicity of 2,4,5-T from Existing Animal Experiments," *Science*, Vol. 174 (1971), p. 1358.
33. "Evaluation of Environmental Carcinogens," *op. cit.*
34. The Mrak Report, p. 657.
35. "Birth Defects and the Environmental Causes," *Medical World News*, January 22, 1971, p. 48.
36. L. Golberg, *op. cit.*
37. The report of the National Cancer Institute/Bionetics Study may be found in the Jl. of the National Cancer Institute, Vol. 42 (June, 1969), pp. 1101–1114.
38. The Mrak Report, p. 655.
39. S. Epstein, *op. cit.*
40. T. D. Sterling, *op. cit.*
41. Joshua Lederberg, letter to Sen. Gaylord Nelson concerning proposed revision of the Food Additive Safety Act, April 29, 1970.
42. "Evaluation of Chemical Carcinogens," *op. cit.*
43. Atomic Energy Commission Rep. TID 25180, p. 1.
44. Frank von Hippel and Joel Primack, "Scientists and the Politics of Technology," *Applied Spectroscopy*, Vol. 25 (1971), p. 403.
45. *Report on 2,4,5-T*, Report of the Panel on Herbicides of the President's Science Advisory Committee, Executive Office of the President, Office of Science and Technology, March, 1971.
46. Report of the EPA Advisory Committee on 2,4,5-T, May, 1971.
47. Epstein, *op. cit.*
48. Sterling, *op. cit.*
49. N. P. Buu-Hoi, et al., C. R. Acad. Sci. Series D. Vol. 273 (1971), p. 708.
50. Hippel and Primack, *op. cit.*
51. *Science*, August 13, 1971.

CHAPTER 8

1. J. H. Davis, "The Changing Profile of Fatal Poisonings," cited the *Report of the Secretary's Commission on Pesticides and Their Relationship to Environmental Health* (the Mrak Report), USDHEW (December, 1969), p. 308.
2. "Parathion Summary," Ecological Investigations Division, EPA, 1971.
3. *Science*, Vol. 171 (January 15, 1971), p. 148.
4. USDA Press Release 2734, 1970.
5. The Mrak Report, pp. 347 ff; *Diagnosis and Treatment of Phosphate Ester Poisoning*, Technical Bulletin for Physicians, California Department of Public Health, 1967.
6. Letter from Federico Hernandez Denton, Director of Consumer Research Center, University of Puerto Rico, May 7, 1971.

7. *The Arizona Republic*, May 6, 1970.
8. The Mrak Report, p. 312.
9. Department of Transportation, Federal Aviation Administration, Southwest Region, Fort Worth, Texas, May 20, 1969.
10. D. G. Clark, *et al.*, "The Toxicity of Paraquat," *British Journal of Industrial Medicine*, Vol. 23 (1966), pp. 126–32.
11. Interview with Dr. William F. Barthel, Chief, Atlanta Toxicology Branch, Division of Pesticide Community Studies, EPA.
12. Dr. Irma West, California State Department of Public Health, *Congressional Record*, October 3, 1969, E8168.
13. *Chemical Insect Control Handbook*, Washington University Cooperative Extension Service (April, 1969), p. 6.
14. E. E. Kenaga and W. F. Allison, "Commercial and Experimental Organic Insecticides," *Bulletin of American Entomological Society*, Vol. 15, No. 85, p. 148.
15. Letter from Dr. R. H. Wellman, Union Carbide Corporation, December 7, 1970.
16. *Ibid.*
17. Personal communication.
18. Letter from Dr. Frederick Plapp, January 3, 1971.
19. Wellman, *op. cit.*
20. Interview with Dr. Cipriano Cueto, Human Safety Branch, PRD, EPA, January, 1971.
21. Metcalf, *et al.*, *Journal of Agricultural Food Chemistry*, Vol. 14, 1966, pp. 579–584.
22. *Farm Chemicals*, July, 1970, p. 19.
23. *Community Study on Pesticides*, FDA, Report 70–40, Hawaii, December 23, 1970.
24. Report on the Secretary's Commission on Pesticides, p. 148.
25. L. R. Weiss and R. A. Orzel, "Enhancement of Toxicity of Anticholinesterases by Central Depressant Drugs in Rats," *Toxicology and Applied Pharmacology*, Vol. 10 (1967), pp. 334–39.
26. *Deficiencies in Administration of Federal Insecticide, Fungicide, and Rodenticide Act*, Hearings before a Subcommittee of the Committee on Government Operations, U.S. House of Representatives, 91st Congress, 1st Session, p. 63.
27. Report of the Secretary's Commission on Pesticides, p. 306.
28. P. C. Mintner, *Benchmarks in the Colorado Agricultural Chemicals Program* (Colorado State University, 1965), p. 36.
29. *Ibid.*
30. Betsy Weiner and Robert Worth, "Insecticides: Household Use and Respiratory Impairment," *Hawaii Medical Journal*, Vol. 28, No. 4, pp. 283–85.
31. *Pesticides*, Report by Colorado Rural Legal Services, Inc. (1971).
32. *Migrant and Seasonal Farm Worker Powerlessness*, Hearings before the Subcommittee on Migratory Labor of the Committee on Labor and Public Welfare, U.S. Senate, August 1, September 29, 30, 1969, Parts 6A, 6B, 6C, pp. 3,007–4,041.
33. *Ibid.*, p. 3185.
34. *Ibid.*, pp. 3396, 3402, 3406.

35. *CBNS Notes*, Center for the Biology of Natural Systems (Washington University, St. Louis), Vol. 42 (January, 1971), p. 14.
36. *Migrant . . . Powerlessness, op. cit.*, p. 3803.
37. *Pesticides, op. cit.*

CHAPTER 9

1. *Pest Control Research*, Hearings, Committee on Agriculture and Forestry, U.S. Senate, September 30 and October 1, 1971, p. 43.
2. *Ibid.*, p. 52.
3. *Progressive Farmer*, September, 1970.
4. L. D. Newsom and J. R. Brazzel, "Pests and their Control," *Advances in Production and Utilization of Quality Cotton: Principles and Practices, 1968*, F. C. Elliot, M. Hoover, and W. K. Porter, eds., (Ames, Iowa, Iowa State University Press), pp. 367–405.
5. W. H. Whitcomb and K. Bell, "Predaceous Insects, Spiders and Mites of Arkansas Cotton Fields," *University of Arkansas Agricultural Experiment Station Bulletin*, 1964, p. 690.
6. Ray F. Smith and Harold T. Reynolds, "Effects of Manipulation of Cotton Agro-Ecosystems on Insect Pest Populations," in *The Careless Technology*, eds. M. T. Farvar and J. P. Milton, (Natural History Press) (forthcoming).
7. *Ibid.*
8. Rachel Carson, *Silent Spring* (Greenwich, Conn., 1962), p. 217 (all references to *Silent Spring* are to the paperback edition).
9. "Diminishing Returns," a report by the staff of *Environment Magazine*, Vol. 11, No. 7, p. 8.
10. *Ibid.*, p. 11.
11. *Hobe Ranches* v. *Collier Carbon & Chemical Corporation*, Civil No. 137793, Fresno County Superior Court, September 29, 1970.
12. *Ibid.*, Leigh Testimony, p. 8.
13. *Ibid.*, p. 8.
14. Luther J. Clark, "Development in the Poor Nations: How to Avoid Fouling the Nest," *Science*, Vol. 163, p. 1047.
15. Teodora Boza Barducci, "Problemas de la agricultura del Valle de Canete," *Vida Agricultura* (Lima), September, 1959, pp. 511–25.
16. Harman Henkin, "Report of a Conference on Ecological Aspects of International Development," *Environment*, January–February, 1969, p. 2.
17. *International Development Review*, March, 1969.
18. Dr. P. L. Adkisson, "Impact of Insecticides' Resistance on Cotton Production in South Texas and Northeastern Mexico," a Working Paper Prepared for the Third Session of the FAO Panel of Experts on Integrated Pest Control, Rome, September, 1970.
19. *Ibid.*
20. "Diminishing Returns," *loc. cit.*, p. 8.
21. Adkisson, *op. cit.*

22. "Here's What's New in Insect Control Practices," *Cotton International Edition*, 1969, p. 81.
23. Smith and Reynolds, *op. cit.*, p. 49.
24. *Agriculture Science Review*, USDA Cooperative State Research Service.
25. Dr. Leo D. Newsom, Louisiana State University, "Ecological Aspects of International Development," *Environment*, Vol. 11, No. 7, p. 11.
26. Ray F. Smith, "Summary Report on Cotton Pests in Central America and Northern South America," in *Report of Second Session of FAO Panel of Experts on Integrated Pest Control*, FAO, Rome.
27. Smith and Reynolds, *op. cit.*, p. 39.
28. *Ibid.*, p. 48.
29. J. C. Headley, *Economic Research on Pesticides for Policy Decision-making*, ERS, UDFS, April, 1970.
30. Robert van den Bosch, *op. cit.*
31. R. van den Bosch, "The Toxicity Problem—Comments by an Applied Insect Ecologist," *Chemical Fallout*, eds. M. W. Miller and G. G. Berg, (Springfield, Illinois, 1969).
32. *Ibid.*, p. 9.
33. Robert van den Bosch, "Statement on Insecticides," testimony before the Committee on Agriculture and Forestry, U.S. Senate, March 26, 1971.
34. Kevin P. Shea, "Cotton and Chemicals," *Scientist and Citizen*, Vol. 10, No. 9, November 1968, p. 209.
35. Frank M. Eaton, "Physiology of the Cotton Plant," *Ann. Rev. of Plant Physiology*, 1955, 6:299–328; L. D. Newsom and J. R. Brazzel, *Pests and Their Control in Advances in Production and Utilization of Quality Cotton: Principles and Practices*, F. C. Elliott, M. Hoover, and W. K. Porter, eds. (Ames, Iowa: Iowa State University Press), pp. 367–407.
36. *Pest and Disease Control Program for Cotton*, Calif. Agr. Exp. Sta. (1968).
37. Kevin P. Shea, *op. cit.*, p. 210.
38. *Ibid.*, p. 211. Also, *Cotton Insect Control*, University of California Experiment Station Report, 1966, pp. 9–15.
39. Kevin Shea, *op. cit.*, p. 212.
40. *Hobe Ranches* v. *Collier Carbon & Chemical Corporation*, *op. cit.*
41. Kevin Shea, *op. cit.*, p. 216.
42. Kevin Shea, *op. cit.*, p. 209.
43. R. van den Bosch, *The Toxicity Problem, op. cit.*, p. 6.
44. Kevin Shea, *op. cit.*, p. 211.
45. R. van den Bosch, "Statement on Insecticides," *op. cit.*, p. 18.
46. *Ibid.*, p. 18.
47. G. M. Beal, J. M. Bohlem, and H. G. Lingren, *Special Report No. 49*, Agricultural and Home Economics Experiment Station, Iowa State University, 1966.
48. M. C. Shurtleff, "The Blight, Facts and Fiction," *Agricultural Chemicals*, March, 1971, p. 24.
49. Peter and Katherine Montague, "The Great Caterpillar War," *Audubon*, Vol. 73, No. 1, (January, 1971), pp. 50–59.

50. *Ibid.*
51. *Hobe Ranches* v. *Collier Carbon & Chemical Company,* *op. cit.*
52. *Banducci* v. *F.M.C. Corporation,* Civil No. 92144 (Kern County Superior Court, January 23, 1969).

CHAPTER 10

1. Frank Graham, *Since Silent Spring* (Boston, 1970), pp. 57–58.
2. Statement of Robert van den Bosch in *Pest Control Research,* Hearings before Senate Committee on Agriculture and Forestry, September 30, and October 1, 1971, p. 44.
3. Robert White-Stevens, *DDT: Selected Statements from State of Washington DDT Hearings and Other Related Papers,* published by the DDT Producers of the United States, May, 1970, p. 351.
4. Norman E. Borlaug, "DDT, the First Domino," *New York Times,* November 21, 1971.
5. Statement of Dr. Perry L. Adkisson (Head, Department of Entomology, Texas A&M University) in *Pest Control Research,* pp. 50ff.
6. Dr. Edward J. Armbrust, "Illinois Natural History Survey," *Congressional Record,* May 13, 1971, S. 6854.
7. *California Farm Bureau Monthly,* May, 1971, p. 16.
8. Statement of Dr. Ned Bailey, Director of the Office of Science and Technology, USDA, in hearings before the Senate Subcommittee on Energy, Natural Resources, and the Environment, June 17, 1970.
9. Hal Lancaster, *Wall Street Journal,* August 10, 1970, p. 14.
10. *Ibid.*
11. Statement of F. R. Lawson, in *Pest Control Research,* p. 87.
12. *Pest Control Research,* pp. 39, 88.
13. Statement of Dr. F. R. Lawson, *Pest Control Research,* p. 88.
14. *Ibid.,* p. 89.
15. *Report of the Secretary's Commission on Pesticides* (the Mrak Report), U.S. Department of Health, Education, and Welfare, December, 1969, p. 57.
16. Velmar W. Davis and Austin S. Fox, *et al., Economic Consequence of Restraining the Use of Organochlorines on Cotton, Corn, Tobacco, and Peanuts,* Product Research Branch, ERS, USDA, 1970, p. v.
17. *Report of the Secretary's Commission on Pesticides,* p. 56.
18. Statement of Dr. Theo F. Watson, Department of Entomology, University of Arizona, in *Pest Control Research,* p. 142.
19. Barry Commoner, *The Closing Circle* (New York, 1971), p. 136.
20. J. C. Headley, *Economic Research on Pesticides for Policy Decision-making,* ERS, USDA, 1970.
21. *Ibid.,* p. 85.
22. Statement of Dr. Theo F. Watson, *Pest Control Research,* p. 142.

23. Statement of F. R. Lawson, *Pest Control Research*, p. 86.
24. Dr. R. F. Smith, "Integrated Control of Insects—A Challenge for Scientists," *Agr. Sci. Rev.*, January, 1969, pp. 1–5.
25. *California Farm Bureau Monthly*, May, 1971, p. 16.
26. Statement of Ernest C. Bay, Head, Department of Entomology, University of Maryland, in *Pest Control Research*, p. 151.
27. USDA News Release (USDA 3265-71), October 4, 1971.
28. Statement of Dr. H. T. Reynolds, Chairman, Department of Entomology, University of California, Riverside, in *Pest Control Research*, p. 162.
29. "Basis of NSF–Agriculture Cooperation in Research on Alternative Methods of Control of Insect Pests," NSF-USDA joint statement, 1970.
30. Statement of Senator Gaylord Nelson in *Pest Control Research*, p. 7.
31. W. M. Upholt, *et al.*, "The Search for Safer, More Selective and Less Persistent Pesticides," *Bio-Science*, Vol. 20, No. 18.
32. *Report of the Secretary's Commission on Pesticides*, p. 162.
33. Communication from Robert van den Bosch.
34. *Science*, December 12, 1969, p. 1386.
35. Rachel Carson, *Silent Spring* (Greenwich, Conn., 1962).
36. Roy Hansberry, "Integrated Insecticides in Industry," paper presented to Western Agricultural Chemical Association, Portland, Oregon, January 10, 1968.
37. R. L. Ridgeway and S. L. Jones, *Jl. Eco. Entom.* Vol. 62 (1969), p. 177.
38. *Environmental Science and Technology* (May, 1971), p. 401.
39. George Irving, "Agricultural Pest Control and the Environment," *Science* (1968), p. 1419.

CHAPTER 11

1. *Senate Hearings Before the Committee on Appropriations, Department of Agriculture and Related Agencies Appropriations*, 1969.
2. Committee on the Imported Fire Ant, *Report to the Administrator*, ARS, USDA, National Research Council, National Academy of Engineering, 1967.
3. F. Bellinger, R. E. Dyer, R. King and R. B. Platt, *Observations on the Biology of the Imported Fire Ant*, Agricultural Research Service, USDA, ARS 33-49:1-21, 1958. See "The Ant War" by Donald W. Coon and Robert R. Fleet, *Environment*, Vol. 12, No. 10.
4. S. B. Hays and Kirby L. Hays, "Food Habits of Solenopsis salvissima richteri Forel," *Journal of Economic Entomology*, 52 (3):455-457 (1959).
5. Kirby L. Hays, "The Present Status of the Imported Fire Ant in Argentina," *Journal of Economic Entomology*, 51 (1): 111-112, 1958. See Victor W. Lambou, Technical Assistance Branch, Division of Technical Support, USDI, "Evaluation of Water Quality Effects of the Program to Control the Imported Fire Ant with Mirex," September 14, 1970.

6. R. L. Rudd, *Pesticides and the Living Landscape* (Madison, Wisconsin: University of Wisconsin Press, 1964).

7. *Report of the Secretary's Commission on Pesticides, The Mrak Report*, U.S. Department of Health, Education, and Welfare, December, 1969, p. 218.

8. *Report of the Secretary's Commission on Pesticides, op. cit.*, p. 111.

9. *Ibid.*, p. 110.

10. Rachel Carson, *Silent Spring* (Greenwich, Connecticut: Fawcett Publications, 1962), p. 147.

11. Donald W. Coon and Robert R. Fleet, "The Ant War," *Environment*, Vol. 12, No. 10, p. 28.

12. Rachel Carson, *op. cit.*, p. 148.

13. *Weaknesses and Problem Areas in the Administration of the Imported Fire Ant Eradication Program*, Agricultural Research Service, U.S. Department of Agriculture, by the Comptroller General of the United States, January, 1965.

14. *Ibid.*, p. 47.

15. *Ibid.*, pp. 34–35.

16. *Department of Agriculture Appropriations for 1966*, Hearings before Subcommittee of the Committee on Appropriations, House of Representatives, Part 2, p. 146.

17. *Ibid.*, p. 114.

18. *Ibid.*, p. 174.

19. *Ibid.*

20. *Department of Agriculture Appropriations for 1969*, Hearings before a Subcommittee of the Committee on Appropriations, House of Representatives, Part 2, p. 146.

21. *Ibid.*, p. 43.

22. *Ibid.*

23. *Science*, April 23, 1971.

24. *Department of Agriculture Appropriations for 1971*, Hearings before Subcommittee of the Committee on Appropriations, House of Representatives, p. 65.

25. P. A. Butler, "Monitoring Pesticide Pollution," *Bio-Science*, Vol. 19 (1969), p. 889.

26. *Chronology of Mirex in Imported Fire Ant Program*, ARS, PPD, MD, U.S. Department of Agriculture, May 15, 1970, p. 4.

27. First Quarterly Report for 1969, Gulf Breeze Laboratory, USDI, see Victor W. Lambou, op. cit.

28. Report of the Secretary's Commission on Pesticides and Their Relationship to Environmental Health, p. 470.

29. T. B. Gaines and R. D. Kimbrough, "Oral Toxicity of Mirex in Adult and Suckling Rats," *Arch. Environmental Health*, Vol. 21:7–14.

30. Letter to USDA from Dr. Thomas Harris.

31. See *Mrak Report* etc.

32. *Evaluation of Environmental Carcinogens.* Report to the Surgeon General, U.S. Public Health Service, by the Ad Hoc Committee on the Evaluation of Low Levels of Environmental Chemical Carcinogens, National Institutes of Health, National Cancer Institute, April 22, 1970, p. 1.

33. *Ibid.*, p. 7.
34. Letter from Walter Hickel, former Secretary of Interior to Secretary of Agriculture, Clifford Hardin, November 16, 1970.
35. Letter from Dr. Tom Harris, Director of Division of Pesticide Registration to Dr. Harry Hays, Director of Pesticides Regulation Division.
36. *Science*, April 23, 1971, p. 359.
37. *Report on the Survey of County Agents on the Imported Fire Ant*, January 15, 1968, USDA, ARS, Washington, D.C.
38. *Atlanta Journal*, February 17, 1970.
39. *Atlanta Journal*, April 27, 1965.
40. *Atlanta Constitution*, March 19, 1968.
41. *Atlanta Constitution*, February 16, 1970.
42. *Port Arthur News* (Texas), 1970.
43. Confidential communication to Polly Roberts.
44. Frank Graham, *Since Silent Spring*, p. 29.
45. The Department of Interior, commenting on USDA's Environmental Impact Statement on February 19, 1971, noted that the fire ant "primarily affects man himself rather than his crops or livestock." The National Research Council, in its 1967 report, found that "there is practically no evidence of direct damage to livestock" and that the fire ant "is not a menace to fish and wildlife."

CHAPTER 12

1. *Deficiencies in Administration of Federal Insecticide, Fungicide, and Rodenticide Act*, Hearings before Subcommittee of the Committee on Government Operations, House of Representatives, 91st Congress, 1st Session, May 1, June 24, 1969.
2. *Ibid.*
3. *Ibid.*, Dr. M. J. Sloan, manager of regulatory affairs for Shell Chemical Company, impugns the committee's competence: "The record will show the group was supplied with very few documents on Vapona and met for less than one full day. Careful review and evaluation of data were obviously impossible in the time available." Personal communication.
4. *Ibid.*
5. See discussion of recall in Chapter 13.
6. Kenneth Culp Davis, *Discretionary Justice* (Louisiana State University Press, 1969).
7. Affidavit of Dr. George Irving, Administrator, Agricultural Research Service, USDA, in *Wellford* v. *Hardin*, U.S. District Court, D.C. Civil No. 740-70, August 5, 1970.
8. *Ibid.*
9. See Chapter 3 for awards to meat inspection officials.
10. Statement of Nicholas Johnson, *Public Counsel Corporation*; Hearings before the Subcommittee on Administrative Practice and Procedures of the Committee on the Judiciary, U.S. Senate, 91st Congress, 2nd Session, July 1970, p. 19.
11. Attorney General's Memorandum on the Public Information Section of the Administrative Procedure Act (June, 1967).

12. "The People's Right to Know," *Congressional Record*, No. 139, September 3, 1969.
13. *Discretionary Justice, op. cit.*, p. 102.
14. Affidavit of Dr. George Irving, *op. cit.*

CHAPTER 13

1. Rothschild, *Washington Monthly*, August, 1970, pp. 1–57.
2. Statement of Nicholas Johnson, *Public Counsel Corporation*, Hearings before the Subcommittee on Administrative Practice and Procedures of the Committee on the Judiciary, U.S. Senate, 91st Congress, 2nd Session, July, 1970, p. 19.
3. *New York Times*, November 14, 1969, p. 46.
4. Interview with Dr. Alan McGowan, Center for the Biology of Natural Systems, Washington University, St. Louis, Missouri.
5. "Reasons Underlying the Registration Decisions Concerning Products Containing DDT, 2,4,5-T, Aldrin and Dieldrin," EPA, March 18, 1971, p. 15.
6. *Ibid.*, p. 14.
7. *DDT: Selected Statements from State of Washington DDT Hearings* held in Seattle, October 14, 15, 16, 1969, published by DDT producers of U.S., May, 1970.
8. *Ibid.*, Statement by Max Sobelman, pp. 220–21.
9. *Ibid.* For McLean's statement, see *Bio-Science* (September, 1967), p. 616.
10. *Ibid.*, Preface.
11. *Ibid.*, Preface.
12. *Seattle Times*, October 5, 1969.
13. *Deficiencies in Administration of Federal Insecticide, Fungicide, and Rodenticide Act*, Hearings before a Subcommittee of the Committee on Government Operations, House of Representatives, 91st Congress, 1st Session, May 7 and June 24, 1969, Section 4.
14. *Environmental Defense Fund, Inc.,* v. *Ruckelshaus* (not yet reported in *Federal Reporter*), 2 ERC 1114, D.C. Circuit, January 7, 1971.
15. See review by Frank Egler, *Atlantic Naturalist*, October–December, 1962.
16. Statement of Dr. Samuel Epstein before the Subcommittee on Executive Reorganization and Government Research, Committee on Government Operations, U.S. Senate, April 6, 1971.
17. Letter from Daniel Mullally, Medical Officer, Office of Pesticides, Public Health Service, to Dr. R. V. Anderson, Deputy Administrator of Agricultural Research Service, USDA, December 4, 1964.

CONCLUSION

1. Frank von Hippel and Joel Primack, "Scientists and the Politics of Technology," *Applied Spectroscopy*, Vol. 25 (1971), p. 412.
2. *Ibid.*

Index